CHANGING RELIGIOUS WORLDS

SUNY series,

ISSUES IN THE STUDY OF RELIGION

———————

Bryan Rennie, editor

CHANGING RELIGIOUS WORLDS

The Meaning and End of
MIRCEA ELIADE

Edited by
BRYAN RENNIE

STATE UNIVERSITY OF NEW YORK PRESS

Published by
STATE UNIVERSITY OF NEW YORK PRESS, ALBANY

© 2001 State University of New York
All rights reserved
Printed in the United States of America

No part of this book may be used or reproduced in any manner whatsoever without written permission. No part of this book may be stored in a retrieval system or transmitted in any form or by any means including electronic, electrostatic, magnetic tape, mechanical, photocopying, recording, or otherwise without the prior permission in writing of the publisher.

For information, address
State University of New York Press,
90 State Street, Suite 700, Albany, NY 12207

Production, Laurie Searl
Marketing, Patrick Durocher

Library of Congress Cataloging-in-Publication Data

Changing religious worlds : the meaning and end of Mircea Eliade / edited by Bryan Rennie.
    p. cm. — (SUNY series, issues in the study of religion)
    Includes bibliographical references (p.) and index.
    ISBN 0-7914-4729-4 (alk. paper) — ISBN 0-7914-4730-8 (pbk. : alk. paper)
    1. Eliade, Mircea, 1907–   I. Rennie, Bryan S., 1954–   II. Series.
BL43.E4 C48 2000
200'.9'2—dc21

                                                                        00-022911

10 9 8 7 6 5 4 3 2 1

Contents

Acknowledgments — vii
Introduction — ix

PART I ✣ CRITIQUE

1. Building on Eliade's Magnificent Failure — 3
   Roger Corless

2. Methods, Theories, and the Terrors of History: Closing the Eliadean Era with Some Dignity — 11
   Russell T. McCutcheon

3. Are There Modern Myths? — 25
   Robert A. Segal

PART II ✣ PHILOSOPHY

4. Eliade, Subjectivity, and Hermeneutics — 35
   Tim Murphy

5. The Phenomenology of Mircea Eliade — 49
   Allan W. Larsen

6. Eliade, the Comparative Method, Historical Context, and Difference — 59
   Carl Olson

PART III ✣ LITERATURE

7. The United States' Response to Mircea Eliade's Fiction — 79
   Mac Linscott Ricketts

8. Romantic Postmodernism and the Literary Eliade — 95
   Rachela Permenter

9. The Man Who Could Read Stones — 117
   Mircea Eliade, translated by Mac Linscott Ricketts

PART IV ✣ PERSONAL REFLECTIONS

10 SMILES AND WHISPERS: NOSTALGIC REFLECTIONS ON MIRCEA ELIADE'S SIGNIFICANCE FOR THE STUDY OF RELIGION 143
    N. J. Girardot

11 METHODOLOGICAL, PEDAGOGICAL, AND PHILOSOPHICAL REFLECTIONS ON MIRCEA ELIADE AS HISTORIAN OF RELIGIONS 165
    Wendell Charles Beane

12 CONVERSATION WITH AN INDIAN NATIONALIST AND INTERMEZZO: FRAGMENTS FROM A CIVIL REVOLT 191
    Mircea Eliade, Translated by Mac Linscott Ricketts

PART V ✣ APPLICATIONS

13 MIRCEA ELIADE'S VIEW OF THE STUDY OF RELIGION AS THE BASIS FOR CULTURAL AND SPIRITUAL RENEWAL 207
    Douglas Allen

14 ELIADE'S INTERPRETATION OF SACRED SPACE AND ITS ROLE TOWARD THE CULTIVATION OF VIRTUE 235
    David Cave

15 THE CONCEPT OF WORLD HABITATION: ELIADEAN LINKAGES WITH A NEW COMPARATIVISM 249
    William E. Paden

PART VI ✣ CONCLUSION

16 THE MEANING AND END OF ELIADE 263
    Bryan Rennie

BIBLIOGRAPHY 283
CONTRIBUTORS 293
SUBJECT INDEX 299
NAME INDEX 303

Acknowledgments

Acknowledgments are first due to the contributors without whom this volume would be empty. If not for their diligence, intelligence, hard work, and patience I would never have been able to bring these ideas together, and I thank them all for permission to use their work. Thanks are also due to the photographer, Jeff Lowenthal, who took the cover photograph of Eliade shortly before the latter's death. Jeff kindly gave permission to use the photograph for much less than the usual professional rate. (Thanks, Jeff.) Permissions were also granted by the following publishers: Harcourt, Inc. for a quotation from Eliade's *The Sacred and the Profane;* Harper Collins for a quotation from Eliade's *Myths, Dreams, and Mysteries*; The University of Chicago Press for excerpts from Eliade's *Journal*, volumes I and III, and from *The Quest*; Taylor and Francis Books for a short extract from Maurice Merleau-Ponty's *Phenomenology of Perception* (Routledge, 1992); and Indiana University Press for a quotation from *American Sacred Space*, David Chidester and Edward T. Linenthal, eds. (Bloomington, Indiana: Indiana University Press, 1995). I particularly want to thank T. David Brent of The Mircea Eliade Literary Estate for permission to publish translations of Eliade's "The Man Who Could Read Stones," "Conversation with an Indian Nationalist," and "Intermezzo: Fragments from a Civil Revolt"; and, of course, Mac Linscott Ricketts for permission to use his translations of these pieces. Finally, and personally, I need to thank my wife, Rachela, for all her help, support, and understanding.

Introduction

Times change and worlds change with them. As many of the contributions to this volume acknowledge, worlds are constituted by us and are manifold, varied, and changeable.[1] Eliade, for example, bemoaned his own inability to inhabit simultaneously the two "universes" of literature and scholarship.[2] The world from which Eliade wrote his fiction[3] was not the same as that from which he wrote his history of religions scholarship. It is increasingly evident that the world from which he wrote his scholarship was not the same as the world into which it was received, especially here in the United States. Nor was the world into which it was originally received the world that we currently inhabit. The question before us now, then, is what is the relevance of the writings of Mircea Eliade for the contemporary world. What is the meaning of Eliade's work and to what end can it be put? Indeed, does his work have *any* meaningful application or is it time to end the Eliadean era as Corless and McCutcheon insist? Has the changing world left Eliade behind or is it

---

1. See especially the contribution of William Paden (but also Girardot, Olson, Cave, and Beane). I must thank William Paden for focusing my attention on the importance and utility of this concept of world. See his *Religious Worlds: The Comparative Study of Religion*. Boston: Beacon Press, 1994.

2. (*Journal*: November 3, 1949) what he called "my fundamental weakness," i.e., that "I am incapable of living at the same time in two spiritual universes: that of literature and that of science." Quoted by Virgil Ierunca in *Myth and Symbols: Studies in Honor of Mircea Eliade*. Chicago: University of Chicago Press, 346.

3. See Mac Linscott Ricketts's contribution for a brief history of Eliade's fiction in the United States.

finally catching up with him? A related question, all-important for scholars of religion, concerns the incommensurability of worlds. Are the different religious worlds accessible to those who do not inhabit them? Or, as Thomas Kuhn claimed to be the case for those possessed of differing scientific paradigms,[4] is it impossible for us to voluntarily "change worlds" and see the world of other from the inside?

This collection of essays grew out of a session at the 1996 Conference of the American Academy of Religion.[5] The success of this session persuaded me to collect together this group of articles with an eye to assessing the significance and effect of Eliade and his thought on the scholarly understanding in the United States of religious phenomena.[6] When they were invited to contribute to the present collection, the authors were told that subjective, personal observations were appropriate and indeed sought. I hoped to learn something of the personal and historical effect and influence that Eliade had exercised. This grows out of my assertion that from a certain point of view the observation of one's fellow scholars constitutes fieldwork in the history of religion (*Reconstructing Eliade* 62, n.1). Russell McCutcheon has similarly said that "[b]ecause I study the way scholars construct religion, I do field work in publications and at national and international conferences on religion."[7] Thus, I feel that we are privileged to read such personal observations and they provide valuable insights into empirical experience. This is in part a historical study and personal observations are historical documents. Whether written from a personal perspective or not, all the papers in this volume seek, each in its own way, to address the same question: What, if anything, is the benefit of applying the thought of Mircea Eliade to our ongoing attempt to understand religious phenomena?[8]

The beginnings of my own answer to this question were given in *Reconstructing Eliade*. There an attempt was made to reveal a coherence in Eliade's writings that

---

4. *The Structure of Scientific Revolutions*. Chicago: University of Chicago Press, 1990, 100.

5. My own researches into Eliade had been published as *Reconstructing Eliade: Making Sense of Religion* (Albany: State University of New York Press, 1996) and my meeting with Thomas Ryba, chair of the History of the Study of Religion Group of the AAR, led to the organization of a session hosted by that group on the response in the United States to Eliade's work. Douglas Allen, Mac Linscott Ricketts, and Russell McCutcheon gave papers (reworked in this volume) and Ivan Strenski and I responded to them.

6. With the exception of Russell McCutcheon (Canadian) and myself (British), all the scholars in this volume are United States citizens. Both Russell and myself now teach in the United States.

7. *Manufacturing Religion: The Discourse on Sui generis Religion and the Politics of Nostalgia*. New York: Oxford University Press, 1997, 7.

8. For my analysis of understanding see "Manufacturing McCutcheon: The Failure of Understanding in the Academic Study of Religion," *Culture and Religion*, 1:1 (2000).

would explain how he could believe what he had written despite the self-contradiction and deep-rooted inconsistency that critics perceived there. This was undertaken as an application of Eliade's own methodology for understanding the religious worlds of others. The phenomenal fact is that there is a plurality of "religious worlds" that the scholar does not inhabit, whose the inhabitants hold as true things that the scholar cannot. If privileging the analyst's position is to be avoided, it must be assumed that alternative positions are perceived by their occupants to be as coherent as the analyst's. Thus, I took it upon myself to find how Eliade might perceive his work as coherent, rather than to show how it might be perceived as incoherent. I explicitly accepted "that what I will describe in this book will never be anything other than my own (creative, I hope) interpretation of the thought of Mircea Eliade" (4). Of course, I also recognize that any reasoning and language-using intelligence will fall prey to some inconsistency and self-contradiction. Our worlds are complex and our intelligence fallible. Yet because of that very fact we are obliged to give one another the benefit of the doubt and attempt to reconstruct the world from which a text has issued. If not, our criticisms will be restricted to constant restatements of our own positions, descriptions of our own world.

Using this method I found that certain themes were axiomatic in Eliade's thought. Central to his understanding is the identity of the sacred and the real. This does not mean that all scholars of religion must accept the absolute and independent ontology of God or gods. Rather, "it is this experience of the sacred, that generates the idea of something which *really* exists and, in consequence the notion that there are absolute intangible values which confer a meaning upon human existence" ("Structure and Changes in the History of Religion" 366). Eliade explicitly states that the "sacred" does not "imply belief in God or gods or spirits . . . it is the experience of a reality and the source of an awareness of existing in the world" (*Ordeal by Labyrinth* 154).

Eliade repeats this definition of the sacred as the real consistently from "Cosmical Homology and Yoga" in 1937 onward. Unfortunately, it is the nature of the real that we tend to take it as always and everywhere the same. Thus, readers tend to read their own real into Eliade's interpretative category. However, thus identified with the sacred, the real is an intentional object, the object of belief. Scholars have tended either to disregard this equation (taking it for an unwarranted a priori assumption whose truth is precisely what is at issue in the study of religion) or have mistakenly assumed it to refer to a particular deity or independent ontology. On the contrary, Eliade also repeatedly states that "the sacred is an element in the structure of (human) consciousness" (*Quest* i; *No Souvenirs* 1; and *The History of Religious Ideas*, vol. 1. xiii). It is that which is *apprehended* as real. It is the intentional object of human experience. Philosophically this is not a novel position—Immanuel Kant had concluded that the real is a category of the understanding in the late eighteenth century.⁹ Do Kant's and Eliade's claims make "the real" into a "vacuous concept" as McCutcheon insists (below 22)? Perhaps it does for some, but Eliade's assumption is not an unwarranted a priori. It is an interpretive move consistent with the empirical observation that myths are precisely those narratives that are held to be true. Applying it to the understanding of religion was a novel strategy that has yet to be fully appreciated. Thus applied, it becomes a powerful tool in understanding other worlds rather than privileging one's own.

His "hierophanies," then, are those events or entities that are perceived to manifest this sacred/reality. Not only could any existing thing become a hierophany but, "[W]e cannot be sure that there is anything . . . that has not at some time in human history been somewhere transformed into a hierophany" (*Patterns in Comparative Religion*, 11). Existence is the only characteristic essential to the revelation of the real.

"The dialectic of the sacred and profane" implies that, while all events and entities could potentially be perceived as manifesting the sacred/real, the fact is that our ascriptions of sacrality to some things is simultaneously and necessarily a denial of the significance of others (see *Reconstructing Eliade*, chs. 1 and 3). Hence the *coincidentia oppositorum:* When the sacred is perceived it is always in profane realities, and profane realities always conceal or camouflage the sacred (ch. 4). The only thing, then, that can be said about "ultimate reality" is that it transcends all dichotomies.

Illud tempus, "that time"—"yon time," as I tend to think of it—is another world, one not normally experienced in the mundane world of the everyday. It is the world of myth, the time of the ancestors, the realm of tales. It may be thought "unreal" in the sense that historical actualities are "real," but, to the mind for which historical actualities are less significant than traditional narrative, it is eminently more real. It is the source of all meaning and of all values in the mundane realm (ch. 8).

Related to this constructivist understanding of the sacred as the real and all that follows from it, is the understanding of myth as "determined by the prevalent attitude to a popular narrative. Myth is the popular narrative which is (either uncritically or with reference to other myths) held to be true, to represent the real, and thus to be exemplary. In Eliadean terms, to be sacred" (*Reconstructing Eliade* 72). Myths tell people why their world is the way that it is in a way that elicits a meaningful response. Myths relate those events that are held to be "the effective determinant antecedents" (90) of the world they experience. In this way not only

---

9. In *The Critique of Pure Reason*, in "The Analytic of Concepts," section III: Of the Pure Concepts of the Understanding or of the Categories (Kant's *Critique of Pure Reason*, trans. Friedrich Max Müller. London: Macmillan, 1900, 58). The *Critique* first appeared in 1781. On Kant's table of types of judgment see Frederick Copleston's *History of Philosophy* vol. I, 250f.

stories about gods, but, say, male superiority (or any unconsidered expression that simply assumes it to be true) would be mythic. The uncritical acceptance of an ethnocentric history that validates perceptions of ethnic superiority would be as mythic as the belief that the physical world was constructed from the corpse of a monster slain by a god. Myth gives access to *illud tempus* in that, via narrative or any other traditional art forms, it brings into the world of experience a world that never existed in terms of historical actuality. For example, a world in which the British were unquestionably superior or a world in which every pious Hebrew was personally liberated from Egypt.

The understanding of the role of "sacred histories" is becoming increasingly well established. Hence William Paden's observation that "historians of religion are finding a large body of sophisticated analysis in other fields that illumine or recontextualize the notion of 'sacred histories.' "[10] This leads to an increasingly complex notion of history in which I have identified

> a reflexively propagating series of interpenetrating "histories" which change on each reflection. History as personal experience, the things which "enter into the lot of each individual and collectivity" ↔ History as the totality of human experiences ↔ History as the (abstract concept of) the chronological succession of unique and irreversible events in the external world ↔ History as the accurate description of all that has come to pass in the course of time ↔ History as (the record of) those events which are held to be the effective determinant antecedents of ↔ History as personal experience. I do not mean to suggest that this is a fixed or closed series, it is rather an unbounded proliferation in which any and every element is contained in any and every element with differing emphasis. "History" is not a simple term, but refers to the real. Human conceptions and constructions of "history" reflect the real with an infinite capacity for nuance and flavor. (90)

This constellation of the sacred/real, myth, and history permits Eliade's identification of humanity as *homo religiosus*, his universalization of religious behavior, and his statement that "to be, or to become, human is to be religious" (*Quest*, preface). It also permits my analysis of Eliade as at least a precursor to a postmodern understanding of religions. This type of constructive thought, particularly the social construction of reality, is one of the few constant features of the constantly shifting

---

10. Below, 256. Paden cites a number of sources (n. 15) to which I would like to add Richard Slotkin, "Myth and the Production of History," in *Ideology and Classic American Literature*, ed. by Sacvan Bercovitch and Myra Jehlen. New York: Cambridge University Press, 1986. Paden also points out that J. Z. Smith makes a call for the kind of complex notion of history that I attribute to Eliade.

constellation of postmodern thought.[11] Eliade's thought can be quite closely related to that of Jacques Derrida.[12] Where Derrida identifies a longing for a center, Eliade sees the nostalgia for paradise and the desire to live in close proximity to the sacred. Where this leads Derrida to the recognition of binary opposites, Eliade recognizes the *coincidentia oppositorum*. Where Derrida considers the longing for the center to spawn a "centering" or privileging of one of the binary pair and to give rise to the play of binary opposites, Eliade has the dialectic of the sacred and the profane in which one of the pair is elevated over the other. Note that in Eliade's thought this elevation is dependent upon the preparation of the subject and could always be different.[13] The "transcendental signified" of deconstructionist criticism may correspond to the traditional institutional characterization of the sacred as God, but all "centered" members of a binary pair partake of sacrality to some degree. Where Eliade concludes that religion is universal, Derrida states that "for me there is no religion."[14] Yet Derrida observes that religious thought, though lost, returns, for example, in the structure of de Saussure's linguistics in which the Western metaphysics of presence values the "presence within" and assumes a "natural bond" between the inner meaning and the outer sound thus repeating the pre-scientific assumptions of religion in which God the Father is the real inner meaning and source of the outer word or *Logos*, Christ. (Derrida's critique of de Saussure occurs in *Of Grammatology*.) Thus, both thinkers destabilize the binary opposition between religious/nonreligious. I do not mean to imply any indebtedness on behalf of either author. They were both the product of the same philosophical genealogy through Hegel, Nietzsche, Heidegger, and de Saussure, and both products of similarly marginalized cultures (Algeria and Romania), and both influenced by Romantic forebears. It would not be in the least astonishing if they came to similar conclusions.

---

11. On Eliade's postmodernism, see the comments by Permenter, passim; Girardot (160ff.), Allen (223), Paden (250), and see *Reconstructing Eliade* 75 and 232–239. For an excellent and very readable introduction to postmodern thought in general see *Reality Isn't What It Used To Be* and *The Truth about the Truth* by Walter Truett Anderson. For readable introductions to Derrida see *Derrida*, by Christopher Norris. Cambridge: Harvard University Press and *Derrida and Deconstruction* by Hugh Silverman. New York: Routledge, 1989.

12. Carl Olson has already made a partial study of the relation of Eliade and Derrida in his *Theology and Philosophy of Mircea Eliade*. (New York: St. Martin's Press, 1992). Olson asserts a radical disagreement between the two. I disagree. See *Reconstructing Eliade*, 234.

13. See *Reconstructing Eliade* chapter 1 and especially page 19. The exact working out of the correspondence between Eliade and Derrida is a project that is too large for the present work. Much remains to be done and I can only make these suggestive comments at this time.

14. *Deconstruction in a Nutshell: A Conversation with Jacques Derrida*, ed. John D. Caputo. New York: Fordham University Press, 1997, 21.

For Eliade, this longing for a center, this desire to live in close proximity to the real, the true, the significant, the sacred, is an innate human characteristic. Even aware of it we cannot resist it. Even the deconstructionist critic, fully aware of the longing for a center and the centering of one binary over the other, cannot prevent that centering, and cannot refuse to apply binary couples. The best that can be done is to accept the "play of opposites" and to de-center and destabilize our own constructions. But in order to apprehend meaning in our experience we are required to judge. We cannot resist the temptation to center, to sacralize, or, if we could, we then could not evaluate the significance of our experiences. Centering or sacralizing ideal and nonhistorical categories, we appeal to *illud tempus* to justify our privileging of one over another, of the sacred over the profane, and thus we evoke mythical structures. The secular modern does this no less than the traditionally religious, but in a different world. "Historical," "physical," "rational," are valorized over "fictional," "spiritual," "intuitive," as if the former were somehow more accessible than the latter. "Nature" is valorized over "culture" as if we could finally and absolutely determine the difference.[15] But none of these distinctions are "natural kinds," things that exist in all worlds independent of the social constructions placed upon them. None of these centerings are irresistible or indefeasible. All can be de-centered, refused, profaned. All must be constantly resacralized by a return *in illo tempore* by means of the narration of myth, the performance of ritual, and the reestablishment of sacred space.

Accepting for the moment that this "postmodern" meaning of Eliade's thought can genuinely be found in his work,[16] what point does it have? To what end can it be put? I have suggested benefits to our field in the destabilization of binary oppositions such as belief/unbelief and religious/nonreligious (*Reconstructing Eliade* 109, 116) and I will not rehearse the obvious here. What needs to be repeated, perhaps, is that the scientific worldview and its concomitant insistence upon empirical "reality" as the ultimate locus of meaning is itself a belief. Its authority, like that of any traditional religious system, rests in our ascription of authority to it. Its powerful compulsion resides in its breadth of acceptance as well as its internal coherence. Perhaps I should point out that this is still my world. I do not find demon possession more credible than quantum physics. But some do, and for comparable reasons. This does indeed emphasize sameness at the expense of difference.

---

15. On a problem with the nature/culture dichotomy: Is the incest taboo natural or cultural? See Christopher Norris, *Derrida*, 136 with reference to Derrida's *Writing and Difference*, trans. Alan Bass. London: Routledge and Kegan Paul, 1978, 282.

16. See the debate between Carl Olson and myself over this point: "Mircea Eliade, Postmodernism, and the Problematic Nature of Representational Thinking," by Carl Olson, *Method and Theory in the Study of Religion*, Volume 11, number 4 and my response in 12:3.

It provides a clear vision of a universal human nature that allows us to conceive the other as the self; that allows the recognition of identity in difference, and thus provides an open door into the world of the other. All human worlds are in contact in that they share this structure of centering and of the dialectic of the sacred and the profane. As we can enter into other worlds of fantasy and fiction, we can enter into the religious worlds of the other by means of the imaginative process that Eliade describes as creative hermeneutics. "Creative hermeneutics" is what I have just attempted to explain and to do in my analysis of Eliade: one assumes the internal coherence of the religious world for its inhabitants and attempts to recognize the apprehensions of the real, the hierophanies and centerings, that are implied by that coherence.

Evidently this evaluation of Eliade ascribes a great deal of meaning to his writings. His scholarship provided a commentary that assisted me in my attempts to understand people who inhabited worlds markedly different from my own, who believed that which I could not. Other scholars, even those whom I admired or found useful and informative, were clearly articulating their own worlds of meaning. Nor were theologians (closet or otherwise) exclusively guilty of this. Dogmatic secularists seemed particularly intent on making readers see the world as they saw it rather than on articulating alternative perspectives. Such critics write as if any coherent articulation of an alternative worldview challenges the rectitude of their own. However, if one is to understand how the Muslim can experience Allah as closer than his own jugular, how Sri Aurobindo could encounter Krishna in his Alipore jail cell in 1908, how the characters in James's *Varieties of Religious Experience* could encounter the absolute in Christ, without making them into fools, frauds, or liars, one cannot take a stance of unmitigated self-righteousness. In this, for me, Eliade's writings proved effective.

In contrast to my own attempt to claim some utility for the thought of Mircea Eliade are the critiques of various scholars who perceive Eliade as a dangerously misleading and tendentious author. My intention is to acquaint the reader with the current critiques of Eliade so that both negative and positive responses to our central question may receive a fair hearing. In the first contribution to the section on critique, Roger Corless frankly calls for an end to the Eliadean era, building on Eliade's "magnificent failure" with "a polymethodic approach to what-you-would-die-for systems, combining these and other investigative tools with those developed by History of Religion(s) under the leadership of Eliade" (9). The only re-publication in this volume, this article remains one of the most succinct statements of some of the problems with Eliade's work, specifically in the religious studies classroom.

Russell McCutcheon takes up Corless's refrain, also calling for the end of the Eliadean era. McCutcheon's is, in many ways, one of the most critical essays included in this volume. Not just critical of Eliade but of defenders of Eliade and of any scholar who would support the "*sui generis* discourse" in religion by maintaining "the autonomy of the sacred,"[17] McCutcheon sees "links between the Eliade, de Man, and Heidegger affairs *not* in terms of any similarity in their individual actions, beliefs, or guilt" but in "the techniques their contemporary defenders use not only to protect their work and influence in academia but to construct and maintain a supposedly ahistorical, totalized scholarly field" (13f). In brief, his argument is that to follow Eliade's advice and study the reports of religious believers "on their own plane of reference" is to give privileged authoritative status to insider judgments—a hallmark of the *sui generis* discourse that treats religion as an essentially independent category. Although McCutcheon permits that "without taking such insider reports and interpretations seriously we would have no descriptive data to study," he insists that "*scholars must carefully devise defensible criteria to determine at what level of analysis they do or do not suspend such first person explanatory authority*" (18, emphasis original). The failure to do so is connected with—if not directly responsible for—the paucity of theory in our field. McCutcheon argues that following Eliade's recommendations and example has not only been of little or no benefit to the field of religious studies; it has actively hindered its development.

It is not surprising that Robert Segal, a prominent theorist on myth, has chosen to write on Eliade's understanding of myth. Behind his choice is his recognition of Eliade's attempt to universalize the religious impulse, presenting it as innate to humanity. Since, in Eliade's understanding, myth is coextensive with religion, his success or failure in arguing the ubiquity of myth indicates the success or failure of his entire program. Segal argues that "[i]f moderns have myths, as Eliade contends, then surely those myths must fulfill the same . . . functions as traditional myths" (27). Eliade has seen the functioning of myths and mythology in secular modern thought, including political ideology, psychoanalysis, and popular culture. In psychoanalysis, "dreams, reveries, fantasies, and so forth" are seen as "private myths," which psychoanalysis "employs . . . as a vehicle for returning to the past" (28). He concludes, "[W]hile private myths may well carry one back to the character-forming, precedent-setting time of childhood, no gods are to be found in this private primordial time" (29). Of the "camouflaged" myths of popular culture Segal asks, "What . . . is religious about these camouflaged myths?" (30). Since they do not provide a charter for contemporary institutions, they do not "serve as models for others." Since "the modern spectator or reader [does not] travel to the time and place of the story" (31), then "Eliade's claim that moderns have myths is less convincing than Jung's or Campbell's" (32). Eliade "faces a key dilemma that Jung

---

17. See McCutcheon's work, note 1 above, and my review in *Zygon* (June 2000), and my response to McCutcheon's review of my own work in *Religion*, 28:4 (1998).

and Campbell avoid: to be acceptable to moderns, myths must be secular, yet to function as myths, they must be religious." Segal concludes that Eliade fails to overcome this dilemma, thus failing to show that modern myths exist. Having failed to show that modern myths exist, Eliade's conception of religion as universal is significantly falsified. For Segal, then, Eliade has little of benefit to say to contemporary scholars.

In a section focused on the philosophical analysis of Eliade's work, Tim Murphy argues that "a transhistorical subjectivity ('humanism' in Eliade's terms) forms the condition for the possibility of the kind of hermeneutic of religion which Eliade both described and practiced" and that this "is Eliade's central legacy in the history of the study of religion" (35). According to Murphy, however, "the subject is, in fact, historical" (36) and Eliade's misplaced acceptance of the universality of the subject informs his acceptance of "the homogeneity of consciousness, [which] then, is the basis for *Verstehen* on this hermeneutical model" (39). Murphy's "argument is that the necessary consequence of Eliade's transcendental subjectivity is that it makes his methodology inherently ethnocentric" (40) and that "Eliade's approach to non-Western cultures is aggressively assimilating in the name of an ethnocentric project" (43). Although Eliade "will say of the term 'primitive,' that it is 'ambiguous and inconsistent,'[18] and he often (though not always) puts it in scare quotes" (43), he groups together all Africans, Oceanians, Asians, archaic, and "primitive" peoples. "In what universe do these peoples belong together?" asks Murphy, and he has to answer, "only in the universe of an essentialist consciousness; only in the universe of a universalist subjectivity" (44). Murphy proposes a Nietzschean/Foucaultian "genealogy" as an alternative to the universalist subjectivity informing Eliadean phenomenology. Thus, while not entirely rejecting the value of studying Eliade, Murphy issues a blunt warning against the vices inherent in Eliade's thought and recommends more salutary fare.

In a more positive assessment of Eliade, Allan Larsen provides a perspective from the discipline of philosophy more or less independent of the History of Religions. His paper gives an interesting insight into the philosophical understanding of phenomenology. So strong is Larsen's conviction of the significance of this phenomenology in Eliade's work that he can suggest that "it would seem that the title 'history of religions' is inappropriate and the 'phenomenology of religion' might be more fitting for his work." Moreover, Eliade's

> purpose is to show, to bring forth into the light that which is closest to a people because for them it is the most real. This bringing forth out of "lived-experience" is parallel to that of the art work. Both the phenomenologist and the artist bring forth the essences that constitute a world,

---

18. *Australian Religions*, n. 2, xii.

but the phenomenologist does not leave these images on an emotional level of intentional feeling but tries to bring these structures of the real and lived world to the mode of ideas, of essential structures. (56)

Carl Olson considers J. Z. Smith's criticism of comparative methodology in general and Eliade's application of it in particular. Olson poses the following questions: "Was Eliade's use of comparison an improvement over prior uses of this method for the study of religion? And is the method of comparison a useful tool for the historian of religions in light of Smith's criticism?" In order to answer, Olson gives us a survey of "a selected group of scholars from the latter nineteenth century until the period of Eliade's scholarly activity" (60). In this context Olson gives an interesting insight into the developing relation between the study of religion and our conception of science. He concludes, among other things, that "Eliade's use of the comparative method was devoid of the positivistic and behavioristic slant of Spencer's method . . . [and] unlike Max Müller, Eliade did not compare religions to determine which one was the best as if comparison was a means of testing one's own faith and religion" (72). In the process of his argument, Olson addresses several of the points raised by Tim Murphy regarding ethnocentrism and the diminution of difference. While Olson shares the opinion that ethnocentrism is finally inescapable, he does consider that "it is at least theoretically possible to begin to overcome it" within the type of hermeneutics exemplified by Eliade. Finally, Olson claims, "Smith is justified to criticize Eliade for neglecting difference and emphasizing sameness, but this does not mean that the method of comparison does not have a viable and useful role to play in cross-cultural hermeneutics" (75).

It is increasingly clear that the distinctions between philosophy, literature, and scholarship in religion are permeable constructs. However, such distinctions are nonetheless applicable and are applied in this volume by separating sections on literature and philosophy. Mac Linscott Ricketts informs us that Mircea Eliade felt that, in the long run, his works of fiction would outlast his scholarly writings and finally prove of greater significance.[19] Matei Calinescu is likewise "certain that one day Eliade's literary work will enjoy the wider readership it deserves."[20] It is evident that some understanding of Eliade's literary output is required in any attempt to assess the man and his work. Furthermore, it may be that the study of the relation between literary

---

19. Stated in Eliade's autograph in Ricketts's copy of *Noaptea de Sanziene*. See *Imagination and Meaning: The Scholarly and Literary Works of Mircea Eliade*. New York: The Seabury Press, 1982, 111.

20. "Imagination and Meaning: Aesthetic Attitudes and Ideas in Mircea Eliade's Thought," in *Journal of Religion* 57:1 (1977): 2.

creativity and the activity of scholarship will itself prove a fruitful application for the study of Eliade.

Mac Ricketts gives us a brief history of Eliade's publishing career in America. Although it is particularly "The United States' Response to Mircea Eliade's Fiction" that occupies Ricketts, he unavoidably relates details of both Eliade's worldwide publishing career and of Eliade's response to his fictional publications in the United States. Although Ricketts seeks to be informative rather than evaluative, this information can be helpful in our attempt to evaluate Eliade. Ricketts's article is not an account of the content of Eliade's fiction, nor an evaluation of its merit, nor a literary critical analysis. While such work remains to be done, it cannot be done without first raising awareness of the fact that Eliade was a writer of fiction, and of the significance of this fact. It should be noted that Ricketts agrees with Walter Strauss that "it would be quite wrong to think of [Eliade's] creative work as 'illustrative' of his scholarly theories" (quoted below 84).

The work of literary-critical analysis is begun for us here by Rachela Permenter, who has used Eliade in her work on "non-duality" in the writings of Herman Melville, D. H. Lawrence, and Louise Erdrich. Here, among other insights, she traces the connection between Romanticism and postmodernism and assesses the presence of "Romantic Postmodernism" in the fiction of Mircea Eliade. She suggests that "[h]is work offers a dependable bridge from Romantic to postmodern thought and by doing so, can help create a postmodernism that includes a protean foundationalism with its antifoundationalism" (97). In the context of reading some of Eliade's published fiction such as *The Old Man and the Bureaucrats* and *Miss Christina*, as well as materials unpublished in English such as the play *Men and Stones* and of the short story, published in this volume for the first time in English, "The Man Who Could Read Stones," Permenter makes clear statements about the lineage and characteristics of both Romanticism and postmodernism and helps the willing reader to enter these worlds and to appreciate their continuity. Declaring that it is paradoxically "our repeated arresting of Proteus that allows us to function" (116), she accepts Eliade's central contradictions as inevitable.

The short story from Mircea Eliade, translated by Ricketts, concludes the section on Literature. Written (in Romanian, of course) some two or three years after Eliade's move to Chicago, this story has been repeatedly published in Romanian, but never before in English. It is no more revealing than his other fiction of either his style as a writer or the presence of certain themes in his writing. It is, however, a convenient length and it does include the common themes of his fiction. In the light of Ricketts's information and Permenter's analysis, this piece of fiction is included to give readers the opportunity to assess for themselves the possible utility of a study of Eliade's fiction.

As already mentioned, the boundaries between scholarship in religious studies, philosophy, and literature are conveniences and can be crossed at will. Placing the contributions of Norman Girardot and Wendell Charles Beane in a separate section labelled "Personal Reflections" indicates the confluence of these various styles in the personal lives of their practitioners. While many are bemoaning the failure of the academic study of religion to exhibit any coherence or relevance and questioning its very right to exist as an independent study, Norman Girardot supplies a deeply sensible observation: "Just at the point when the study of religion has finally gained some meager acceptance within the academy, the whole nature of higher education seems poised on the brink of a major sea-change" (144). It is not only the study of religion that is suffering in this way, but the whole of the Academy and religious studies along with it. This "age of erasure" as Girardot neatly labels it, has seen loomings of a failure of nerve[21] in many disciplines. This is significant to our study because

> the current rush to repudiate Eliade may be more symptomatic of problems related to the stunted professionalization and permanent "identity crisis" of the academic study of religion and its furtive struggle for institutional acceptance than with Eliade's supposed moral and intellectual unsuitability for the contemporary situation. [In fact] Eliade often appears to be dismissed because he is an unfashionable and politically incorrect dead white male with an unsavory past, not because of any careful assessment of his approach to the study of religion. (160)

Girardot's assessment is that "the ongoing significance of an Eliadean approach to the study of religion is its multidisciplinary nature, its unabashedly 'comparative' sensibility, its concern for chaotic concreteness over abstract theory, its struggle to combine an outsider's and insider's understanding of religion" (161). Girardot points out that this has already provided concrete benefits. His conclusion is that "[d]espite all the understandable disappointment, embarrassment, and dismay regarding Eliade, we are incongruously left in a post-Eliadean age that calls for some semblance of an Eliadean approach to the study of religion" (162).

Wendell Beane's argument reveals that there is an inherently inescapable romantic dimension in the truly historical quest and an inherently inescapable historical dimension in the ideal romantic quest. Beane thus alerts the reader to the complexity of the issues that confront the historian of religion and warns against the folly of attempting analyses that seek to be purely historical or purely philosophical. "Neither philosophy nor the history of religions can ever afford to ignore each other," he concludes (188).

Since he does refer to "the dimension of mystery that the sacred presents to us" (188), Beane is sure to raise the ire of commentators who abhor the inherent

---

21. The reference is to Donald Wiebe's "The Failure of Nerve in Religious Studies," *Sciences Religieuses* 13:4 (1984): 401–422.

vagueness of such terms and the abuses to which it can lead. This suspicion has sound cause, but Beane is irrefutable in his contention that religion insists on talking about things that we do not and arguably cannot know. It is a method of mapping terra incognita and, like it or not, it thus deals with what is mysterious. The greatest danger for the study of religion remains the same danger for all areas of knowledge. That is the great mistake of assuming that our mapping of the unknown is identical to the territory.

Two brief excerpts, previously unpublished in English, from Eliade's Indian journals of 1929–1930 complete this section. Eliade brings to life the realities of the India where he lived for three years. In our attempt to assess the value of his writings it is well that we should be aware of some of his personal reflections on the experiences that formed his early life and thought.

Douglas Allen's paper is the first of those I have grouped together because of their suggestions as to the applicability of Eliadean thought. In this paper Allen "focus[es] on some of the boldest and most controversial claims in Eliade's theory of religion: his claims that the study of religion can serve—or even, must serve—as the basis for the cultural and spiritual renewal of modern human beings." He "examine[s] Eliade's proposals for overcoming modern anxiety, meaninglessness, and provincialism through a radical cultural and spiritual renewal" (209f). Allen insists that Eliade's antihistorical judgments involve an ontological stance and philosophical claims that go far beyond the usual boundaries of the history and phenomenology of religion. However, Allen does not thus claim that Eliade's "entire study of religion is based on his own religious orientation, on his normative assumptions and judgments." Rather, "in most of his studies, Eliade is attempting to interpret the religious meaning of phenomena for *homo religiosus*, not the religious meaning for Eliade" (210).

Allen is evenhanded in his conclusions as to the value of Eliade's work. While recognizing its value he concludes that:

> Eliade's approach ... needs to be enlarged for at least three reasons: he dismisses or devalues achievements of modernity; he excludes the voices of many "others" suppressed by the modern West; and he does not address how "others" have been and still are suppressed in traditional religious cultures. (231)

In another attempt to consider some positive applications of Eliadean thought, David Cave looks at "Eliade's Interpretation of Sacred Space and its Role Toward the Cultivation of Virtue." Cave indicates that, although not without faults, "Eliade's view of sacred space contributes to the cultivation of virtue in two ways: sacred places provide a context for learning and experiencing the virtues, and sacred places require virtuous actions to uphold the integrity of the places as sacred places" (236).

Cave continues, however, by pointing out that Eliade does not provide the "how-to" of sacred space—he does not tells us how we craft, maintain, and protect it. Finally, Eliade's view is inadequate because he attends to virtues but not to vices. In this way sacred space is always sacred and never profaned. It cannot lose its sacredness. Cave, on the other hand, would insist that "while sacred spaces or places can contribute to virtuous behavior, they can also spawn corresponding vices" (247) and thus be profaned.

In an essay with a sound suggestion to offer for the continued study of religion, William Paden calls for a "new comparativism" that focuses on "religious world habitation." He identifies two differing voices in the writings of Eliade:

> The first is the one most commonly associated with Eliade, where "the sacred" refers to hierophanies of the transcendent.... It is the Eliade who ... at places seems to associate his category of the sacred with the "Wholly Other" of Otto and other classical religious phenomenologies. (250)

Because "[r]eaders scan texts in terms of the categories and horizons they already possess" (251), Paden contends, many have seen this as Eliade's only voice. In his second voice, however, "Eliade is not theological at all, but postfoundationalist and to some extent postmodern" (250). This is Eliade's "world-construction voice," which "owes more to the French School figures ... than it does to the Dutch, German, and Scandinavian phenomenologies" (251) and this is "the relevant Eliadean discourse for our present secular, comparativist generation" (252). Many of Eliade's statements are thus seen as "existential descriptions of how cultures construct their lenses" rather than "implicit ontology on the author's part" (253).

Paden attempts a formal characterization of this notion of "world," which "not only marks a clear shift to a post-theological model of comparativism, but also provides a foundational term for addressing the main issue surrounding comparativism, namely, doing justice to difference as well as commonality" and "gives a frame for seeing both commonness and difference" (255).[22] He even hazards the identification of "a universal case of worldmaking behavior" (256) in the construction of sacred histories. Any such identification of universals invites unkind attention in this "age of erasure" (Girardot's phrase, 160), but it also marks the presence of robust theorizing of the kind whose absence is bemoaned by many of Eliade's critics (especially McCutcheon). Paden suggests the need for a reconsideration of the idea of universals based on world construction and concludes that "the concept

---

22. On this issue see the articles by and my concluding responses to Tim Murphy and Carl Olson.

of plural world habitation receives some direction and vision from Eliade but needs to be worked out on a broader canvas" (258). He makes a courageous beginning to that work and issues an attractive invitation for our participation.

The subtitle of the volume, *The Meaning and End of Eliade*, is taken from Wilfred Cantwell Smith's classic work *The Meaning and End of Religion*.[23] Under this title the concluding essay elucidates certain parallels between our study of Eliade and the study of religion itself. It also attempts to respond to all of the arguments involved, particularly to those calling for an end to Eliadean thought or "the Eliadean era." Focusing on the meaning that Eliade has had for me and for other contributors to this volume, and suggesting the possible meaning of our interpretation for the study and understanding of religious phenomena, I attempt to put Eliade to another end. Some carefully constructed arguments for both positions inform the following essays and readers should consider each one and the world from which each one comes in assessing the very possibility of thus changing worlds.

---

23. London: SPCK, 1962.

Part One

CRITIQUE

Chapter One

BUILDING ON ELIADE'S MAGNIFICENT FAILURE

ROGER CORLESS

The publication of *The Eliade Guide to World Religions* together with the re-publication of *Essential Sacred Writings from Around the World* (formerly *From Primitives to Zen*) allows us to get what Mircea Eliade once called "a bird view" of his work. *Essential Sacred Writings* is a topical anthology, unchanged from its first edition except for its title. The *Guide* is a sort of digest of the magisterial *The Encyclopedia of Religion* with a stimulating and all too brief methodological essay called "Introduction: Religion as System" by Eliade's disciple Ioan Petru Culianu (here spelled Couliano). The *Guide* is not backward in coming forward: its subtitle (which, however, appears only on the jacket, not on the flyleaf) is *The Authoritative Compendium of the 33 Major Religious Traditions*, and the blurb on the flap assures us that "the essence of Eliade's monumental lifeswork [*sic*] is here made available to all through this single-volume alphabetical guide."

Since I am myself not backward in coming forward, let me put my cards on the table at the very beginning. I agree with Ninian Smart that "Maybe we are at the end of the Eliadean era, and, grateful for his great contributions, are also turning to new questions and themes,"[1] but I wish to be even more forthright. Mircea Eliade, I would claim, was the seal of the prophets in that religion or

---

1. Ninian Smart, reviewing *The Encyclopedia of Religion*, in *Religious Studies Review* 14:3 (1988): 197.

tradition known as "The History of Religion(s)" and, after him, the canon is closed. We must completely rethink what we mean by "religion(s)" and what we think we are doing when we "study" "it/them." But, unlike Muhammad, who brought us a clear message to seal the tradition of Islam, Eliade has left us a perplexing message. I am bold to say that Eliade's lifework was a failure, but it was a magnificent and invaluable failure, like the failure (technically, the "null result") of the Michelson-Morley experiment to find ether, which opened the way for us to discover electromagnetic radiation.[2] Before Eliade, there had been attempts to find out what is religious about religion. Some, as Couliano puts it in his Introduction to the *Guide,* saw religion as *heteronomous,* that is, they wished to reduce it to something else (economy or society, he says, but also, surely, mental disorder or some other kind of mistake), whereas others saw religion as "*autonomous* . . . [that is] that religion in its origin and function is not the by-product of other systems . . . does not depend on them, and does not generate them" (1f.)—and of these, surely, Eliade was the leader and, in the event, the capstone. The breadth and depth of Eliade's learning, which astonished all who met him, his reverence toward the traditions he studied, and his intense, infectious enthusiasm, were an assurance that, if anyone could find what was religious about religion(s), he could. I believe the record shows that he could not. As a result, we now know a great deal more about religion(s) and we can ask totally new questions about it/them.

Well, dear reader, if you are still with me, how do I support this accusation, hoping at least to preserve my academic kneecaps intact, in the brief space of an article? Let us try a thought experiment. Imagine that you are (as, indeed, you probably are) a professor who has been asked, once again, to teach the introductory course on religion. Like a person facing any major disaster, you go through the phases of shock, denial, anger, and despair, and eventually settle into acceptance. Then you start looking for textbooks and decide that the *Guide* and the *Essential Sacred Writings* would make a manageable and complementary pair. But then you ask yourself upon which book to structure the course. The *Guide* follows, in the positivistic tradition of the *encyclopédistes,* the order accidentally provided by the haphazard and unscientific Roman alphabet. *Essential Sacred Writings,* on the other hand, is more systematic, and seems to be telling us something about what Eliade thought was religious about religion(s). So, you look at it first.

---

2. The Michelson-Morley Experiment was "an attempt to detect the velocity of the Earth with respect to the hypothetical luminiferous ether, a medium in space proposed to carry light waves. First performed in Berlin in 1881 by the physicist A. A. Michelson, the test was later refined in 1887 by Michelson and E. W. Morley in the United States." *Britannica Online,* sub "Michelson-Morley."

At the outset, you wonder about the title, and you notice what there isn't—Judaism and Christianity—so the selection belies the phrase "from around the world" in the subtitle. However, the title may have been just a fancy conceived somewhere in the dark recesses of "Harper San Francisco" in New York (or wherever they are) since Eliade was entirely aware of the omission[3] and it bears no obvious relation to the original title, *From Primitives to Zen*, another misnomer that seems to imply some sort of evolution from people who don't write anything to people who tear up things that other people have written. To see what, in fact, there is in the anthology, you look at the "Ethnic and Geographic Cross-Reference Index" (pages 644–645) and note that there are selections from Ancient Europe, Ancient Near East, Asia, and Primitives (Pre-literate Societies). Within Primitives, you find Asia again, along with Africa, Australia, the Americas, Oceania, and General. Not quite sure what to make of this mixture of area and phenomenology, you turn to the table of contents (ix–xxv), where you find the following groupings: Gods, Goddesses and Supernatural Beings; Myths of Creation and of Origin; Man (this was written before anyone knew they were being sexist, of course) and the Sacred; Death, Afterlife, Eschatology; Specialists of the Sacred—From Medicine Men to Mystics and Founders of Religions; and, last but not least, Speculations on Man and God. Something seems familiar. Oh, yes! Back in your seminary days, you did Christian Theology this way! First, God, the Creator; then, the Creation, beginning with humans; then, death, heaven and hell; then, some of the saints, mystics, founders of orders, and reformers; and finally, if there was time, a bit of philosophy.

You realize that if you structure your course on the *Essential Sacred Writings*, your students will be confirmed in the common error that religion has to do, largely or even wholly, with God or god[desse]s and human responses to Him/them, such that Christianity would appear as a typical, rather than an eccentric, religion, and that they will fail to see the uniqueness of, say, Buddhism, Jainism, and Confucianism, which in their own distinctive ways deny or refuse to take seriously one or other of these constructs. So, you turn to the *Guide* and, as it happens, it falls open at page ninety-one, where the author is getting into a muddle about Confucianism. Although (we are told) Confucianism is part of the "three religions" of China, it is not a religion, and, it turns out, it is not a philosophy either. Maybe we shouldn't

---

3. "A more serious omission it [*sic*] that of Judaism and Christianity. But it seemed unwise to increase the bulk and price of this source book considerably by reproducing such well-known texts. However, a companion volume presenting the Judaic and Christian documents on a somewhat similar thematic basis would be timely." *Essential Sacred Writings*, vii. Such a companion volume (if indeed Eliade ever really considered producing it himself) never appeared.

bother with it, then. Would Taoism be better? It has a separate entry, which starts off comparing it to Christianity and Plato, then gives up and goes on to the Three Religions, but it doesn't tell us how they interrelate, just that there were, or are, three. So, you look at Buddhism, the remaining member of this mysterious triad. The article on Buddhism begins by discounting Theravāda as incomplete and praising Tibetan Buddhism as complete, although the account of Tibetan Buddhism (40–41) is brief, woolly in the extreme, and pays undue attention to the color of the practitioner's headgear. There is a section on Chinese Buddhism, but it is almost all history, and you are disappointed to find that the most important Chinese Buddhist school is dismissed in a single baffling sentence.[4]

Going at things another way, you decide to note down the length of each article in the *Guide*, to see how much importance you should attach to each. There is no contest: Christianity, once again, but now explicitly, comes in the clear winner, with thirty-one pages. Buddhism, Islam, and Judaism arrive somewhat breathlessly as second, third, and fourth, with, respectively, eighteen, seventeen, and sixteen pages. Hinduism and African Religions tie for fifth place, with twelve pages each. But, wait! Three of the pages purportedly on Hinduism are in fact on Sikhism, so Hinduism really has only nine pages, one behind Greek Religion (eleven pages) and level with South American Religions. Tibetan Religion is last, with one page dealing with the preliterate, or pre-Buddhist, tradition.

In regard to treatment, you find that Christianity is discussed largely as a history of detailed Christological controversies; within Islam, great attention is paid to the technicalities of the Sufi path; and Hinduism and Shintō are sketched broadly and unproblematically from a unified, Great Tradition perspective. That is, the treatment is in all cases abstract and conceptual.

As for the arrangement, looking beyond the happenstance of the Roman alphabet, and simply taking the number thirty-three for granted, since it was arrived at "after considerable deliberation" (*Guide*, page xi) and you don't want to be tiresome and start all *that* again, you find the standard list of "the great world religions," some regional clusters, and some arrangements that you may never have thought of (Quick! What was the name of the sky god of the Geto-Dacian Thracians? Give up? See page 243), and cross-systematic or cross-cultural clusters such as Shamanism and Dualistic Religions—this last being a tantalizing introduction to Couliano's brilliant *The Tree of Gnosis*, the only really new thing to come along on Gnosticism, despite all the work on Nag Hammadi, since *The Gnostic Religion* by Hans Jonas.

---

4. "Another influential school was T'ien-t'ai (Japanese Tendai), founded on the eponymous mountain in Chekiang by Chih-I (531–597)." *Guide*, 36.

So, in the end, you relapse into despair. How *are* you going to teach your introductory course on religion(s) when these two books, which summarize such an enormous amount of scholarship on religion(s), are so unhelpful?

If I might now come back as myself, let me make clear once again that my criticisms are not in any way intended to belittle the achievements of Eliade and Couliano. I regard Eliade as one of those very few scholarly giants whom to meet was an unforgettable experience, who made invaluable and irreplaceable contributions to our understanding of religion(s), and who died more or less with his lifework completed. Couliano bid fair to become a worthy successor, but was tragically cut down just as he was beginning to be his most productive. I sincerely believe that we do in fact have, in the *Guide* and the *Essential Sacred Writings*, the authoritative compendia of the discipline that Americans call History of Religion(s) and the French sometimes, and perhaps more accurately, call *Science des Religions*. The fact that these two books are confused and confusing leads me to criticize the discipline, to place my strictures on, that is to say, the structures. As Augustine said about time, we all know what religion is until we think about it.

Couliano is quite right to characterize the genius of Eliade as his ability to show the inaccuracy, or rather the incoherence, of the heteronomous approach to religion, that is, the attempt to show that religion is not really religion but a misinformed way of classifying something else. The problem with the heteronomists (if I may call them such) is that they are absolutists: they claim autonomy for themselves but deny it to others. Freud and Marx at their worst, we might say, regard everything, not only religion, as a mental or a social disorder. To sort ourselves out, we must, they seem to say, worship Freud and Marx themselves and convert to their several creeds. Thus, Marxism (and why not Freudianism?) is sometimes called a pseudo-religion. So, what is a *true* religion? Sorry, nobody knows for sure.

If the heteronomous approach to religion is in fact a pseudo-autonomous approach, what is the truly autonomous approach? That is, if religion is really religion (or, perhaps, Religion), something uniquely itself, what is it and how do we study it? This is what Eliade, building on suggestions from his teachers, assayed. He went about it by looking for similarity of content. There might be, he reasoned, something in "myth" and "symbol" that was distinctively, or autonomously, religious. In order to test this hypothesis, Eliade had to embark on the breathtaking academic odyssey the marks of which appeared in the extensive footnotes to his publications and in the arrangement of his office at Chicago, which was so piled with books that when he sat down at his desk he disappeared from view. When he put his data together synchronically, as in *Patterns in Comparative Religion*, it seemed to work. But, as he said once, whenever he tried to situate the data chronologically, that is, *contextually*, "I get a pain in my head." Finally, he produced *A History of*

Religious Ideas and oversaw *The Encyclopedia of Religion*, both of which are in effect summarized in the two books here under consideration.

We can now step back and see where we are. Similarity of content has not been shown. Had it been, these two books would be clearly and simply organized. But, they are chaotic at best and pseudo-Christian at worst. The claim to autonomy, however, has been sustained, but what has been found to be autonomous is not something called by that/those Western word(s) "religion(s)" but, as Couliano suggests, *systems*.

Couliano tells us that "*all* religions are maps of the human mind," and that "this explains the basic question . . . Why do religions have so many things in common?"[5] However, it doesn't. In order to prove his point about similarity, Couliano cites not a religion or group of religions, but a structure or, indeed, a system—in this case, reincarnation—and elegantly shows how many different teachings on reincarnation can be derived from a kind of transformational grammar of two basic propositions.[6] In *The Tree of Gnosis*, he does the same thing on a grander scale for Dualism. This certainly results in a way of looking at systems, but what is religious about them? The approach ignores the boundaries supposedly drawn by labels such as Hinduism and Manichæanism, so it is not about "the great world religions," and it would work equally well for understanding some Christian teachings on the Rapture together with scientific proposals for space colonies, which are structurally similar systems of leaving a planet that has for one or another reason become unsatisfactory.

As Jacob Neusner would say, "Take Judaism, for example." It is certainly a system. Is it a religion? Is it even religious? How about Buddhism? One way to understand the teaching of the Buddha is to say that he came to put an end to religion, for religion, he said, while promising freedom, actually enslaves. And Marxism? Christians may regard Marxism as pseudo-religious, but Marx regarded religion as pseudo-Marxist. So, here is the point: if a system is autonomous it is able, at least to its own satisfaction, to explain all other systems as heteronomous. To study such a system *as autonomous*, we need to enter into its circle of discourse while somehow remaining critically outside it.

This is what Eliade tried to do, but he had an implicit list of systems that were religious and systems that were not. Wilfred Cantwell Smith also tried this, and realized, in a famous simile, that there is something "fishy" about the distinction between these lists (which he sees in terms of a false dichotomy between religion

---

5. *Guide*, 7. Italics original.

6. Some teachings on reincarnation cannot be derived from these transformations. Buddhism, for example, does not accept Couliano's premises, and so escapes his net.

and culture), but he has been unable to make a clean break of it. Ninian Smart has suggested that we discard the distinction between religion, philosophy, and ideology altogether, and just ask, in effect, "Would you die for it?"[7] Then, he proposes that we should use the tools developed by the discipline called History of Religion(s) to examine "what-you-would-die-for-isms," but he does not tell us how to do it.[8]

With the introduction of the notion of system, however, things start to clear up. Systems theory is now fairly sophisticated, and can be plundered for insights, as long as we are armed with postmodernist suspicions and regard systems as important but not as serious—so long, that is, as we do not reify them and thus slip back into the dreaded Foundationalism. A polymethodic approach to what-you-would-die-for systems, combining these and other investigative tools with those developed by History of Religion(s) under the leadership of Eliade, would allow us to close the Eliadean era with dignity, building upon the null result of his indispensable investigation, and go on to other questions.

---

7. Ninian Smart, *Beyond Ideology: Religion and the Future of Western Civilization,* Gifford Lectures, 1979–1980. San Francisco: Harper and Row, 1981. See especially chapter 7, "Secular Ideologies: A First Anatomy."

8. Smart, *Beyond Ideology,* especially pages 64–68 and 311–313.

Chapter Two

METHODS, THEORIES, AND THE TERRORS OF HISTORY

Closing the Eliadean Era with Some Dignity

RUSSELL T. MCCUTCHEON

> What is at stake in these debates is a struggle over what the study of religion itself should be. Eliade has [simply] become a focal point for the on going identity crisis in the field.
>
> —Tim Murphy, *Wesen und Erscheinung*

Since the early 1980s a number of allegations have been made regarding the personal politics of Mircea Eliade. In many regards, the "Eliade affair" is similar to other cases of notable European intellectuals of the interwar generation whose political pasts emerged only after they had established themselves as influential figures in their respective scholarly fields. The names of the literary critic Paul de Man and the

---

An earlier form of this paper was presented to the History of the Study of Religion Group of the American Academy of Religion, New Orleans, November 24, 1996. Portions of this paper rely on work published in greater detail in McCutcheon, *Manufacturing Religion: The Discourse on* Sui Genesis *Religion and the Politics of Nostalgia*. Oxford: OUP, 1997.

philosopher Martin Heidegger come to mind as two of the better known examples of scholars with, in the least, questionable, and at most, extreme, political backgrounds. But in one important regard the case of Eliade differs from de Man and Heidegger; whereas news of de Man's antisemitic wartime newspaper columns and Heidegger's explicit association with Nazism continue to spark considerable debates within such fields as literary criticism and philosophy,[1] the case of Eliade remains largely marginal to the work of the vast majority of scholars of religion.

Although some specialized articles and book chapters have examined aspects of Eliade's early years, his political writings and relationships, and, more importantly, their possible relations to his mature work as a scholar have received little extended debate. Instead, troublesome categories and abstractions popularized in Eliade's work such as "the sacred," "hierophany," "*coincidentia oppositorum*," and "*homo religiosus*" continue to be used uncritically by a surprisingly large number of writers in the field. Precisely because of the central role played by Heidegger's and de Man's writings in their respective fields, reassessments of their work have been necessary and widespread. Simply put, for good or ill it has become virtually impossible to cite the work of either scholar without taking into account, implicitly or explicitly, the Nazi past of the one and the, at least early, antisemitism of the other. However, contemporary representations of Eliade as a disembodied Great Man, or, better put, Great Mind, coupled with the virtually unquestioned authority his work yet exerts in contemporary scholarship on religion suggests the existence of a critical blind spot in the study of religion.[2]

---

1. Specifically, I have in mind the degree to which the most prominent deconstructive critic, Jacques Derrida, has been explicitly involved in both debates. See what Christopher Norris has termed Derrida's compassionate essay, "Like the Sound of the Sea Deep within a Shell: Paul de Man's War," *Critical Inquiry* 14 (1988): 590–652, on de Man and his wartime articles, as well as Derrida's response to the critical reception of this very article, "Biodegradables: Seven Diary Fragments," *Critical Inquiry* 15:4 (1989): 812–873. See also the other essays published in the same issue of *Critical Inquiry* that respond to Derrida's essay on de Man. On the de Man affair see also Werner Hamacher et al., *Wartime Journalism, 1939–1943*. Lincoln, NB: University of Nebraska Press, 1988, and *Responses: On Paul de Man's Wartime Journalism*. Lincoln, NB: University of Nebraska Press, 1989. Concerning the case of Heidegger, see the essays by, among others, Hans-Georg Gadamer, Jürgen Habermas, and Derrida, in *Critical Inquiry* 15:2 (1989). On the controversy surrounding Derrida's wishes to remove one of his own essays from Richard Wolin's collection on Heidegger (as documented in Richard Wolin, *The Heidegger Controversy: A Critical Reader*. Cambridge, MA: MIT Press, 1993, ix–xx), see Thomas Sheehan's *New York Review of Books* review of Wolin and the many spirited subsequent letters to the editor written by those involved in this controversy, published in the early months of 1993.

2. This is a claim I addressed in small measure in my earlier survey of the Eliade affair— "The Myth of the Apolitical Scholar," *Queen's Quarterly* 100 (1993): 642–646.

The problem, then, is to discern how scholars of religion have withstood the critical assessments of the politics of Eliade's life and his scholarship.³ That Eliade's life was political should be apparent from the fact that he, like all of us, lived and acted in complex social and institutional networks where we must continually negotiate power and privilege. That his scholarship has a politics embedded within it, what Armin Geertz and Jeppe Sinding Jensen have aptly termed the "politics of nostalgia" (Geertz and Jensen 1991), I have argued elsewhere and therefore take for granted here (McCutcheon 1997b). Accordingly, my concern here is not with Eliade so much as with the reception of his work in the North American context. Given that his scholarship continues to comprise an almost paradigmatic model for the field, we must not forget that we are not talking simply about an isolated critique of a marginal scholar in the otherwise rich history of the study of religion; instead, we are talking about an entire scholarly field successfully sidestepping its engagement with the politics of its own representations—in this case, its representation of Eliade.

From the outset, then, I must make it clear that I am not particularly concerned with Eliade's personal political views, his actions, his supposed guilt or culpability. Although his personal politics has attracted the attention of other critics (the work of Ivan Strenski [1982, 1987] and Adriana Berger [1989, 1994] being two of the foremost examples), whether he was or was not a card-carrying Romanian fascist is largely irrelevant to my current interests. Instead, I see significant links between contemporary defenses of Eliade and his work, on the one hand, and the ways in which scholars of religion routinely marginalize issues of context, power, and conflict in their studies of religion, myth, ritual, scriptures, and the like, on the other. In other words, the particular way in which Eliade and his work are represented in these various defenses is simply the most recent instance of a wider, more pervasive problem in our field, a field where the dominant strategies of representation construct not only a privileged datum (*sui generis* religion) and methods (phenomenology and hermeneutics) but also the field's own privileged, apolitical context and history. I term this the discourse on *sui generis* religion.

Therefore, let me repeat: in this chapter I am not concerned with Eliade's personal culpability for I see in the various defenses of his life and work much larger and more intriguing issues pertaining to the politics of this scholarly discourse (a similar point to that made by Allen 1994, 345). Quoting Tim Murphy, we must recognize that "there are more options [in the Eliade affair] than 'for or against' Eliade" (Murphy 1994, 383). Accordingly, I see the links between the Eliade, de Man, and Heidegger affairs not in terms of any similarity in their individual actions,

---

3. My thanks to Charles Lock, of the University of Toronto's English Department, who first put the matter in precisely this way in a conversation we had in January 1995.

beliefs, or guilt—whether such links are present is a separate debate; rather, the links pertain to the techniques their contemporary defenders use not only to protect their work and influence in academia but to construct and maintain a supposedly ahistorical, totalized scholarly field.

My thesis is simply this: the very way in which scholars of religion have responded to the debate on Eliade and politics is itself representative of the de-historicizing strategies that routinely construct religion as an autonomous, irreducible, personal experience that cannot be explained but only described, interpreted, and ultimately appreciated "on its own plane of reference." Accordingly, the field constructed in this way is more akin to the practice of religious pluralism than a scholarly study of human beliefs, behaviors, and institutions. Just such a field results when scholars of religion warn against the dangers of social scientific reductionism and, instead, recommend that we "take religions seriously"—a common plea heard throughout the field. That such de-historicizing strategies have not only intellectual but institutional, social, and even geopolitical implications and effects is a related thesis I have argued elsewhere (*Manufacturing Religion*, chapter 6).

Perhaps there exists no better example of how this presumed irreducibility and autonomy of the religious datum affects the reception of Eliade than the work of David Cave. He writes:

> I am largely sympathetic to Eliade's cultural and pluralistic vision and I consider informative, insightful, and valid many of his interpretations of religious experience. I have tried to read Eliade as much as possible *on his own terms* and to place him within the framework of reference he himself was trying to construct, which I contend is the new humanism. (Cave 1993, 12; emphasis added)

Agreement with the views of one's subject is not necessarily troublesome; what is problematic, however, is the position that maintains that Eliade's work is somehow *sui generis*, and can sufficiently be studied on its own terms. Come to think of it, what precisely does this mean? Just how does one determine the intentions of an author or the "framework of reference he himself was trying to construct"? Moreover, would Cave extend the same interpretive privilege to all historical subjects we as scholars study? I am reminded here of the recent documentary entitled *The Architecture of Doom*, which deploys a similar method in virtually maintaining that Nazism was an aesthetic movement that simply got out of control.

In the second sentence of his Introduction, Cave makes it clear that his concern is to examine "the *visionary impulse behind the totality* of Eliade's prolific and manifold life work" (3; emphasis added). All connections and associations with larger issues of context, politics, and power are thereby effectively excluded from the outset, for Cave is dealing with private visions, impulses, and totalities—whatever they may be—

rather than with publicly available practices and institutions. In his study of Eliade, Cave immediately turns our attention to abstract totalities that can only be glimpsed as they are manifested in this or that passing moment. Starting out with the textual remains of what I would simply term Eliade-the-hierophany, Cave works toward discerning the transcendental essence (i.e., the totality) to Eliade's so-called program of cultural and spiritual renewal (i.e., the new humanism). Such a methodology prevents his readers from ever seriously entertaining that the new humanism might instead be understood as a potent and ethnocentric political program.

In fully accepting Eliade's own troublesome terminology and methodologies—Eliadean jargon, if you will—and then using these as the basis for his own study of Eliade's life and work, Cave effectively precludes from the outset any form of social, political, and economic analysis; for, as the old argument goes, such reductions throw the proverbial baby out with the bathwater by missing the deeper spiritual impulse supposedly present in the abstract totality. However, Cave's routine talk of such things as totality, visions, essences, experiences, the sacred, the real, Being, and authentic versus inauthentic existence arises from, and makes sense only within, an interpretive context that accords some sort of privilege to certain conceptions of reality that we as scholars of religion should analyze rather than presuppose. To borrow two terms from psychology, in reading Eliade on his own level—whatever that may turn out to be—commentators take for granted the self-evident meaning of the manifest level of analysis and forsake any analysis of latent functions and implications. Such scholarship corresponds to the penchant in our field for phenomenological, descriptivist studies that forgo developing theories of religion.

For another example of this general trend of privileging internal, sympathetic exegesis and commentary over analysis and critique, take the case of Bryan Rennie's book on Eliade where, in the opening, he writes: "Secondary scholars have all too often criticized what on closer inspection turns out to be their own interpretations of Eliade's thought rather than his actual thought" (1996, 4). Much like Cave who tries to assess Eliade in terms of what Eliade himself was supposedly trying to do and achieve (1993, 3), Rennie's defense and reconstruction of Eliade's thought is implicitly based on delivering the real goods unavailable to so-called secondary scholars; Rennie—who waffles on whether he is himself among the group of "secondary scholars" since he offers an authoritative reading of "primary texts"—aims, much like Cave, to provide his readers with the coherent and meaningful whole as contained in Eliade's "actual thought." Rennie also achieves this essential re-reading of Eliade by using an exclusively Eliadean methodology: not the new humanism, as in the case of Cave, but the related creative hermeneutic; Rennie writes in his opening chapter: "My approach will also be an attempt to clarify *by application* Eliade's creative hermeneutics" (1996, 5; emphasis added).

Much as Eliade maintained that religion could only be studied on its own plane of reference, so too Cave and Rennie study Eliade on his own plane of reference. Presuming that talk of such things as the whole, totality, the real, unmediated experiences, and, one of my personal favorites, Rennie's discussion of Eliade's notion of symbols as expressing "an otherwise non-sensory modality of the real" (1996, 51), actually make sense, both writers demonstrate not only the ease with which the Eliadean jargon lulls readers into a noncritical stupor but also the primary means by which this entire debate is constrained from the start. Certainly, I acknowledge that Eliade's work is filled with such vaguely defined terminology and, further, that any commentary on his work will of necessity address such terms. However, any commentary on his work must also address the vacuous and obscurantist nature of claims regarding such things as "non-sensory modalities of the real."

A very useful example of the obscurantism that results from the application of this ideological posture to the Eliade affair can be found in Carl Olson's book, *The Theology and Philosophy of Mircea Eliade* (1992).[4] In his opening chapter, Olson writes:

> Even if Eliade was a hard-core Fascist throughout his life, for which I have not found any evidence, this political ideology did not affect his scholarship to any sinister extent, and it is unjust to taint someone and to judge them guilty by association. How can we come to grips with Eliade's prewar association with the Iron Guard? Before and after the war, it can be concluded, by reading his *Autobiography*, that he was a patriot and a Rumanian nationalist concerned with his nation's historical past, present dictatorial bondage, and uncertain future; he was also concerned with preserving its culture during its period of diaspora for its artists and intellectuals after the Second World War. Eliade's patriotic fervor is evident in his notion of "Romanianism," a non-political nationalism that embodied a messianic sense of the divinely-chosen nature of the Rumanian nation with a special mission to fulfil in the world. (Olson 1992, 4–5)[5]

It is gratuitous, to say the least, to assert that any scholarly work remains unaffected, or at least unaffected to any "sinister extent," by political ideologies. Just as in the case of other interpreters of Eliade's time in Romania, Olson attempts to limit any of his political involvements to early or youthful indiscretions, thereby protecting his later scholarly works from exposure to any sinister indictment. (Another common strategy is to limit political influence to Eliade's journalism, thereby protecting

---

4. For a related critique of Olson's depoliticizing strategies, see the closing pages of Tim Murphy's review essay, *Method & Theory in the Study of Religion* 6:4 (1994): 382–389.

5. Olson notes that Ricketts (*Romanian Roots*, 903, 912) covers these same issues.

his "serious" scholarship.) Olson presumes a problematic notion of just what political means, as if it only refers to organized party politics as opposed to the more pervasive ways in which we routinely construct and contest social power and authority. Even more troubling is Olson's understanding of the relations between patriotism and nationalism; according to him, only the latter seems to be related to political motives or intentions while the former seems to be nonpolitical or merely cultural. In terms of how dominant ethnic, social, and political groups use these concepts, "patriotism" (e.g., British or American patriotism) is understood as essentially positive, inspiring, and as affirming some sort of neutral cultural heritage, whereas "nationalism" (e.g., Québécois or Serbian nationalism) is interpreted as threatening, politically and militarily loaded, and therefore dangerous. I would suggest that there is no difference whatsoever between the two for when someone on our side dies in an effort to maintain or destabilize certain political, social, or economic practices they are a patriot; and when someone on their side does the exact same, they are a nationalist zealot or a terrorist. It should be apparent that there is much at stake, both politically and socially, in maintaining the illusion of difference.

Furthermore, it is astounding that Olson could interpret such profoundly political assertions as those regarding the so-called mystical and messianic mission of a divinely chosen nation as being in any way apolitical or merely patriotic. Simply put, I have no idea what "non-political nationalism" means. It virtually amounts to reading the divine right of monarchs as a purely spiritual or cultural claim, as if that makes any sense at all. Although such a claim may make sense to those with a stake in such rhetoric—an American audience comes to mind where claims regarding the country's divinely chosen mission, or Manifest Destiny, have a long, rich history—our role as scholars is not to perpetuate such rhetoric but to contextualize, to historicize, to explain it. As a byproduct of this type of analysis we end up deauthorizing it as well.[6] Surely few modern scholars of religion would fail to recognize the highly political nature of such claims if, for example, they were made in the rhetoric of a fundamentalist context. Therefore, Olson's exclusion of potent political implications from critical examination is itself a highly suspicious strategy.

And last, Olson's uncritical use of Eliade's *Autobiography* betrays an important aspect of our field already seen in the work of Cave and Rennie: presuming religion to be an essentially personalistic, irreducible experience, actors are granted first-person interpretive authority when it comes to accounting for the details, meanings,

---

6. I have elaborated on this role for the scholar in my essay, "The Default of Critical Intelligence? The Scholar of Religion as Public Intellectual," *Journal of the American Academy of Religion* 65:2 (1997): 443–468.

and origins of their experiences and lives (on the complexities of this issue, see Godlove [1994]). This is precisely what we see happening when commentators read Eliade on his own "plane of reference." Now, this is not to say that scholars should instead routinely suspend the informant's right to interpret and explain his or her own actions and beliefs, but that *scholars must carefully devise defensible criteria to determine at what level of analysis they do or do not suspend such first person explanatory authority.*

This is the crucial methodological point that such writers as Robert Segal and Wayne Proudfoot told us some time ago; without taking such insider reports and interpretations seriously we would have no descriptive data to study, for much of our scholarship theorizes and redescribes not simply other people's observable behavior but also their own understandings of, and explanations for, their behavior. Despite the fact that we as scholars might find certain sorts of physical behavior to be of interest, what we are often more attracted to is the fact that some people explain their behavior by appealing to demonic possession. Were we to offer such people the same interpretive privilege that Cave affords Eliade, we as scholars would have little to do but report on insider accounts. Instead, these reports are the data for our theoretically based redescriptive efforts. As phrased by Bruce Lincoln in the last of his thirteen theses on method:

> When one permits those whom one studies to define the terms in which they will be understood . . . one has ceased to function as historian or scholar. In that moment, a variety of roles are available: some perfectly respectable (amanuensis, collector, friend and advocate), and some less appealing (cheerleader, voyeur, retailer of import goods). None, however, should be confused with scholarship. (Lincoln 1996, 227)

The way in which many commentators seem to find no good reason to read Eliade's various published journals and his two volume autobiography as data rather than as an authoritative, transparent accounts of his motivations and intentions is, once again, evidence of the general suspicion of theorizing, explanation, and analysis that abounds in the regnant discourse. Indeed, Eliade's journals and the autobiography provide important points of access into this debate but surely they are not to be taken as self-evidently authoritative, read simply as Eliade's "actual thought," or as his unvarnished self-disclosures. Such a prioritizing of the insider's claims at the expense of the outsider's analytic perspective is characteristic of an undefended scholarly intuition regarding what we can only term an essential experience that apparently grounds all behavior; such an intuitive basis for the field leads the way for scholars simply to become, in Lincoln's words, collectors, cheerleaders, and voyeurs, or in Burton Mack's apt words (1989), caretakers for religion rather than critics of culture.

Explicitly related to Olson's obscurantism, is the defense of Eliade offered in an earlier article by Rennie. In his otherwise useful response to Berger's critique of Eliade's wartime activities (Berger 1989), Rennie obscures the wartime nationalist and xenophobic activities of certain elements of the Romanian population by painting a sympathetic picture of their historical lot as an oppressed people continually striving to deal with the burden of foreign domination (see Rennie, *Reconstructing Eliade*, 149–159). With its annexation of Transylvania, which contributed to the doubling of Romania's size after World War I, the Romanians, according to Rennie, were finally "free from foreign domination . . . [and] were determined not to cede Romanian self-determination to internal foreign influences" (1992, 376). That the rhetoric of "internal foreign influences" begs questions of the criteria used to determine ethnic and nationalist purity seems wholly lost on Rennie. As well, it is unlikely that one could find a better example of the relations between nationalism and the devaluation of others than in his comments on the Transylvanian annexation: with that annexation in mind, we can see that Rennie's comment on Romanians finally being "free from foreign domination" takes on an ironic tone. His description sounds remarkably like a rationalization for the later ethnic and religious oppression and victimization in Romania. Simply put, one can assume that the Transylvanians who awoke to find themselves part of Romania were not as pleased with the new geographic, nationalist realities as were the newly "liberated" Romanians.

Much as Olson excuses Eliade by understanding his actions as arising from "patriotic fervor" and a sense of "non-political nationalism," Rennie goes on to excuse Eliade from lending his explicit support to the cause of the Romanian fascist movement on the grounds of ethnic purity; that is, because, according to Rennie, the Archangel Movement was "at least *genuinely* Romanian" (italics added) as opposed to the new Romanian King's Italian- and German-influenced policies. According to Rennie's interpretation, then, Eliade's stand at this time is not so much political but ethnic and cultural—as if this troublesome distinction somehow assists us to understand the situation any better. However, at no time does he question just what is genuine about one's ethnic status and why such a status implies an apolitical privilege of some sort. Such claims are based on a spurious, essentialist understanding of social identity.

Also like Olson, Rennie explains away the eventual violent antisemitism of the Iron Guard to such attitudes as "blind nationalism" and "fanatical nationalism" (1992, 386; 387), both of which are akin to what he later characterizes as "virulent nationalism." These various causes are implicitly contrasted with Eliade's own motivations, termed by Rennie "essential humanism" (1992, 388)—I am reminded here of the opening of Olson's quotation where we found the implicit distinction between fascism and hard-core fascism, a distinction not that far from certain defenders of Heidegger who labeled him simply a "normal Nazi." Through speculation and arbitrary distinctions Rennie protects Eliade from all accusations of fanaticism or nationalism and portrays his ambitions as somehow nonvirulent and insightful rather than dangerous and blind. The use of the adjectives blind, fanatical, and virulent are evidence of a baseless, normative judgment that ensures that the actions of some people are held at the margins, far from the privileged cultural, spiritual, and apolitical center. Accordingly, this one representation of Eliade, and its possible uses, benefits tremendously from this implicit and unquestioned construction of a margin far removed from what we must simply accept as self-evidently and purely cultural and apolitical commitments and motives. As implied by Rennie, one appears to be held accountable for one's actions and beliefs only at the margin.

Although it is highly questionable to what extent one can determine Eliade's intentions and motivations concerning his early associations and how such associations affected his later work in religion, what is of particular interest are the ways in which Cave, Olson, and Rennie have constructed their replies to such criticisms. (If space allowed we could include the seemingly critical work of Norman Manea [1991, 1992] in this list as well). Instead of discounting Strenski's and Berger's criticisms as being based on amateur psychologizing and utter speculation—which is not to say that I would make such a critique of their work—all three defenders engage in their own form of psychologizing, speculation, and obscurantism to construct elaborate interpretive schemes that function to privilege and isolate a portion of Eliade's history and/or his work, thereby ensuring that a highly abstract, essential image of Eliade qua intellectual remains aloof from the taint of historical or political life. Implicitly, in all three cases the phenomenological *epoché* is employed to segment, isolate, and thereby protect Eliade's life, work, and the field at large from the kind of critical scrutiny made possible by social scientific analysis.

In fact, such protection is so effective that it is the basis for Rennie's recent attempt to rehabilitate Eliade's ideological program of conceptualizing religion as an essential, universal, and total human experience capable of saving Western civilization by appropriating supposedly archaic values. In his foreword to Rennie's *Reconstructing Eliade*, Mac Linscott Ricketts goes so far as to suggest that Rennie's reconstruction of Eliade's thought provides "a guide in religious studies for years to come, in an increasingly secular and postmodern twenty-first century" (Rennie 1996, ix). I do not agree: the future of the post-Eliadean field will have much more to do with a critical inquiry into the theoretical as well as the social and political origins and implications of the very categories and tools that such scholars as Cave, Olson, Rennie, and Ricketts—not to mention Eliade—employ in their studies of human behavior and institutions (e.g., we will study the very distinction between the so-called sacred and secular for it has been one of the most effective rhetorical means for constructing a privileged realm of nonpolitical human behavior). If anything, Rennie's book is not so much a guide for the future, as suggested by

Ricketts, but possibly the end of the Eliadean era.[7] Therefore, its appearance in the late-twentieth-century study of religion makes it all the more difficult, in the words of Roger Corless, to "close the Eliadean era with dignity" (1993, 377, above, 9). Instead of uncritically deploying such categories as the sacred, the real, Being, and experience, the post-Eliadean study of religion ought to be concerned with the ways in which power and authority are constructed and legitimated through so-called religious claims and practices *as well as* through the very scholarship on such beliefs and behaviors. The recent work of Bruce Lincoln on authority (1994) comes to mind as one of the leading examples of the critical potential of just such a post-Eliadean study of religion.

Because of such features as the strategically useful distinctions between scholarship and journalism, politics and spirit, the suspect limitations placed on sociopolitical origins and influences, and the elevation of insider reports to the status of authoritative analysis, the representations of Eliade's defenders invite further scrutiny. Their virtual dismissal of contextualist or so-called external and secondary criticism is unwarranted inasmuch as it is based on an uncritical use of Eliade's own troublesome categories and existential judgments. To paraphrase Christopher Norris commenting on similarly suspect defenses of Heidegger, the works of Cave, Olson, and Rennie cause us to ask why "certain intellectuals—among them thinkers of great acuity and power . . . should have gone to such great lengths of ingenious argumentation" (Norris 1990, 242) to protect Eliade's work from criticism and debate. For although Cave acknowledges that indeed Eliade was "right-wing" (1993, 6), although Olson recognizes that Eliade's scholarship was indeed affected by political ideologies, and although Rennie comes to agree that Eliade was "fiercely nationalistic" (1996, 143), all three construct elaborate and ingenious ways of marginalizing and lessening the impact of these admissions. For Cave, the genius of Eliade forces us to accept the tares along with the wheat (1993, 21); Olson asserts that Eliade's nonpolitical nationalism did not affect his scholarship to any sinister extent; and Rennie maintains that Eliade's texts, when read exclusively in an Eliadean fashion, present a "deliberate statement of the author's intentions" (1996, 148). In fact, Rennie goes on to defend Eliade by arguing that he was no more nationalist or antisemitic than his peers, for he "was just as opposed to Bulgarian and Hungarian usurpation of Romanian autonomy as he was of Jewish" (1996, 151). Defending Eliade by maintaining that he disliked "the Jews" as much as many other groups simply serves as a biting indictment of both Eliade and his defenders.

---

7. For a more extended analysis of what is sure to become one of the standard commentaries on Eliade's extensive body of work, see my review of Rennie's *Reconstructing Eliade*, in *Religion* 28:1 (1998): 92–97. See Rennie's response, *Religion* 28:4 (1998):413–414 and his review of *Manufacturing Religion* in *Zygon* (June 2000).

Whether or not Eliade was an antisemite, a nationalist, and a fascist—let alone a hard-core one—the presence in his defenders' works of such weak arguments, unfounded assertions, the rhetoric of primacy, actuality, autonomy, and authenticity, as well as the use of such vacuous concepts as "unmediated experience," "the real," and "non-political nationalism," all suggest that there is much at stake in the Eliade affair. What is at stake is not simply the reputation of Eliade, as some may think, but also the ability of a group of scholars to continue to define their object of study by means of assertion and intuition rather than by means of explicit theories, evidential criteria, and rational argumentation. As stated by Tim Murphy in the epigraph to this essay, "what is at stake in these debates is a struggle over what the study of religion itself should be. Eliade has [simply] become a focal point for the on-going identity crisis in the field" (Murphy 1994, 383). This struggle, then, is over the fate of the study of religion defined as an apolitical, autonomous, and irreducible intellectual and institutional pursuit. Accordingly, all scholars of religion have a stake in the Eliade affair.

The study of religion conceived as the description of a private, *sui generis* experience exists precisely by camouflaging and obscuring not only the social, political, and economic origins and implications of so-called religious experiences but also the political origins and implications of the academic discourse on these experiences.[8] Because the very means by which Eliade has been defended are the same means by which scholars established and continue to maintain the autonomous study of religion in North America, addressing claims of extreme politics in the field in any systematic manner will entail a far greater and more sustained effort than we have so far seen.

Ironically, however, the very strategies of exclusion, isolation, and protection that in the Eliade affair most deserve critique are the same strategies that provide what, along with Norris we can term, the discourse's conditions of possibility and its unthought axiomatics (1990, 257); the theoretical and methodological means by which "religion" is conceptualized and inductively studied as a seemingly autonomous, self-evident essence are therefore the strategies that also allow scholars of religion to construct a discourse that evades the terrors of their own history.[9] These

---

8. Most recently, the explicit colonial history of comparative religion has been critically examined by David Chidester. "Anchoring Religion in the World: A Southern African History of Comparative Religion," *Religion* 26 (1996): 141–160 and " 'Classify and Conquer': Friedrich Max Müller, Indigenous Religious Traditions, and Imperial Comparative Religion," unpublished paper, 1996.

9. For a survey of the various ways in which "religion" is used by scholars, see McCutcheon, "The Category 'Religion' in Recent Publications: A Critical Survey," *Numen* 42/3 (1995): 284–309.

inductivist methods and ideological strategies simultaneously comprise the opening for one way of defining and studying religion as well as the blind spot that prevents its practitioners from addressing questions of extreme politics. This suggests that it may in fact be utterly impossible for members of the discourse on *sui generis* religion to address the issues raised in this paper, insulated as they and their datum are from the pressures of historical, political existence. If this is indeed the case, and, further, if it is only by addressing these theoretical, methodological, and ideological strategies that we can close the Eliadean era in the study of religion with any dignity at all, then it means that we also need to reconceive how we define, describe, compare, and explain religion in the public university.[10] Therefore, Murphy was correct in pointing out that the critique of Eliade's politics and the reception of his work in North America is implicitly a critique of the way the majority of scholars of religion continue to carry out their work in the academy. Accordingly, ending the Eliadean era in the study of religion entails redescribing issues of theory, definition, method, and data. In a word, it means redescribing "religion" itself.

---

10. I have elaborated on this argument in my paper, "Lumbering Through the Academy? Redescribing the Study of Religion in the Public University," in *Critics not Caretakers: Redescribing the Study of Religion*, forthcoming from the State University of New York Press.

Chapter Three

ARE THERE MODERN MYTHS?

ROBERT A. SEGAL

In all his writings Mircea Eliade strives to show that religiosity is innate to human beings and, more, that it is as insatiable a drive as hunger. Rather than arguing the case philosophically, by analyzing the concept of human nature or of religion, Eliade argues it empirically, by amassing evidence of the universality of religion. The two main expressions of religion for him are myths and rituals.

Eliade's greatest challenge is to demonstrate the presence of religion among modern Westerners, who for him are almost by definition professed nonbelievers.[1] To be able to show that even those who spurn religion still evince it would surely be a strong, whether or not clinching, argument for the ineluctability of it. This chapter evaluates Eliade's claim that moderns harbor myths in particular.

TRADITIONAL MYTHS

According to Eliade, in "primitive" and "archaic" societies myth is "the very foundation of social life and culture."[2] Operating at its fullest, myth here fulfills several

---

1. To cite but one statement: "the situation of modern man, who believes himself—or wishes to be—without religion" (*The Two and the One* [*Mephistopheles and the Androgyne*], trans. J. M. Cohen. New York: Harper Torchbooks, 1969. Eng. tr. 1965, 20–21).

2. *Myth, Dreams, and Mysteries*, trans. Philip Mairet. New York: Harper Torchbooks, 1967, Eng. tr. 1960, 23.

functions. First, it explains the origin of present-day phenomena, tracing them back to the primordial deeds of gods:

> Myth narrates a sacred history; it relates an event that took place in primordial Time, the fabled time of the "beginnings." In other words, myth tells how, through the deeds of Supernatural Beings, a reality came into existence, be it the whole of reality, the Cosmos, or only a fragment of reality—an island, a species of plant, a particular kind of human behavior, an institution.[3]

Second, myth provides models for behavior. The deeds of gods recounted in myth serve as norms to be imitated: "[T]he myth becomes exemplary, and consequently repeatable, for it serves as a model, and by the same token as a justification, for all human actions" (*Myths, Dreams, and Mysteries*, 23).

Third, either the outright imitation of a primordial deed or the sheer recounting of it takes one out of present time and, as if on a magic carpet, carries one back to the time of the deed itself: "In imitating the exemplary acts of a god or of a mythic hero, or simply by recounting their adventures, the man of an archaic society detaches himself from profane time and magically reenters the Great Time, the sacred time" (*Myths, Dreams, and Mysteries*, 23). The payoff is less escapism than rejuvenation: "What is involved is, in short, a return to the original time, the therapeutic purpose of which is to begin life once again, a symbolic rebirth."[4] That rejuvenation comes from returning to the time when, it is believed, the gods were close at hand. The rejuvenation comes not from becoming divine oneself—Eliade stresses the hiatus between the human and the divine, between the profane and the sacred—but from brushing up against divinity. Humans are rejuvenated by *encountering* the sacred, not by *becoming* sacred. What Eliade says of creation myths, which for him are the fundamental myths, applies to other myths as well:

> *In illo tempore* the gods had displayed their greatest powers. The cosmogony is the supreme divine manifestation, the paradigmatic art of strength, superabundance, and reality. Religious man thirsts for the real. By every means at his disposal, he seeks to reside at the very source of primordial reality, when the world was *in statu nascendi*. (*Sacred and Profane*, 80)

---

3. *Myth and Reality*, tr. Willard R. Trask. New York: Harper Torchbooks, 1968, Eng. tr. 1963, 5–6.

4. *The Sacred and the Profane*, trans. Willard R. Trask. New York: Harvest Books, 1968, Eng. tr. 1959, 82.

MODERN MYTHS

If moderns have myths, as Eliade contends, then surely those myths must fulfill the same three functions as traditional myths. By modern myths, he means both new, distinctively modern myths and, even more, earlier myths that continue to exist in modernity. Most often, he means a combination of the two: distinctively modern *versions* of older, "archetypal" myths.[5] To use one of his favorite examples, Marxism represents an updated version of the traditional mythic motifs of an original golden age, a fall, a battle between good and evil forces, the triumph of good, and the restoration of the golden age:

> For whatever we may think of the scientific claims of Marx, it is clear that the author of the *Communist Manifesto* takes up and carries on one of the great eschatological myths of the Middle Eastern and Mediterranean world, namely: the redemptive part to be played by the Just (the "elect," the "anointed," the "innocent," the "missioners," in our own days by the proletariat), whose sufferings are invoked to change the ontological status of the world. In fact, Marx's classless society, and the consequent disappearance of all historical tensions, find their most exact precedent in the myth of the Golden Age which, according to a number of traditions, lies at the beginning and the end of History. Marx has enriched this venerable myth with a truly messianic Judaeo-Christian ideology; on the one hand, by the prophetic and soteriological function he ascribes to the proletariat; and, on the other, by the final struggle between Good and Evil, which may well be compared with the apocalyptic conflict between Christ and Antichrist, ending in the decisive victory of the former. (*Myths, Dreams, and Mysteries*, 25–26)

Similarly, modern literature evinces perennial mythic motifs in contemporary guise:

> The successive stages of myth, legend, epic and modern literature have often been pointed out and need not detain us here. Let us merely recall the fact that the mythical archetypes survive to some degree in the great modern novels. The difficulties and trials that the novelist's hero has to

---

5. On modern myths, which Eliade often mixes with rituals, see esp. his *The Sacred and the Profane*, 201–213; *Myth and Reality*, 181–193; *Myths, Dreams, and Mysteries*, ch. 1; *Cosmos and History (The Myth of the Eternal Return)*, trans. Willard R. Trask. New York: Harper Torchbooks, 1959, Eng. tr. 1954, ch. 4; *Rites and Symbols of Initiation (Birth and Rebirth)*, trans. Willard R. Trask. New York: Harper Torchbooks, 1965, Eng. tr. 1958, 127–136; *Patterns in Comparative Religion*, trans. Rosemary Sheed. Cleveland: Meridian Books, 1963, Eng. tr. 1958, 431–434; *Images and Symbols*, trans. Philip Mairet. London: Harvill Press, 1961, 16–21; *The Quest*. Chicago: University of Chicago Press, 1969, ch. 7; *Occultism, Witchcraft, and Cultural Fashions*. Chicago: University of Chicago Press, 1976, chs. 1–4.

> pass through are prefigured in the adventures of the mythic Heroes. It has been possible also to show how the mythic themes of the primordial waters, of the isles of Paradise, of the quest of the Holy Grail, of heroic and mystical initiation, etc., still dominate modern European literature. Quite recently we have seen, in surrealism, a prodigious outburst of mythical themes and primordial symbols. As for the literature of the bookstalls, its mythological character is obvious. Every popular novel has to present the exemplary struggle between Good and Evil, the hero and the villain (modern incarnation of the Demon), and repeat one of those universal motives [*sic*] of folklore, the persecuted young woman, salvation by love, the unknown protector, etc. Even detective novels, as Roger Caillois has so well demonstrated, are full of mythological themes. (*Myths, Dreams, and Mysteries*, 35)

Eliade finds mythic themes everywhere in modern culture, even if he sometimes takes rituals as myths (see *Myths, Dreams, and Mysteries*, 28). The question is whether the themes amount to myths: whether they constitute stories, and stories that fulfill Eliade's three mythic functions. Eliade tries to fend off the charge that would-be modern myths fall short by characterizing them as "private" and "camouflaged." But do these diminished cases still qualify as myths?

PRIVATE MYTHS

Eliade regularly compares psychoanalysis with religion. Both activities seek to reconnect human beings to a reality from which they have become severed:

> Two of Freud's ideas are relevant to our subject: (1) the bliss of the "origin" and "beginnings" of the human being, and (2) the idea that through memory, or by a "going back," one can relive certain traumatic incidents of early childhood. The bliss of the "origin" is, we have seen, a quite frequent theme in the archaic religions; it is attested in India, Iran, Greece, and in Judaeo-Christianity. (*Myth and Reality*, 78)

Psychoanalysis as well as religion employs myth as a vehicle for returning to the past. But psychoanalytic myths—"dreams, reveries, fantasies, and so forth"—are merely "private mythologies." They "never rise to the ontological status of myths, precisely because they are not experienced by the whole man and therefore do not transform a particular situation into a situation that is paradigmatic" (*Sacred and Profane*, 211). Private myths help solve personal problems, but they do not link their creators or users to anything cosmic. They open up human beings to the unconscious but not, like traditional myths, to the sacred:

> [T]he nonreligious man of modern societies is still nourished and aided by the activity of his unconscious, yet without thereby attaining to a

properly religious experience and vision of the world. The unconscious offers him solutions for the difficulties of his own life, and in this way plays the role of religion. (*Sacred and Profane*, 212)

By Eliade's three functions of myth, private myths fail altogether. First, they do not explain anything. Dreams and fantasies may express unconscious wishes, but they do not account for them. Psychoanalytic theory accounts for the wishes, but dreams and fantasies are not themselves the explanation. The wishes expressed by dreams and fantasies may explain adult feelings and actions, and explain them as the legacy of childhood, but again the explanation is not provided by dreams and fantasies themselves, which typically do not even appear in coherent form.

Second, dreams and fantasies, as the repositories for Freud of antisocial impulses, hardly provide models for behavior. Moreover, since private myths are autobiographical, the model offered would be one oneself!

Third and most important, while private myths may well carry one back to the character-forming, precedent-setting time of childhood, no gods are to be found in this private primordial time. In childhood, parents do take on the role of gods, but parents are in fact mere human beings—one of the lessons to be learned in analysis. It might be argued that private myths do put subjects in touch with the psychological counterpart to the sacred—the unconscious—but the payoff is still merely psychological: one encounters not god but only another side of oneself.

Jungian psychology would here work better for Eliade than Freudian since Jung both characterizes the unconscious as godlike and makes the unconscious largely independent of consciousness. Even so, the payoff for Jung no less than for Freud is psychological and not religious: one encounters a god*like* side of oneself, not a god independent of oneself. Eliade recognizes Jung's psychological reductionism and consequently distances himself from Jung. Only the later Jungian concept of synchronicity, which Eliade never mentions, reconnects humans to the world, but even that world remains profane. In fact, synchronicity, as the coincidence of inner reality with outer, presupposes the differentiation of the two, and that differentiation presupposes the withdrawal of the divinity projected onto outer reality.

CAMOUFLAGED MYTHS

Eliade by no means limits modern myths to private ones, which he recognizes barely qualify as myths. He gives more weight to public myths. He calls them "camouflaged" because they go unrecognized by their adherents. They are to be found above all in plays, films, and books:

> A whole volume could well be written on the myths of modern man, on the mythologies camouflaged in the plays that he enjoys, in the books that he reads. The cinema, that "dream factory," takes over and employs countless mythical motifs—the fight between hero and monster, initiatory combats and ordeals, paradigmatic figures and images (the maiden, the hero, the paradisal landscape, hell, and so on). Even reading includes a mythological function . . . because, through reading, the modern man succeeds in obtaining an "escape from time" comparable to the "emergence from time" effected by myths. Whether modern man "kills" time with a detective story or enters such a foreign temporal universe as is represented by any novel, reading projects him out of his personal duration and incorporates him into other rhythms, makes him live in another "history." (*Sacred and Profane*, 205)

Eliade is labelling "mythic" two related elements in plays, movies, and books: superhuman figures, and escape to another time and place. Myths here are public because they are shared. They are camouflaged because theatergoers, movie fans, and readers, as moderns, miss the religious nature of the themes:

> The majority of the "irreligious" still behave religiously, even though they are not aware of the fact. We refer not only to the modern man's many "superstitions" and "tabus," all of them magico-religious in structure. But the modern man who feels and claims that he is nonreligious still retains a large stock of camouflaged myths and degenerated rituals. (*Sacred and Profane*, 204–205)

What, however, is religious about these camouflaged myths? Are the figures in them gods? The figures in, say, science fiction may be supernatural, but surely the characters in most modern plays, movies, and books are not. Most are merely human, even all too human. Even if some human heroes verge on the superhuman—for example, Rambo—most do not.

The divinity of the characters aside, do the stories in modern drama, film, and literature function as myths? First, do they trace the establishment long ago of a natural or social phenomenon of any kind that continues to exist today? Certainly historical plays, movies, and books often describe the establishment of enduring social institutions such as nations, forms of government, ideologies, occupations, laws, and customs. But clearly many plays, movies, and books are not historical. Most take place in the present or even in the future. And even those that take place in the past by no means always involve the establishment of any lasting phenomenon.

Second, do the characters in modern plays, movies, and books serve as models for others? Some may, but surely many modern protagonists are antiheroes rather than heroes. Many live on the margins of society. Many reject society rather than seek to alter it.

Third and last, does the modern spectator or reader travel to the time and place of the story? It may be true that stories work only when one gets lost in them, forgetting where one is and getting caught up in the events described. Doubtless the emotions that stories elicit—fear, pity, admiration, love—require absorption in the lives of the characters, even identification with the characters. A horror movie works only when the audience as well as the victims on the screen is scared, only when the audience imagines itself to be part of the action. Still, the spectator or reader is scarcely carried away for more than the duration of the story. When it is over, the emotion stirred may linger, but only as a memory. Reality takes over. Furthermore, few think that they have *really* been carried to the time mid place of the plot. They only feel as if they have been.

Those who continue to identify themselves with the story are considered crazy. They have confused fiction with reality. By no coincidence it is nowadays a commonplace to ask whether children who harm, even kill, others have taken their cues from movies. The contrast between impressionable children and detached adults reinforces the common assumption that movies are not the real world. The saddest lesson learned by the adult Toto in *Cinema Paradiso* is exactly that movies are no guide to the real world. Indeed, movies are often seen more as sheer escapism than as a perspective on reality. A committed fan may see the same movie again and again, but ordinarily the fan still distinguishes the movie from reality. The fan may wish reality to be like the movie, but ordinarily manages to differentiate the two.

Finally, what payoff would a fan derive from somehow managing to enter the world of the movie, play, or book? Eliade insists that immersion in the time of myths provides rejuvenation and not mere escapism. But how many filmgoers, theatergoers, or readers feel permanently rejuvenated after their experiences? Are their lives transformed?

Far closer to gods are not the characters in movies but the actors. Movie stars are not merely revered but "worshiped." Even more than celebrities from other walks of life, movie stars are associated with the traditional characteristics of gods: they are bigger, handsomer, and richer than ordinary folk. After all, they are seen writ large on the screen, and with physical flaws and limitations erased. Thus, it comes as a shock to fans to learn that "in reality" Mel Gibson is not very tall. Movie stars are free of the constraints that bind the rest of us, so that it comes as a shock, not least to them themselves, to discover that even they cannot always get away with, for example, drug or spouse abuse. At the same time, everyone wants to be a movie star, and the behavior of stars influences others. Like gods, movie stars are inaccessible, off screen as well as on, and if one ever does get near them, the thrill is simply to touch them, to brush up against them. Above all, movie stars, like gods and unlike other kinds of celebrities, are immortal: they live on in their movies.

Unfortunately, movie stars are not usually linked to myths—one reason perhaps that Eliade ignores them. With exceptions like James Dean, stars are not usually credited with establishing phenomena, except for the most fleeting of trends. Furthermore, stars live in the present as well as in the past. Some fans may think that today's stars are no match for those of yesteryear, but any precedent that present-day stars set would not hark back to primordial time. Consequently, getting close to the stars does not require going back in time. Indeed, the divide between ordinary folks and movie stars is more spatial than temporal, and our connection to stars involves more rituals than myths. We seek out the places where they live—for example, maps and tours of stars' homes—more than any precedents they have forged. In short, movie stars do not save Eliade's claim of modern myths.

For some theorists of myth—notably, Edward Tylor and James Frazer—myth is a wholly primitive or at least premodern phenomenon, and "modern myth" is an oxymoron. For other theorists, including C. G. Jung and Joseph Campbell as well as Eliade, myth is eternal. Yet Eliade's claim that moderns have myths is less convincing than Jung's or Campbell's. Where they allow for fully secular myths, in which case modern adherents need not be religious to employ them, Eliade insists that seemingly secular myths are really religious, in which case modern adherents must themselves be religious to use them. Where Jung and Campbell read myth symbolically and can thereby interpret it in ways that are palatable to moderns, Eliade reads myth literally and is thereby stuck with the incredulity that accompanies many modern myths—for example, that of Superman, to note one of his favorites. Where Jung and Campbell take myth to be an expression of the human mind, in which case both the function and the subject matter of myth run askew to those of science, Eliade takes myth to be foremost an explanation of the physical world, in which case it clashes with natural science, which Eliade no less than Jung and Campbell equates with modernity. Even as an explanation of the social world, myth still clashes with social science. Above all, where Jung and Campbell deem secular myths, especially for Jung private myths, the equal in power to religious ones, Eliade deems or must deem seemingly secular myths hapless inferiors to overtly religious ones. He thereby faces a key dilemma that Jung and Campbell avoid: to be acceptable to moderns, myths must be secular, yet to function as myths, they must be religious. Failing to overcome this dilemma, Eliade fails to show that modern myths exist.

Part Two

PHILOSOPHY

Chapter Four

ELIADE, SUBJECTIVITY, AND HERMENEUTICS

TIM MURPHY

What has been the effect, or perhaps the cost, of the concept of the subject in religious studies? What is Eliade's legacy in relation to this conjunction of "religion" and "subject"? What will the study of religion look like *after* the subject? This chapter proposes some answers to these questions.

The problem of Eliade's relation to subjectivity is usually dealt with in religious studies in one of two ways. Either he is read in the tradition of Wach and Kristensen vis-à-vis the "insider/outsider" problem, or he is read in the tradition of Popper and Nagel in which he is seen as a "soft subjectivist" in the pejorative sense. This paper proposes another reading: Eliade's emphasis on the relation between subjectivity and hermeneutics can be fruitfully read within the larger context of the "subjective turn" of the modern human sciences and culture. This recontextualization explains how it is that a transhistorical subjectivity ("humanism" in Eliade's terms) forms the condition for the possibility of the kind of hermeneutic of religion that Eliade both described and practiced. This, I argue, is Eliade's central legacy in the history of the study of religion. Once this is established, I will suggest what is wrong with this paradigm.

PRELUDE: THE "SUBJECT" OF MODERNITY

The philosopher Robert Solomon explains what is meant by "the modern subject" (or self):

> The self in question is no ordinary self, no individual personality, nor even one of the many heroic or mock-heroic personalities of the early nineteenth century. The self that becomes the star performer in modern European philosophy is the transcendental self.... The transcendental self was *the* self—timeless, universal, and in each one of us around the globe and throughout history.[1]

The by now familiar narrative of the subject's coming to be usually cites Descartes's *Cogito* as the first full articulation of the modern subject, or perhaps Luther's "interior man"; finds this same subject in Locke's theory of rights and as the foundation for Liberalism (and hence, capitalism); shows that it is the bedrock notion of Romanticism;[2] ties it to both the art and literature of the nineteenth century, as well as much of the twentieth century; and sees it as the foundation for consummately modernist phenomenological approaches to thought as a whole, especially in that lineage of writers from Hegel to Merleau-Ponty (though not exclusive of Anglo-American empiricism). Phenomenology is, from this perspective, the logical culmination of the history of the subject.

Two points emerge from this narrative. First, that the subject is, in fact, historical—which is as much to say that it is not transcendental, universal, nor inherent in "Man." To think that it is, is to reiterate the *Wirkungsgeschichte*, or "effective history," of the subject from within. This reiteration of the transcendentality of the subject is precisely what is refused in its historicization. Second, this is a very distinct concept of human being, and must not be taken as simply another name for the soul, *homo sapiens*, or "Man." That is, the contention of those who write this history of subject is not simply that the modern concept of the subject should be appended to the traditional history of ideas. Rather, the appearance of the subject in Western history represents a dramatic "paradigm shift" in human self-understanding. Martin Heidegger puts the point thusly:

> What is decisive [in the modern age] is not that man frees himself to himself from previous obligations, but that the very essence of man itself changes, in that man becomes a subject.... when man becomes the primary and only real *subiectum*, that means: Man becomes that being upon which all that is, is grounded as regards the manner of its Being and its truth. Man becomes the relational center of that which is as such.[3]

---

1. Robert Solomon, *Continental Philosophy Since 1750: The Rise and Fall of the Self*. New York: Oxford University Press, 1988, 4.

2. On the connection between modernity, subjectivity, and Romanticism, see Victor Burgin, "The End of Art Theory," in *The End of Art Theory: Criticism and Postmodernity*. Atlantic Highlands: Humanities Press International, 1986, 188.

3. Martin Heidegger, "The Age of the World Picture," in *The Question Concerning Technology and Other Essays*. New York: Harper Torchbooks, 1977, 128.

It should be clear, then, that what is claimed by the phrase "subjective turn" is no mere fad in philosophy, but a fundamental, epochal transition in the manner in which Western humans organize and understand reality as a whole. How does this notion of the modern subject work in Eliade's hermeneutics?

SUBJECTIVITY AND HERMENEUTICS IN ELIADE'S METHODOLOGY

"Ultimately, the historian of religion cannot renounce hermeneutics."[4] Eliade's methodology is a hermeneutics of the sacred. He goes about finding, analyzing, and understanding the objects of his investigation by applying to them concepts drawn from the German hermeneutical tradition, which goes back to Schleiermacher and Dilthey, and which is mediated to *Religionswissenschaft* by Wach, van der Leeuw, and others.

Like Schleiermacher and Otto before him, Eliade sees religion as a *sui generis* phenomenon, a category independent of other categories: "[A] religious phenomenon will only be recognized as such if it is grasped at its own level, that is to say, if it is studied *as* something religious."[5] "The sacred," in turn, is the irreducible element in religion: "To try to grasp the essence" of religion by other means "or any other study is false; it misses the one unique and irreducible element in it—the element of the sacred" (*Patterns*, xiii). To attempt to apprehend religion as something other than a manifestation of the sacred is to misapprehend it, because the sacred is not reducible to anything else.

The crucial question is, then, how does Eliade account for the *sui generis*, a priori, universal nature of the sacred? The answer, in short, is consciousness: "the 'sacred' is an element in the structure of consciousness."[6] This small phrase, I would argue, is the key premise to Eliade's hermeneutics. Its meaning can be made clearer by seeing that in this statement, Eliade is reiterating one of Rudolf Otto's foundational methodological proposition, viz.: "It follows from what has been said that the 'holy' in the fullest sense of the word is a combined, complex category . . . it a *purely a priori* category," and with it "we are referred away from all sense-experience back to an original and underivable capacity of the mind implanted in the 'pure reason' independently of all perception."[7] Otto further argues that with the category, "we are referred back to something still deeper than the 'pure reason,' at least as this is

---

4. *Australian Religions: An Introduction*. Ithaca: Cornell University Press, 1973, 200.

5. *Patterns in Comparative Religion*. London: Sheed and Ward, 1958, xiii.

6. "Preface" to *The Quest: History and Meaning in Religion*. Chicago: University of Chicago Press, 1969, i.

7. *The Idea of the Holy*. New York: Oxford University Press, 1958, 112. The connection between the position Otto takes here and the concept of the "religious a priori" in the theological tradition of Schleiermacher, Ritschl, and Troeltsch is well known.

usually understood, namely, to that which mysticism has rightly named the *fundus animae*, the 'bottom' or 'ground of the soul' (*Seelengrund*)" (*Idea of the Holy*, 112).

By arguing that the sacred is a category of consciousness Eliade is not only evoking this historical concept within *Religionswissenschaft*, but he is claiming that the sacred is part of the very structure of human being. The *sui generis* nature of the sacred and of religion, the universality of religion, which allows one to see all historical manifestations as manifestations of the sacred, have their grounding in a transcendental conception of consciousness. Every particular, empirical instance of the sacred is correlated to a universal, a priori category. Eliade's hermeneutics of the sacred is predicated on a distinct philosophy of mind, or, as he himself calls it, a "philosophical anthropology,"[8] by which he means a systematic explication, or even exegesis, of the structures of consciousness, mind, or the human spirit.

The central methodological task of a hermeneutics of the sacred will be to forge linkages between externalized data and the transcendental consciousness that produces such data, or to see the former as "expressions" of the latter: "Hermeneutics is of preponderant interest to us because, inevitably, it is the least developed aspect of our discipline. Preoccupied, and indeed often completely taken up, by their admittedly urgent and indispensable work of collecting, publishing, and analyzing religious data, scholars have sometimes neglected to study their meaning. Now, these data represent the expression of various religious experiences" (*Quest*, 2). Religious data, then, for Eliade must not be seen as merely historical documents. As "expressions of" they are meaningful, that is, indicators of that transcendental consciousness: "But if we are to avoid sinking back into an obsolete 'reductionism,' this history of religious meanings must always be regarded as forming part of the *history of the human spirit*" (9; emphasis added).

Eliade is here repeating a point that Gerardus van der Leeuw held as central to *Religionswissenschaft*, namely, that as expressions, religious data are intelligible, that is, their difference from us is bridgeable: "Certainly the monuments of the first dynasty [of Egypt] are intelligible only with great difficulty, but as an expression, as a human statement, they are no harder than my colleague's letter."[9] This is because, as a human expression, "there is something that is intelligible in accord with our own experience" (677). Van der Leeuw is, in turn, repeating a fundamental tenet of Dilthey's hermeneutical program for the *Geisteswissenschaften*: "What is given [in historical research] are always expressions of life; occurring in the world of the senses they are always expressions of a mind which they help us to under-

---

8. See, e.g., "A New Humanism," in *The Quest*, 9.
9. *Religion in Essence and Manifestation*. Princeton: Princeton University Press, 1964, 677.

stand."[10] The homogeneity of consciousness is the basis for *Verstehen* on this hermeneutical model.

Consequently, the historian of religion is not content with mere "facticity," but seeks the *meaning* of religious expressions. The historian of religion does not act as a philologist, but as a hermeneutist. He endeavors to understand the materials that philologists and historians make available to him in his own perspective, that of the history of religions (*Quest*, 58–61). The shift away from "mere" philology to hermeneutics, from historical texts or data to "expressions" opens up an entirely different domain of investigation for the history of religion. It is, finally, concerned with what meaning expressions reveal. This delineation of the object-field is what makes hermeneutical phenomenology a specific approach to the study of religion, different from other approaches, or, for that matter, different from other approaches to the study of "meaning." We must be careful not to allow ourselves to feel that this concatenation of "consciousness/expression/meaning" is natural, just because it has become so widespread. It is, both analytically and historically, a very distinct, or specific operation effected upon historical materials.

It is on the basis of transcendental subjectivity that the science of religion does not deal with a merely "regional ontology," as do other humanistic disciplines (such as psychology or sociology), but with *homo religiosus*, and "*homo religiosus* represents the 'total man'" (*Quest*, 8). Religious meanings express the very structure of man's mode of being-in-the-world, or "existential situations," and are therefore all-encompassing in what they tell us about man: "[B]y attempting to understand the existential situations expressed by the documents he is studying, the historian of religions will inevitably attain to a deeper knowledge of man. It is on the basis of such knowledge that a new humanism, on a world-wide scale, could develop" (3).

As opposed to a regional ontology, the study of religion should aim at what Eliade calls a total hermeneutic: "The history of religions is not merely a historical discipline, as, for example, are archaeology or numismatics. It is equally a total hermeneutics, being called to decipher and explicate every kind of encounter of man with the sacred, from prehistory to our day" (58). The philosophical foundation for the *simile in multis* that Eliade believes the "total hermeneutic" can find in history is none other than "human spirit," human nature, consciousness, or "Man." In a long passage, he fully indicates this philosophical ground:

> The historian of religion recognizes a spiritual unity subjacent to the history of humanity; in other terms, in studying the Australians, Vedic Indians, or whatever other ethnic group or cultural system, the historian

---

10. Dilthey, *Pattern and Meaning in History*. New York: Harper and Row, 1961, 117.

of religions does not have a sense of moving in a world radically "foreign" to him. Certainly, the unity of the human species is accepted *de facto* in other disciplines, for example linguistics, anthropology, sociology. But the historian of religions has the privilege of grasping this unity at the highest levels—or the deepest.... Today history is becoming truly universal for the first time. (69)

In spirit, all differences are subsumed and history becomes universal history: *allgemeine Geschichte*. Spirit, for Eliade as with Hegel, is the *subiectum* and *substancia* of history, that which by its "subjacency" gives unity, even identity, to all of the various forms of difference that appear in time. The history of religions culminates in philosophical anthropology, that is, a "New Humanism": "More than any other humanistic discipline, history of religions can open the way to a philosophical anthropology" (9). "Man" is the philosophical ground and center of all phenomenological structures and essences and all hermeneutical meanings. All meaning is, finally, "Man's" meaning; it points to him; it is his "expression." Consequently, reductive historicism gives way to a new universalism, and now, "Western consciousness recognizes only one history, the Universal History," and "the ethnocentric history is surpassed as being provincial" (52). Philosophical anthropology, understood as the science of spirit, is the basis for a new universalism: "From a certain point of view, one could say that a new *Phenomenology of the Mind* awaits elaboration by taking account of all that the history of religions is capable of revealing to us" (64). In Eliade's view, this universality entails overcoming the narrow, ethnocentrism of Western history: "How to assimilate culturally the spiritual universes that Africa, Oceania, Southeast Asia open to us?" (70). The total hermeneut has no sense of moving in any area foreign to him; all cultures are now available to him for the enrichment of each. The use of materials from "Oriental and archaic societies," then, "will not only show us the point of view of the *'others,'* the non-Europeans: for any confrontation with another person leads to enlightenment about one's *own* situation."[11] The goal of Eliade's total hermeneutic, then, is the same as that of Hegel's Science of Wisdom, viz., "the pure self-recognition in absolute otherness."[12]

THE FERTILE OTHER

The necessary consequence of Eliade's transcendental subjectivity is that it makes his methodology inherently ethnocentric. This can be seen in Eliade's repeated

---

11. *Myths, Dreams, and Mysteries.* New York: Harper and Row, 1960, 233; emphasis added.

12. Hegel, *The Phenomenology of Spirit.* New York: Oxford University Press, 1977, 14.

citation of the positive and creative influence of primitive art on the European art world of the early twentieth century. A typical passage reads as follows:

> It is the meeting with the "others"—with human beings belonging to various types of archaic and exotic societies—that is culturally stimulating and fertile.... We have in mind the discovery of the exotic and primitive arts, which revivified modern Western aesthetics. We have in mind especially the discovery of the unconscious by psychoanalysis, which opened new perspectives for our understanding of man. *In both cases alike*, there was a meeting with the "foreign" the unknown, with what cannot be reduced to familiar categories—in short, with the "wholly other." (*Quest*, 3)

I want to look at each aspect of this statement carefully. First, on the influence of primitive art on cubism and surrealism. He praises as "creative" the contact between the art worlds of Europe and those of "exotic," or "archaic," or "primitive" peoples: "Let us recall the effect the first exposition of Japanese painting had on the French impressionists, or the influence of African sculpture on Picasso, or the consequences of the discovery of 'primitive art' for the first generation of surrealists" (*Quest*, 57). For Eliade this encounter is not strictly, nor even primarily, an aesthetic encounter. Rather, it produces knowledge, and from this kind of knowledge comes the possibility for the transformation of modern man: "It is naïvely believed that six months of 'field work' among a tribe whose language one can scarcely speak haltingly constitutes 'serious' work that can advance knowledge of man—and one ignores all that surrealism or James Joyce, Henry Michaux, and Picasso have contributed to the knowledge of man" (*Quest*, 65). The reason for this is that, like "archaic man," and like *homo religiosus*, the artist re-presents the unconscious. The artist, therefore, is a kind of "primitive," and the primitive, in "his" creativity, is a kind of artist.

Secondly, is Eliade's view of the discovery of the unconscious. The equation of the primitive, the child, and the neurotic, is of course, one familiar to readers of Freud. In a famous passage from *Moses and Monotheism*, Freud makes this same conjunction: "The essential point is, however, that we attribute to those primeval people the same feelings and emotions that we have elucidated in the primitives of our own times, our children, by psychoanalytic research."[13] Eliade, of course, rejected the kind of reductive explanation implied here by Freud. That is not in dispute. What is more interesting, however, is the commonality of the move to juxtapose a present, modern phenomenon (artists, children) with a past, "archaic" one. In the larger terrain of the modernist imaginary, Freud and Eliade perhaps

---

13. *Moses and Monotheism*. New York: Vintage Books, 1939, 103.

share more than is sometimes assumed. Eliade notes of Freud, that: "Freud's discovery of the unconscious encouraged the study of symbols and myths, and has been partially responsible for the modern interest in the archaic and oriental religions and mythologies."[14] The juxtapositions, "unconscious," "archaic," and "oriental" are relatively constant in Eliade.

Eliade's "validation" of primitive art is arguably not as benign as it appears or as he intended it. James Clifford has shown how "modernist primitivism, with its claims to deeper humanist sympathies and a wider aesthetic sense, goes hand-in-hand with a developed market in tribal art and with definitions of artistic and cultural authenticity that are now widely contested."[15] Clifford offers us an ethnographic tour of the Museum of Modern Art's 1984 " 'Primitivism in 20th-Century Art: Affinity of the Tribal and the Modern." The express intent of the exhibition is very much in line with Eliade's remarks about the "creative contact" between early modern art and African and Oceanic art.

What the exhibition does not do, Clifford says, is situate the tribal objects on display within the wider contexts of either their production or collection. As Clifford notes: "Cultural background is not essential to correct aesthetic appreciation and analysis: good art, the masterpiece, is universally recognizable. The pioneer modernists themselves knew little or nothing of these objects' ethnographic meaning. What was good enough for Picasso was good enough for the Museum of Modern Art" (200). This decontextualization via aestheticization is not merely a problem of correct interpretation of the meaning of the tribal objects in questions, nor is it simply a matter of methodological neatness. What it does is elide "a more disquieting quality of modernism: its taste for appropriating or redeeming otherness, for constituting non-Western arts in its own image, for discovering universal, ahistorical 'human' capacities. The search for similarities requires justification" (193). In other words, "the scope and underlying logic of the 'discovery' of tribal art reproduces hegemonic Western assumptions rooted in the colonial and neocolonial epoch" (197).

Mutatis mutandis, we must conclude that Eliade's valorization of the surrealist recovery of the primitive participates in a system defined by Edward Said (and others) as "colonial discourse." Before we can turn this inference into a claim, however, we must look at Eliade's own view of the study of non-Western cultures by Westerners, as well as his use of such terms as *primitive* and *archaic*.

---

14. "The History of Religions in Retrospect: 1912 and After," in *The Quest*, 21.

15. Clifford, "Histories of the Tribal and the Modern," in *The Predicament of Culture: Twentieth-Century Ethnography, Literature, and Art*. Cambridge: Harvard University Press, 1988, 198.

Eliade displays an ambivalence about the study of non-European cultures. He is very self-conscious about the problem of intercultural translation and very critical of the tendency toward cultural imperialism demonstrated by the West toward the non-West. He says of anthropologists: "It is to be expected that some time in the future the political and cultural representatives of the new states of Africa or Oceania, that is, the descendants of what we still call 'primitives,' will strongly object to the anthropological expeditions and the other varieties of field work. They will rightly point out that their peoples have too long been the 'objects' of such investigations, with rather disappointing results" (*Australian Religions*, xviii). In another place where he reiterates this same argument, he says such representatives will "regard many social scientists as camouflaged apologists of Western Culture." Why? "Because these scientists insist so persistently on the sociopolitical origin and character of the 'primitive' messianic movements, they may be suspected of a Western superiority complex, namely, the conviction that such religious movements cannot rise to the same level of 'freedom from sociopolitical conjuncture' as, for instance, a Gioachino da Fiore or St. Francis."[16]

What is "colonialist" about the social sciences is not that they extract cultural materials from foreign societies, but that they explain these extracted materials on reductive, nonspiritual, and nonreligious, principles. It is to this that Eliade objects. As for the extraction of cultural materials, he is absolutely unambiguous in his advocating of this: "How to assimilate *culturally* the spiritual universes that Africa, Oceania, Southeast Asia open to us?" (*Quest*, 70). It is, after all, Eliade's own claim that the social sciences compartmentalize religious and cultural data, and that the history of religions demands a "*total hermeneutics*, being called to decipher and explicate *every kind* of encounter of man with the sacred, *from prehistory to our day*."[17] Eliade's hermeneutics, then, is a totalizing discourse, that is, a discourse that subsumes all otherness into itself.

That Eliade's approach to non-Western cultures is aggressively assimilating in the name of the ethnocentric project of the modern, Western subject is further evidenced by his use of terms such as primitive and archaic. Again, *prima facie*, he seems to evince a critical self-consciousness on this issue. Thus, he will say of the term *primitive*, that it is "ambiguous and inconsistent," (*Australian Religions*, xii, n.2) and he often (though not always) puts it in scare quotes. However, his own

---

16. *Quest*, 7. His argument here is based on a distinction that most anthropologists would not share. That is, religious essentialists such as Schleiermacher, Hegel, and Otto would argue for such a difference, whereas a reductive anthropologist such as Weston LeBarre, who compared Plato to the Cargo Cults and the Ghost Dance, would not grant such a difference.

17. Ibid., 58; some italics added, and again, requoted for emphasis.

descriptive, taxonomic practice belies this appearance of sensitivity. In a number of places, he recites a concatenation of "peoples" such as "archaic and Asian," or "African and primitive," or "African, Oceanic, and archaic," and so forth. Our question is this: In what universe do these peoples belong together? In what universe do Africans—of all kinds, apparently!—and Native North Americans, the peoples of Oceania—all of them—and the Aborigines of Australia belong together? Only in the universe of an essentialist consciousness; only in the universe of a universalist subjectivity that can assume that *"homo sum, humani nil a me alienum puto*: this is no key to the deepest comprehension of the remotest experience, but is nevertheless the triumphant assertion that the *essentially human always remains the essentially human, and is, as such, comprehensible,"*[18] are these various cultures moments in a history of the same. Eliade could say as easily as did Hegel: "Thus, what in religion was *content* or a form for presenting an *other*, is here the *Self's* own *act*. . . . Our *own* act here has been simply to *gather together* the separate moments, each of which in principle exhibits the life of the Spirit in its entirety."[19]

In short, Eliade's move to inclusiveness is bought by the elision of the difference of the other. These groups, completely distinct from each other, and complexly plural in themselves, are all the same vis-à-vis European "Man." They are images of the other of Europe. Their sameness is nonexistent other than as a construct of the universalist ambitions of the modern European subject.

THE END OF "MAN"

In order to fully assess the implications of Eliade's hermeneutics—and of religious studies, insofar as it has appropriated his hermeneutics—it is necessary to locate it within a larger history of phenomenological discourse, and to see how the correlations between humanism, meaning, and Eurocentrism can be understood.

Derrida and others have convincingly argued that, rather than overcoming traditional, a priori views of human nature, the move to a phenomenological ontology ultimately served to reinstate anthropology, or, "Man": "To the extent that it describes the structures of human-reality [or "existential situation"], phenomenological ontology is a philosophical anthropology. Whatever the breaks marked by this Hegelian-Husserlian-Heideggerian anthropology as concerns the classical anthropologies, there is an uninterrupted metaphysical familiarity with that which, so naturally, links the

---

18. van der Leeuw, *Religion in Essence and Manifestation*, 675. For the connection between this statement and Eliade, see Tim Murphy, "*Wesen und Erscheinung* in the History of the Study of Religion: A Poststructuralist Perspective," *Method and Theory in the Study of Religion* 6/2: 119–146.

19. Hegel, *Phenomenology of Spirit*, 485, all italics Hegel's.

we of the philosopher to 'we men,' to the *we* in horizon of humanity."[20] The problem here lies in the fact that "the history of the concept man is never examined. Everything occurs as if the sign 'man' had no origin, no historical, cultural, or linguistic limit" (116). Without this history, it becomes easy, even necessary, to move from "we" to "we men." Historicizing the concept of "Man" and the discursive operations within which it lives is a necessary first step to overcoming the ethnocentrism that results so casually from this "uninterrupted metaphysical familiarity."

Although the phenomenological-hermeneutical tradition sought to avoid the constructivistic metaphysics so characteristic of the nineteenth century, as Derrida notes, this was not so. Rather than an atheoretical analysis of the given in human experience, insofar as it was a restoration of the a priori universalism that so thoroughly saturates the name of "Man," "Phenomenology's critique of the state of metaphysics was aimed only at its restoration."[21] As is well known, for Derrida (and others), the history of metaphysics is not merely the "history of ideas." It is, rather, the basis for understanding the history of the West's relation to its others. The key to metaphysics, for Derrida, is presence: "The history of metaphysics, like the history of the West . . . is the determination of Being as presence, in all senses of this word."[22] It is this notion of presence that is reinstated by the humanism of phenomenology's return of "Man": "the name of man being the name of that being who, throughout the history of metaphysics or of ontotheology—in other words, throughout his entire history—has dreamed of full presence, the reassuring foundation, the origin and end of play" (292). It is this longing for the uninterrupted fullness of presence that forces phenomenological hermeneutics into its narcissistic, ethnocentric quest to find sameness in all forms of otherness.

It is also within this history of phenomenological hermeneutics that we must understand the methodological centrality of consciousness. As noted above, consciousness as the *Seelengrund*, the essence or core of "Man," and as the firmament of the "sacred." However, as Derrida has pointed out, in the centrality of consciousness, the privileging of consciousness as the unique site of the truth of man is part of the history of phenomenology: "Consciousness is the truth of man, phenomenology is the truth of anthropology" (*Margins*, 120). Consciousness is taken as the essence of "Man," and intentionality and meaning as the essence of consciousness. These are the basic premises of phenomenological hermeneutics.

---

20. Jacques Derrida, "The Ends of Man," in *Margins of Philosophy*. Chicago: University of Chicago Press, 1982, 115–116.

21. Derrida, "Form and Meaning: A Note on the Phenomenology of Language," in *Margins*, 157.

22. Derrida, "Structure, Sign, and Play in the Discourse of the Human Sciences," in *Writing and Difference*. Chicago: University of Chicago Press, 1978, 279.

Elaborating and extending this notion, David Hoy has, perhaps, given the most comprehensive and accessible account of the role of consciousness in the history of modern philosophy: "Although consciousness thus seems to some to be the pre-eminent topic of modern philosophy, others have suspected that the history of modern philosophy has disclosed not what consciousness really is, but that it is really not anything at all, or at least not much more than a matter of stipulative definition. On this view, a history of consciousness could only be a postmodern history of 'consciousness,' that is, a history not of some real thing but of a technical term."[23] "Consciousness" is a historical category, and its dominance in phenomenological-hermeneutical discourse names nothing other than the era of the subject.

Finally, we are in a position to see how the history of hermeneutics is, by and large, the history of the problem of the subject's relation to something outside of itself; that is, the history of hermeneutics is—with some qualification—a chapter within the history of the modern subject. What Richard Palmer says of Schleiermacher and Dilthey could also, *mutatis mutandis*, be said about Eliade and the tradition of hermeneutical "understanding" associated with him in Religious Studies:

> In Schleiermacher, understanding was grounded in his philosophical affirmation of the identity of inner realities (*Identitätsphilosophie*) so that in understanding, one vibrated in unison with the speaker as one understood; understanding involved both comparative and divinatory phases. In Dilthey, understanding referred to that deeper level of comprehension involved in grasping a picture, a poem, or a fact . . . as more than a mere datum, as an "expression" of "inner realities" and ultimately of "life" itself.[24]

Which is as much to say, in the tradition of hermeneutics, which Eliade both inherited and advocated, the subject is central. This tradition of hermeneutics is a hermeneutics of the subject, of "his" expressions on the one hand, and of "his" empathy as hermeneut on the other hand. Or, as Gadamer has said of Dilthey: "Historical understanding expands to embrace all historical data and is truly universal, because it has a firm foundation in the inner totality and infinity of the mind. Here Dilthey is following the old theory that understanding is possible because of the homogeneity of human nature."[25] We can substitute "Eliade" for "Dilthey" and lose nothing.

---

23. David Hoy, "A History of Consciousness: from Kant and Hegel to Derrida and Foucault," *History of the Human Sciences* 4:2 (1991): 262.

24. Palmer, *Hermeneneutics: Interpretation Theory in Schleiermacher, Dilthey, Heidegger, and Gadamer*. Evanston: Northwestern University Press, 1969, 131.

25. Gadamer, *Truth and Method*. New York: Crossroad Publishing Co., 1989, 232.

In sum: the legacy of Eliade in religious studies is synonymous with the era of the subject, and the era of the subject has been, if not synonymous with, then deeply complicit in, an aggressively assimilative history of the same. Although space does not allow me to substantiate this claim fully, insofar as religious studies adopts a paradigm of postmodern genealogy, it will move into a post-subject era, an era marked by the end of "Man." Genealogical difference does not eliminate ethnocentrism, but it reduces its power over us by foregrounding and naming it as such. Insofar as religious studies moves into a post-subject era, it will also move into a post-Eliadean era.

Chapter Five

THE PHENOMENOLOGY OF MIRCEA ELIADE

ALLAN W. LARSEN

From the beginning of my reading of Eliade many years ago, it has always seemed to me that his work on the history of religions was consistently a response to the existential question, "What does it mean to be religious?" At the same time it also seemed to me that his method was essentially phenomenological. Hence, the purpose of this chapter is not so much a scholarly presentation of the thought of Mircea Eliade in the typical social science manner, but an exposition of the fruitful use to which he put the phenomenological method. There have been a sufficient number of divergent understandings of phenomenology to warrant a disclosure of phenomenology that is true both to its development in Martin Heidegger and Maurice Merleau-Ponty and to its fruitful use as an essential description of the phenomenon of the sacred.

There are those critics of Eliade who say that a phenomenology of the sacred is impossible because the sacred is by definition beyond experience. Such an understanding of experience is positivistic, that is, experience is reduced to what is repeatable, quantitatively measurable, formulatible, or categorizable. The positivistic understanding of experience is reductionistic but more importantly it is a *concept* of experience that is the result of a rational analysis with its own discernible history and it is a *concept* of profane experience. Eliade's interest is neither in the concept of profane experience nor in the derived concept of the sacred, but rather in the way these two are actually experienced. It is the phenomenological method that claims to describe these experiences of the sacred and the profane.

Hans Penner's analysis of Husserl's phenomenology is a good example of this "positivist" tendency and may indeed miss the whole point of the phenomenological revolution. Is Husserl trying to solve the questions of epistemology and metaphysics within the modern philosophical tradition or has he put aside those assumptions, upon which the modern tradition rests, and developed an entirely different way? It is a difference between detachment (the subject in opposition to the object) and involvement, the difference between an analytic reflection and a perception in which I am inextricably involved.[1]

When Eliade defines myth as a "true story"[2] he is giving us a phenomenological description. For the people for whom the myth is a true story, it is not a figment of the imagination or merely a subjective belief but the perceived reality in which they live out their lives. What constitutes one's life, is the world fraught with meaning and value. It is the living perception of a people. That and that alone is what is meant by phenomena.

It is important at the outset to identify the salient elements of phenomenology that show it to be at once a genuine philosophical process and an overcoming of metaphysics. The overcoming of metaphysics is a rejection neither of speculation nor of the central importance of reason, but rather the overcoming of the metaphysical subject. Heidegger calls the history of Western metaphysics a history of "subjectism."[3] It seems to me that it is René Descartes who substantiates the subject in opposition to medieval theology and the prevailing Aristotelianism. Although the idea of the soul as substance predates Descartes, it is his unique construction of the rational mind that sets the stage for the metaphysics of "subjectism" and its consequence of modern science. This is a complex and difficult issue that cannot be pursued in this context. Let it suffice to be said that Descartes's radical separation of the mind from matter is necessary for the objectification of nature. Such objectification requires a subject that gives categorical structure to experience, that is, a transcendental subject that gives the necessary conditions for the possibility of an object as known. Knowledge of the object is a knowing beforehand, the conditions, the categorical structures that make an experience a possible object of knowledge are a priori. But if we suspend judgment (in the Kantian sense of judgment), that is, we do not make the movement to categorical objectification but remain on the level of experience, is there still some form of knowledge possible? Such knowledge would not have the nature of logical certainty, it would not be clear and

---

1. Hans Penner, "Is Phenomenology a Method for the Study of Religion?" *The Bucknell Review* 18:3 (1970): 29–54.
2. *Myth and Reality* (New York: Harper and Row, 1963), 8f. Hereafter *M & R*.
3. *Being and Time*. New York: Harper and Row, 1962, 41ff.

distinct because we have suspended these criteria. The suspension of logical certainty should be understood in terms of priorities. Of course, reason's logical criteria must continue to play a role, but when confronted with a contradiction, an ambiguity, a paradox, or an absurdity in the very experiences that constitute my life I need not clear them up, reduce them to an artificial consistency. Indeed, in many cases it is precisely the contradictory character of much of a person's life that calls for our attention and concern. It is, after all, a matter of priorities.

Hans-Georg Gadamer says phenomenology's task is not to understand the individual case as an instance of a general rule—as is the method of the natural sciences. Rather, its ideal is to understand the individual situation "in its uniqueness and historical concreteness."[4] Nonetheless, there is still a universality in the phenomenological method, but it does not belong to the abstract universality of the mathematical, but rather to the existential or lived situation as it gives itself in the phenomena. It is a question of starting points. Is it the experience itself that directs our understanding or is it the mathematical demand of simplicity, clarity, and distinctness?

Following Husserl's dictum "return to the things themselves," Heidegger describes phenomenology as the logos within the phenomena that gives itself as distinct from the scientific process of what he calls *mathesis* or a "knowing beforehand," that is "imposed" on the object.[5]

In a more literary form Erwin Strauss says,

> The eye of man, emancipated from the bondage of catching, grabbing, and gobbling, can dwell on the things themselves.... In the attitude of composure we reach the visible and yet leave it as it is. Distance is the condition of seeing the other in its uniqueness.... The distant opens itself to our gaze in contemplative regard, not in aggressive action.... The first great abstraction of suchness is achieved in the beholding gaze: The *eidos* discerned from the *hylé*.[6]

If we do not take the transcendental subject (the categorization of objects) as prior but rather recognize that there is a knowledge that is both ontologically and chronologically prior we will be opening the door to the realm of phenomenology. Perhaps phenomenology can be further clarified by a contrast with the modern tradition from Descartes to Kant in terms of the nature of perception. In every case

---

4. *Truth and Method*. New York: Crossroads Publishing Co., 1989, 6.

5. Martin Heidegger, "Modern Science, Metaphysics and Mathematics," in *Basic Writings*. New York: 1977, 249ff.

6. Erwin Strauss, "Born to See, Bound to Behold...," in *The Philosophy of the Body*, ed. Spicker. Chicago: Quadrangle Books, 1970, 341–343.

in this tradition perception is understood in terms of an analytic reflection. In the first place, so this story goes, there are sensations, then a series of syntheses and then, Voila! Perception is the result. But these sensations and syntheses have no prior reality and are all the artificial products of analysis. We do not live in a world of neutral objects. Rather, we find ourselves inextricably related and immersed in a world of meaning before any reflection. The world of meaning and value, in other words, the real world, is first and foremost the perceived world.

Perhaps a distinction can be made between two senses of subjectivity that will be helpful: First let's put together Kant's transcendental subject with Descartes's cogito as subjectivity number one. This subject is without gender, race, ethnicity, or nationality (at least as it is so conceived) and in like manner its object is also neutral, without meaning or value. It is also important to note that this subject is an impersonal, universal subjectivity even though Descartes's cogito is an "I" that thinks. In Descartes, all qualities that would ordinarily constitute an individual are put aside as unreliable witnesses to the truth. As a shorthand expression, we might simply call this the rational subject. Let us now think of a second sense or type of subjectivity that is first and foremost an experiencing subject that is inextricably involved in a lived world of meaning as a feeling conscious body. It is in this sense that Merleau-Ponty retrieves simultaneously both the human person and the earth in all of its diversity, richness, and mystery.[7]

In *Myth and Reality*, Eliade describes the essential difference between the space experienced as profane and space experienced as sacred. Sacred space is homogeneous in that a single meaning of the highest sort becomes the ground for a people's understanding of reality. It is indeed the place of the gods, but more important to the actual experience is the felt fullness and richness of the space. The contrast *as experience* is the heterogeneity of profane space. Here one moves about as if they were lost in a seeming infinite number of possibilities whose values vary without consistency. Kierkegaard calls this the essential condition of despair, and for Eliade it is the condition of the modern world. A sense of power is experienced when one finds oneself in sacred space and it is an irony of the secular world of today with all its assumed power over nature that one feels a profound sense of powerlessness. Of course there is no mystery here, for the power/control that is achieved through technology is only for the rational subject. The living person is just another "resource," manipulated by the forces of time.

Considered from a different perspective Eliade explains in the *Sacred and Profane* that sacred space is heterogeneous in that certain places are special and give an orientation to the person living in this world. "The profane experience," he says,

---

7. *Phenomenology of Perception*. New York: Humanities Press, 1962. Hereafter *P of P*.

"on the contrary, maintains a homogeneity and hence the relativity of space. No *time* orientation is now possible, for the fixed point no longer enjoys a unique ontological status; it appears and disappears in accordance with the needs of the day." The homogeneity of profane space signifies that all places are equal in value, which means they have no value. The conceptualization of space in geometry is exactly parallel to the experience, that is, that all spaces are exactly identical to each other. No one is superior or inferior to any other. An experience in such a space is disorienting and indeed does not constitute a world at all since all spaces are neutral. However, it should be immediately added that such a world or rather non-world of neutral spaces is seldom experienced as such; rather, we are thrown back upon our own special experiences of a birthplace, a first love, or some other significant event that is only for the individual. Such a device is hardly capable of giving us a sufficient orientation for a world.

The distinction of the sacred and profane is most relevant in societies based on agriculture/farming. In hunter/gatherer societies, the distinction has little or no meaning because all things and all activities exist without a context of meaning that has a reference to a primeval time (*in illo tempore*), that is not in a fixed historical past, but rather in a dynamic present that continues both past and future. It seems that in an agriculturally based society, there is an inevitable hierarchy where only the privileged few enjoy the freedom and plenty gained on the labor of the many. Given the hard labor and misery of the many, a radical distinction would have to be made between the sacred (freedom and plenty) and the profane (suffering and slavery). Even without a hierarchy the very nature of agriculture would entail an alienation, distrust, or even hatred of "wild nature," that is, nature not under cultivation/control.[8]

When Edmund Husserl was developing his phenomenology he said it would be an *apodictic* science. This apodicticity seems to follow the Cartesian meditations that sought for a certain foundation for the sciences. But such a parallel is more misleading than helpful. As was noted above, Descartes's certainty rested upon a "knowing beforehand," the a priori categories of reason structuring the given data of experience. Husserl's apodicticity, on the other hand, is precisely in the other direction. It rests entirely upon the given, the phenomenon itself. When Eliade speaks of the sacred as a hierophany he wishes to express first and foremost that it is an appearance, a phenomenon of the sacred. The usual objection is that

---

8. Paul Shepard, "A Post-Historic Primitivism," in *The Wilderness Condition*. San Francisco: Island Press, 1992, 40 ff. Also see Herbert N. Schneidau, *Sacred Discontent*, for a most convincing argument on this distinction between agriculturally based societies and hunter/gatherer people.

what might appear to one person as a sacred place can to another be merely another geographical location on a map. Therefore, it is up to the individual. First of all, it is never a matter of "free choice"; that is clearly an illusion. If we take these two options of a place as sacred or merely a spot on a map, both require considerable previous education. One is able to see a place as a spot on a map only because one has acquired specific knowledge and skill. In like manner a place as a hierophany, requires considerable knowledge in a particular sacred world. On the other side, that is, on the side of the other, there is a reality beyond any solipsistic argument. But what is it? Phenomenology's response is neither objectivistic nor subjectivistic. It bypasses the pitfalls of both metaphysical positions by returning to the phenomena.

Before any reflection, Husserl writes "I am aware of a world, spread out in space endlessly. . . . I discover it immediately, intuitively, I experience it . . . corporeal things somehow spatially distributed are *for me simply there* . . . present."[9] This is the basis for his call to "return to the things themselves." My consciousness of things as I perceive them is not in my head, but out there in the world. Husserl, therefore, calls the nature of consciousness "intentionality." My consciousness is always directed toward something. There is no pure consciousness as in Descartes's cogito. But intentionality is never simply neutral, it is not a pure light. Here we might take the next step to Heidegger's existentially founded human consciousness as "care" (*Sorge—Being and Time*, ch. VI). This existential understanding speaks to the essence of human behavior in terms of its involvement in and with the world. This involvement is not one of cause and effect, not a mechanistic view of human behavior but an involvement in terms of meaning. Eliade's descriptions of human behavior in terms of the sacred begin here, with one's immersion in a world of meaning structured around the central experience of the sacred.

Eliade's phenomenological descriptions include both the religious dimensions of archaic societies as well as the secular modern world, a distinction that occupies many of his works and always seems to hover just behind all of his writings. Eliade sees the difference between archaic societies and modern society as one between a culture of eternal recurrence and historicism respectively; however, historicism as a concept in its pure or idealized form never exists in an actual or real society because he believes that the human being is always in some sense *homo religiosus*. This means that even in a society such as the modern world that is consciously secular there are nonetheless more or less conscious constitutive intentions and ideals that fulfill Eliade's idea of the religious. For our purposes that means there are transhistorical ideals that are believed to be real. However, the problem for Eliade

---

9. *Ideas*. New York: Collier Books, 1931, ch. 1.

lies elsewhere. He says, "[H]istoricism arises as a decomposition product of Christianity: it accords decisive importance to the historical event (which is an idea whose origin is Christian) but to the *historical even as such*, that is, by denying it any possibility of revealing a transhistorical, soteriological intent."[10] The attitude of modern natural science which is intended to reveal a neutral objective world, is now applied to the human sciences, to history, which first and foremost means a desacralization of historical events. Such historicism for Eliade contains a built-in terror. We can identify three characteristics of historicism that Eliade considers decisive and interconnected in his judgment of the horror and terror of historicism: 1) historical events are indeterminate, which is implied by the modern world's understanding of the "openness of the future"; 2) they are irreversible, which means they are unredeemable; and 3) they are neutral in themselves, i.e. an event is the result of blind social, economic, or political forces.

By contrast, Eliade elevates the value of archaic societies that live within the structural meaning of eternal recurrence, and consciously rejects historicism. Within the meaning of eternal recurrence events take on a meaning in reference to a myth that took place before historical time, the pain, suffering, and evil that occurs will be washed away at the new year and life is renewed as nature is renewed in the spring. This is not a mere theoretical freedom that is promised by the "open future" of historicism, where very few, if any are really free, but an actual freedom of creativity that may be experienced by all within eternal recurrence. In summary form, that is Eliade's argument. But how is this "valorization of archaic societies" related to phenomenology?

First of all, Eliade as a Romanian of eastern Europe has experienced firsthand the terror of history, in the hands of the great powers from the west (Germany), the south (Ottoman Empire), and from the east (Soviet Union). The Romanians suffered the terror of history only because of their geographical location. A geographical location is merely an accident of history. This signifies that there is no justification, no meaning, no sense to it from the vantage point of historicism. However, within the archaic world of meaning, a meaning derived from the all-encompassing structure of mythology, the terror, the absurdity of history as just so many accidents is kept at bay. This does not mean that if Romania were a mythological society, rather than a modern one, that it would have avoided the terror at the hands of conquering armies, on the contrary it has been often pointed out that archaic societies based on myth are typically fragile in nature, especially with regard to cataclysmic occurrences.

---

10. *The Sacred and the Profane*. London: Harcourt Brace Jovanovich, 1959, 112. Hereafter *S & P*.

Another irony of the modern world might be noted here: its preoccupation with history. It is as if the study of history, as the cataloguing of past events, were to ensure that it is a dead past. Given Eliade's understanding of historicism as noted above, it would seem that the title, "history of religions" is inappropriate and the "phenomenology of religion" might be more fitting for his work.

The phenomenologist does not have to experience these possibilities directly; indeed, a phenomenological description requires a distance. However, this distance takes up neither the explanatory stance of the sciences nor the evaluative position of the early studies in comparative religion (e.g., Max Müller) that presupposed a kind of evolution culminating in today's dominant monotheisms. On the contrary, the phenomenologist is like an actor who reenacts, in Paul Ricoeur's words, in *imaginative sympathy* the role of a person in a play or story. In this stance of a "reenactment in sympathetic imagination" the phenomenologist at once achieves a distance and an involvement.[11]

Eliade often attempts his phenomenological reenactments by reiterating statements made by members of different archaic societies about sacred phenomena—the sky, water, the earth, etc. He then brings these statements together and describes sacred structures that form the worlds of these archaic peoples, but without explanation or evaluation. Rather, his purpose is to show, to bring forth into the light that which is closest to a people because for them it is the most real. This bringing forth out of "lived-experience" is parallel to that of the art work. Both the phenomenologist and the artist bring forth the essences that constitute a world, but the phenomenologist does not leave these images on an emotional level of intentional feeling but tries to bring these structures of the real and lived world to the mode of ideas, of essential structures.

For example, in a study of the "celestial sacred": although Eliade gathers statements from various sources (social scientists), he always tries to refer this information to original statements made by natives themselves. The experience of the transcendent is derived from an "awareness of infinite height." The sky shows itself as unbounded, and "spontaneously becomes an attribute of divinity" (*S & P*, 118) Eliade says:

> [T]his is not arrived at by a logical, rational operation. The transcendental category of height, of the super-terrestrial, of the infinite, is revealed to the whole man, to his intelligence and his soul. It is a *total* awareness on man's part; beholding the sky, he simultaneously discovers the divine incommensurability and his own situation in the cosmos. For the sky, *by its own mode of being*, reveals transcendence, force, eternity. It *exists absolutely* because it is *high, infinite, eternal, powerful.* (*S & P*, 119)

---

11. *The Symbolism of Evil.* New York: Harper and Row, 1967, 3.

The point here is that for the archaic man the experience of the sacred is found in the other, in the sky itself before any conceptualizations, before any flights of the imagination. Such an experience includes both poles of subject and object. The subject's consciousness (as was said earlier) is not a neutral gaze but, rather, intentional; it may be conceived as a light but it has a color or direction. On the other side of the other it spontaneously reveals itself in terms of its various possibilities. The phenomenologist describes the relation between these two, that area of meaning that is the very foundation and starting point for all theory, for all conceptualizations. Eliade does not deny the significance of the social sciences, of history, but he continually tries to reach down beneath the presuppositions to the actual experiences upon which the results of these sciences are based. For this reason it seems to me that Eliade's work, his lifetime efforts to understand religion as the human being lives it, makes him a philosopher and not a social scientist.

I would like to conclude with a few words from Merleau-Ponty's Preface to the *Phenomenology of Perception*, where he describes the legacy of phenomenology that he has taken on himself.

> [W]e cannot subject our perception of the world to philosophical scrutiny without ceasing to be identified with that act of positing the world, with that interest in it which delimits us, without drawing back from our commitment which is itself thus made to be a spectacle, without passing from the *fact* of our existence to its *nature*, from the *Dasein* to the *Wesen*.... The need to proceed by way of essences does not mean that philosophy takes them as its object, but, on the contrary, that our existence is too tightly held in the world to be able to know itself as such at the moment of its involvement, and that it requires the field of ideality in order to become acquainted with and prevail over its facticity. (xiv, xv)

This means that phenomenology is always, as Husserl says, *eidetic*. Its understanding is in the form of ideas, ideas as essences. Kant calls scientific knowledge representational. Experience is mediated through the logical categories of reason. It is therefore a secondhand knowing that is based upon the veracity of reason. The phenomenologist does "not rediscover an already given rationality, [phenomena] establish themselves," as Husserl says. "The phenomenological world is not the bringing to explicit expressing of a pre-existing being, but the laying down of being. Philosophy is not the reflection of a pre-existing truth, but, like art, the act of bringing truth into being" (xx).

It might seem that we tread here on dangerous ground, that Eliade's phenomenology of the religions of the world lacks objectivity, that his writings do not correspond to the actual religions. Such charges precisely reflect the presuppositions of a pre-existing world ordered by reason which the subject can view with a neutral gaze. For one last time let us return to the subject matter of phenomenology, that is, the world as it is lived. The phenomenological essences that Eliade reveals to us of the religions of the world are the result of a dialectic between what we usually call "the given" and the creative act of bringing that "material" to fruition, to our understanding. It is a matter of attentive listening and imaginative sympathy—perhaps only in this way can we begin to understand the religions of the world.

Chapter Six

ELIADE, THE COMPARATIVE METHOD, HISTORICAL CONTEXT, AND DIFFERENCE

CARL OLSON

Among Mircea Eliade's numerous critics, Jonathan Z. Smith[1] tends to stand out because his criticism calls attention to problems that are central to Eliade's methodology that involve his use of morphological classification and the comparative method, which are two aspects of his method that are tied together. Smith claims that morphology, a logical arrangement of particular items organized into a complex whole for Eliade, tends to ignore the categories of space and time and assumes an a priori "fitting economy," and thereby neglects the historical dimension.[2] With respect to Eliade's comparison of data, Smith thinks that this process is also done in a nonhistorical way. According to Smith, comparison is not a method for inquiry because it is more akin to memory and impression (*Map*, 259; *Imagining*, 22).

---

1. For his most recent statements, see J. Z. Smith, "Acknowledgements: Morphology and History in Mircea Eliade's *Patterns in Comparative Religion* (1949–1999), Part 1: The Work and Its Contexts; Part 2: The Texture of the Work," *History of Religions* 39:4 (2000): 315–351.

2. *Map Is Not Territory: Studies in the History of Religions*. Leiden: E. J. Brill, 1978, 259; *Imagining Religion from Babylon to Jonestown*. Chicago and London: University of Chicago Press, 1982, 23.

Moreover, comparison is a method that requires the acknowledgment of difference because it is the difference between data that makes an inquiry interesting and enables it to accomplish "some stated cognitive end."[3] Smith suggests that Eliade failed to pay enough attention to difference when he compared religious phenomena because he was overly concerned with sameness to the extent of neglecting or ignoring their differences. From another perspective, Smith is suggesting that Eliade's methodological use of morphology and comparison is nondiachronic and that its synchronic aspect is atemporal.

Smith is not the only such critic of Eliade, and these charges must be taken seriously. If we assume for the sake of argument that Smith is correct in his criticism, we need to ask the following questions: Was Eliade's use of comparison an improvement over prior uses of this method for the study of religion? And is the method of comparison a useful tool for the historian of religions in light of Smith's criticism of Eliade and his use of comparison? Since the first question is historical, it will be necessary to attempt to answer this question by giving some historical context. Thus, we will begin by reviewing a selected group of scholars from the latter nineteenth century until the period of Eliade's scholarly activity. This approach will allow us to see the prior uses of the method of comparison and the common features that Eliade shared with his predecessors and the differences between them. The latter result will enable us to recognize any improvements made by Eliade over prior religious theorists. We will then be in a better position to determine whether or not the use of comparison contains any future benefit for the study of religious phenomena.

QUEST FOR THE ORIGINS OF RELIGION

In the nineteenth century, the notion of comparison was used within the context of a quest for the origins of religion, a search framed by the theory of evolution. In the first volume of his work entitled *The Principles of Sociology* (1879), Herbert Spencer (1820–1903) tried to trace, for instance, the origins of religion in ancestor worship, to higher forms of religion, and argued that remnants of this practice can still be discovered in Christianity in such notions as the Holy Ghost and funeral customs. By comparing earlier religious beliefs and practices with historically later ones, Spencer, an advocate of positivism and social Darwinism, thought that he could rationally argue a priori for the evolutionary development of certain similar

---

3. *To Take Place: Toward Theory in Ritual*. Chicago and London: University of Chicago Press, 1987, 14.

notions into different conceptions.⁴ This position was based on the axiomatic conviction that evolutionary development consisted of a process of increasing differentiation, although increased differentiation was regulated by a tendency toward ultimate integration, a scholarly position that he thought placed him in agreement with his contemporary Tylor.

Edward B. Tylor (1832–1917) was concerned with religious development because it was part of his attempt to outline a "science of culture" by writing a history of the human mind in his major work entitled *Primitive Culture*. He began with the following question: "Are there, or have there been, tribes of men so low in culture as to have no religious conceptions whatever?"⁵ Tylor wanted to base his own method on objective observation and not speculation, an approach that led him to identify animism as the basis for the religion of lower tribes that originated in the belief of the existence of the deceased souls of creatures and represented a deeper theory of the origin of spiritual beings. Tylor's theory embodied a twofold conviction: primitive religion was inferior and lower on the evolutionary scale than that of the civilized world.

Although it is strongly suggested by the work of Tylor and his use of the notion of comparison, Lucien Lévy-Bruhl (1857–1939) compared primitive mentality to modern Western modes of scientific thinking and found the former lacking in rigor and rationality. Lévy-Bruhl called primitive or archaic mentality "prelogical reasoning," although he later rejected the differences between modern and primitive mentality in his posthumously published work entitled *Les Carnets* (1949) where he argued that the mental differences were not matters of principle but more indicative of nuances of mentality. In his earlier works, he used, however, comparison to measure modern Western modes of thinking with that of the primitive thought that focused on collective representations, tended to ignore necessity, and identified the one and the many by means of the principle of participation.⁶ Lévy-Bruhl described this type of mentality as mystical, prelogical, and pervaded by a sense of affectional participation because some primitives think of themselves as animals or birds without thinking metaphorically or symbolically about this kind of identity.

Derogatory terms such as *savage*, *heathen*, and *primitive* used by Tylor, Lévy-Bruhl, and other Western scholars were also part of the vocabulary of Sir James G.

---

4. *The Principles of Sociology*, 3 Vols. New York: D. Appleton and Company, 1898, I: 304–305.

5. *Primitive Culture: Researches into the Development of Mythology, Philosophy, Religion, Language, Art, and Customs*, 2 Vols. Third Edition. New York: H. Holt & Company, 1883, I: 1.

6. *Primitive Mentality*, trans. Lilian A. Clare. London: George Allen & Unwin Ltd., 1923, 5, 130–131.

Frazer (1854–1941), an acknowledged founding father of anthropology and equally a pioneer of comparative religion. Religion, which represented a propitiation and conciliation of assumed superior powers to human beings, was fundamentally opposed to magic, a necessarily false discipline and basic mistaken application of the association of ideas and an erroneous system of natural law, and science. In contrast to science, magic is more of an art to the savage and never a science, a notion that is lacking in the mind of the primitive because he/she reasons in ignorance of intellectual and physiological processes.[7] Frazer thought that this mode of argument enabled him to expose the myth of the noble savage and promote his own political agenda. There was no truth to the belief that the savage was the freest creature of humankind, because the primitive was limited by custom and tradition. The basic problem with tribal societies can be traced to their political systems, which tend to be democratic, whereas Frazer preferred a monarchical form of government because it represented symbolically and practically the emergence of humankind from the bondage of savagery with its prevalent ignorance and superstition. The truth discovered by Frazer about the cultural and political status of the primitive can be enhanced by a comparative study of the beliefs and institutions of humankind. More than a way of simply satisfying the curiosity of scientifically enlightened and culturally sophisticated humans, the comparative approach can become a powerful tool to expedite progress by exposing weak points of modern society (*Golden Bough*, I, xiv). Thus, Frazer's use of the comparative method within the context of his overall evolutionary and encyclopedic approach embodied a not so latent political agenda.

THE POSSIBILITY OF A SCIENCE OF RELIGION

Friedrich Max Müller (1823–1900) called for a science of religion within the context of his vision of the human discovery of the underlying purpose of the religions of humankind and a reconstruction of a genuine *Civitas Dei* that would encompass East and West. This final science to be developed by humans will change the world and renew Christianity from Müller's perspective.[8] The science of religion envisioned by Müller essentially represented the comparative study of religions. Müller stressed the comparative and pluralistic nature of his new science. But why did Müller think that this new science must be comparative and pluralistic? He quoted the Church Father Basilius on the purpose of comparing religions to the effect that it was to learn how religions differ and to ascertain which one was better than the

---

7. *The Golden Bough: A Study in Magic and Religion*, 3 Vols. Third Edition. London: Macmillan, 1951, I: xxii.

8. *Chips from a German Workshop. Volume I. Essays on the Science of Religion*. New York: Charles Scribner and Company, 1869; reprint Chico, CA: Scholars Press, 1985, xix–xx.

remainder (xix). If this new science of religion needed to be comparative in order to be scientific, what precisely made it scientific? Eric J. Sharpe provides an answer to this question by stating that it is scientific because of its inductive method and adherence to laws of cause and effect and "comparative because it claimed comparison to be the basis of all knowledge."[9]

From Müller's perspective, it is only from a pluralisitic context that one can discern the reasons for the superiority of Christianity. Citing Goethe's remark about not knowing any language unless one knows more than one, Müller claimed in probably his most well-known assertion that the same formula can be applied to religion: *"He who knows one, knows none."*[10] This type of assertion was grounded in Müller's conviction that all higher forms of knowledge were acquired by comparison and were based on comparison (12). By using the comparative method, a scholar gained a broader cultural perspective that gave the comparative scientist of religion a chance to also gain a better understanding of common assumptions about the origin, character, development, and inevitable decay of religion by comparing their natures. Overall, Müller grounded his theory of religion in a finite perceptual epistemology that implied something greater than the finite entities that were connected with the primary data of religion.[11] What Müller called Natural Religion, a possession of all humankind, developed from the combining of moral sensibility with religion, which in turn had its roots in the perception of the infinite (169). Müller's efforts were to influence other scholars, who attempted to develop further a science of religion.

Cornelius Tiele (1830–1902), a Dutch scholar and pioneer of the science of religion, wanted to extricate religious scholarship from the hermeneutical circle by avoiding formulating an ideal of the nature of religion, a phenomenon that was grounded in human nature and originates from the human soul.[12] Rather than proceed from an ideal of religion, which was neither an entirely natural nor artificial product of human beings, he conceived of the science of religion as a universal investigation that involved a multiplicity of facts and invited a scholar of religion to classify them and to draw inferences. The multiplicity of religious facts was united by the human mind within the context of an objective stance by the scholar that enabled him/her to distinguish the forms of religion from religion itself (I, 6). The path for this new science was paved by historical research with the overall goal of understanding and explaining religious facts. This can be accomplished by

---

9. *Comparative Religion: A History*, Second Edition. La Salle, IL: Open Court, 1986, 31.

10. *Introduction to the Science of Religion*. London: Longmans, Green & Company, 1873, 16.

11. *Natural Religion*. London: Longmans, 1890, 123.

12. *Elements of the Science of Religion*, 2 Vols. New York: Charles Scribner's Sons, 1897, 1899, I: 15.

observation, collection, classification, and comparison (I, 13). The exact method of the natural sciences cannot be applied to the science of religion, although this new science did use a deductive method that utilized reason to unlock results that were given by induction, empirical analysis, historical research, and comparison (I, 18). This suggested that comparison must be done in accord with the development of religion. Thus, Tiele envisioned his version of the science of religion to include a method that was empirical, historical, and comparative. This science was also cognizant of the psychological, social, and human dimension of religion.

Another Dutch scholar named Pierre D. Chantepie de la Saussaye (1848–1920) called for a science of religion. A basic presupposition of this science of religion was that there existed a unity among all religions.[13] In order to develop a science of religion two conditions were necessary: a general philosophy of history, and making religion an object of philosophical knowledge. With a firm foundation in these disciplines, a scholar of religion was prepared by means of the philosophy of religion to find the manifestations of religion and also by using the history of religion, which included not only historical development but also ethnography, to determine the essence of religion. Like Müller and Tiele, Chantepie de la Saussaye conceived of this new science of religion as having a comparative component that will function to sharpen the focus of the scholar (5). Chantepie de la Saussaye was opposed to the type of comparison that compared Christianity to tribal forms of religion. In fact, he even inverted this kind of comparison to make a point: "If on one side the views and customs of savages may everywhere be detected amongst civilized races, traces and indications of higher ideals are not wanting amongst savages" (36). The scientific spirit of Chantepie de la Saussaye's project was emphasized by his introduction of the notion of a phenomenology of religion, a discipline closely connected to psychology, that received its material from religious acts, cults, and customs. Since religion cannot be reduced to problems of its origin or essence, a phenomenology of religion was necessary in order to describe and classify the phenomena of religion.

COMPARISON AND THE SOCIOLOGICAL PERSPECTIVE

Unlike some earlier theorists and their quest for the origins of religion in some kind of primordial practice of a tribal group, Emile Durkheim (1858–1917) thought that the objective of the science of sociology was to explain religious and cultural realities in order to understand the people within that culture as social beings. Just as social facts are a product of a collective consciousness, religion is also a result of a collective mind.[14] Even though Durkheim boldly proclaimed that all religions

---

13. *Manual of the Science of Religion*, trans. Beatrice S. Colyer-Fergusson (Née Max Müller). London: Longmans, Green, and Company, 1891, 9.

14. *The Rules of Sociological Method*, trans. Sarah A. Solovay and John H. Mueller, Eighth Edition. Chicago: University of Chicago Press, 1938, 16–17.

were true in their own way because all provided an answer to the problem of human existence, he still thought that all religions can be compared. Thus, comparison and classification of phenomena played an important role in the approach of sociology because they enhanced human understanding by connecting ideas and unifying knowledge. In collaboration with his nephew Marcel Mauss, Durkheim viewed classification as a "first philosophy of nature" that was rooted in social relations that provided the distinctions for such a system.[15] If religions shared many common features, Durkheim thought these external similarities were often indicative of deeper underlying differences.[16] By means of comparing religions, another lesson drawn by Durkheim was that simpler, more elementary societies reduced differences because everything was common to everyone else in the tribe, the movements of tribal members were stereotyped, and conformity of conduct was indicative of congruity of thought.

In contrast to the type of sociology developed by Durkheim and his school, Max Weber (1864–1920) took the new discipline in a different direction and away from the positivist stance of those thinkers influenced by the theoretical work of Auguste Comte, who assimilated sociology to the natural sciences. Unlike the holistic and functional approach of Durkheim, the German scholar shifted fundamental analysis away from society as a unitary whole to the individual, which led Weber to emphasize social action over social structure. Weber's sociology was a science that attempted to interpret social action to gain a causal explanation of its cause and effect without neglecting the subjective aspect of the individual: "Action is social in so far as, by virtue of the subjective meaning attached to it by the acting individual(s), it takes account of the behavior of others and is thereby oriented in its course."[17] This type of an approach allowed Weber an opportunity to examine the interrelationship between human motives and intentions.

Several aspects of Weber's work shaped his method of inquiry that he called *Verstehen*, a way to comprehend social action by an empathetic understanding of another person's values or culture. This extra-empirical method was not devoid of the use of comparison, although a predominant theme was the gradual evolutionary development of rationalization within Western society. The comparative features of Weber's work can be recognized in his analytical construct called the "ideal-type," which represented a rational construction of given elements of social reality into a comprehensible conception. The priest, prophet, magician, and

---

15. *Primitive Classification*, trans. Rodney Needham. Chicago: University of Chicago Press, 1963, 82–83.

16. *The Elementary Forms of the Religious Life*, trans. Joseph Ward Swain. London: George Allen & Unwin Ltd., 1954, 5.

17. *The Theory of Social and Economic Organization*, trans. A. M. Henderson and T. Parsons. New York: Free Press, 1947, 88.

shaman were all examples of ideal-types, which were configurations of meaning that functioned as abstractions to assist sociological analysis and ultimately enhance understanding. These ideal-types can be compared with each other and actions of various religious figures can be compared in order to determine into which type it fitted best. Weber's cross-cultural studies were also important examples of his comparative approach and the important role that it played in his scholarship.

The role of comparison also played an even more central role in the scholarship of Joachim Wach (1898–1955), a teaching predecessor of Eliade at the University of Chicago. Wach began by raising a rhetorical question: Can a sociology of religion reveal the nature and essence of religion itself? Although he gave a negative response to his own question, Wach argued that the specific aim of a sociology of religion was to examine the interrelations between religion and social phenomena in order to understand how religion functioned within the context of the varied interrelationships and interdependencies of its numerous components. A more general aim of the discipline was to elucidate the overall cultural significance of religion.[18] Wach advocated an impartial and objective approach because the facts must be studied without bias, although he curiously viewed the sociology of religion as a supplement to phenomenology, psychology, theology, and the history of religions (6). In fact, Wach called his approach topological, whose purpose was the study of the interrelation and interaction of religion and society. When studying religion Wach advised scholars not to limit their focus to a single religion because this type of an approach led to insufficient and perverted conclusions (9).

By incorporating the comparative approach, Wach did not think that this implied indifference to the subject, rather, he argued, comparative studies "contribute toward the gaining of perspective, as well as of discernment and understanding."[19] Wach believed that one gained stages of understanding that he identified as partial, integral, and comprehensive. But before one gained any of these levels of understanding, it was necessary to bring certain equipment with one to the practice of comparison: extensive information; an adequate emotional condition that was devoid of indifference but embodied an engagement of feeling, interest, and participation; a volition directed toward a constructive purpose; and broad experience (12–13). In this manner, Wach sought to make the application of Weber's notion of *Verstehen* broader by making it more cross-cultural and more sensitive to the religious nature of the phenomena studied and interpreted.

---

18. *Sociology of Religion.* Chicago and London: University of Chicago Press, 1971, 4.

19. *The Comparative Study of Religions*, ed. Joseph M. Kitagawa. New York and London: Columbia University Press, 1969, 9.

ELIADE, COMPARISON, AND HIS PREDECESSORS

Without reconstructing his entire method, it is important to consider the role of comparison in Eliade's approach to the study of religion in order to demonstrate his different and similar uses of the comparative method in contrast to his predecessors. Eliade understood himself as a historian of religion, although such a scholar must exceed the intellectual grasp of an ordinary historian who attempted to reconstruct a historical event. The intellectual reach of the historian of religion surpassed the common historian because the former "must trace not only the history of a given hierophany, but must first of all understand and explain the modality of the sacred that that hierophany discloses."[20] Thus, Eliade's approach was not merely concerned with historical accuracy, but he was also involved with understanding and explaining the material. Besides being historical, the methodological approach of the historian of religion must be as encyclopedic and all-encompassing as possible in its scope, which rendered the discipline impossibly difficult because a practitioner had to know everything, refer to other disciplines for help, and always seek genuine sources.[21] Although one needed to consult a specialist on a given topic that one was investigating, Eliade strongly emphasized going back to the original sources such as primary texts.[22] Even though Eliade wanted to ground his method on the historically concrete, he thought that it was necessary to examine all the manifestations of a religious phenomenon, not merely to discern its message, but the historian of religion also "attempts to decipher whatever transhistorical content a religious datum reveals through history."[23] Any attempt to interpret a transhistorical message has been problematic for some of Eliade's critics.[24]

---

20. *Patterns in Comparative Religion*, trans. Rosemary Sheed. Cleveland: The World Publishing Company, 1968, 5.

21. *Journal II. 1957–1969.* trans. Fred H. Johnson, Jr. Chicago: University of Chicago Press, 1977, 43.

22. *Ordeal by Labyrinth: Conversations with Claude-Henri Rocquet*, trans. Derek Coltman. Chicago and London: University of Chicago Press, 1982, 144; "Autobiographical Fragment," in *Imagination and Meaning: The Scholarly and Literary Worlds of Mircea Eliade*, ed. Norman J. Girardot and Mac Linscott Ricketts. New York: Seabury Press, 1982, 114–115.

23. *Shamanism: Archaic Techniques of Ecstasy*, trans. Willard R. Trask, Bollingen Series LXXVI. New York: Pantheon Books, 1964, xv.

24. Some of these criticisms can be discovered among the following scholars: John A. Saliba, *Homo Religiosus*, in *Mircea Eliade: An Anthropological Evaluation*. Leiden: E. J. Brill, 1976; Ioan Culianu, *Mircea Eliade*. Assisi: Cittadella Editrice, 1977; Ninian Smart, "Beyond Eliade: The Future of Theory in Religion," *Numen* XXV, Fasc. 2 (August 1978): 171–183; Robert D. Baird, *Category Formation and the History of Religions*. The Hague: Mouton, 1971; Guilford Dudley III, *Religion on Trial: Mircea Eliade and His Critics*. Philadelphia: Temple University Press, 1977; Ivan Strenski, *Religion in Relation: Method, Application, and Moral Location*. Columbia, SC: University of South Carolina Press, 1993.

Nonetheless, the history of religions represented a total hermeneutics for Eliade because it was "called to decipher and explicate every kind of encounter of man with the sacred."[25] This total hermeneutics reached beyond understanding and interpreting religious phenomena because it was concerned to think about the religious facts in a potentially creative way, which could lead to the creation of new cultural values. This creative hermeneutics possessed the potential to change us, to stimulate us, to nourish us, and to revitalize our philosophical thinking. By creative hermeneutics, Eliade meant more than a method of interpretation, because it was also "a spiritual technique that possessed the ability of modifying the quality of existence itself" (62). Thus, hermeneutics, a never-completed task, was creative in a dual sense: It was creative for the particular interpreter by enriching his/her mind and life, and it was creative because it revealed values unavailable in ordinary experience. This type of awareness was liberating for Eliade. Besides its potential ontological implications for the individual interpreter, the study of unfamiliar religions more than broadened one's horizon of understanding because one encountered others representing foreign cultures, which results in culturally stimulating one.

For Eliade, hermeneutics was also a risk and an adventure because the historian of religions was confronted with numerous strange situations during the course of his/her investigations that were extremely complex and needed to be interpreted in order to be understood. The various boundary situations that were opened before our hermeneutical gaze often challenged us to rethink our own ontological situation. By learning as many boundary situations as possible from different religious cultures, the interpreter was able to abstract the structure of the different kinds of behavior that he/she encountered. Eliade understood this search for symbolic structures as a form of integration into a larger whole or system and not a form of reduction. But it was insufficient to discern the structures of religious phenomena or behavior; it was also necessary to understand their meaning. If religious phenomena revealed new and unexpected perspectives by means of which they could be grasped and articulated into a pattern or system, Eliade claimed that "[t]his makes possible not only the intuition of a certain mode of being, but also the understanding of the 'place' of this mode of being in the constitution of the world and of the human condition."[26] Eliade implied that he followed this type of approach because

---

25. *The Quest: History and Meaning in Religion*. Chicago and London: University of Chicago Press, 1969, 58.

26. "Methodological Remarks on the Study of Religious Symbolism," in *The History of Religions: Essays in Methodology*, ed. Mircea Eliade and Joseph M. Kitagawa. Chicago and London: University of Chicago Press, 1959, 100.

the dialectic of the sacred, a tendency to indefinitely repeat a series of archetypes, demanded it. Due to the fact that hierophanies repeated themselves and inherently sought to reveal the totality of the sacred, it was possible for us to distinguish religious facts and to understand them (*Shamanism*, xvii). This process implied a comparative approach to the study of religious phenomena.

If meaning became obscured, it was possible to restore it by means of comparison and exegesis (*Journal II*, 162f.). Moreover, Eliade claimed in his journal the following: "[I]n the history of religions, as in anthropology and folklore, comparison has as its function to introduce the universal element into 'local,' 'provincial' research" (298). With respect to the use of comparison, Eliade made a distinction between the historian of religions and the strict phenomenologist. According to Eliade, the phenomenologist rejected using comparison because such a scholar confined him or herself to finding the meaning of a particular phenomenon. "Whereas the historian of religions does not reach a comprehension of a phenomenon until after he has compared it with thousands of similar or dissimilar phenomena, until he has situated it among them; and these thousands of phenomena are separated not only in time but also in space" (*Shamanism*, xv). This did not mean that the historian of religions was content to compare elements in his/her typology or morphology. The historian was also aware that religious phenomena were not exhausted by history, although he/she needed to remember that religious phenomena developed within and revealed their meanings within history.

The historical aspect of religious phenomena was often neglected by some of the predecessors of Eliade. The embrace of the theory of evolution, along with its concomitant scientific aura, by scholars such as Spencer, Tylor, Lévy-Bruhl, Frazer, and Durkheim obscured the historical nature of religious phenomena. And their own approaches to the study of religion were ahistorical, an approach that was consistently criticized by Eliade. Furthermore, the quest for origins was a misguided endeavor because there was no way to investigate primordial religion from the perspective of Eliade (*Quest*, 25). If the human mind simply responded to the laws of nature as Tylor claimed, there was no place for human creativity from the viewpoint of Eliade.

The embrace of the theory of evolution also led to a tendency among many scholars before Eliade to reduce the origin of religion to a particular phenomenon such as: the souls of deceased humans developing into supreme beings, according to Spencer; identifying animism as the basis of religion, as did Tylor; the argument by Frazer that religion developed from magic; and the single-minded focus on the social aspects of religion by Durkheim. To these examples of a tendency to reduce religious phenomena by some scholars, Eliade emphatically replied:

Indeed, there is no such thing as a "pure" religious fact. Such a fact is always also a historical, sociological, cultural, and psychological fact, to name only the most important contexts. If the historian of religions does not always insist on this multiplicity of meanings, it is mainly because he is supposed to concentrate on the religious signification of his documents. The confusion starts when only one aspect of religious life is accepted as primary and meaningful, and the other aspects or functions are regarded as secondary or even illusory. Such a reductionist method was applied by Durkheim and other sociologists of religion. (19)

Another danger to which the theory of evolution contributed in the scholarship, for instance, of Tylor and Frazer was to gather material from all around the world and arrange it into a sequential pattern that accorded with a preconceived plan. Tylor, Frazer, and Spencer shared a tendency to view religious phenomena and actions as natural phenomena that developed out of human reason and not supernatural intervention. From the perspective of Eliade, there are three problems with such tendencies for the study of religion: the illegitimate use of scientific models; a misuse of primary sources; and the danger to overemphasize rationality, found in such scholars as Tylor, Lévy-Bruhl, and Weber. Eliade elucidates the problematic nature of relying on scientific paradigms: "Neither the history of religions nor any other humanist discipline ought to conform—as they have already done too long—to models borrowed from the natural sciences, still more as these models are out of date (especially those borrowed from physics)" (60–61). Thus, since a fundamental premise of the philosophy of positivism associated with Auguste Comte that perceived a logical and methodological unity between the natural and social sciences was a product of a confusion between what German scholars called *Naturwissenschaft* and *Geisteswissenschaft*, respectively disciplines of the natural science and humanistic studies, Eliade was convinced that no humanistic discipline should conform to models taken from the natural sciences. The positivistic aversion to metaphysical thinking was an obstacle to grasping the nature of religion, and its claim that science was focused on empirical facts irrespective of the human subject were anathema to Eliade's method and personal philosophical convictions, although he perceived a structural analogy between the scientific method and literary imagination in which the human mind is free to play outside of the process of logical thinking.[27] With respect to the second problem associated with the use of sources, Eliade's emphasis on focusing upon primary sources has already been mentioned. Moreover, he thought that the history of religions, an empirical method of the study of

---

27. *Symbolism, the Sacred, and the Arts*, ed. Diane Apostolos-Cappadona. New York: Crossroad Publishing Company, 1986, 155.

religion, represented a multitude of past messages waiting to be deciphered and understood by the scholar.

Late nineteenth-century theorists concerned with the quest for the origin of religion used the method of comparison in an illegitimate way from the perspective of Eliade because they used it to attempt to prove the theory of evolution and to support their contention that earlier forms of religion were inferior to Christianity or Western modes of thinking. If earlier forms of religion were discovered to have survived to the present moment, these were labelled modes of superstition by Tylor or exposed weak points of modern society according to Frazer—to cite just two examples. This line of argument manifested a cultural and religious arrogance by Western scholars. With respect to surviving beliefs and practices from an earlier period of religious history, Eliade referred to these things as camouflaged in the banality of the modern world.[28] There were also numerous examples of mythical survivals in the modern world that could be discovered in the notion of Aryanism in Germany; the adoption of eschatological myths by Marxists; the figure of Superman in comic books; the exodus to suburbia, which reflected a nostalgia for primordial perfection; the modern embrace of the novel, which represented a desire to hear desacralized but mythological narratives, whereas reading itself suggested to Eliade an escape from time.[29] With the possible exception of Wach, the hermeneutics of Eliade demonstrated a sensitivity to the use of Western categories when interpreting archaic religious beliefs and practices in sharp contrast to most of the scholars that have been reviewed in this essay. Moreover, although Eliade has been criticized for his use of the comparative method, his use of it represented an important improvement over that of most of his predecessors. If it is possible to agree that Eliade's use of the comparative method represented a significant or even a small improvement over the use of this method by his predecessors, this single example, although other examples could be cited, begins to refute any exaggerated and scurrilous assertion that Eliade's scholarly career was an abject or grandiose failure.[30]

Eliade's use of the comparative method was devoid of the positivistic and behavioristic slant of Spencer's method, which tended to exclude meaning and human subjectivity. Eliade seemed to have scholars like Spencer in mind when he stated, "It is impossible to imagine how consciousness could appear without conferring a *meaning* on man's impulses and experiences" (*Ordeal*, 153). For Eliade,

---

28. *Autobiography. Volume I: 1907–1937. Journey East. Journey West*, trans. Mac Linscott Ricketts. San Francisco: Harper and Row, 1981, 274.

29. *Myth and Reality*, trans. Willard R. Trask. New York: Harper and Row, 1963, 181.

30. Roger Corless, "After Eliade, What?" *Religion* 23 (1993): 373–377. (Reproduced in this volume as "Building on Eliade's Magnificent Failure"—Ed.)

meaning was intimately linked with what it meant to be a human being. Eliade's work also stood against the penchant for using comparison to demonstrate the inferiority of primitive religion, as in the work of Tylor and Frazer, or using it to prove that primitive mentality is prelogical because it lacks the rigor and rationality of Western thinking. Unlike Max Müller, Eliade did not compare religions to determine which one was the best, as if comparison was a means of testing one's own faith and religion against others or assumed the guise of a game with a winner and a loser. Although Eliade attempted to avoid Durkheim's reductionism, they agreed that comparison helped to demonstrate that religions shared common features. And Eliade thought that the use of comparison was more helpful than just sharpening the focus of the scholar as did Chantepie de la Saussaye. Eliade was, however, closer in spirit regarding the use of comparison to the scholarship of Tiele, Weber, and Wach with their respective emphasis on historical research to pave the way for classification, the empathetic understanding of Weber, and Wach's advocacy of an impartial and objective approach, the need to avoid insufficient or distorted conclusions, and using comparison as an aid to understanding, although Eliade was a bit leery of the emphasis on rationality found in the methods of Tiele and Weber.

For the most part, Eliade and his predecessors avoided the individualizing type of comparison that is used to "contrast specific instances of a given phenomenon as a means of grasping the peculiarities of each case."[31] With the exception of Weber and Wach, they also neglected the variation-finding type of comparison that was intended "to establish a principle of variation in the character or intensity of a phenomenon by examining systematic differences among instances." Many of Eliade's predecessors engaged in the universalizing type of comparison because its overall aim was to "establish that every instance of a phenomenon follows essentially the same rule" (82). Eliade's method of integrating elements into his system of morphological classification and his emphasis on an encyclopedic approach to the history of religions suggests that he used the encompassing type of comparison that operates by placing different instances of a phenomenon "at various locations within the same system, on the way to explaining their characteristics as a function of their varying relationship to the system as a whole" (83). This suggests that the encompassing type of comparison commences within a large structure or process, and Eliade's morphological classification of myths and symbols in his work the *Patterns in Comparative Religion* is a good example of the use of this type of comparison. When using this type of comparison, the scholar can select particular locations or phenomena within the structure or process and explain similarities or differences

---

31. Charles Tilly, *Big Structures, Large Processes, Huge Comparisons*. New York: Russell Sage Foundation, 1984, 82.

between them as a result of their relationship to the entire structure. If the encompassing type of comparison is historically grounded, it can assist the scholar to explain large structures or processes, connect these explanations to the temporal and special context, and enhance our understanding of the overall structures or processes and better understand their particular parts. Thus, whatever type of comparison a scholar chooses to employ it possesses the potential to enhance our understanding of religious actions and phenomena.

REFLECTIONS ON DIFFERENCE AND COMPARISON

There are still, however, problems with comparison, according to Jonathan Z. Smith's criticism of Eliade's use of the method. Smith claims that the use of comparison reflects a recollection of similarity, explained as contiguity, constructed on contagion, a subjective experience, and represents an invention and not a discovery because the latter implies finding something, whereas invention is an unintended realization of novelty. Smith concludes that comparison is an impressionistic matter of memory and not a sound method, although Smith does think that a limited or controlled use of comparison is useful if it is limited to cultural items that are spatially and temporally contiguous (*Imagining Religion*, 21–24). Moreover, since comparison enables the scholar to bring differences together within his/her mind, it is the scholar who makes possible their sameness, which suggests that comparison does not inform us how things are but rather how they might be conceived.[32] From the perspective of Smith, a consequence of the use of comparison is that difference tends to be forgotten, which leads him to call for a discourse of difference (42).

Responding to such a call is not without its dangers, if one's method for the study of religion has been shaped in part by neo-Kantian philosophy and its representational type of thinking, as is the case for Eliade.[33] Depending on one's point of view, both the dangers and potential for liberating the mind from representational modes of thinking are reflected especially in the early philosophy of Gilles Deleuze, who attempts to develop a philosophy of difference. Without going into great depth, Deleuze wants to restore difference to thought just as Smith wants to restore the importance of difference in the comparative method, but it is first necessary to overcome the tendency to represent "difference through the identity of

---

32. *Drudgery Divine: On the Comparison of Early Christianities and the Religions of Late Antiquity*. Chicago: University of Chicago Press, 1990, 51–52.

33. Eliade shares with the neo-Kantian and Enlightenment philosophical tradition a number of convictions such as the following: the universe is intelligible; truths are fixed, uniform, permanent, absolute, and universal; religion is a *sui generis* reality that is unique and irreducible.

the concept and the thinking subject."[34] Within his philosophy, Deleuze rejects notions such as the one, universal being, the multiple in general because such terms are too all-encompassing or abstract. In place of these kinds of terms, Deleuze stresses the specific, particular, and singular. Difference is an aconceptual notion for Deleuze that undermines the certainties traditionally associated with rationality in the West. Since difference eludes reason, Deleuze finds himself at the limits of the Western philosophical tradition, whereas a more conservative scholar such as Eliade is more symbolically and ontologically comfortable at the center. At these limits of philosophy, the radical nature of difference becomes even more apparent when Deleuze claims that difference inhabits the *Aion*, a past and future with no present, which means that difference is always past or about to be future. From Eliade's perspective, this type of approach makes it impossible to make comparisons and to ultimately understand religious actions, beliefs, and phenomena. This is also not the type of discourse about difference that Smith would appear to favor because he wants to preserve at least a limited role for comparison. If Deleuze's philosophy of difference undermines hermeneutics and the comparative method, is there another alternative that is sympathetic to both Eliade and Smith and does not neglect difference?

There is another hermeneutical option, which involves altering and expanding one's understanding by remaking its forms and limits. Normally, we understand without articulating what or how we comprehend something, a pattern of behavior or unawareness that shapes our judgments. By means of past experiences, prior decisions, and previous modes of understanding, we develop an inarticulate and unaware mode of comprehension that is akin to a kind of preunderstanding, which shapes our mode of understanding without our being cognizant of its operation. This makes it very difficult, if not impossible, and even undesirable to enter into the viewpoint or worldview of another person. If it is extremely difficult or impossible to get into the mind of another, we should, then, not foolishly think that we can rise above or transcend our own point of view.[35] We must also recognize that our understanding can change over the course of a period of time. Life experiences cause us to adopt, for instance, different modes of understanding our own behavior or that of another person depending on one's stage of life and experiences prior to the moment of interpretation. An interpreter's state of mind during the process of interpretation can also unconsciously shape his/her interpretation. This alternative hermeneutical option is more than a self-conscious examination or a mode of becoming aware of our pre-understanding.

---

34. *Difference and Repetition,* trans. Paul Patton. New York: Columbia University Press, 1994, 66.

35. *Truth and Method.* New York: Crossroad Publishing Company, 1982, 238.

If we are to interpret the religious actions and beliefs of another person or community, it must be acknowledged that other-understanding changes our personal self-understanding. This implies that by attempting to understand the religion of another culture we must also become aware that our understanding is a single possible mode of understanding among other possibilities. To a greater or lesser degree the scholars discussed in this essay exhibit some form of ethnocentrism. Although it is very difficult to completely eradicate one's ethnocentrism in practice, it is at least theoretically possible to begin to overcome it by becoming aware that our individual understanding possesses limits and of how it fits within a wider context of attempts to understand the other. Furthermore, there is always a comparative component to other-understanding: "This is because we make the other intelligible through our own human understanding."[36] Within the context of this comparative process of recognizing, identifying, and articulating differences, we liberate ourselves by increasing our self-awareness, and we liberate the other by letting them be who they are. If we can recognize the differences between their understanding and our own, we are on our way to the termination of interpreting the other through our personal mode of understanding and allowing them to stand, undistorted by our understanding, in their own authentic mode of being. Thus, by contrasting and comparing, we can make progress understanding the other, strive to escape our ethnocentrism, and transcend our previous personal understanding.

This does not mean that our newly discovered or acquired understanding will be without limits. The philosopher Charles Taylor makes this clear: "When we struggle to get beyond our limited home understanding, we struggle not toward a liberation from this understanding as such (the error of the natural science model) but toward a wider understanding which can englobe the other undistortively" (150–151). This implies that our prior narrowness is overcome, while ethnocentrism is conquered by inclusiveness, which suggests understanding the other within the context of his/her own world. Therefore, the role of the comparative method in understanding possesses an important value by elucidating cross-cultural misunderstandings and distortions, which represents a way to not only liberate oneself but also the other. It is thus not necessary to embrace the philosophy of difference espoused by Deleuze in order to emphasize the importance of difference and committing the error of neglecting or not recognizing similarities. Smith is justified to criticize Eliade for neglecting difference and emphasizing sameness, but this does not mean that the method of comparison does not have a viable and useful role to play in cross-cultural hermeneutics. Although it is probably not totally possible to overcome one's ethnocentrism, the comparative method does have a useful

---

36. Charles Taylor, *Philosophical Arguments*. Cambridge: Harvard University Press, 1995, 150.

hermeneutical role to play in understanding the religious beliefs, actions, and phenomena connected with the other when it is used in such a way that sameness and difference are kept in creative tension with each other within an overall historical context.

Part Three

LITERATURE

Chapter Seven

THE UNITED STATES' RESPONSE TO MIRCEA ELIADE'S FICTION

MAC LINSCOTT RICKETTS

On April 12–14, 1978, a conference entitled *"Coincidentia Oppositorum:* The Scholarly and Literary Worlds of Mircea Eliade" was held on the campus of Notre Dame University. The university's press had just released *The Forbidden Forest,* an English translation of the novel Eliade considered his masterwork, *Noaptea de Sânziene,* and Norman Girardot, then a member of the Notre Dame religion faculty, had organized the conference partly to promote the book by publicizing the little-known literary side of Eliade's oeuvre. About a dozen "Eliade experts" were gathered to present or respond to papers, three of which were devoted entirely to Eliade's literary activity.[1] On the second evening, the university's drama department staged

---

This is an abridged version of a paper presented at the 1996 American Academy of Religion Annual Meeting. (Ricketts originally entitled his paper "America's Response to Mircea Eliade as a Writer." With his permission I have changed this. Obviously it is the response to Eliade's literary fiction that is Ricketts's concern. Furthermore, although he does make one reference to *The Toronto Review,* his focus is on reviews and responses from the United States, omitting as he does any reference to French Canadian responses and considering Mexico, Argentina, and Brazil to be outside his immediate frame of reference, Ed.)

1. Matei Calinescu (Indiana University), "Narrative and Meaning: The Literary Universe of Mircea Eliade"; Mac Ricketts (Louisburg College), "Fate in *The Forbidden Forest*"; and Virgil Nemoianu (University of California, Berkeley), "Wrestling with Time: Eliade and Nabokov's Later Novels."

a reading of a play by Eliade, *The Endless Column (Coloana nesfârsita)*, as translated by Mary Park Stevenson. For the first time in the United States, Eliade was celebrated not only for his achievements as a scholar, but also for the creations of his imagination.[2]

At the time this conference was held, students and readers of Eliade in the United States should at least have been aware of the fact that the world-renowned historian of religions was also the author of a body of fictional works. One section of the Festschrift published in 1969 for Eliade's sixtieth birthday, *Myths and Symbols: Studies in Honor of Mircea Eliade*,[3] was devoted to his literary accomplishments, and a portion of his journal, *No Souvenirs,* which appeared in 1977,[4] contained numerous references to his fiction. The situation, then, was somewhat better than it had been in 1959–1964 when I was a student of the University of Chicago Divinity School. I do not remember ever hearing anything said, in those five years, about my professor's being the author of novels, plays, and short stories. If I did, I ascribed no importance to the fact. About 1968, one of my former classmates, H. Byron Earhart, presented a paper at an AAR meeting dealing with Eliade's *Fôret interdite* and two or three shorter fictional works in French or German translations.[5] This, as I remember, was my introduction to Eliade as an author.

In 1970, there appeared the first book of English translations of stories by Eliade to be published in the United States: *Two Tales of the Occult*—translations by William Ames Coates of a pair of fantastic novellas of 1939–1940 vintage.[6] Eliade wrote a short but important preface for the book in which, among other things, he says he would have preferred to have seen *Fôret interdite* translated first: "But what publisher would undertake the risk of bringing out a 640-page novel

---

2. See Norman Girardot and Mac Ricketts, eds., *Imagination and Meaning: The Scholarly and Literary Worlds of Mircea Eliade.* New York: Seabury Press, 1981, ix, and Mary Park Stevenson, "Report of Conference on the Work of Mircea Eliade," in *Romanian Bulletin* (July–August 1978): 9–10.

3. Edited by Joseph Kitagawa and Charles H. Long. Chicago: University of Chicago Press, 1969. The book contains an extensive bibliography, including literary items.

4. *No Souvenirs: Journal, 1957–1969*, trans. from the French by Fred H. Johnson Jr. New York: Harper and Row, 1977. New Edition: *Journal II.* Chicago: University of Chicago Press, 1989.

5. "The Novel of Mircea Eliade and His Contribution to the History of Religions." The paper is undated.

6. Published by Herder and Herder, New York; reissued as *Two Strange Tales.* Boston: Shambala, 1986. One year earlier Eric Tappe of the University of London had brought out a book, *Fantastic Tales*, in Romanian and English (London: Dillon's), containing two stories by Eliade and one by M. Niculescu. Printed in Romanian and English on facing pages, it was intended for language students and had very limited circulation, especially in the United States.

written by an author primarily known as an historian of religions?" He makes it clear that it was the translator's idea, not his, to publish these stories, but he concludes, "I am grateful to Professor Coates that, thanks to his enthusiasm, I have had an opportunity [in this preface] to touch on an aspect of my writing which for a long time I have almost kept as a secret." Thus did Eliade, rather reluctantly and almost apologetically, make his literary debut in the United States![7]

Apart from brief notices in the *Library Journal* and *Christian Century*, I know of only two significant reviews of this book: one by a former student of Eliade's, Charles S. J. White, in *Journal of Asian Studies,* and another by Jay Bail in *The Book Review, An Alternative Magazine from California.*[8] The review by Charles White is perceptive, as would be expected, relating the themes of the stories to Eliade's history of religions writings. White recognizes that *littérature fantastique* is an excellent medium for illustrating the dialectics of the camouflage of the sacred in the profane, a basic Eliadean concept. For him, one of the stories, "The Secret of Dr. Honigberger," "gives access, perhaps for the first time . . . to an inner perspective upon the drama of yogic change in mode of being." White believes that "additional translations . . . of Eliade's literary *oeuvre* will be recognized as imperative in the English-speaking world for understanding the relationship between the scientific and artistic motivations of the man who has in a special way reopened access for modern sensibility to the mythic and the religious." Bail gushes from a "Zenist" perspective: "Eliade dives into personalities, splashes with dialogue, always swimming closer until nothing is left but the strangeness of the mind." I do not know how large the original edition was, but in late 1977, when Eliade tried to buy a copy for himself, he was told by the publisher that it was sold out.[9]

Two papers on Eliade as an author were presented during the seventies at AAR annual meetings: "The Fantastic and the Sacred in the Writings of Mircea Eliade," by

---

7. Eliade makes no mention of this book in his published "Journal fragments."

8. White, *Journal of Asian Studies* XXX, 3 (May 1971): 717–719; and J. Bail, "The Spiritual Revolution," in *The Book Review* 18 (March 1971): 32–33, 39. White's review was condensed in *Contemporary Literary Criticism* 19 (1981): 147. Two other minor reviews should be mentioned: Marvin Mudrick made a few supercilious remarks about it in a ten-book review article, "Scrupulous Permutations and Occult Resemblances," in *The Hudson Review* XXIV, 2 (Spring 1971): 185–200; and Allen J. Hubin devoted a paragraph to it in a group review of several mystery novels (!), "Criminals at Large," in *The New York Times Book Review*, December 20, 1970: 10. Mudrick is of the opinion that: "Claptrap and mystification—whether or not under religious auspices—were never very promising literary materials." Hubin finds the plots "not spectacular when viewed against the body of fantastic literature," but says that Eliade writes "graceful and often intricate prose." I have found no reviews of the 1986 Shambala edition.

9. Letter to me, December 5, 1977, published in *Manuscriptum* (București), no. 86–89, (1992): 291.

myself in 1974, and "The Royal Road toward the Center: Fictional Hermeneutic and Hermeneutical Fiction in Eliade's *Two Tales of the Occult*," in 1977—a well-written study by Mary Zeiss Stewart, then a graduate student at Syracuse University.[10]

As in the case of *Two Tales of the Occult*, the publication of *The Forbidden Forest* in 1978 also came about at the initiative of the translators, Mary Park Stevenson and myself. We began the translation in 1972, shortly after its publication in Romanian.[11] The correspondence between myself and Eliade at this time shows that Eliade was very dubious about our finding a publisher in the United States for such a large volume. Although by now his literary works were having considerable success on the continent in German and French translations, he doubted that they would be received the same way here. On February 9, 1975, he wrote to me: "Only a *great* success with another book (say, the *opus magnum [A History of Religious Ideas]*) could convince an editor to take a risk on *Forbidden Forest*." And in his next letter of March 25, 1975, he says: "The 'hour' of my literature in the U.S.A. has not yet arrived."[12] Although the University of Chicago Press was eagerly publishing his scholarly books, the editor there was not interested in producing the novel. Near the end of 1976, Mrs. Stevenson and I, with much help from Norman Girardot, succeeded in having *The Forbidden Forest* accepted by the University of Notre Dame Press. Eliade was, of course, delighted (cf. letter of February 10, 1977—289). And a year later, the novel appeared.

Eliade furnished a short but revealing preface for *The Forbidden Forest* in which, among other things, he speaks frankly about the role that literary creation has played in his life since youth. It is, he says, "my only means of preserving my mental health." He cites specific times in his career when, after prolonged periods of intense scholarly labor, he was "tempted" or "obsessed" by the desire to write a novel, to "escape from the prison" and regain "*freedom*—that freedom which the writer knows only in the act of literary creation."[13]

---

10. Published in *The Ohio Journal of Religious Studies* VI, 1 (April 1978): 29–44.

11. *Noaptea de Sânziene*, two vols. Paris: Ioan Cusa, 1971–1972. The novel was published first in a French translation: *Fôret interdite*, trans. by Alain Guillermou. Paris: Gallimard, 1955.

12. *Manuscriptum*, 1992: 286.

13. *The Forbidden Forest*. Notre Dame: University of Notre Dame Press, 1978, v–vi. See also Eliade's "Autobiographical Fragment" in *Imagination and Meaning*, 113–127. Cf. Seymour Cain, "Poetry and Truth: The Double Vocation in Eliade's Journals and Other Autobiographical Writings," in the same book, 87–91. Referring to Eliade's personal comments in his journal, Cain says, "By far the majority of his complaints and most of his angst about unfulfillment come from the nonconsumation of his literary work, and his negative remarks are almost entirely directed against scholarship as an annoying, frustrating obstacle to his true metier" (91).

The Forbidden Forest received almost unanimous praise in the numerous reviews and notices that followed its publication. It must be admitted, however, that many of the reviewers were personally acquainted with Eliade, and that nearly all the review articles were in religious periodicals. Virgil Nemoianu, a Romanian-American literary critic, reviewed it for the *Times Literary Supplement*, the most prestigious periodical to acknowledge it with more than a note. Joseph M. Kitagawa furnished a review for *Parabola*, Matei Calinescu (another Romanian-American critic) wrote two long and excellent review articles on it, while Jerry Cullum, a former student of Eliade's, contributed short reviews to two periodicals. John Miles Foley, then of the English department at Emory University and *not* personally acquainted with Eliade, wrote a fine review for *Balkan Studies*. And there were others in *Choice, Library Journal*, etc.[14]

Nemoianu considers *The Forbidden Forest* Eliade's "most ambitious" literary effort, but he personally regards his post-1940 novellas as his "best" creations. Calinescu stresses the novel's "fairytale" quality, classifies it as a peculiarly Romanian example of magic realism, and relates it specifically to three major Romanian folktales. Foley identifies the plot structure as "paratactic, a characteristic of all early epics." Harry J. Caragas tells readers of *Catholic Library World* that the novel "shows affinity" to Jung's thought. The *Library Journal* note says simply: "A superb novel—though not for every taste," and *Choice* states that "it is worthy of comparison with Dostoevsky or Proust." Cullum rightly observes: "Although the novel is more likely to be read by students of religion than by literary critics, it deserves consideration in its own right, rather than as a footnote to Eliade's scholarly works." However, it is probable that the majority of its readers came to it, as did nearly all the critics, with a prior knowledge of Eliade's history of religions writings and therefore viewed it as the avocational effort of a professional scholar.

Even after the novel was published, Eliade remained skeptical of its popularity: "I *hope* it will have some success—although, frankly, I don't think so," he wrote to me.[15] Referring to what he considered the poor sales of *No Souvenirs* (less

---

14. Nemoianu, "Time out of Time," *TLS* (13 October 1978): 1183; Kitagawa, *Parabola* (August 1978): 112–114; Calinescu, "The Disguises of Miracle," *World Literature Today* (Autumn 1978): 558–564; idem., "Between History and Paradise," *Journal of Religion* (April 1979): 218–223; Cullum, *Religious Studies Review* 4, 3 (July 1978): 226; and in *Christian Century* (20 Sept.): 864. Other reviews: Francis Sullivan, *America* (10 March 1979): 203–204; J. M. Foley, *Balkan Studies* XX, 2 (1979): 507–509; H. J. Cargas, in "Evaluating Eliade," *Catholic Library World* (Nov. 1978): 176; brief notices appeared in *Choice* (October 1978), and in *The Library Journal* (15 May 1978); etc.

15. Letter of March 10, 1978; in *Manuscriptum* 94–97 (1994): 245.

than half the original five thousand copies sold in the first year), he wondered how a big book costing $20.00—a large sum then!—would sell. More optimistically, he added, "At any rate, a *great step forward* has been taken. When other translations of fiction will appear, perhaps my name will make headway among readers of *literature*."

Sales of *The Forbidden Forest* were relatively brisk for the first year and a half: more than a thousand copies were purchased. However, another eight years would pass before the second thousand sold.[16]

Eliade's fame on the continent, especially in France, was at an all-time high in these last years of the decade. He received numerous prestigious honors, and in 1979 and 1980 his name was proposed for the Nobel Prize in Literature.[17] His novellas were being snatched up quickly when they appeared in German and French translations.[18]

Encouraged by the sales of *The Forbidden Forest* and other developments, the University of Notre Dame Press was optimistic enough to publish in late 1979 Mary Stevenson's translation of *Pe strada Mântuleasa*, titled in English *The Old Man and the Bureaucrats*. Considered by many to be one of the best examples of Eliade's short fiction, it was reviewed quite favorably in three literary periodicals: *World Literature Today*, by Romanian-born Marguerite Dorian; *Studies in Short Fiction*, by William Buchanan; and *The Western Humanities Review*, by Walter A. Strauss.[19] Dorian calls it a "little masterpiece of brilliant craft and exuberant imagination," and Strauss praises it as an example of magic realism. Strauss stresses the point that Eliade began his career as a *homme de lettres* in Romania and that it would be quite wrong to think of his creative work as "illustrative" of his scholarly theories. Rather, he says, Eliade's literary and history of religions writings are both "creative transformations" of personal experience. As in the case of *The Forbidden Forest*, no reviews

---

16. Royalty statements, University of Notre Dame Press.

17. Proposed by Gheorghe Bulgar, a Romanian linguist who was visiting professor in those years at the University of Lyons. See Mircea Handoca, "Convorbire cu prof. univ. dr. Gh. Bulgar, despre Mircea Eliade," in *Ateneu* (București), Oct. 1984. The prize in 1979 went to the Greek poet Odysseus Elytis, and in 1980 to the Lithuanian-born Polish poet Czeslaw Milosz.

18. For example, the first edition of *Le vieil homme et l'officier* (*Pe strada Mântuleasa*), placed on sale in France in the spring of 1977, was sold out in three weeks. Letter from Eliade to me, May 11, 1977: in *Manuscriptum*, 1992: 290.

19. Dorian, *World Literature Today* (Autumn 1980): 615; Buchanan, *Studies in Short Fiction* (Spring 1981): 196–197; Strauss, *Western Humanities Review* (Autumn 1981): 276–280; also J. P. G., *Chronicles of Culture* (July–August, 1980).

appeared in any major U.S. newspaper or magazine but several "religious" periodicals carried reviews, all enthusiastic.[20]

In 1981 the Westminster Press brought out a slim paperback volume called *Tales of the Sacred and the Supernatural*, featuring two of Eliade's novellas: "With the Gypsy Girls," translated by William Ames Coates,[21] and "Les Trois Grâces," translated by myself. I had hoped for a much larger book that would contain five or six novellas, but the editor cautiously limited it to about one hundred pages. Eliade, who was consulted about the contents (Coates was deceased), again furnished a short foreword, about half of which was taken from a book he had published in 1932![22] *Tales of the Sacred and the Supernatural* was reviewed positively though briefly in *Science Fiction and Fantasy Book Review* and *Religious Studies Review*.[23] Morton Kelsey, who reviewed it for *New Catholic World*, was less than enthusiastic, however. He found it "difficult to shift gears and listen to [Eliade] as a novelist of the fantastic," wondering if he should look for "some deeper meaning" in the stories. While they held his attention and "created an atmosphere of mystery," he says they do not "take one into the supernatural as the novels of Charles Williams or C. S. Lewis," and he calls them "somewhat risqué."[24] I was never given any figures on sales, but they could not have been large. A book of this genre was an anomaly for the Westminster Press, and it received little publicity.

When *Imagination and Meaning* appeared in 1982, it contained one short story by Eliade, "Good-bye!" None of the brief reviews of this book made any mention of the story, however.

Professor Walter Strauss, chairman of the Department of Modem Language and Literature at Case Western Reserve University and author of a review article

---

20. D. Atkins, *Christian Century* (May 21, 1980): 585; Kathleen Verduin, *Christianity and Literature* XXIX, 4 (Summer 1980): 81–83; and Matei Calinescu, *Notre Dame English Journal* XIII, 1 (Fall 1980): 74–78. (Verduin, writing for an "evangelical" readership, feels obliged to say: "Perhaps some might regret the absence of anything distinctly Christian in this book, but let us take the author on his own terms: he is concerned not so much with the Christian reader as with the more universal *homo religiosus* at the core of all of us which has never quite been secularized out of existence.")

21. First published in *The Denver Review* VIII, 2 (Summer 1973): 13–58; a translation of "La ţiganci."

22. *Soliloquii*, Bucureşti: Cartea cu Semne, 1932, 47–50.

23. Robert Galbreath, *Science Fiction and Fantasy Book Review* (May 1982); and Seymour Cain, *Religious Studies Review* (April 1983): 166. Jill Baumgartner, who contributed a carefully worded, one-sentence review to *Christian Century* (May 26, 1982: 637), also reviewed it for *The Cresset* (May 1982): 27, a publication of Valpariso University—a review I have not seen.

24. Morton Kelsey, in *New Catholic World* (May–June 1982): 141–142.

cited above, was so interested in Eliade as an author that he organized a session for the Midwestern Modern Language Association in 1982 on "Mircea Eliade and Literature." Honoring Eliade in the year of his seventy-fifth birthday, the purpose of the session, as Strauss explained in his letter inviting me to participate,[25] was: "[t]o explore the importance of Eliade's studies in the history of religions, especially his highly important contributions to the knowledge of myths and symbols . . . ; to recognize and appreciate his creative writings . . . and his autobiographical writings. [In short], to *connect* Eliade's work with literary studies—a task that should have been performed long ago."

Four papers were presented at the conference: "Creative Writing as *Imitatio Dei:* The Book and the Fall," by Lawrence E. Sullivan; "Time and Myth in *The Forbidden Forest,*" by John Miles Foley; "Eliade's Novella *Domnişoara Christina (Mlle. Christine),*" by Norman Girardot; and "Reading Eliade's Stories as Myths for Moderns," by myself. All of us but Foley were "religionists" and former students of Eliade's; Foley was a member of the English department at the University of Missouri, Columbia. These papers—all solid works of scholarship—unfortunately were not published, except for Sullivan's which appeared in *Unirea*,[26] an obscure Romanian émigré paper out of Toronto.[27] Their impact, therefore, was limited essentially to the small audience attending the session.

Another session devoted to Eliade as author was held at the national MLA meeting in Washington in November 1989, sponsored by the Romanian Studies Association. Only three papers were presented: "Eliade's *Forbidden Forest* and Postwar Existentialism," by Peter Christensen, then of Marquette University; *"Maitreyi: Le nuit bengali,"* by Ramonde Bulger of Graceland College; and "Eliade's View of Human Existence in 'Un om mare,' " by Maria Pia Chisu. Christensen's paper subsequently was published in *The Journal of the American-Romanian Academy,* 1990 (128–144).[28]

To my knowledge, no other session on Eliade has been conducted at a national or regional MLA meeting.* That Eliade is known rather widely and considered important in United States literary-academic circles is attested by the fair number of dissertations and articles that turn up on data bases for "Eliade" with the

---

25. Letter dated April 13, 1982.
26. No. 2 (March 1984): 21–22.
27. Foley's paper was an expanded version of his review article mentioned above (note 16).
28. *PMLA* 104, 6 (Nov. 1989): 1082. My thanks to Bryan Rennie for this information!

*After Prof. Ricketts wrote this, the Romanian Studies Association of America arranged a session at the National MLA meeting in Chicago in 1999. Christian Moraru presided over a panel on "Eastern Fantasies: Memoir, Romance, and Transactions of Identity in Mircea Eliade's and Maitreyi Devi's Fiction." *PMLA* 114, 6 (Nov. 1999): 1235 [ed.].

indication that "use" or "application" has been made of his theories. Indeed, extensive and intelligent use of his theories on myth, symbol, and the sacred/profane dichotomy sometimes is made, but in many cases one finds no more than a few brief allusions taken from one or two of his books. Eliade has become a "good reference to cite" in scholarly literary articles and dissertations. In general, his major theoretical works seem much better known than his fiction. To my knowledge, no dissertation based exclusively on Eliade's literary writings has been written in any university in the United States, but one exists that deals in part with a novel of his. Jeanette Mercer (now Sabre) received a doctorate in 1981 from Pennsylvania State University with a dissertation entitled *The Sacred Wood in Four Twentieth-Century Fictional Narratives*—one of the works studied being *The Sacred Forest*.[29]

Matei Calinescu, Romanian-born professor of comparative literature at Indiana University, was commissioned in 1987, one year after Eliade's death, by the Ohio State University Press to direct a series of books of Romanian translations. The first volume, by his decision, is comprised of three of Eliade's fantastic-genre stories: "Youth without Youth," "The Cape," and "Nineteen Roses," all translated by myself, with an excellent introduction written by the editor. Entitled *Youth without Youth and Other Novellas,* it was released in a handsome, hardcover edition in the summer of 1988. Appearing, as it did, about the same time as Volume II of Eliade's *Autobiography,* the two books frequently were reviewed jointly. Calinescu and the press were quite pleased by the strongly positive review in the *New York Times* by novelist Robert Irwin.[30] Other favorable reviews were given by Marguerite Dorian,[31] and Carol Zaleski of Harvard.[32] Initial sales were rather encouraging: more than 1,500 copies in the first six months; but since then fewer than a thousand more have been sold.[33]

In 1994 the University of Chicago Press, in conjunction with Carcanet Press, Ltd., of Manchester, England, launched the most ambitious effort to date to put a literary work by Eliade before the English-reading public. A translation of *Maitreyi,* Eliade's most popular novel in Romania from its appearance in 1933, was released together with a "companion" volume, *It Does Not Die,* written by Maitreyi Devi, the real-life heroine of Eliade's highly autobiographical novel that bears her name.[34]

---

29. See also Jeannette Mercer Sabre, "The Sacred Wood in Three Twentieth-Century Narratives," in *The Christian Scholar's Review* 13, 1 (1983): 34–47.

30. "Sympathy for the Archangel," *New York Times Book Review*, March 3, 1989: 24; reviewed together with *Autobiography,* vol. II.

31. *World Literature Today* 64, 1 (Winter 1990).

32. *Parabola* XII, 4: 100–104; reviewed with *Autobiography,* vol. II.

33. Ohio State University Press royalty statements through June 1996.

34. *Bengal Nights: A Novel,* trans. from the French (*La nuit bengali,* Gallimard, 1950) by Catherine Spencer. Chicago: University of Chicago Press, 1994, and Manchester: Carcanet Press Ltd., 1994; Maitreyi Devi, *It Does Not Die: A Romance,* same publishers, 1994.

The English translation, curiously, is from the French version, *La nuit bengali*, rather than from the original Romanian, and bears the title, *Bengal Nights*.[35] Published with much fanfare in both cloth and paperback editions, the two books were reviewed extensively in tandem (I know of at least seventeen reviews). The senior editor at the University of Chicago Press reported to me that as of May 1996 some 2,200 clothbound and 5,000 paperback copies of *Bengal Nights* had been sold, plus 1,600 and 4,800 copies respectively of Maitreyi's book.[36]

The two novels need to be read together to be well understood, since neither book is furnished with an introduction. Maitreyi's book explains Eliade's to some extent. The dust jacket paragraphs also help a little. Eliade's "novel" was written shortly after his return from India, and it won a literary prize and brought him fame as an author. He admits that in writing it he used passages from his journal almost verbatim, making little effort to disguise the identities of the leading characters.[37] Maitreyi herself did not learn the contents of the book until nearly forty years later. She considered that Eliade had slandered her by claiming they had been intimate—a point she denied—and she came to Chicago unannounced, to confront him in his office one spring day in 1973. Then, after returning home, she wrote her version of the romance—and continued her life story up to the point of their meeting again in Chicago. Neither account claims to be purely autobiographical, but where fact ends and fiction begins in either book is impossible to say.

More than half the reviews were written by women, four of them of Indian birth[38] and another someone who knew Maitreyi Devi personally.[39] Virtually all the reviewers dwell mainly on the plot details, treating the books as essentially autobiographical, with Maitreyi's account being considered the more straightforward. Literary criticism, where it arises, relates mostly to the genre of Eliade's novel, dubbed by one reviewer (Kamani) "colonial fantasy," adjudged now somewhat outmoded. Most reviewers rate Eliade the better writer, complaining of Maitreyi's imperfect

---

35. Where I have taken the trouble to compare the English translation with the Romanian, I have discovered serious departures from the original text owing to the double translation. Strangely, none of the reviewers have raised any questions about this matter.

36. Letter from T. David Brent, May 20, 1996. "These are very satisfactory if not spectacular sales."

37. *Autobiography*, vol. I. New York: Harper and Row, 1981: 239–240; cf. *Journal* III: 96–97.

38. Anita Desai (*The New Republic*, Aug. 15, 1994), Nita Mehta (*Chicago Tribune Books*, May 8, 1994), Tilottama Mina Tharoor (*Washington Post Book World*, May 22, 1994), and Ginu Kamani (*The Toronto Review*, Summer 1996).

39. Carolyn Wright (*Boston Globe*, July 11, 1994). The more notable of the male reviewers: K. E. Fleming (*The Nation*, October 10, 1994), Ian Buruma (*New York Review of Books*, September 22, 1994), and Richard Eder (*Los Angeles Times Book Review*, March 27, 1994).

English (she wrote her book in Bengali and translated it herself—but Eliade's book, of course, is also a translation!). Otherwise, criticism, where it arises, is mainly *ad hominem*, directed at Eliade's behavior and attitudes—the reviewers assuming an identity between the author of *Bengal Nights* and the male protagonist of both books. Eliade is faulted for exhibiting colonial arrogance, male chauvinism, condescension, and ignorance of Indian customs. Most critical is Anita Desai (in *The New Republic*), who accuses Eliade of racism. She, like nearly all the reviewers, does not seem to be familiar with Eliade's scholarly works on Indian thought and religion.

Much more could be said about these reviews, but for our purposes we need only observe that Eliade, at last, has been widely recognized as an author. His first novel to gain considerable notoriety in the United States was, coincidentally, the same one that made him a "popular author" in Romania—more than sixty years earlier! But, in many respects *Bengal Nights* is not typical of Eliade's literary work—certainly it is quite unlike his fictional writings since World War II. Reading *Bengal Nights* in no way prepares one for *The Forbidden Forest, The Old Man and the Bureaucrats,* or the novellas in *Youth without Youth*. What will be the long-range impact of the publication of these "Maitreyi" books on Eliade's recognition in the United States as a writer is, therefore, highly uncertain.

When *La nuit bengali,* which was Eliade's first novel to be published in France, failed to meet with success at its appearance in 1950, Eliade concluded, after reflection, that it was a good thing that it had not sold well. He wrote then in his journal: "[T]he novel represents only one aspect of my literary *oeuvre,* and not even the most significant one. It would not be convenient for me to be *identified* as the author of *this* novel. . . . It is *not appropriate* that I should be discovered as a writer *today* through a novel written at age twenty-five."[40] I believe that Eliade would say the same thing today, that he would be dubious about the value of the relative "success" of this novel, as compared to that of *The Forbidden Forest* which he regarded at his most significant literary creation.

This, then, has been a hasty survey of "The United States' Response to Eliade's Fiction" or "literature" (to use the term by which he always referred to his fictional writings). Summing up, we can say that the response, in general, has been considerably less enthusiastic here than on the continent of Europe—especially in Germany, France, and Italy where nearly all his novels and novellas are now available in translation, and where sales are strong.[41] In Italy, in 1984, Eliade received two

---

40. *Journal I, 1945–1955,* trans. M. L. Ricketts. Chicago: University of Chicago Press, 1990, 148–149: entry dated only "1951."

41. For example, Herder Verlag reports that its translation of *Nunta în cer, Hochzeit im Himmel* (1992), has been the best seller of its Eliade literary titles—which include translations of *Huliganii, Şarpele,* and *Noaptea de Sânziene*. (Letter to me of May 22, 1996, signed by Ingrid Keßler.) Most of the novellas have been published at other presses, apparently with much success.

literary awards: the Dante Alighieri Prize and the Isola d'Elba Prize, the latter for *Nozze in Ciello* (*Nunta în Cer* [Marriage in Heaven], 1938), judged the best foreign novel published in translation in Italy in 1983. The growing number of titles translated into Spanish and Portuguese and published not only in Europe but also in Mexico, Argentina, and Brazil attest to a popularity on both sides of the Atlantic. Needless to say, he is avidly read in his native Romania, where he was first known as a literary personality. All his fiction, moreover, was written in Romanian, and the novellas from the years of Eliade's exile seem to have been composed with his compatriots strongly in mind.

With these facts before us, it is time to ask: Why has Eliade not enjoyed the "literary success" in the United States that he has had in continental Europe and Latin America? This is a question about which only speculation is possible, but I think several probable reasons can be adduced.

First, in contrast to his situation in Romania where his initial popularity was as a novelist and man of letters, and where his history of religions writings were regarded as of secondary value in the 1930s, in the United States he was known first and foremost as a scholar, a theorist, a savant. When his fictional works began to appear, it was inevitable that they should be regarded as the avocational, "amateurish" efforts of a scholar—or perhaps a secondary way for him to put across his "message." That a man of science can also be also a man of letters is hard for us to accept.

However, Eliade had this same "handicap" to overcome in Europe, outside Romania. He had begun to be known, in certain circles at least, as an Indianist and historian of religions before his literary writings started to appear in French and other languages.[42] The French translation of *Maitreyi, La nuit bengali*, published in 1950, was not initially successful, owing, perhaps, to the failure of a prominent literary critic, Marcel Brion, to review it in *Le Monde* as he had promised.[43] However, the publisher of his *Traité d'histoire des religions* (Payot, 1949) was indignant that he had published a novel. Eliade remembers: "Your name, he told me, evokes in the minds of readers an Orientalist and historian of religions. You must not disorient them!"[44] It would take another twenty years or so for his literary writings to "catch on" in Europe, and by this time he was a world-renowned scholar. Why he did gain literary fame there may be explained by cultural differences between the Old World and the United States, by differences in "literary taste," or by the kinds

---

42. It is true that translations of *Maitreyi* were published in Italy in 1945 and in Germany in 1948, but these did not attract much attention in the postwar chaos.

43. See comments in *Journal I*, 148: undated 1951.

44. *Autobiography*, vol II, 148.

of publicity he received in the two areas (see below). To answer this question adequately would require much additional research and would lead us beyond the limited scope of this chapter.

Second, there is the fact that Eliade himself did not take the initiative in publishing English translations of his fiction, seeming indifferent or even reluctant to have them appear. Matei Calinescu, commenting in 1977 on the lack of awareness in the United States of Eliade's work as an author, suggested that "this may be due, among other things, to Eliade's own curious disinterest in the promotion of his fiction, a disinterest that is in perfect contrast to his passion for writing."[45] All the English translations of Eliade's literary works were made on the initiative of the translators (Tappe, Coates, Stevenson, and me), and their appearance in print also was at our initiative—with the concurrence and cooperation of the author himself, to be sure, but not at his urging. The same seems to have been the case, at least at first, with the European translations, after what he considered the "failure" of *La nuit bengali* in 1950 and of *Fôret interdite* in 1954.

In his autobiography, Eliade says that the lack of success of *Fôret interdite* "reconciled me to the decision I had made: from here on I would write for Christinel and myself and for a few Romanian friends."[46] In 1963 one of his students in the University of Chicago's Social Thought program, after discovering the German translation of *Şarpele*, expressed interest in reading more of his fiction. Eliade says, "I didn't encourage him."[47] When Mary Stevenson in 1972 proposed translating and publishing some of his fiction, he was not enthusiastic. "I doubt she will find an editor. In the United States, as in Europe, I am known and accepted *exclusively* as an historian of religions. And if my literary works ever appear, even in part, they will provoke bewilderment—and probably will upset the publishers of my 'serious' books."[48] As late as 1976, when the first English translation of a part of his journal *(No Souvenirs)* was about to be released, he expressed misgivings. "For many of my English-language readers, the discovery of 'the writer' will surprise them, maybe even baffle them. The cliché, 'man of science,' still terrorizes academic circles. Many believe that the poetic imagination, literary creativity, cannot be reconciled with 'objective,' scientific research. . . . It will be ten or fifteen years before the homology of scientific and artistic creativity will become obvious to everyone, including academic circles."[49] In 1977 he told an interviewer that he had often postponed

---

45. "Imagination and Meaning: Aesthetic Attitudes and Ideas in Mircea Eliade's Thought," in *Journal of Religion* 57, 1 (January 1977): 2.
46. *Autobiography*, vol. II, 175.
47. *No Souvenirs*, 191 (24 June 1963).
48. *Journal*, 14 August 1972 (my translation from the Romanian).
49. *Journal*, 30 March 1976 (my translation).

translation of his novels to avoid possibly damaging his credibility as a historian of religions.[50]

Judging from these candid statements, Eliade's reluctance to publish his literary works in English seems to have stemmed from his fear of their not being taken "seriously"—to the possible detriment of his reputation as a scholar. Or perhaps, unconsciously, he wished to avoid another experience of rejection. In the last ten years or so of his life, however, with his literary prestige in Europe waxing, and with his being considered for the Nobel Prize in literature in 1979, he seems to have become more interested in seeing his fiction published, at least on the continent.[51] I like to think that had Eliade lived another five or ten years, he might have taken a more active part in getting his literary works published in English translation.

Third, as a consequence of his unwillingness to seek publishers for these translations, the task of finding them fell upon us, his translators—who, unfortunately, were ill-prepared for the responsibility. He deserved much better. The result, as I have shown above, was that the publication of Eliade's works of fiction in English was a rather haphazard affair—at least, prior to the 1994 release of the "Maitreyi" books by the University of Chicago Press.[52] Moreover, the publishers did not publicize the books vigorously, and they appear not to have sent review copies to the leading "secular" newspapers and magazines. Had we, the translators, been able to interest a major publishing house in Eliade's literary works, the story might be very different. Eliade was right, of course, about the difficulties his creative writings would face in the United States. This is not to say that advertising and

---

50. *Ordeal by Labyrinth. Conversations with Claude-Henri Rocquet.* Chicago: University of Chicago Press, 1982, 143.

51. However, in a Journal entry for 29 May 1979 Eliade records that a friend has informed him that he is better known in West Berlin today as a writer than as a historian of religions. Eliade's comment: "which doesn't please me; my ideal is to be known 'totally' " (*Journal IV*, 16).

52. In addition to publications in books discussed above, I published "A Fourteen Year Old Photograph" in the *Louisburg College Journal of Arts and Sciences*, 1971; and Mary Stevenson's "The Endless Column" appeared in *Dialectics and Humanism* (Warsaw, Poland) I, 1 (1983): 44–48. East European Monographs (Boulder) currently distributes *Mystic Stories: The Sacred and the Profane*, edited by Kurt Treptow (București: Editura Minerva, 1992), which is a book containing four of Eliade's novellas (*Domnișoara Christina, Secretul doctorului Honigberger, La țiganci,* and *Tinerețe fara tinetețe*) translated into rather stilted English by a Romanian, Ana Cartianu. "In the Shadow of a Lily" ("La umbra unui crin"), trans. by me, is found in the second edition only of *Waiting for the Dawn: Mircea Eliade in Perspective*, eds. David Carrasco and Jane Marie Law. Boulder: University of Colorado Press, 1991, and "The Captain's Daughter" ("Fata čapitanului") is included in *The Phantom Church and Other Stories from Romania*, eds. Georgiana Farnoaga and Sharon King. Pittsburgh: University of Pittsburgh Press, 1996.

recommendations by leading critics alone will make an author popular, but without such aids even a writer of great talent may remain unappreciated.

As for the future, I hesitate to prophesy. Personally, I hope that the success of *Bengal Nights*—even though it is not typical of Eliade's literary oeuvre—has been sufficient to convince the editors at the University of Chicago Press—or some other major house—to risk publishing some of his other novels and novellas. I heartily agree with a statement Matei Calinescu made in 1977: "I am certain that one day Eliade's literary work will enjoy the wider readership it deserves,"[53] and I believe that it could even prove, in the long run, to be of more enduring value than many of his scholarly writings.

---

53. "Imagination and Meaning: Aesthetic Attitudes and Ideas in Mircea Eliade's Thought," loc. cit.

Chapter Eight

ROMANTIC POSTMODERNISM AND THE LITERARY ELIADE

RACHELA PERMENTER

> The current debate between organicist and deconstructionist critics over the nature of Romanticism was originally waged by the Romantics themselves and was not resolved in favor of either side.
>
> —Tilottama Rajan, *The Supplement of Reading*

In 1967 Allen Ginsberg insisted on meeting Mircea Eliade. Surrounded by snow-drifted Chicago, in the apartment of a mutual acquaintance, Ginsberg recited verses of Prajnaparamita to Eliade in Japanese and English "while singing and striking two little bronze bells" (Eliade, *Journal II*, 295). The image aptly introduces the complex and provocative relationship between Eliade's work and the field of literary studies. His devotion to literature is clear by his having written volumes of short fiction and more than a dozen novels. His 1933 novel *Maitreyi* gave him national stardom in Romania and *Nunta în Cer* (*Marriage in Heaven*) won the 1984 Elba-Brignetti prize for the best translated novel in Italian.[1]

---

1. Some of Eliade's novels are actually novellas. In this volume see Mac Linscott Ricketts, "The United States' Response to Mircea Eliade's Fiction," for publication and reception details. Ricketts has also translated *Nunta în Cer* into English (unpublished) and has written a précis of that novel in *Mircea Eliade: The Romanian Roots*, 2 vols. New York: Columbia University Press, 1988, 1160–1178.

Because Eliade was known mainly as a fiction writer of folk-hero proportions in Romania[2] and solely as a celebrated academic in the United States, the topic of his work's relationship to current literary studies is certainly engaging. Moreover, since most twentieth-century literary scholars in the areas of myth and archetype theory, symbolism, and Romanticism either encountered or used references to his scholarly work, the topic as a retrospective assessment is pertinent.[3] Finally, and perhaps most pragmatically, because Eliade's fiction is linked to Romanian folklore, magic realism, and diaspora studies,[4] the current academic reassessment of a world literary canon may benefit from the continued translation of his fiction into English.

Discussion of Eliade's literary contributions offers more ancillary paths than direct appraisals. The idea of such an inevitably circuitous description of reality, not coincidentally, is a key to Eliade's fiction and scholarship. His enthusiastic appreciation of Eastern thought and of Goethe, for example, led him to believe Goethe's statement that whenever we speak "outside of poetry," we are "bound for the moment to become one-sided. There is no communication, no theory, without separation" (Wilkinson, 143). For Eliade, art is beyond the divisive limits of language; it is in fact "a liberation" and "victorious bursting of the iron band."[5] Eliade, like Goethe, never seems to veer from that imposing Romantic dictum: *Although poetry as art offers the creation of a new world, all language separates.* Much more than coincidentally, this pronouncement has a distinct poststructuralist/postmodern fa-

---

2. Eliade noted the "unreality" of his literary fame: "They all, without exception, assure me that in Rumania I am the widest-read, the most admired writer, etc. . . . Of course, I'm aware that under the current circumstances it is impossible to write about me, and I must consider myself lucky that at least I can be spoken about. . . . In Rumania I belong to the oral culture, just like characters in folklore" (*Journal III*, 81).

3. The complementary interests of literary theorists and historians of religion is a central assumption of this paper. Eliade wrote in 1970, "[The] majority of the historians of religions . . . have some puritanical or bourgeois prejudices against literature, thus neglecting or ignoring the tremendous work done in the last twenty years by literary critics and theoreticians" (*Two Strange Tales*, xiii). Eliade was probably referring to the archetypal criticism of Northrop Frye and perhaps to structuralists and formalists such as Tzvetan Todorov, Vladimir Propp, Roman Jacobson, and the early Roland Barthes; Romantic theorists such as M. H. Abrams; and to Eliade's University of Chicago colleagues, neo-Aristotelians Wayne C. Booth and R. S. Crane. He refers to Ferdinand de Saussure in his *Journal* (III, 311). See also Eliade's *Journal III*, 225 where he criticizes extremely "positivist" literary theory.

4. Eliade wrote in 1948, "The Romanian diaspora. . . . The role of pastoral nomadism in Romanian folk-spirituality. . . . Someday someone will make precise the tension between the diaspora (emigration) and the zealots" (*Journal I*, 79).

5. Foreword, *Tales of the Sacred and the Supernatural*. Philadelphia: Westminster, 1981, 7.

miliarity, an affinity revealing what I see as Eliade's most currently relevant cross-disciplinary contribution. His work offers a dependable bridge from Romantic to postmodern thought and by doing so, can help create a postmodernism that includes a protean foundationalism with its antifoundationalism.[6] In this way Eliade helps us read Romantic and postmodern literature and theory. Reciprocally, since much of Eliade's work evinces a strong base in Eastern and Romantic thought, the study of Romantic theory can contribute to the debate about further use of his work in religious studies.

Like Emerson and Coleridge, Eliade discusses the sacred in a scholarly Romantic context, inevitably forcing his work to be regularly misunderstood and misappropriated. This is further complicated by the paratextual factor of Eliade's youthful connections to a right-wing nationalist group that eventually became the antisemitic Iron Guard[7] and by strong textual evidence of his implacable complicity with the mainstream sexism of his generation. It follows to ask if the addition of Eliade's fiction to literary studies in English-speaking countries and the renewed use of his scholarship in literary criticism can be sufficiently contributive to warrant all the turmoil. I believe it can. Significant studies would place Eliade among those literary Romantic men who cause us so much trouble with their mixture of patriarchal privilege and generous pluralism, their commingled love and appropriation of the "fluid feminine," and their jarring assortment of mystical, empirical, ideal, pragmatic, rigidly conservative, and hospitably liberal stances—particularly William Blake, Herman Melville, William Butler Yeats, and D. H. Lawrence. Moreover, scholars must make attempts at unravelling or at least noting the tortuous political knots that entwine both artistic and scholarly writing. Even allowing that Eliade cut himself free when his ties with the Legion of the Archangel Michael were soon to be tangled with the Iron Guard, his scholarly work, his fiction, and his journals can help us study narrative and its place in the relationships of nationalism and tribalism, patriotism and racism, myth and oppression, theory and dominance, language and power. We have a lot of work to do.

---

6. Oversimplifications of poststructuralist and postmodern thought often show that they combine into a turn-of-the-millennium worldview that (1) explodes the unity of structuralism's binary oppositions into chaotic fragments, (2) denies metaphysics, (3) forgoes closure and consensus, (4) deprives language and action of meaning, and (5) discredits "centers" or "foundations," thus erasing the plausibility of metanarratives. Although these descriptions (other than #4) are at least partially appropriate, this chapter argues that Romantic "foundationalism" has been too narrowly equated with absolutism and a static idealism. Foundationalism when informed by Romanticism has a place in descriptions of the postmodern.

7. See Rennie, *Reconstructing Eliade*, chapter 13.

Thankfully, the much smaller focus of this chapter is Eliade's Romantic postmodernism as it overlaps his scholarly and literary work, with specific analyses of the short story "The Man Who Could Read Stones"[8] and the play *Men and Stones*.[9]

In reading Eliade's scholarly works and his fiction, I agree with Matei Calinescu's assessment that the "other worlds" of his fantastic tales represent the sacred or the mythical by which "we go beyond the inherent meaninglessness of quotidian life." With recognition of the interpretive disagreement about what exactly Eliade means by *myth* and by *the sacred*, Calinescu insists that "[f]or Eliade, this *other* world does not exist objectively... materially, physically... 'out there,' waiting to be discovered: rather, it is an invention or a creation but one that paradoxically, entirely mysteriously, carries ontological weight" (*Youth without Youth*, xiv).[10] In other words, those worlds *exist* even though they are invented and are *sacred* because they have been born as such by the Imagination. This is an integral point in reading Eliade's fiction and in my explication of his literature as contributive to the study of Romanticism and postmodernism.

I believe Eliade was quite literal about this human re/invention of sacred worlds. In terms by which one can recognize Coleridge, Shelley, and Emerson, for example, he relates a personal observance of "the creative function" of scenery and of art: "I had only to escape everyday tedium, its routine, and to feel as free as at the dawn of a new life, to recover the spontaneity and joys of the imagination" in order to participate in the "feeling of resurrection" whereby "the world one discovers belongs to another universe, with its own finality and values" (*Journal* III: 163–164). It is through human creativity, the Imagination, that "space becomes sacred, hence preeminently *real*" (*The Sacred and the Profane*, 45, hereafter *SP*).

Also integral is an understanding of what Eliade believes to be the use of those other worlds in myth and in his fiction. As Calinescu argues, "Eliade's fantastic not only refers to myth (myth being a paradigmatic act of creation) but aspires to function like myth, that is, to create new worlds, meanings, and realities... his literary use of the supernatural is meant to disclose 'various and sometimes dramatic irruptions of the sacred into the world'" (*Youth without Youth*, xv). The use of

---

8. Translated by M. L. Ricketts in this volume, 185.

9. From an unpublished translation also by Ricketts.

10. In defense of his interpretation, Calinescu quotes Eliade: "Every real existence reproduces the Odyssey.... That means: seeing signs, hidden meanings, symbols, in the sufferings, the depressions, the dry periods in everyday life. Seeing them and reading them even if they aren't there; if one sees them, one can build a structure and read a message in the formless flow of things and the monotonous flux of historical facts" (*No Souvenirs, Journal 1957–1969*. New York: Harper and Row, 1977, 84).

fiction, according to Eliade's commentaries, is to experience a momentary deliverance from history or time by engaging the Imagination and thus, quite paradoxically, to make the timeless real, to re/invent the sacred. Romantic and postmodern theory can help us understand this "impassable" paradox.

Partially because of this creation of other worlds, Eliade would not be considered a great writer of fiction. Writing about the supernatural as much as he has will place him perhaps as a Romanian Stephen King or as one who uses the themes of Poe without Poe's power of language. In addition, he seems to try too hard to put ideas, symbols, and metaphysical "points" into his work. Yet Eliade insists clearly and repeatedly in his commentaries, "I do not want to leave the impression that I write literature to 'demonstrate' such and such a philosophical thesis" ("Autobiographical Fragment," in *Imagination and Meaning*, 125, hereafter AF and *IM* respectively). He explains that "the writer" in him "refused any conscious collaboration with the scholar and interpreter of symbols," and that in fact "the free act of literary creation can ... *reveal* certain theoretical meanings" (123; italics mine). He gives the striking example of how he discovered his ideas about the "camouflaged intrusion" of the sacred into the world while reading his novel *Sarpele* (124). Almost anyone who has written extensively is aware that the very act of writing teaches us what we think and can "reveal" meaning.

Eliade seemed aware, however, that clear theoretical meanings do not necessarily make good art. He defended his nervous explanatory introductions to his works by stating simply, "I do not see how I can otherwise avoid some misunderstanding" (*Two Strange Tales*, vii). Saddened that "only a *commentary* can communicate to a reader of today a meaning which should, however, be *obvious*" (III: 86), he sensed how symbolism should work on its own, but lamented our lost ability in the twentieth-century to connect to our "collective memory."[11] Possibly due to this need to articulate the symbolic or to the problem of translation for a non-Romanian-reading audience (he wrote his scholarship in French and his fiction in Romanian),[12] Eliade's fictional prose appears stilted, devoid of poetic language and detailed character development. This is not surprising, however, when considering the folklore quality of his tales, which create new worlds in order to make philosophical points. Eliade's character Alexandru, a writer in the play *Men and Stones*, reflects

---

11. The "collective memory" can be associated with Jung's collective unconscious and archetypes, but does not necessarily suggest an absolute ideal realm of some kind, as many readers of Eliade (and of Romanticism in general) assume.

12. As he explains in the introduction to *Two Strange Tales*, "I could not decide how a rather large and literary production should best be introduced to the English-reading public. . . . Meanwhile I continued to write fiction in Rumanian, even though for many years my only readers were my wife and a few friends" (viii).

Eliade's consciousness of the difficulty of his task when Alexandru and his audience see a ghost girl in a cave and he says, "Fairies, dwarfs—banal, banal! Pseudo-poetry, cheap 'literature!' Folklore! Cheap, cheap . . . I must see something else, something *new*. Something not . . . imagined by anyone" (11). Despite or because of the redundant use of "banal" symbols to say something newly created in the "repetition of history," however, akin to Native American legends, and surely to Romanian folklore, there is something compelling about Eliade's almost alchemical tales.

ELIADE, THE EAST, AND ROMANTICISM

> The mystery of this *total* attraction felt for Goethe still fascinates me. A thought or a page of his . . . projects me into a sthenic, luminous, familiar universe. . . . That is my world.
>
> —Eliade

Art, according to Eliade and the Romantics, can take the artist and the perceiver momentarily out of the constraints of time. As a summary of the purpose and inherent themes of his fiction, Eliade writes, "I could say that all these works try to uncover the same central mystery of the rupture provoked by the appearance of Time and the 'fall into History' which followed of necessity" (AF, 124). Eliade's use of the terms *fall* and *rupture* suggests a metaphor by which art, the imagination, or human creativity can provide a momentary "return" (this is a metaphor, remember) to prelapsarian wholeness, not to be confused with a static absolute, but rather associated with Romantic organicism. The Fall as separation from God or from the organic whole—the act of "naming" things because we can only observe them in our separateness—is a clear trope for the human drive to cross the barrier of skin to unite with something other in an attempt to feel "whole." This is a central Romantic concern.

The terms *Romantic* and *Romanticism* refer to a category broader than that of a poetics or a periodization. As Harold Bloom and Leon Chai among others use the word, it is a philosophy commingled with literature, a "notion or perspective" almost "a metaphysics, a theory of history, a way of life."[13] Julie Ellison's classification for the Romantic includes most writings with the "habit of reference to forms of post-Kantian idealism" (ix). Hans Eichner reminds us that defining Romanticism

---

13. Leon Chai, *The Romantic Foundations of the American Rennaissance*. Ithaca: Cornell University Press, 1987, 6, and Bloom, *The Breaking of Vessels*. Chicago: University of Chicago Press, 1982, ix.

and attempting to differentiate its characteristics from those of both classicism and modernity has been an undertaking as anxiety-ridden as our attempts to distinguish postmodernism from modernism. Classification is always somehow incorrect. "Romanticism," he asserts, "is not a technical term . . . but a word with a long and confused history."[14] Its complex history certainly does not permit a succinct definition nor a simple lineage, but the tracing of the English Romantic writers and the American Renaissance writers to the German Romantic philosophers was fruitful enough to become commonplace in scholarship.[15]

Tilottama Rajan's summation of Romantic theory is helpful to a discussion of Eliade's work. As she suggests, the Romantics are credited with giving back to Calvinist humanity direct access to the ideal or the noumenal. She explains,

> Art, as the power to invent. . . . Indeed the historical and etymological connection of the term "Romanticism" with "romance" points to a view of literature as an idealizing rather than a mimetic activity, a mode of consciousness that envisions the unreal and the possible across the barrier of the actual.[16]

In opposition to the Duchamp/avant-garde aesthetic, Eliade seems to work for a rather cerebral, almost coerced reader interpretation of his fiction which, oddly enough, is designed to take readers beyond the cerebral. He writes, "A literary work is an instrument of knowledge. The imaginary universes created in novels, stories, and tales reveal certain values and meanings unique to the human condition which, without them, would remain unknown, or, at the very least, imperfectly understood" (*Journal* III, 283). This defines his Romantic belief in the function and process of literature and art. He explains further in descriptions very similar to those of Rajan:

---

14. "The Rise of Modern Science and the Genesis of Romanticism." *PMLA* 97 (1982): 8.

15. Abrams, for example, wrote that Blake "sketched out a world-view which came remarkably close to that of German Romantic philosophy: a view based on the generative power of opposites . . . and terminating in the concept of an organically inter-related universe" (*The Mirror and the Lamp: Romantic Theory and the Critical Tradition.* New York: Oxford, 1953, 216). In no way minimizing the significance of the Puritan heritage upon the American Renaissance (as evidenced by Sacvan Bercovitch and Richard Poirier), Chai convincingly traces *The Romantic Foundations of the American Renaissance* to "the cultural legacy of European Romanticism from roughly 1780 to 1830" (xi), an endeavor pioneered by F. O. Matthiessen.

16. *The Dark Interpreter: The Discourse of Romanticism.* Ithaca: Cornell University Press, 1980, 13.

> [T]he literary imagination is the continuation of mythological creativity and oneiric experience. Narration has infinite possibilities . . . both in life or in history and in the parallel universes forged by the creative imagination. . . . I did not emphasize sufficiently the similarities between religious phenomena and literary creation. Just as all religious phenomena are hierophantic (in the sense that they reveal the sacred in a profane object or act), literary creation unveils the universal and exemplary meanings hidden in men and in the most commonplace events. (*Journal* III, 284)

Eliade's descriptions of the hierophany of the sacred and profane are clearly indicative of the affinities of Eastern philosophies and Romantic thought. Romanticism grew as a consideration of consciousness and with the rescue of the "self" from its orphaned state in the mechanized Newtonian-Lockean worldview. For decades scholars have noted the Romantic preoccupation with the imagination and nature, self and perception, wholeness and organicism, the endless voyage and story, and the eternal flux of time and truth at the center of the Romantic vision.[17] In wrestling with these ideas, many thinkers have been scissor-locked by the puzzle of nonduality. How can subject and object be both divided and undivided? How can fragments reveal the whole? How can the cosmos be both chaotic and unified? How can the universe become what it already is? How can truth be ambiguous? How can the life process be the death process? How can we be both spirit and flesh? Romanticism, postmodernism, and Eliade seem to answer with "the two and the one" as expressed in Eastern thought. To understand this, "one must remember the dialectic of the sacred" and, Eliade maintains, must understand the way that "any object whatever may paradoxically become a hierophany, a receptacle of the sacred, while still participating in its own cosmic environment (a *sacred* stone, e.g., remains nevertheless a *stone* along with other stones)" (*Images and Symbols*, 84–85, hereafter *IS*).

When Goethe, the "king of Romantics,"[18] tried to formulate a new science to correct the unnatural division between observer and observed, he led a secular turn against the valorization of empiricism. Abrams summarizes this key force behind Romantic thought when he maintains that Wordsworth and Coleridge "attempt to revitalize the material and mechanical universe of Descartes and Hobbes" and at the same time aspire to "overcome the sense of [our] . . . alienation from the world by

---

17. It can be argued in this context that the Romantic ideal of the individual (especially in line with Rousseau and American Romanticism) differs from the Enlightenment and modern views of individualism in its rebelliousness against the subjugation of the individual by society as it supports the organic unity of the whole.

18. Owen Barfield, *Romanticism Comes of Age*, Middletown, CT: Wesleyan University Press, 1967, 16.

healing the cleavage between subject and object" (65). Wordsworth expresses that healing in *The Prelude* by declaring that the mind is

> Creator and receiver both,
> Working but in alliance with the works
> Which it beholds. (II, 258–260)

Romantic and Eastern preoccupations repeat this propensity toward painful struggles with dualities, which are occasionally eased by an acknowledgment of nonduality whereby "the two are one."

I use the term *(non)duality*[19] to indicate "the two-and-the-one," as it is presented in many philosophical constructs. It is the coexistence of "two" and "one," a concept and a mode of perception that embrace both duality and oneness in one thought. Eliade stresses in much of his work that "the *summum bonum* is situated beyond polarities" (*Quest*, 169). Postmodern feminists Hélène Cixous and Luce Irigaray express a similar contention. Cixous calls it "thinking of/on both sides." Irigaray explains, "We are luminous. Beyond 'one' or 'two.'"[20] The concept of (non)duality is part of a perennial thread some would label Romantic, which ties East to West and pre-Socratics and primitive to postmodern. When Eliade describes the Eastern spiritual drive to annul bipolar oppositions, he writes, "By identifying all the 'opposites' in the one and only universal Void (*śunyā*), certain Mahayānic philosophers (Nāgārjuna, for example) and above all the various tantric schools, Buddhist (Vajrayāna) as well as Hindu, have come to similar conclusions" (*IS*, 90, diacritical marks as original).

Many Romantic and Eastern thinkers, as well as many other Westerners, have attempted to use words and images to help even the nonmystical among us form concepts of (non)duality. Despite the claims that the experience or the true understanding can only be apprehended nonrationally, it is also claimed that an

---

19. With the parentheses, the prefix (non) does not annul the duality, but adds oneness to the twoness. This is a crucial addition. See David Loy, *Nonduality: A Study in Comparative Philosophy*. New Haven: Yale University Press, 1988; for a comprehensive explanation of Mahayana Buddhism, the Vedanta branch of Hinduism, and Taoism as asserting a condition or perception of nonduality. Loy also uncovers the nondual in an impressive gathering of Western thinkers, which begins with the pre-Socratics and ends with Gadamer and Derrida.

20. Hélène Cixous, *Root-prints*, with Mireille Cale-Gruber, trans. Eric Prenowitz. New York: Routledge, 1997, 25. In "The Laugh of the Medusa," Cixous calls it "the other bisexuality" (*New French Feminisms*, ed. Elaine Marks and Isabelle de Courtivron. Brighton: Harvester, 1980, 255). The concept does not purport a fantastic disappearing act of sexual difference, but a "non-exclusion either of the difference or the one of sex," a perception that "doesn't annul differences, but stirs them up" ("Medusa," 155). Luce Irigaray, "When Our Lips Speak Together," trans. Carolyn Burke, *Signs* 6 (1980), 71.

intellectual acceptance of the condition of nonduality is possible, desirable, and close to understanding—at least somehow more "true" than a rational denial of it. Eliade calls this the "intermediate situation" as described in Indian thought—"that of the [person] who, while continuing to live in . . . historic time . . . keeps a way open into the great time. . . . 'bad action' is to believe that nothing else exists, nothing outside of Time" (*IS*, 90–91).

So, in line with the Romantics, Eliade refers to "escaping from time," "the favourable moment," or "a break through the planes" (*IS*, 82–83) that describes or corresponds to Eastern and literary descriptions of transcendental moments: Hindu and Buddhist nirvana, Buddhist satori, Emerson's moment of "perfect exhilaration," Whitman's moments of "peace and knowledge that pass all the argument of the earth"; and Harold Bloom lists,

> Stevens's "irrational moment," Wordsworth's "spot of time," Pater's "privileged moment," Joyce's "epiphany," Yeats's moments when he is blessed and can bless, Browning's "good moment," Blake's "moments in each day that Satan's Watch Fiends cannot find," Lawrence's moments of breakthrough, Hart Crane's sudden revelations."[21]

Eliade describes in a 1974 journal entry, "certain 'revelations' . . . that occur before certain natural sites" whereby "I feel outside time, outside that which is mine . . . I am moved, but also calm (III, 163–164). As he explains, "this eternal present is no longer a part of time . . . all symbolism of transcendence is paradoxical, impossible to conceive at the profane level" (*IS*, 82–83).[22]

In line with Western tradition, Eliade repeatedly uses women in his fiction to represent this timelessness beyond history and the fluid, primordial realm beyond language. It is particularly evident in *The Old Man and the Bureaucrats* where Oana and numerous female characters are associated with female muses and the feminine principle of the formless, and in *Miss Christina*,[23] a tale of female vampires who display the negative side of experiencing the death/life nonduality. In *Men and Stones*, the unseen Adriana/Adria is muse/artist who has creative genius and encourages Alexandru to write. Petrus tells him to believe Adriana because "[s]he sees things better than either of us. Both as a woman and as an artist, she has an

---

21. *The Ringers in the Tower.* Chicago: University of Chicago Press, 1971, 327.

22. When Eliade relates this paradox to myth, he reminds us that "for the Australian as well as for the Chinese, the Hindu and the European peasant, the myths are true because they are sacred. . . . Consequently, in reciting or listening to a myth, one resumes contact with the sacred" (*IS*, 59).

23. For references to this usage in *Miss Christina* see Eliade's references to the small "wife-spirit [who] causes a true metamorphosis in her husband" in the "mystical marriage of Johann-George Gichtel and Sophia 1673" (*Journal III*, 75–76).

intuition we can't have" (15). It is customary to explain this use of women by revealing the reverence with which Romantic males held the "feminine" world of the nonrational. We should not overlook, however, the problems of male appropriation of the "feminine" as evidenced by the wish "to become creatively empowered in the feminine" and of encoding the nonrational as female.[24]

In many ways, Romantic writers appear inconsistent as they valorize the nonrational apprehension of life or "truth" yet often foreground rational thought. On the other hand, many contemporary scholars detect a note of Romantic irony rather than naivete in the seemingly conflicting espousals of wholeness and fragmentation or of intuition and logic within a text. Such inconsistencies confirm an emerging postmodern viewpoint amenable to Eliade's theories of nonduality, which tries to balance form and formlessness. When Romantics speak of the nonrational, the unified, and the One, they often do not deny the rational, the chaotic, and the multiple. Not steadfastly, but often, they suggest instead the "two and the one."[25]

BRIDGES TO POSTMODERNISM

> Blake and Derrida are, for me, allies in a culture of artistic and social radicalism that grows out of the Enlightenment and the French Revolution, and that emerges as a strategy for "keeping the Divine Vision in a time of trouble" after the failure or betrayal of revolution . . . as Milton did after the English Revolution, Blake after the French, and Derrida after the experience of the sixties.
>
> —W. J. T. Mitchell

The Romantic notion of "primary faith"—an individual apprehension of the universe and an equating of the life force with consciousness—survives from the Romantics in the writings of modernists such as D. H. Lawrence, E. M. Forster, William Butler Yeats, and Wallace Stevens; of "beats"[26] such as Jack Kerouac, Allen

---

24. Leland Persons (*Aesthetic Headaches*. Athens: University of Georgia Press, 1988) defends Romantic writers. Anne Mellor's study of Romantic men, on the other hand, argues that "in moving from an 'Age of Reason' to an 'Age of Feeling,' male writers . . . colonize[d] the conventionally feminine domain of sensibility" (*Romanticism and Feminism*. Bloomington: Indiana University Press, 1988, 133). Certainly, current readers of Eliade's fiction would consider, as Eliade and many writers of his era apparently did not, that the "rational" and the "nonrational," the powerful mythic principles of Male and Female, should be strictly divorced from gender associations.

25. See especially his *The Two and the One* and chapter 4 in Rennie's *Reconstructing Eliade* for Eliade's explication of the *coincidentia oppositorum*.

26. When asked to define the term *Beat*, Kerouac linked it to "a Catholic beatific vision, the direct knowledge of God enjoyed by the blessed in heaven" (*Jack Kerouac*. New York: Viking Penguin, 1993, ix).

Ginsberg, and Lawrence Ferlinghetti; and through the Western experience of Buddhism in poets such as John Cage, Diane di Prima, Lucien Stryke, and Gary Snyder. Some of the best contemporary American poetry has been directly touched by the ineffable questions of Buddhist thought and has greatly influenced postmodernity. Cage writes, for example, "Zen changes in different times and places and what it has become here and now, I am not certain. Whatever it is it gives me delight." He further explains what was to become his legacy to postmodern art: "I introduced silence. I was a ground, so to speak, in which emptiness could grow."[27]

This statement by Cage suggests, as does Ginsberg's brass bells in a Chicago apartment, how the nondualism in Buddhism, Taoism, and Hinduism contributed to what became postmodernism. Stryke writes about Shinkichi Takahashi:

> Like all awakened Zennists he found no separation between art and life, knowing the achievement of no-mind led not only to right art but to right living. . . . He always cautioned . . . against dualism, assuring that little by little one learns to know true seeing from false. (*Beneath a Single Moon*, 290)

Such a comment seems quite plausible since many believe the practical goal of Zen is the "thinking of no-thinking," the overcoming of dualistic, subject-centered modes of being that limit experience.

Eliade describes this "overcoming" at great length. In listing instances of images used for ways in which "we try to express the paradoxical act of 'escaping from time,'" Eliade refers to how poets describe its difficulty in phrases such as "it is hard to pass over the sharpened blade of the razor"[28] and of an initiation tale in which the hero has to go "where the night and the day meet together" or "up to Heaven by a passage that half-opens for only an instant." He emphasizes that all these images represent "the necessity of *transcending the 'pairs of opposites,'* of abolishing the polarity that besets the human condition" (*IS*, 83–84). Using the example of Indian thought, Eliade writes,

> Indeed, for Indian thought the human condition is defined by the existence of opposites, and liberation from the human condition is equivalent to a non-conditioned state in which the opposites coincide. . . . To illustrate this paradoxical situation attained by the abolition of the "pairs of opposites," Indian thought, like all archaic thinking makes use of

---

27. *Beneath a Single Moon: Buddhism in Contemporary American Poetry*, ed. Kent Johnson and Craig Paulenich, introduction by Gary Snyder. Boston: Shambhala. 1991, 43. Not coincidentally, Cage revealed his enthusiasm for American Romantics by writing a musical arrangement of Thoreau's writings.

28. *Katha Upanishad* (III, 14) as quoted in Eliade, *IS*, 83.

images whose very structure includes contradiction (images of the type of "finding a door in a wall where none is visible"). (*IS*, 84–85)

I would argue that for Eliade this "ultimate reality" is the *coincidentia oppositorum* (the invisible door itself and not merely "the other side") and that this attitude of paradox is certainly the postmodern condition. In the film *The Truman Show* (a comment on this condition),[29] the protagonist literally finds "a door in a wall where none is visible." After discovering that his entire life since birth has been a television show, a constructed reality, he sails across a bay into a vinyl horizon, walks from his boat to a camouflaged "stage door," opens it, and goes out. One of the "jokes" of the film, of course, is that those people outside the set, to where Truman is escaping, also have their reality constructed by their televisions and their stories.

This paradoxical "condition" expressed in *The Truman Show* and associated with postmodernism by theorists such as Jean-Francois Lyotard is most commonly described as being characterized by: indeterminacy, the deferral of definite meaning, nonlinearity, accommodation to ambiguity and fragmentation, pluralism and the assimilation of the past, carnival, self-conscious construction of reality, the culturally formed self, antifoundationalism, and the implosion of binary oppositions. The last, of course is from Derrida's deconstruction of de Saussure, but has not been used strongly enough to describe the world view of a postmodern culture; instead, it has been assumed that poststructuralism's effect on that culture is limited to the belief in the indeterminacy of language and meaning.[30] The awareness of (non)duality itself, however, is a central characteristic of postmodernism; more specifically, the awareness of the fullness/void of silence. Silence is perhaps the most difficult aspect of the postmodern to grasp because it is the one most dependent upon some perception of either "double affirmation" or of (non)duality; thus, all explanations appear as attempts at "continental" cleverness. We try, according to many postmodern artists and theorists, to speak and hear the unspeakable, the unrepresentable, the silent. Since de Saussure strongly suggests that language refers to a void of meaning (in that it cannot speak "the truth"), we know that language (the noise we make) is silent.[31] We see the "carnival," which is our shuffling and banging around, our finding or making pragmatic meanings as we "fill" the void; and the cacophony

---

29. *The Truman Show*. Directed by Peter Weir, Paramount, 1988.

30. In addition to Loy's *Nonduality*, see Harold Coward's *Derrida and Indian Philosophy* and *Derrida and Negative Theology*, ed. Harold Coward and Toby Foshay, for excellent, detailed arguments concerning Derrida, the East, and postmodernism.

31. Such is the dominant application in literary theory of de Saussure's work, based on his idea that "in language there are only differences" in his *Course in General Linguistics*, trans. Wade Baskin. New York: McGraw-Hill, 1966.

silences us. The postmodern struggles with apparently conflicting concepts: our noise is nothing *and* everything, and the noise and the silence are both meaningless and meaning*full*. Maurice Blanchot argues that "[l]anguage can only begin with the void; no fullness, no certainty can ever speak" (43). In keeping with the postmodern proclivity toward double affirmation, fears of nihilism and of the destructiveness of poststructuralism are only half of the postmodern story.[32] In the other half, we are filling the void. We are making meaning, revealing the sacred. We are like Farama in Eliade's *The Old Man and the Bureaucrats*, telling a never-ending story that interlaces with the listeners' and speaker's reality enough to help create it. The search for "truth" and "order" is not in conflict with the recognition of indeterminacy and fragmentation. Rather than dismissing all transcendental stances toward existence, postmodern art and theory are approaching complex new (ancient) ways of perceiving immanence, presence, truth, and reality.[33]

Deconstruction was not "finished" in the '80s. Although we no longer "do" deconstruction, it has left an opening for nondual vision.[34] Hermeneutics can be viewed as the creation of meaning, deconstruction as the reminder that those created meanings, though perhaps partaking of some ineffable creative force, are at the same time mutable. In the ultimate nondual mode, neither "side"—neither interpretation nor the transiency of interpretations—is superior. As in Eliade's hierophany, meaning is created when a text is interpreted, transforming the profane into the sacred.[35] Yet when anything is created, it concurrently begins to die. Viewed in this way, meaning investment both gives life to and destroys (makes static) the creative force of interpreting. As Derrida makes clear, echoing hundreds of Romantic and Eastern voices before him, stasis and death are absurd in a vital, protean universe.[36] In this respect Derrida's "trace" can be seen as a zygote, having resulted from the "little deaths" of the language act. It is Queequeg's life-buoy coffin being shot out

---

32. Hassan points out that there are coexisting "deconstructive" and "reconstructive" tendencies of postmodernism ("Pluralism," 20) and Eagleton writes about "the characteristic post-structuralist blend of pessimism and euphoria" ("Capitalism, Modernism, and Postmodernism," *New Left Review* 152 (1985): 64).

33. In *Myth, Truth, and Literature: Towards a True Post-Modernism*, Colin Falck uses an intricate philosophical argument to expose the absurdity of interpreting poststructuralism to mark the abolishment of reality or meaning. He argues that most of those readings are based on "a fairly simple philosophical fallacy" (Cambridge University Press, 1989, 6).

34. When told that his ideas sound as though Blake can be a cure for Derrida, W. J. T. Mitchell responded, "[T]he ones who need this cure are those who think that Derrida is a nihilist . . . who think that he brings a message of despair" ("Visible Language," 88).

35. Sacred can in this context be defined as "invested with meaning."

36. Coward and Loy argue that Derrida actually does not go far enough, that Nagarjuna does, finding a place beyond language and dualities, where Derrida does not tread (see, for example, Coward, *Derrida and Eastern Philosophy*, 139).

of the whirlpool on the last page of *Moby-Dick*. In Eliade's *Men and Stones*, it is the voice of the poet saying, "I can't describe it," as he is carried out of the "void" of "troglobes, living fossils" into the daylight.

"Opening" to a new meaning beyond polarity implies that such a meaning will be a never-ending interrogation, an ongoing creation of centers. In that poetic, fluid mode of thought and communication "on the other side of words," duality is at least temporarily overcome. "The other side" can be considered as that formless mass "before" the classifications of thought.[37] Eliade uses water symbolism as a central motif to express this inexpressible formlessness. In *The Old Man and the Bureaucrats*, the underworld is reached through the waters in an old cellar. In "The Man Who Could Read Stones," Adriana jumps off a yacht to emerge out of Timelessness onto the dock in front of Emanuel. It is also used in *Men and Stones* where "in the waters of these caves . . . are preserved forms of life" (18). As Eliade explains the use of water symbolism in myths, he writes,

> The Waters symbolise the . . . reservoir of all the potentialities of existence; they *precede* every form and *sustain* every creation. . . . [I]mmersion in the waters symbolises a regression into the pre-formal, reintegration into the undifferentiated mode of pre-existence. Emergence repeats the cosmogonic act of formal manifestation; while immersion is equivalent to a dissolution of forms. That is why the symbolism of the Waters includes Death as well as Re-birth. Contact with water always goes with a regeneration. (*IS*, 151)

When Cixous describes the mode of being and communicating in the "fluid formlessness," she does so in terms of nonduality, as experiencing "tendencies which unite . . . , an aptitude for thinking a thing and its opposite."[38] In this case thinking itself is on the boundary of form and formlessness, where creation and death take place.

THE PHILOSOPHER'S STONE

> [T]he regeneration of plants out of their own ashes. The alchemists, whose eschatology was always present in Goethe's mind, pursued no other goals. The quest for the Philosopher's Stone was only the legitimate application of this mysterious palingenesis.
>
> —Eliade

As Eliade acknowledges "a real dependence of some literary writings on theoretical ones, and vice versa," he gives as one example the play *Oameni si pietre* (*Men*

---

37. The suggested chronology of "before" refers loosely to a possible sequence of perception in the individual: "I experienced the undifferentiation of all there is, and then I thought about it."

38. *Illa*. Paris: Editions des femmes, 1980, 40.

and Stones) coming out of his ideas in "the chapter on sacred stones in *Traité*" (*Patterns*) (AF, 122–123). Perhaps referring to his belief that theory grew from his fiction, he mentions his use of the motif of the Philosopher's Stone in his first published story at age fourteen ("The Philosopher's Stone") as well as in *Noaptea de Sanziene* (*Forbidden Forest*—AF, 124). Central to his play *Men and Stones*, this motif is used to present what Calinescu calls Eliade's "existential alchemy" as an answer to the question "How does one transform everyday meaninglessness into something meaningful?" ("The Function of the Unreal," 150). This rephrases the theme of the unrecognizability of the sacred camouflaged in history and its re/invention through the Imagination.

As Eliade describes it, "all these works try to uncover the same central mystery of the rupture provoked by the appearance of Time and the 'fall into History' " (AF, 124). A "rupture" is a (the) way out, a space or "opening" that is always central, always created, always changing. These indeed are the shifting centers of meaning creation that most theorists of postmodernism discuss. Eliade explains in terms of Australian aborigine myth where openings are "at the Center *always*" such as the Alchipa who carried with them the "sacred pole, the *axis mundi* . . . so that they should never be far from the center and should remain in communication with the supraterrestrial world." Eliade refers to mythological "centers" created from the human necessity for a cosmos, places where universes are born, spreading from a central point. He relates what "Rabbi Ben Gorion said of the rock of Jerusalem: 'it is called the Foundation Stone of the Earth, that is, the navel of the Earth, because it is from there that the whole Earth unfolded" (*SP*, 43–44).

In Eliade's 1943 play *Men and Stones,* the scientist Petrus and the poet Alexandru attempt to travel to this navel of the Earth as "the first persons to enter such a cave after who knows how many thousands of years" (4).[39] Eliade uses metaphoric interplay with myths of the "lower regions" and "the waters of chaos before Creation" (*SP*, 41). The play mixes existential angst with Romantic idealism and mythical archetypes. It seems an awkward clash of *Waiting for Godot* and the tale of The Fisher King. Norman Girardot also sees this aspect in Eliade's story or mock drama "Adio!" (Goodbye!—"God's first and last word to man"). Girardot writes about "Adio!":

> The problem is that in "Waiting for Godot," modern man must, because of the crushing weight of his very historicity and secularity, find some meaning in boredom or just be bored to death. . . . [I]t is the most

---

39. I would rather not confuse the discussion at this point with Eliade's problematic theories about primitive and modern "man," but certainly the reference is clear.

> accidental, the most utterly banal and ordinary experiences of secular life, that potentially disclose a meaningful message of the hidden spiritual continuity of culture, nature, and history. But this is the case only if men are historically and imaginatively prepared to see and hear meaning in what appears to be completely absurd. (*IM*, 9–10)

Humans, therefore, must make meaning in their discovery/creation of "the hidden spiritual continuity of culture, nature, and history." The modern recognition of universal absurdity and Girardot's interpretation of Eliade as saying that most "modern" individuals "can only be saved by discovering the sacrality of the mundane" are also evident in *Men and Stones*. Alexandru, the poet, is dry of creativity and therefore unable to discover/create any sacrality. His Romantic heroic trek to the center of the earth has shown him only the "Heart of Darkness." He laments, "Nothing's worth anything. . . . Everything's absurd and useless" (28), and his perspective on his own life reveals the modernist's uselessness in the waste land, realizing that "whatever I might have done, however I might have lived, the result probably would have been the same. Ashes. Nothing has any sense" (28). He asks, "If nothing lasts, if everything ends *here* (*pointing to the cave*), don't you agree that it's better to negate, to trample underfoot, to profane?" (31). In the darkness, Alexandru cannot "hear or see meaning in what appears to be completely absurd."

Writing a detailed job description for the poet, both Shelley in "In Defense of Poetry" and Emerson in "The Poet" make it quite clear as spokespersons for Romanticism that seeing and making meaning is the poet's responsibility (which Alexandru, moping in the center of the earth, is shirking). Shelley's poetry unbinds Prometheus and uses repeated images of the creative imagination as skylark or as "legion'd rooks," finding those centers where Eliade's ruptures between planes occur. Rooks change instantly from mundane black birds, "gray shades" in a rainy mist, to "fire and azure" by the poetry of their hail to "the unfathomable sky," until "all is bright, and clear, and still" ("Lines Written Among The Euganean Hills"). Similarly, Romantic Emerson campaigns for an American poet who can do the same. "The poet," he writes, "is the sayer, the namer . . . and stands on the center" where the world "is from the beginning beautiful" ("The Poet," 225). So the artist takes the quotidian and makes it sacred by dipping down to the earthly mundane to lift a bit momentarily toward heaven in that "rupture" between the two. Alexandru, however, having one of his "numerous attacks of nihilism," forgets this, or at least believes that only the genius of Shakespeare or Milton are capable of being "blythe spirits."

In one respect *Men and Stones* is existential, but in one respect, so is Romanticism. We create our reality out of what is here by reaching for something that is and is not here.[40] In *Men and Stones*, Alexandru, the poet, sees images of people from past millennia on the stone of the cave walls, reminiscent of Plato's allegory, but more strikingly, the audience sees them as a rather intriguing visual synthesis of humans and stones, past and present, and certainly of human creativity and Promethean ability. Alexandru and Petrus have assured their safe return by the use of a large phosphorous spool of thread, which like the thread of Ariadne allows their escape from the labyrinth. One could imagine that if this play were performed, the audience would see before curtain a black stage with a tangled phosphorous web that would have marked their poststructuralist path.

Alexandru describes the Romantic quest of the artist as first "a descent to the deepest level of consciousness and cosmic life." You can descend anywhere, and as deeply as possible, provided only that you return fuller and richer" (15). The "truth" that Alexandru wants to relate, however, is silent. He wants the stones to speak: "When the stones begin to move and the vault of the cave becomes animated . . . just the stones, without any human profile, without anything being added to them . . . then, maybe then I'll begin to see" (16). The next stage direction, however, is "Darkness." This silence is full of the unspeakable.

Petrus finds living fossils or "troglobes," evidence of how life began on Earth. These creatures, Alexandru realizes, are from "the beginning," having propagated "here in this misery . . . in this darkness . . . for millions of years," and are also alive as our contemporaries. "If this is life," Alexandru insists, "I'd rather be a stone." Petrus tells him he has been "and you will be again. . . . Stone, soil, and troglobe. It's the same cosmic circuit. The only one" (19).

Petrus the scientist wants to see the cave "created by" Alexandru the artist as Prometheus, as shining rook and skylark, who instead has discovered that "No action and no gesture makes any sense. This is the truth! This is the only truth!" (27). "It's so absurd," he has learned, that "our language can't express it. Language, unfortunately, is made for conventional lies" (28). Like Marlow in *Heart of Darkness*, Alexandru, the poet, finds that "the truth is that we judge the world better" in the absurd blankness than in the light "where we all deceive ourselves as best we can, any way we can" (28). The play ends with Petrus carrying Alexandru out of the cave after his "fall." Evidently having fallen back into History, into the profane.

---

40. Calinescu calls it "existential alchemy" as an answer to "how does one transform everyday meaninglessness into something meaningful?" (150). Eliade's comments about Parsifal and the Fisher King should also be developed in reference to this play ("A Detail from Parsifal," in *IM*, 191–195). Petrus finds comfort in the opium he takes to alleviate the pain of the truth at the center. Eliade writes, "In the case of opium, you yield in order to annihilate yourself as an individual, as a separate and suffering being . . . to discover another reality" (*IM*, 190).

He explains, "there exists something ... which gives meaning to everything" and this truth cannot be written, no matter how much genius one has, "or how much imagination." There's something extraordinarily important he wants to say, but the play's last line is Alexandru repeating, "You have no idea how clearly I see ... but I don't have any way ... to tell you." The last stage direction is "Darkness."

As Goethe insisted, no system, no theory can contain the nonduality of the formed and the formless, the profane and the "made sacred." According to Loy's and Eliade's analyses of Eastern thought, we can be led by logic to the (non)concept of nonduality, but we must break through that logic on our own, and not for long. Eliade attempts to record and offer glimpses, but like the Romantic hero, like Melville's Queequeg and Conrad's Marlow, and like Alexandru in *Men and Stones*, he must fail to maintain or describe any glances into the void, which is always also the sacred whole.

When Eliade writes elsewhere about stones in mythic traditions, he explains that a stone's "reality is coupled with perenniality"; it is "incompressible, invulnerable, it is that which man is not." For archaic man, "neither of the objects of the external world nor human acts, properly speaking, have any autonomous intrinsic value. Objects or acts acquire a value, and in so doing become real." Consequently, "among countless stones, one stone becomes sacred ... and hence instantly becomes saturated with being ... because it constitutes a hierophany ... or because it commemorates a mythical act" (*The Myth of the Eternal Return*, 4, hereafter *MER*).

Eliade succinctly explains the stone as metaphor in his comments about the sculptor Brancusi's *Endless Column*: "The problems that obsess me with respect to Brancusi. ... First, his passion for stone. ... His desire to transfigure stone, to abolish its mode of being, and above all its weight, to show us how it ascends and flies." Eliade is conflating, as Emerson and Coleridge do so well, his Romantic theory of art's purpose and his belief of human religiosity in terms of the sacred/profane hierophany. He asks, "Does not one intuit here a certain archaic form of religiosity, long since inaccessible on our continent?" He asserts that Brancusi compared his stone column "to the Column of Heaven, to the cosmic pillar which supports the sky and which makes communication possible between heaven and earth; in a word, Brancusi considered it to be an *axis mundi* ... by which one could reach heaven ... and that after having achieved this masterpiece he created nothing further which was worthy of his genius" (*Journal* II, 292–293). For archaic man, Eliade further explains, a stone "appears as the receptacle of an exterior force that differentiates it from its milieu and gives it meaning and value" (*MER*, 4).

As such, stones have a central presence in the short story "The Man Who Could Read Stones."[41] An old man, Beldiman, has "the strange gift" of being drawn

---

41. Included in this volume, below, 117.

to stones in the proximity of where people have been. He "reads" them, and "knows what awaits the person who sat beside them." In effect, then, in Eliade's terms, Beldiman invests the material world with meaning that would otherwise not exist; he creates a "center," a cosmos. Beldiman meets the protaganist Emanuel on a beach where Beldiman discloses to him what awaits a couple who have just left. Upon hearing Beldiman explain his "gift," Emanuel cannot resist asking him what the stones say about what will come to pass for him in the near future. The story that unfolds and enfolds from this beginning leaves the reader continuously questioning what is actual, what is lie, what is prophesy, and what is past, until finally the present becomes so enmeshed that it too is indistinguishable.

Through this story a reader can discover Eliade's contention elsewhere that "after the first 'fall,' the religious sense descended to the level of the 'divided consciousness'; now, after the second, it has fallen even further, into the depths of the unconscious; it has been 'forgotten' " (*SP*, 213). If we live too long in duality only, we forget. Beldiman's prophecies are spoken in the past tense, commingling separate but parallel worlds, just as the past and present are commingled in the postmodern milieu. The motif of falling is used in parallel with Beldiman's (and eventually Emanuel's) moves in and out of "history." In one of Beldiman's portentous stone-reading vignettes, two women (Adriana/Ariana and Adina) are met by Emanuel "somewhere, at a skating rink or on an icy street" and one of them slips as the other "appears from out of the blue and picks her up" (5). Adriana *falls* into "history" or into the "formed" from the formlessness of the sea.

Parallel worlds collide as Adriana emerges and walks toward Emanuel, seeing past him to Adina, who the reader surmises, is there to "pick her up" after her fall, and the telling of the tale begins as Emanuel is caught between two worlds. According to Eliade, "It is only when we recognize the presence of the *other* world (miracle, primordial time) that we are saved from meaninglessness.... From the point of view of the writer, this *other* world must be created ... to *present* a new universe, by which everyday life is delivered from its arbitrariness" (*IM*, 150). One universe ends and another begins repeatedly, at the end the tale, where for Romantics and postmoderns, ends are beginnings.

ELIADE IN THE END

Eliade's relationship with Romanticism and postmodernism meets at the intersection of radical social rebellion and calm acceptance of the paradoxical human condition. The Romantic "spirit," in the style of Rousseau and Blake, is the perennial drive to break free of mortal limitation in the face of our unavoidable death sentence. Closely related is the need to believe that periodically, by the power of individual human creativity, we can transcend the limits of our constructed social boundaries. Quite simply, Romantic writers have believed (Imagined) that in some way by the power of human creativity (perhaps as the individual chip off the block of "all that is" or off the block of some noumenal "mind"), it is possible to transcend the boundaries of our skin, to move out of the container, so to speak, to demonstrate in the most "favourable moments" (at the very least just by thought itself) that we are somehow free, and to believe so even as we bemoan our inescapable imprisonment. This drive manifests in a wild variety of ways—Goethe's alchemy, Kerouac's road, the French Revolution, Gautama's broken shell,[42] the Declaration of Independence, Kant's *Critiques*, Cixous's laugh, Eliade's escape, Shelley's Aegean lines, the American transcendentalists, Cage's silence, magic realism, the 1960s counterculture, Wordsworth's intimations, Derrida's trace, Truman's show, the Prajnaparamita's verses, Ginsberg's howl, Melville's whale.

In the 1980s it was thought that Derrida's poststructuralism was a nihilistic attempt to destroy some sacred whole. In the late '90s we have settled into seeing it more as a correcting balance to a rather naive and extreme absolutism that we had been taught to see as "natural." It is clearer now that the Romantics themselves, while valorizing a "sacred" organicism, simultaneously accepted and bemoaned the separate and fragmented human experience. Modern writers howled in the alienation of that separation anxiety while many of them nevertheless were still reaching for the whole and were still "making sacred." Postmodern writers sit more comfortably in the chaos, somewhat content with crossed paths of phosphorous thread. They accept more easily the necessary constructions of sacred centers, which do not make those centers any less central or any less real. It is clearer now that a sacred whole can be protean and unfathomable rather than static and absolute, can be made by carrying a pole around and repeatedly starting at center, but nevertheless can still be sacred and still be whole. In the turn of the socially constructed millennium, many have taken on Eliade's Romantic attitude of paradox: "If I should have the choice between a truth and a paradox, I should choose the paradox," as "an insurrection against established or imposed 'truths' " and "being an attitude, [it] never loses its elasticity and vitality" (*IM*, 188).

Also paradoxical is the extent of Eliade's limitations. Eliade's fiction and scholarship demonstrate the Romantic notion that conceptual images and rational approaches to the "ungraspable phantom" abound even if they offer no final word. The latest consensus in linguistic theory, that language is only schizophrenically referential, seems to agree with that Romantic mode. Yet we are obsessed. If we pass a flower in the woods, we need its name so that we can hold it in our minds. It

---

42. According to Eliade, "[T]ranscending the world is illustrated by Buddha proclaiming that he has 'broken' the cosmic egg. The 'shell of ignorance' " (*SP*, 176).

seems humans are incessantly occupied with making order and then forgetting that our taxonomies are creations. Classifying was Eliade's scholarly job. His material, however, was so frustratingly outside the constraints of language, that he tried to *not say* it in his fiction.

Whether or not Eliade's fiction is artful, it is dynamic and it reveals a belief that art, nature, and language can provide "new openings" to nonduality beyond the reach of the rational mind. That is how symbols work. His disappointment with a "modern" world that seemed to forget mythic symbols perhaps belied his belief in the "unformed" by denying its mutability. Both Goethe and Eliade insisted that symbols, like words, change in meaning and form, yet their classifications of symbols insist on universality of the sign. If saying opposite things at the same time is truly an indication of wisdom, as descriptions of (non)duality indicate, it is our Sisyphean classifying that keeps us from "favourable moments" and our repeated arresting of Proteus that allows us to function. Consequently, Eliade wrote both fictional and scholarly texts. His fiction demonstrates how we can point to formless other worlds that are always created, always changing, yet are "paradoxically, entirely mysteriously" real.

Chapter Nine

THE MAN WHO COULD READ STONES

MIRCEA ELIADE

He saw him at a distance, walking slowly toward him along the beach. The man had a strange gait. Sometimes he trod cautiously, almost with fear, stopping, looking down at the sand as though searching for something; then, suddenly, he would change direction and head toward the sea, walking fast on the wet sand, or else he would make for higher ground where the sand was mixed with clay and where briars with pale blue blossoms were growing amidst rocks. As he drew near, Emanuel was surprised to discover that he was rather elderly. Draped over his shoulders was a summer jacket, faded, almost white. He was wearing trousers of an indefinite hue, tennis shoes, and a cloth hat with the brim turned up so that from a distance it resembled a sailor's cap. He stopped again about ten paces from Emanuel and glanced at the couple who had just gotten up and were walking toward the dunes with beach robes over their shoulders. Then, very carefully, as though he were afraid he might step on something of great value, he started walking around the places where traces of their bodies could still be distinguished in the sand. Bending over, he picked up a stone, examined it closely, and smiled sadly, shaking his head. He

---

First published as *Ghichitor in pietre* in Mircea Eliade, *Nuvele*. Madrid: Colecţia Destin, 1963. Republished in Mircea Eliade, *La ţiganci si alte povestiri*. Bucureşti: Editura pentru Literatura, 1969, 415–440; and in idem., *În curte la Dionis*. Bucureşti: Cartea Romanesca, 1981, 73–100. Translated from the Romanian by Mac Linscott Ricketts.

searched again for traces they had left in the sand, looking more and more downcast. For a moment he remained undecided, playing with the stone, tossing it in the air. Suddenly he turned toward the sea and flung it as far as he could over the waves. Then he spat and began walking in Emanuel's direction.

"Do you know them?" he inquired, indicating the young couple with a nod.

"By sight. Domnul and doamna Valimarescu.[1] From Focsani, I believe. He's a lawyer, I understand, and his wife's a teacher."

"It's a shame about them. They're young, and if they don't enjoy life now, in their youth, when will they enjoy it?"

He faced toward the water and spat again with anger.

"But why?" asked Emanuel. "Has something happened to them?"

"Something is about to happen to them. They haven't much longer to stay here. They're leaving. Tomorrow or the day after they'll go."

Emanuel put down the book he was reading and looked at him, smiling.

"They've scarcely come," he said. "They arrived last Saturday. Not even a week ago."

"They're leaving," the other man repeated firmly. "They'll receive a telegram and they'll go."

"Some misfortune in the family," Emanuel suggested without interest.

"No, that's not it. Because, although they'll leave together, they will soon separate and he will go far away, very far. And stay a long time. He will have no idea how long he'll stay there. And it's a great pity, since they're both young. They won't see each other again in a blue moon."

"Then I understand. And you may be right. When I was talking with them I saw they were worried about something; they were afraid he'd be called to military service."

"Then that's it!" exclaimed the other. "That's why they're leaving."

"They said he was lucky in everything except the military lottery. His lot fell to the antiaircraft division, and so far he's escaped being called to duty only through the protection and intervention of friends. But I sensed that he's afraid."

"He won't escape any longer!" the other declared.

"Two or three months away from his wife," Emanuel observed with a smile.

The other man shook his head emphatically.

"It's not a matter of two or three months. I tell you, that young man won't return home for years. Tomorrow or the day after, the war will come, and if he's in the antiaircraft group. . . ."

"War is coming?" Emanuel repeated. "But why am I surprised? Everyone knows this. Today, tomorrow, in a year or two, the war will come."

---

1. Mister and Mrs. Valimarescu. The abbreviations are d-l and d-na.

"It's worse for him, because he'll be far from his wife even before the war starts. And he'll stay a long time..."

"But how do you know these things?" Emanuel asked, suddenly lifting his head and looking straight at him.

The man slipped his jacket off his shoulders, folded it carefully, looked all around, and took several steps toward a large, reddish rock. He placed the jacket on the sand in the shadow of the rock, then turned around and sat down facing Emanuel, with his back to the sea. Emanuel offered him a cigarette.

"No, thank you, I haven't smoked in a long time. When I did, in my youth, I smoked a pipe. You know, for a good while I was a sailor," he added. "Then for five years I was a lighthouse keeper at Tuzla. Now, I'm sort of a *rentier*. But I still like living here, between Tuzla and Mangalia... I like Dobrogea," he added after a pause. "I'm Vasile Beldiman, grandson of Leonida Beldiman—the famous Leonida Beldiman, if the name means anything to you."

"No," replied Emanuel, embarrassed.

"I understand. You're not from around here. But the Beldimans are among the oldest families of Dobrogea. The famous Leonida Beldiman was my grandfather. I also claim Hagi Anton for my greatgrandfather. And I can say that everyone in my family has had this gift, from Hagi Anton on. He was the first to have it."

"What kind of gift?"

"Ah," Beldiman began hesitantly. "How can I tell you? It's a strange gift. I call it a gift because no one teaches it to us. It happens like this: at the age of twelve or thirteen one of the boys begins to like stones. That's how it was with my father: at twelve he fell in love with stones. All kinds of stones—large, small, boulders, pebbles—stones of all shapes and descriptions. One day his father, Leonida, found out about it and began to help him. But he couldn't teach him, properly speaking. He just helped him to read them."

"I don't exactly understand," said Emanuel with a perplexed smile.

"Yes, I realize it seems very strange. It's a curious gift. What can I say? There are people who read the stars, or coffee grounds, or grains of corn. We Beldimans read stones."

An oversized wave broke deafeningly and washed white water over the beach. Beldiman turned his head. His eye caught some children tumbling in the surf, and he smiled.

"Take, for instance, how it happened a little while ago with your friend Valimarescu," he continued. "I saw the two of them from afar, and they seemed so young and happy that I wanted to see what the future holds for them. I examined the place where they'd been sitting. Seldom does it happen that there will be nothing but pure sand, without a single stone, without pebbles. Just a few rocks are enough for me. Right where the person was sitting, or nearby. Sometimes the stones with meaning are located rather far from the place where the person chose to sit.

I look for them, and when I find them I know what is going to happen. I know by their shape, by certain corners and angles, and by the color of the stone, because on one side it's darker and on others it's bright, a different color, or variegated. And then I read the stones and I know what awaits the person who sat beside them or, sometimes, right on top of them. Because, as I've explained, no one ever sits down by chance. Each person sits according to a predestined plan. Haven't you noticed? You start toward a place and it seems nice to you, and you get ready to sit down; then you spy a nicer place next to it. But no sooner do you sit there than you sense that something doesn't suit you, and you change your position until all at once you feel right. You stretch out, and suddenly it seems that everything is good and beautiful, as though the whole world were yours! You have found the place destined for you, which was waiting for you."

Emanuel extinguished his cigarette, grinding it slowly into the sand until it was completely buried.

"All right, let's say it's so, that everyone seeks the place that suits him. But how can you divine his or her future by examining the stones?"

"I don't know very well how to explain it. It's a gift from God. I look at the stones or pebbles and I begin to see. But wait, I started to tell you about Valimarescu and I got to talking and forgot. Let me tell you how it was. I examined the place and suddenly I saw a bad stone—an unlucky one. It was half-buried in the sand with a black corner pointing toward the south, grinning like an evil omen. I understood that those young people wouldn't be staying here long. But only after I picked it up and turned it over on all sides did I see how much misfortune was revealed in it. Today or tomorrow they will receive a telegram and leave . . . What a pity!" he sighed, pulling his hat down on his forehead.

Emanuel had been listening intently, looking deeply into his eyes. When Beldiman stopped speaking, he let his hands drop to the sand and began running his fingers through it idly.

"It must be terrible to be able to read these sad, tragic things . . . "

"They're not always sad," Beldiman interrupted. "Take, for instance, this morning, when I was walking at the far end of the beach. The face of a certain young woman caught my eye. She was the only silent one in a merry, talkative group—silent, looking out over the sea—and at intervals she would turn to steal a glance at a nearby family, especially at the children. I hung around there for better than an hour until I saw her get up and leave—by herself. Then I went to the place where she had been sitting and examined it. I sensed that the others in the group were eyeing me inquisitively, and some of them were laughing under their breath and making gestures to each other, but at my age I'm used to many things. And all at once I understood, as if I had read it in a book. That young woman had been married for several years and she had no children. She wanted children, but she hadn't had any. And recently someone, perhaps a doctor, had told her that she could never have children. But they both were wrong, both she and the doctor. She *will* have children—not one, not two, but four! So, you see, sometimes I find out good news."

"Didn't you run after her and tell her?"

Beldiman shook his head, smiling. "No, that wouldn't have been proper. I'm not a professional fortuneteller. I have no right to meddle in the lives of others, strangers, and give them information not requested of me. Besides, I might be wrong. I know very well that I was wrong once. True, it was on a mountain, Pietre Arse. Boulders which haven't been moved for hundreds of years. But I believed that there also, according to how a man sat down, with his face or his back toward such and such a rock, I should be able to read something. Indeed, I saw many things, but the most significant ones I didn't know how to read, so you could say I didn't see. I was with a good-sized group. They weren't friends of mine—just people I'd met on the road."

If he had been looking at him, Beldiman would have realized that Emanuel had stopped listening to him. He kept shifting his position, and he was drawing hard and often on his cigarette.

"So you see," Beldiman said, concluding his story, "I can be wrong."

"I don't want you to misunderstand me," Emanuel began abruptly, "or think I'm being curious or indiscreet. But, you see, this is the first time this extraordinary thing has happened to me—how to say it—to meet a reader of stones . . ."

"I know what you want," Beldiman interrupted. "You want me to tell your fortune too."

"Exactly."

"Yes, but I don't know if I have any right to," Beldiman continued very seriously. "I cannot meddle in another person's destiny. That right was not given me. I can read in stones what will happen to various persons around me, but except in cases of absolute necessity, I've never revealed to the persons in question what I found out."

"Maybe this time it's a case of absolute necessity," Emanuel persisted. "I'm staying here just a few days; then I leave for a foreign country. I go to Stockholm. I'm in the Consular Service. Who knows when I'll return home again?"

Beldiman pushed his hat back on his head and gave him a long, searching look.

"Well, if that's so . . . But you know," he added quickly, "you know I won't tell you anything but the first part of it."

"What do I have to do?"

"Get up slowly, step here," he said, pointing to show him where to walk, "and sit down beside me."

When he saw him seated, Beldiman raised himself on his knees and leaned forward as far as he could, resting on his hands. He stayed in that position for some time, not moving. Then he reached out and picked up the book.

"Sea Voyage" he said, reading the title aloud. "What about this book?"

"It's a novel. I didn't have anything to read, so I bought it in Constanța."

"It doesn't bode good luck for you," said Beldiman, letting the book fall to the sand.

"But you said that you only read stones . . . "

"That is correct, but the way the book was situated with this broken seashell to the south and these pebbles intersecting the road of good luck . . . It's strange," he added, perplexed, rubbing his chin slowly. "I don't understand very well myself what's going on. I see two girls who bring you misfortune, and yet I don't understand why, because you're not in love with either of them. But there are two girls who do indeed bring you misfortune . . . And it's strange," he resumed after a pause. "It seems that you meet one of them somewhere, at a skating rink or on an icy street, and she slips. And just as you are running to help her, a second girl appears from out of the blue and picks her up. Then you start to say something, but at the same time the girl who helped the other says something, and then you start to laugh . . ."

"D-l Beldiman," Emanuel cried, putting his hand on the other man's shoulder, "you, sir, are an extraordinary man! Either you're a magician or else a seer, a clairvoyant, or whatever it's called. But you'll never convince me that you read these things in the pebbles and seashells here!"

He stopped as though his voice had suddenly failed him and began swallowing hard. His face paled slightly, and without realizing it he ran his fingers through his hair.

". . . Because everything you've just told me," he managed to continue after a little while, "has already happened!"

"Impossible!" Beldiman interrupted, "Absolutely impossible. If these things have happened once, then they'll happen a second time, exactly!"

"No, you don't understand," Emanuel said, trying to smile. "They happened in a dream, in my imagination."

Beldiman pulled his hat down over his forehead again and looked at him questioningly, frowning.

"You see," Emanuel began after lighting another cigarette, "about two or three hours ago, after I'd come to the beach and started reading this novel, I realized all at once that I wasn't following what I was reading. I don't know if I was really asleep or not, but I was stretched out on the sand and my eyes were shut. Suddenly I saw a street with which I'm familiar in București, in the dead of winter. And I saw a girl fall. A young woman she was, wearing a dark-blue overcoat and a beret. When she fell, her hat came off and slid along the icy pavement. I crossed the street to assist her, but a girl came out of a courtyard just then and helped her up. I was planning to say for a joke, 'Behold, a fallen woman!' when I heard the second girl saying exactly the same words! For a moment I was disconcerted, and then I began to laugh involuntarily... And with that laughing the vision came to an end."

"It was a vision," Beldiman said, "but you will live to see it in reality. And that's too bad, because those girls do not bear you luck."

Emanuel stared at him, but with a curious expression, as though he did not understand him.

"This is extraordinary," he said. "You succeeded in seeing what I had imagined two or three hours before! By what miracle you were able to see all this, I don't know. But I can't believe you saw it in the sand and the pebbles."

Beldiman said nothing for some time, seemingly scrutinizing the area for other signs.

"May God grant that I'm mistaken," he began at length. "In any case, if, in the near future, you should meet two girls, one helping the other to her feet, then get yourself away from that place as fast as possible! They will not bring you luck!"

He stood up slowly and went to get his jacket.

"By the way, what is your name?" he asked.

"Emanuel. Alexandru Emanuel. But of course my family and friends call me Sandi."

"Strange," murmured Beldiman, slipping his jacket over his shoulders.

And without another word, without even so much as a good-bye, he ambled off toward the sea.

Emanuel opened the window, feeling depressed. The sky was ashen and low, and the sea was lost in mist. He went downstairs to the lobby without enthusiasm. Aron, the proprietor's nephew, motioned to him from the desk.

"There's a telegram for you, sir," he said. "It just now arrived."

Emanuel took it excitedly, read his name and address with disbelief, and then began fumbling with it absently.

"Was this the only telegram that came?" he inquired. "I mean, were there other telegrams for other people? For *domnul* Valimarescu for instance?"

"No, we didn't get any telegrams but this one."

"Perhaps last evening," Emanuel persisted. "Didn't *domnul* Valimarescu receive a telegram last evening?"

Aron thought for a few moments. "No, I don't remember any."

Emanuel stuffed the telegram in his pocket and started for the door, but after a few steps he stopped and turned around.

"Do you, by any chance, know a d-l Beldiman?" he asked.

"Oh, you've met him too, have you? That's quite surprising. He doesn't like to make conversation with summer visitors. The man's something of a misanthrope. Likes to go for walks by himself."

"But what sort of man is he? I mean, what do you know about him? What do people say?"

Aron shrugged and began fidgeting with his pencil, touching it first to his chin, then to his lower lip.

"As you might guess, people talk about him a lot. He's an old man. Some say he may have killed his wife when he was lighthouse keeper at Tuzla. Others, to the contrary, say that since then, since his wife drowned, he's become a misanthrope and is a little out of his head."

"But what else do you know about him?" Emanuel persisted. "For instance, does he have any exceptional characteristic, some unusual gift?"

"What sort of gift?"

"How should I know? Let's say, for instance, if he knows how to read . . . if he can foretell the future?"

Aron shook his head emphatically. "No, I've never heard that. They say all kinds of things about him, that he inherited an enormous fortune, that he's filthy rich, that the woman who was drowned was not his wife . . . They say all kinds of things."

"Anything to do with stones?" Emanuel interrupted.

"Stones? What kind of stones? Precious stones?"

"I don't exactly know. I'm asking you . . ."

"There might be something to do with stones," he said, "if it's true that he inherited that terrific wealth abroad."

Emanuel smiled, lit a cigarette, and started for the door. On the sidewalk, the intense heat struck him in the face. He hesitated a moment, then took the way to the beach. After walking about two hundred meters he stopped, crossed the street, and entered Vidrighin's. Only later, after he had downed two cups of coffee and finished reading the newspaper, did he take the telegram from his pocket and open it. His face brightened suddenly and he began to laugh. The wire was from Alessandrini in Constanţa, inviting him to dinner that evening. It was not hard to guess why he had been invited. Undoubtedly, friends from Bucureşti had arrived unexpectedly.

When he returned to the hotel, it had begun to rain. Large, warm drops, soon swallowed up by the dust . . . He ate his lunch absently, without much appetite, listening to the rain falling harder and harder. There would be a bus at five. He went up to his room and lay down for a nap.

When he came down to the lobby later, the rain was falling fine and thick, as in autumn. In order not to wait for the bus in the rain, he sat down on a sofa with his raincape on his lap and lit a cigarette. He was looking around for an ashtray when he saw at the door the telegraph boy shaking the water off his coat. The dinner has been cancelled! thought Emanuel, and he started toward the desk.

"No, it's not for you," Aron said. "It's for domnul Valimarescu."

Emanuel grinned sheepishly, then returned to the sofa and continued smoking absently. From time to time he turned to glance at the grandfather's clock. When it struck five times he sighed with relief. Draping the cape over the back of the sofa, he went to select a magazine from the pile of old numbers on the table. It began to grow dark, and Aron lit the large lamp suspended directly above the table with the magazines. A sad, gloomy, dusty light now hung over the lobby. Valimarescu came downstairs and passed by without seeing him, on his way to the desk. Emanuel kept standing with a magazine in his hand, not daring to move.

"I've come to inform you that I have to leave," he heard Valimarescu saying.

Aron attempted to say something, but Valimarescu stopped him, raising his voice in exasperation. "It's a matter of absolute necessity! Let me show you this telegram."

Emanuel took a whole stack of magazines under his arm and returned to the sofa. He started leafing through them idly, stopping now and then to gaze at a picture, but without being aware of what it was about. Suddenly, he threw the magazines down on the sofa and strode to the desk.

"If only I'd known about it this morning!" Aron said with annoyance. "I turned down five potential guests this morning. If only he'd have received the telegram five or six hours earlier..."

"Mobilization orders," Emanuel remarked with considerable gravity.

"I beg your pardon?"

"I said, he must have been called up for military duty."

"No, it was something else. It was a telegram from the tribunal. He has to appear in court on the twentieth of August, at eight in the morning—tomorrow morning, in other words."

"In court? At eight o'clock in the morning!" Emanuel repeated in surprise. "But I thought the tribunal was in recess... Then he's leaving alone."

"No, they're both going," said Aron, irritated.

Emanuel watched as he leaned his left arm on the register, dipped the pen deeply in the inkwell, and began to write slowly, letter by letter, in a fine hand.

"Is there something you wish?" he asked at length, looking up from the register.

"Oh, yes," replied Emanuel, as if he had been awakened. "I want to ask if you know by chance where I can find d-l Beldiman."

"At this hour?" said Aron with astonishment, glancing at the big clock. "I have no idea."

Emanuel returned to the sofa, stuck a magazine under his arm, picked up his cape with the other hand, and set off for his room. But after climbing a few steps he changed his mind, replaced the magazine on the table, slipped into his cape, and went out onto the street. The fine rain was falling steadily, and the few street lamps were burning. Emanuel headed in the direction of the beach. The sea seemed drowned in fog, but the billows were rolling in faster than usual. He was not alone. On the dock two couples were strolling dejectedly. A young man who had just stepped out of the water donned a beach robe over his wet bathing suit. A few hundred yards up the beach, a man was walking away at a brisk pace. He had rolled up his pants legs and with bare feet was treading directly along the line where the waves met the sand. Emanuel stopped, quickly pulled off his shoes, turned up the legs of his trousers, and started running after him. When the man heard him a few steps behind him, he turned around quickly.

"Oh!" said Emanuel, unable to conceal his disappointment. "I thought you were *domnul* Beldiman. From a distance I mistook you for *domnul* Beldiman."

The man smiled but made no reply.

"Good evening," said Emanuel.

When he reached the pier again he shook the sand from his feet, rolled down his trouser legs, and carrying his shoes in his hand he set off for Vidrighin's. The terrace and the two rooms were jammed with summer visitors. A few patrons looked up at him and smiled as he walked through the room barefooted, wearing a raincape over his almost formal clothes, carrying his black shoes in one hand. There were no free tables now, so Emanuel made his way to the bar, sat down on a stool, and commenced wiping his feet with his handkerchief. After putting on his shoes, he removed the cape, laid it on the edge of the bar, and asked for coffee. He drank it sitting on the stool, smoking dreamily, watching the drops dripping off the cape.

"There's a free table on the terrace," Vidrighin whispered when he passed by. "Would you like something else to drink?"

"Bring me a cognac."

On the terrace, at the table next to his, someone in a group waved to him. Emanuel smiled back, but he did not move, waiting for Vidrighin.

"Do you know a gentleman named Beldiman?" he asked, pulling out his billfold to pay.

"I know him, but we're not well acquainted . . . He trades with the competition, if you know what I mean," Vidrighin added, winking. "He's a customer of Trandafir's. You'll find him at Trandafir's place."

Emanuel drank his cognac quickly and left. It was fully dark now and the light of the street lamps seemed less sinister in the fine, cool rain. There were only a few people at Trandafir's, almost all of them locals. Trandafir did not have a radio, only a phonograph. When he entered, Trandafir had just put on a new record, "Blue Heaven." Emanuel stopped in the middle of the room and began to examine the tables one by one.

"I'm looking for d-l Beldiman," he informed the waiter who came to take his order.

"Haven't seen him today. If the weather's too bad, he doesn't come. Goes to his villa... What'll you have?"

"A cognac."

He sought out a more secluded table and sat down, deep in thought.

"Yes," Trandafir explained to him a few minutes later. "When it rains or snows or the weather's bad, especially in the winter, he goes to his big country house. The rest of the time you'll find him either at home—that is, at the house of his first wife, by the town hall—or else here with us or on the beach."

"But where is his villa? Maybe I'll run out there and find him."

"Oh," Trandafir replied, shaking his head, "it's 'way off, towards Tuzla. And now, with all this rain, you can't get there even by car. The roads are bad and unlighted. It's a very desolate place where the house is."

"But how is he able to get there?"

"Ah, with him it's another matter! He knows when bad weather's coming, a rain or a storm, and he leaves in time. Sometimes he goes on foot and other times he takes the Tuzla bus, which drops him off nearby."

"But how does he know when bad weather is on the way?"

"Ah, that's a long story. He used to be a sailor. He was also a lighthouse keeper at Tuzla. He knows the weather; he knows how to get ready!"

"Do you know him well?" asked Emanuel after a pause.

"I've known him ever since his first wife was living—which is to say better than thirty years."

"What sort of man is he?" Emanuel persisted. "Is it true that he has unusual gifts, that he knows how to foretell the future?"

"Ah," Trandafir said with a smile full of meaning. "*Domnul* Beldiman knows everything! I tell you, he was a sailor."

It was past midnight when he decided to return to the hotel. The rain had let up, but the dock and the beach were long since deserted. He walked in vain from one end of the dock to the other, waiting for someone to appear with whom he could strike up a conversation. Nothing could be heard but the sound of the waves pounding ever more furiously and, at intervals, the moaning of the fog horns. Whenever a group emerged from Vidrighin's, bits of jazz music, voices of young people, and laughter drifted to the pier.

A taxi stopped directly in front of the hotel and Emanuel quickened his pace.

"No," the driver said, "I'm from Constanţa I brought a gentleman here from Constanţa and now I'm going back."

"That's just what I want!" exclaimed Emanuel, almost pathetically. "Take me to Constanţa!"

"It'll cost you a fortune!" he warned. "To what part of the city?"

"To d-l Alessandrini's place. It's on . . . "

"I know," the driver interrupted, opening the door. "Get in."

By the time they reached Constanţa the rain had stopped. The lights of the harbor shone unusually clearly, and in the streets there hovered a strong scent of the sea and wet grass. Alessandrini's house was still lighted. Emanuel paid his fare, bounded up the few stone steps, and pressed long and hard on the doorbell button. Presently the voice of an older woman asked in disbelief who was there.

"It's me, *domnul* Sandi. Sandi Emanuel."

The maid turned the key and opened the door. "He waited for you until just a little while ago. Now they've all gone to the Albatros."

"Who are 'they'? Are they people from Bucureşti?"

"No, they're artists. I believe I understood that one of them is a painter. They arrived this morning from Balcic."

"How many women are there?"

"Oh, two or three."

"Think carefully, now," Emanuel insisted. "Are there two or three?"

"Three," the maid replied after a short pause. "First two came, then two more, but one of the young ladies left before dinner. I'm not sure just when she left."

"In other words, three. Good!" he exclaimed, and hurried down the steps.

In front of the Albatros he hesitated a few moments, pacing back and forth on the sidewalk with his hands in the pockets of his raincape. Just when he had decided to go inside, the door bust open and the bouncer shoved two drunken sailors onto the sidewalk. Emanuel quickly turned his back and crossed the street; but a few minutes later he returned, entered, left his raincape at the cloakroom, and purchased a pack of Lucky Strikes.

"Mlle. Odette is singing," the doorman said.

He lighted a cigarette and waited by the door until the end of the song. When he heard applause, he tiptoed in. Alessandrini was seated at the table of honor, surrounded by men and women of all ages in various attire: some were clad in bright-colored beachwear and others in elegant evening clothes. Alessandrini saw him and stood up.

"Excellent!" he cried, motioning for him to come.

But Emanuel drew back, left the room suddenly, and asked for his raincape from the cloakroom. Approaching the doorman, he slipped him a bill and offered him a Lucky.

"I came to meet *domnul* Beldiman," he whispered, "but I didn't see him. Has he by chance already gone?"

"I don't think he's left," replied the doorman. "Marieto," he said to the attendant, "have you see *domnul* Beldiman?"

"He left," the attendant said. "About two. The gentleman neither drinks nor smokes," she added, smiling meaningfully. "He only comes for the program."

"I'm speaking of *domnul* Vasile Beldiman," Emanuel specified.

"I know him well," said the doorman. "When he gets bored with his villa, he comes to Constanța, to his house in Porumbari, and on the second or third day he comes to see us. He comes for the program."

Alessandrini opened the door and stood on the threshold, theatrically stretching out his arms, ready to embrace Emanuel. "Excellent!" he exclaimed. "At last!"

"I'm returning immediately," said Emanuel, starting to leave. "I've got to see Beldiman."

"Why, he was here with us, at our table!" said Alessandrini, pronouncing the words haltingly and with considerable difficulty. "If you'd have come an hour or two earlier, you'd have found him."

"I'm returning immediately," Emanuel repeated and went out onto the street.

He turned up the collar of his cape and began walking fast, taking any street he came to. After about a half-hour he stopped, as though he had remembered something, and headed toward the promenade. Just as he arrived, he heard the clock strike four times. It was still fully dark and the sky seemed as overcast as before. The breakers approached the seawall black and high, crashing against it with a deafening roar. After staring at them blankly for a long time, he looked for a bench and sat down. It had become rather cold, and he blew on his hands, then lit a cigarette to warm himself. After a while, fatigue began to overtake him, and he rested his head in his hands against the back of the bench. He did not, however, succeed in falling asleep. From time to time waves would break high and foam would splash over him. He stood up, stretched all his joints, yawned deeply, and started up the street toward the Albatros with a firm step. Before entering, he glanced once again at his watch: it was a quarter to five.

The bar was deserted. At a table, with his face cupped in his hands, Alessandrini sat waiting for him.

"Ah!" he exclaimed when he saw him approaching. He said nothing more, but gazed steadily into his eyes for a long while in silence.

"Please don't be angry with me, but it was really an important matter," Emanuel began, drawing up a chair and sitting down beside him. "Can I rely on your powers of observation and memory? Can you swear that you recall *everything that happened last evening?*"

Alessandrini was frowning as he listened, but gradually his face brightened and he smiled dreamily. "She spoke that way too," he said. "It's as though I hear her speaking!"

"Who spoke this way?" Emanuel demanded, blanching slightly.

"She, Adriana, Ariana," Alessandrini murmured, still smiling. "And not only that, she talked all the time. At first I thought her name was Adina. But she's not called that. Her name's Ariana . . . or Adriana . . . "

Emanuel took out his pack of cigarettes, then changed his mind and laid it on the table. "It's very important," he began again. "Please tell me frankly, can I rely on you?"

Alessandrini turned toward him suddenly and started laughing. "You're extraordinary!" he exclaimed, speaking with considerable difficulty. "You're simply extraordinary!" he repeated,shaking his head.

Then his smile faded, and folding his arms on the table he bowed his head in thought. Emanuel stared at him for some time, hesitating to speak. Finally, he picked up the pack of cigarettes and began to turn it over and over nervously between his fingers.

"Alessandrini," he began gravely, "this is a very important matter. Please tell me just this much: if last evening, here or at your villa, one of your friends—one of the girls—slipped and fell, and when one of you hurried to lift her up, another girl or woman *was already there* and helped her?"

Alessandrini tried to listen to him, but he soon gave up and shook his head firmly.

"No," he broke in, "you don't understand. It was nothing of the sort. I meant to say something else."

"Maybe she slipped when she was dancing," Emanuel continued excitedly, "or maybe someone on the dance floor bumped into her by accident and she tripped and fell."

"No, nobody fell. But you know, the story's not over! They haven't left yet. They've just gone to the house to change. Their yacht isn't leaving 'til ten. They're waiting for you."

"For me?" asked Emanuel in astonishment, smiling. "But I don't even know them!"

"It was Adriana's idea," continued Alessandrini. "Ariana's, I mean. She saw you when you came in here earlier tonight . . . Ah, excellent!" he exclaimed, almost pathetically. "What an extraordinary woman! I tell you, it was enough for her just to glimpse you. A moment! She didn't need more than a moment!"

Emanuel opened the pack absently and slowly removed a cigarette.

"I don't exactly understand," he said. "I don't see what connection she could have . . . "

"Just that she saw you a single moment, and then she talked about you for a solid hour. What intelligence! She figured you out immediately. She said, 'That young man's afraid of me! He's running away from me!' "

Emanuel lit his cigarette and drew the first smoke hungrily.

"I had no reason to run from her," he said. "I don't know her. I don't even know what her face looks like."

"She knows you very well," Alessandrini asserted. "She guessed immediately that you were afraid. I wanted to send Gib out to hunt for you. I thought that probably you were on the promenade, but Adriana wouldn't let me. 'No matter,' she said. 'We'll wait for him, and tomorrow morning we'll take him with us to Balcic.'"

"That's absurd!" Emanuel said, beginning to laugh. "You know very well I can't go. In two weeks I have to leave for Stockholm."

"That's just what Adriana said herself. She said, 'But if he doesn't want to come with us to Balcic, it doesn't matter; in two weeks we'll meet in Stockholm anyway!'"

"In Stockholm?!" Emanuel fairly shouted. "But what business does she have in Stockholm?"

"I don't know. I didn't ask. But I'll tell you one thing: she's an extraordinary woman! She figured you out completely! . . . How about a cup of coffee?" he asked, turning toward him. "Since I have to stay here a while. I'm waiting for Botgros."

Emanuel shook his head absently. "But who is she?" he asked suddenly in a different voice, as if he had just awakened. "What's her name?"

"Ah," said Alessandrini, "that I don't know. I believe she told me her name, but I didn't retain it. At first I thought she was called Adina, but Adina was the other one, the one who left. Incidentally, I believe she left for Movila, to look for you," he added, suddenly remembering. "She said that she knew you—knew you very well, in fact!"

"Adina?" Emanuel asked in astonishment. "Adina who?"

Alessandrini shrugged. "To tell you the truth, I haven't retained the name. But she said that she knew you very well. And if a certain event had not intervened, you two would have been engaged."

"Then she's got me confused with someone else!" Emanuel declared, his face suddenly brightening.

"No, I don't think so. She told us a lot of things about you. And now that I think of it . . ."

But the sentence remained unfinished. He had caught sight of Botgros coming through the doorway and he motioned to him. Botgros approached unhurriedly, walking with a rather unsteady gait and smiling.

"So this is the man in question," he said, taking a seat and looking at Emanuel with interest. "I imagined you differently."

"You can tell him everything," Alessandrini suggested. "I've prepared him."

Embarrassed, Emanuel began to laugh, and not knowing what else to do, he held out the pack of cigarettes across the table.

"No thanks, I don't want to smoke anymore," Botgros said. "I smoked all night... So, you're the one, eh?" he added, continuing to look at him with a mysterious grin.

"Don't dilly-dally any longer," Alessandrini interrupted him. "I told you that I've prepared him."

"I'm telling you, sir," Botgros began, "don't ever trust descriptions given by a woman! If you want to know what someone looks like, always ask a man. For instance, if I'd asked you instead of listening to Adina, I'd have recognized him immediately."

Alessandrini took Emanuel's arm and whispered to him, pointing toward Botgros: "If I've understood rightly, he's engaged to Adina."

"Oh, no," Botgros corrected him, smiling bitterly. "I know she said so, but it's not true. Perhaps, if a certain event hadn't intervened in our lives... But, after all, what has been, has been. Let's say no more of the past... She left for Movila to look for you," he added after a short pause, turning toward Emanuel. "She said she hadn't seen you for a long time. Wondered if you'd recognize her after so many years."

Emanuel listened intently, doing his best to understand. He wiped his hand across his cheek, as if to regain contact with reality by touching himself. Then he began to laugh again.

"I believe it's all a simple mistake," he managed to say at last, trying to seem casual.

"What did I tell you?" Alessandrini exclaimed triumphantly to Botgros. "I told you Adriana had figured him out immediately! A moment was enough for her."

"Yes, it's curious," Botgros replied, fixing his gaze on Emanuel again. "Even though she knew him very well, Adina described him to me in such a way that I'd never have been able to recognize him. But the Empress saw him for only a moment in the doorway!"

"A fraction of a second!" Alessandrini interjected. "What an extraordinary woman! What intelligence!"

"The Empress?" Emanuel echoed.

"Yes, we call her that for fun," Botgros explained.

"Adriana," added Alessandrini. "I explained to you who she is."

"But who is she? Emanuel burst out in exasperation. "What's her full name?"

"Adriana," Botgros resumed. "Until a few months ago she was Adriana Palade, but now that she's been divorced, she's just Adriana again. Or the Empress, as we call her. She and Adina are good friends. They met each other last winter ice skating, and ever since they've been inseparable."

"She's an extraordinary woman!" Alessandrini exclaimed again.

Emanuel sat staring into space. "Ice skating," he repeated slowly, mostly to himself.

"You can tell him the rest, too," Alessandrini persisted. "I've forewarned him."

With an effort, Emanuel raised himself suddenly from his chair. "I've got to be going," he announced, attempting to smile. "I have a bus to catch at eight."

But Alessandrini caught hold of his arm and held him back. "What's wrong with you? Didn't I tell you we're all going to Balcic?"

Emanuel shook his head with obstinacy. "Impossible! I have a room engaged at Movila. I'm staying just one week longer. Then, to București, to my duties!"

The other two suddenly started to laugh. Botgros snickered discreetly, peculiarly, almost without making a sound, squinting slightly, but Alessandrini seemed shaken by a deep, inner convulsion until he choked and began coughing.

"This is simply extraordinary!" he managed to say finally, exhausted.

He began to wipe the tears with the back of his hand. Just then the bartender brought the tray with the coffee. Alessandrini hurriedly picked up a glass of water and started drinking it.

"Yes," said Botgros, looking down, no longer staring, "it's truly extraordinary. Those were the Empress's very words, exactly!"

Emanuel flushed and twisted the pack of cigarettes unconsciously between his fingers. "I don't understand what you mean," he said slowly, stressing each word.

"Excellent!" Alessandrini burst out with sudden enthusiasm. "She's a simply extraordinary woman! You absolutely must meet her!"

"I'm deeply sorry," said Emanuel, "but before lunchtime I have to be in Movila."

Alessandrini turned suddenly to Botgros. "Then it's on account of Adina," he declared. "So Adina might have been right after all!"

Botgros smiled again, then began sipping his coffee. "As far as I'm concerned," he said without looking up, "Adina's free to make any decision she wishes. What was in the past is of no interest to me."

Emanuel tried to laugh. "I give you my word of honor that I'm hearing now for the first time about this dr-a* Adina!"

"Her name isn't really Adina," Botgros announced gravely. "We call her Adina—we, her friends. Gib called her that once, and ever since she's been Adina."

"She was confused with Adriana," Alessandrini interjected.

"Yes, she was confused with the Empress. And yet, they don't look anything alike."

Emanuel remained on his feet, perplexed. Moistening his lips, he looked from one to the other.

"But she liked that name," Botgros continued, "and ever since then, Adina she's been!"

---

domnisoara—miss.

At that instant Alessandrini threw his arms in the air. "Stop, stop!" he shouted, speaking to someone who had started to enter the room. "Don't you all come—we're not finished yet!"

Emanuel paled and looked toward the door in alarm. A blond youth with a freckled face was approaching their table. He was wearing shorts, as though dressed for the beach.

"The Empress sent me to tell you we're making port at Movila," he said as he drew near.

Turning toward Emanuel, he stared at him curiously, smiling.

"This man is Ioniţa," Alessandrini explained hastily. "A talented painter."

Emanuel took his outstretched hand and shook it perfunctorily.

"I didn't imagine him this way," Ioniţa said. "I pictured him as shorter . . . and more animated," he added after looking over him again.

"The Empress prejudiced you," Botgros said. "The way she described him to us last night."

"No," Ioniţa continued without taking his eyes off Emanuel's face. "I was going by Adina's description."

He pulled up a chair and sat down. "Have you told him everything?" he asked.

"I haven't had time to," Alessandrini replied. "He arrived just a little while ago, about five."

"The Empress insists that you tell him especially about how he tried to escape by jumping into the water and swimming toward the shore."

Alessandrini and Botgros exchanged meaningful glances, and their faces shone as though illumined by the same smile.

"That was the most beautiful part," whispered Botgros, half-closing his eyes. "You tell him, sir!"

"Not I!" Alessandrini said, shaking his head. "I'm rather tired and I don't know how to tell stories well."

"How he arranged with Botgros to have him bring the yacht near the shore," Ioniţa began, "and at the opportune moment—a kiss, a few words: 'Goodbye! You'll never know how much I love you!'—and then, splash! He's in the water!" Ioniţa started laughing, quite pleased with himself, and glanced at Emanuel again.

"But what came next was even more beautiful," Alessandrini broke in. "Because, after a few kilometers he became tired, tried to float, and when the water started getting in his mouth and nose, he got scared and began yelling for help."

"It was lucky the Empress had jumped in right after he had and was swimming behind him, unseen, ready to come to his rescue!"

Botgros turned toward Emanuel with a somewhat sheepish grin. "Really, that was the most beautiful part. It's too bad Adina wasn't there to help him too!"

"Oh, no!" exclaimed Ioniţa. "If Adina had been there, the Empress wouldn't have dared do it. Adina claims that he swims very well. For a good swimmer, a kilometer or two is nothing. If Adina had been there, the Empress wouldn't have been able to say that he'd get tired and call for help after a kilometer or less."

"Pardon me," Alessandrini interrupted, "but Adriana explained to us that he was very tired, and she was right. Look at him now, and it's not even six o'clock yet! What will he be like in a few hours? Remember how Ariana described him walking on the docks at Movila in the rain, and then here, on the promenade, smoking one cigarette after another? He was extremely tired."

Emanuel listened to them, trying to appear nonchalant but quite obviously blushing. "About whom are you speaking?" he inquired in a dry, caustic tone of voice.

"Ha! As if you didn't know!" Alessandrini retorted. "Who else could we be talking about?"

"The Empress told us last night what would happen," Botgros explained. "How you'd come back here, find us, and in the end let yourself be persuaded to come with us on the yacht to Balcic."

"Impossible!" Emanuel exclaimed. "Alessandrini can assure you that in no event will I let myself be persuaded . . ."

"I can see you don't know her!" Alessandrini broke in.

"It's obvious he doesn't know her," Ioniţa chimed in.

"At any rate, you will be coming with us on the yacht," Botgros continued. "But the feeling of duty and especially the fear of the Empress . . ."

"I'm telling you for the last time . . . " Emanuel began, his voice choked with emotion.

"Please, don't interrupt him!" shouted Alessandrini, taking him by the hand.

"You aren't telling it very well," Ioniţa spoke up. "You've forgotten the most important thing: how he stood there on the yacht in the bathing suit that you, sir, had lent him," he said, turning to Alessandrini, "shivering from the cold, but not daring to make a move, because the Empress had her arm around his shoulder and was whispering in his ear . . . "

"Oh, how beautiful!" exclaimed Alessandrini, closing his eyes and visualizing the scene. "It's as though I'd been there and had seen you. Because, I had a role in this story too! I'd wired the hotel to send your baggage to Balcic."

"I had the most disagreeable role," said Botgros wistfully. "I felt sorry for you. I'd heard you were going to Stockholm as vice-consul, that it's your first foreign posting, and I felt sorry for you. I wanted to help you out of the predicament. I was at the helm. I brought the yacht to within a kilometer or two of the shore . . . "

Alessandrini took his arm. "And I shouted, 'Hey, Botgros! Hold the tiller to port—you're taking us onto the rocks! To port!' "

"And then you jumped into the sea," Botgros continued, "and you started swimming for the beach."

"But you grew tired," Alessandrini resumed, "and after about a kilometer you began to swallow water, and you got scared and called for help."

"The Empress had dived into the water too," Ionița broke in, "but you hadn't seen her. She was swimming back of you."

"Luckily, Beldiman was there too," Alessandrini continued, "and he saw you."

Emanuel suddenly turned deathly pale. "Beldiman! But what's Beldiman doing in this story?"

"He was there, on the beach, and he saw you," Alessandrini went on quite animatedly. "He called out to you to float. Then he slipped off his clothes, dived into the water, and swam toward you!"

"But what's Beldiman doing in this story?" Emanuel repeated in a dry, hoarse voice. "How do you know about Beldiman?"

For a few moments the three men just sat there, dumbfounded, as though they couldn't believe their ears.

"Now, that's a good one!" exclaimed Alessandrini, slapping his hand on the table. "That beats everything!"

He erupted into a fit of laughter, his whole body convulsed. Emanuel glared at him savagely, then turned his back and strode away from the table. "So long!" he shouted from the doorway.

He could have taken the eight o'clock bus, but on approaching the station he caught sight of a young woman who seemed to be waiting for him, sitting on a bench, pretending to be reading. He noticed how she kept glancing up all the time from her magazine, looking around inquisitively, sometimes turning her head toward the tables on the sidewalk. Emanuel took the first side-street he came to. Soon, spotting a barbershop, he slipped inside.

When he returned to the bus station it was half past eight, and the woman was still there on the bench, leafing through her magazine and looking bored. Emanuel hesitated a few moments, then retreated in search of a cafe. He asked for a cup of tea and drank it slowly, pensively. The sky began to clear, heralding a hot morning. After about half an hour he got up and walked slowly back to the station. The girl was pacing up and down on the sidewalk. Emanuel felt his heart begin to pound, but he held his course and looking steadily ahead he made straight for the bus. Finding a seat immediately behind the driver, he sank into it and began to breathe more easily.

It was almost eleven when he arrived at his hotel. As soon as Aron saw him, he motioned to him.

"You have a surprise," he said in a confidential tone, after carefully surveying the lobby. "I can't tell you who it is, but you'll be pleased!" He smiled mysteriously, half-closing his eyes.

"What's her name?" Emanuel asked sharply.

"I can't tell you, since then you'd guess. She came last evening and looked everywhere for you—at Vidrighin's, at Trandafir's . . . Then she waited for you here in the lobby 'til two."

"Can't you describe her for me?"

"No, that's a surprise. She didn't go to the beach, so she could wait for you. And we made an agreement that as soon as you came, without telling you anything, I'd send Marina up to her room to inform her."

Emanuel stared at him, unconsciously moistening his lips. "Good," he said. "I'll be back directly."

He went outside and headed straight for the beach. Beginning to feel the heat, he walked slowly, stopping now and then to rest. At the dock he took off his jacket and shoes, put his socks in his pocket, and set off again with the jacket over his arm and the shoes in his hand. After about a hundred meters he stopped and reached for his handkerchief to wipe his forehead, but he changed his mind and made for a kiosk. There he bought a newspaper and folded it into a hat to shield him from the sun. Then he started off again.

Soon, however, he felt extremely tired, exhausted to the marrow, and he sat down on the edge of the dock. For a long time he sat there, staring blankly out over the water.

After a while he sensed that someone had come up behind him and had stopped. He turned his head in alarm. Seeing it was Beldiman, his face brightened and he sighed deeply.

"I looked for you all night," he began quickly. "I looked for you at the Albatros. I wanted to tell you—you were right! He received a telegram and he left . . . Valimarescu," he added, observing Beldiman's blank look. "A telegram summoning him to appear in court immediately!"

Beldiman took off his jacket and sat down beside him on the dock. He seemed lost in thought.

"It wasn't the mobilization order, as we supposed," Emanuel resumed, smiling. Then, because Beldiman still didn't say anything, he asked him in a much lower voice, "Why didn't you tell me? If you knew, why didn't you tell me?"

Beldiman turned to face him and looked him up and down with curiosity, as though he were seeing him for the first time.

"What should I have told you?"

"Everything that came afterward. All that mix-up with Alessandrini and his friends from Balcic."

"Oh," said Beldiman as if he had suddenly remembered, "you're speaking about Alessandrini. I met him last night at the Albatros . . . He ought to arrive any minute now," he added, pointing out to sea.

Emanuel followed his gesture and saw a yacht gliding slowly a few kilometers offshore.

"If you knew, you should have warned me," he continued, lowering his voice still more. "It's a very important matter. My career's at stake... My first foreign posting," he added in a whisper.

"As you see it there," Beldiman began with a glimmer of pride in his eyes, "it would cost ten or twelve million today. And I bought it two years ago for less than four million. What a bargain!"

"It's yours?" asked Emanuel in surprise.

"It was mine when I bought it. But I didn't buy it for myself. I bought it for that scatterbrain, Adriana... The sins of old age!" he added after a pause, in a whisper.

As in a dream, Emanuel pulled on his socks and then began putting on his shoes.

"Look now," Beldiman went on, his gaze fixed on the yacht, "she's going to jump into the sea and swim right over to us! She's done this ever since I can remember. That's why I chose this spot—there aren't any rocks here. Look now! She's jumping!"

Emanuel sat holding one shoe in his hand, straining his eyes to see across the waves. "I don't see her," he said.

"She's swimming under water. But in three or four minutes she'll surface. She'll pop up right here in front of us!"

Trembling, Emanuel put on the other shoe, adjusted the newspaper hat on his head, and with difficulty got to his feet.

"The sins of old age!" Beldiman repeated, mostly to himself. "He said it well, whoever said, 'Don't make children in your old age!'"

Emanuel was standing beside him, listening. "Is she your daughter?" he asked after a moment.

Beldiman looked up surprised and grinned.

"So everybody claims," he said. "And so it pleases me to believe also."

"They call her the Empress," Emanuel added, trying to smile.

"Yes," replied Beldiman gravely. "She's as lovely as an empress, and she's not afraid of anything. But so what? She belongs to another world!"

"I've got to be going," Emanuel announced suddenly.

"... to another world," Beldiman repeated, mostly to himself.

"I'm glad to have met you," said Emanuel, starting to leave. "So long!"

But he had already seen her, swimming exceptionally fast, some twenty meters from the shore, and he no longer dared to move. It was as though all the blood had been drained suddenly from his veins. He had removed the paper hat without realizing it and had let it drop at his feet on the dock. Coming to his senses, he realized that he was waiting for her, smiling and happy. But when their eyes met, she looked away quickly, indifferently, as though she did not recognize him. Moments later her whole face brightened in a big smile, and she began waving to someone at other end of the end of the dock.

"Adina!" she shouted. "Adina!"

Chicago, March 1959

Part Four

PERSONAL REFLECTIONS

Chapter Ten

SMILES AND WHISPERS

Nostalgic Reflections on Mircea Eliade's Significance for the Study of Religion

N. J. GIRARDOT

"How should we interpret it?" I heard from the group of students in the rear, who had by now gotten to their feet. I approached the director. "I know now why I didn't want to write for the theater," I whispered to him. "I'm bashful. I don't know how to speak in public. The public intimidates me. Especially the learned public, the public of today. They know things, they've studied, they've reflected. Symbols, deep meanings... I know why I didn't want to write this play." The director looked at me and smiled. "If you don't want to, don't write it." I breathed more easily. "Then I won't write it," I said. He continued to smile, but I could tell he was disappointed.

—M. Eliade, "Goodbye"

WHISPERS AT THE END OF AN AGE

This chronicle about Mircea Eliade is constructed from autobiographical vignettes. The first of these involves a portentous moment in my education that I was able to recognize only in hindsight. Other stories come from my years as a graduate student and from my early career as a teacher and scholar. In the course of this meandering narrative, I will sketch out some of Eliade's influence on my academic odyssey, confess my own gradual estrangement from the Eliadean faith, and consider why it has only been with this essay that, after almost two decades, I have been able to write again about my indebtedness to, and renewed appreciation of, Eliade's vision for the history of religions.

It is not that I feel myself born again in some old-time religion. Contrary to some conspiratorial readings of academic history, there never was any kind of Eliade-imposed true belief during the cosmogonic time of the 1960s and '70s. Nor was Chicago much of an *axis mundi*. Nothing remains the same in time or memory—Eliade, Chicago, discourse, culture, or the sacred. Eliade insists that our experience of time results in a mythic fall back into chaos. Bittersweet nostalgia is the mother of meaning. These realizations have, as most everyone now knows, special poignancy in light of postmortem accusations regarding Eliade's affiliation with the fascist Iron Guard in pre–World War II Romania.[1]

Although I have grown old and jaded in an era of startling academic pettiness and revelations about the shameful secrets of prominent immigrant scholars, I find that, along with real disappointment, I can view the now bludgeoned and bloodied Eliade corpus with renewed sympathy. Let me make it clear that my muddled feelings about this issue are affected both by my weary reaction to Eliade's blemished heritage and by my generation's discovery that, in these last days of the millennium, we may be witnessing the end of higher education as we have known it. Just at the point when the study of religion has gained some meager acceptance within the academy, the whole nature of higher education seems poised on the brink of a major sea-change. The very idea of a university seems to be passing away in these postmodern times.[2] Where the academic study of religion will fit into this new cybernetic realm of heightened vocational interests and pragmatic methods remains to be seen. There is an increased fascination with the peculiar vitality of religion and the role of the creative imagination on the part of individual students, yet at the same time many departments of religion face extinction by institutional downsizing.

---

1. See especially: A. Berger, "Fascism and Religion in Romania," *The Annals of Scholarship* 6 (1989): 455–465; I. Strenski, *Four Theories of Myth in the Twentieth Century*. London: Macmillan, 1989; D. Dubuisson, *Mythologies du XXe Siècle* (Dumezil, Lévi-Strauss, Eliade). Lille: Presses Universitaires de Lille, 1993. For contextualizing discussion of these accusations see Bryan Rennie, *Reconstructing Eliade: Making Sense of Religion*. Albany: State University of New York Press, 1996; Nancy Harrowitz, *Tainted Greatness: Antisemitism and Cultural Heroes*. Philadelphia: Temple University Press, 1994; and Leon Volovici, *Nationalist Ideology and Antisemitism: The Case of Romanian Intellectuals in the 30s*. New York: Pergamon Press, 1991.

2. See the discussion in a special issue of *The Oxford Review* 17 (1995) devoted to the theme of "The University in Ruins."

My personal tales will illustrate Eliade's contribution to my own sensibility as a comparative religionist during these last dark days. But they also suggest something more general about Eliade as a scholar and man. Having experienced pangs of self-doubt and methodological malaise in a field that has never achieved full disciplinary acceptance within the academy, I have learned to embrace my marginal status (and impending virtuality) and to speak up once again for an Eliadean approach to the comparative history of religions.

In the midst of continuing whispers concerning Eliade and new (self-inflicted) questions about my own Taoistic turn toward visionary outsider art and the sublimely ridiculous area of "Elvis Studies," I have learned to smile once more.[3] It is my nostalgic remembrance of Eliade's own sly smile (and the fact that I have tenure and supportive departmental colleagues!) that gives me encouragement to pursue these matters and to be my own comparatively unserious myth-and-ritual self.

IN ILLO TEMPORE

HOLY CROSS

The first time I ever heard Mircea Eliade's name was in a sophomore theology class in 1962 at the Jesuit College of the Holy Cross in Worcester, Massachusetts. I had attended a full range of Catholic elementary and secondary schools and grown up a good Catholic boy with a regimental crew cut and nerdish habits of study. The saving grace in my Catholic upbringing was probably that I never became an altar boy and that I read too much, especially an abundance of trashy science fiction—the lush horror stories of H. P. Lovecraft and the quirky existential occultism of Colin Wilson. In the pre–Vatican II 1950s, my formative religious experiences were an odd lot of mandatory masses, excruciatingly prolonged recitations of the rosary, Latin missals and tattered "holy cards," scapular medals and other odd bits of material religion, Sunday morning and Good Friday fasting, May Day crownings of the Blessed Virgin, the duplicitous thrills of the postpubescent confessional, and so on.

I remember most fondly the quaintly absurd folklore that surrounded so much of the Eucharist and the magical-mystery spookiness of the "real presence" (the special gold plated sinks that drained directly into the center of the earth,

---

3. Regarding my involvement with visionary folk art see my catalog essays for *The Finsters at Lehigh*. Bethlehem, PA: LUAG, 1986; and *Natural Scriptures*. Bethlehem, PA: LUAG, 1990. My work on Elvis has coincided with other quasi-shamanistic ritual events at Lehigh University and is discussed in "But Seriously: Taking the Elvis Phenomenon Religiously," *Religious Studies News* 11 (November 1996): 11–12.

sworn accounts of mistakenly biting into a consecrated host and feeling a warm spurt of blood, and the red-alert conditions of panic that prevailed if one were accidentally to drop a consecrated host). Also remembered, though less fondly, were the ridiculously arcane theological and sacramental matters of the faith meticulously memorized and scholastically analyzed in catechism classes in elementary and high school (for some reason the pressing question of the possibility of using watermelon juice for baptism and the correct methods for dealing with smegma are lodged in my memory). In many ways, I suppose that I am still unconsciously living out the wonderfully foolish implications of that damnable linkage of sin, sex, salvation, sacraments, and smegma.

This was delightfully wacky stuff and a powerful manifestation of the popular religiosity of traditional American Catholicism in the 1950s, but unfortunately it also meant that I had an extremely parochial perspective on the nature of religion, on other religious traditions, and on the teaching of religion. In my first year with the Jesuits at Holy Cross, I was disappointed to discover that the required college theology course was still only a glorified catechism class. Although like many ambitious, middle-class, third generation Catholic boys I was enrolled in the biology pre-med. curriculum, I was looking forward to something more stimulating in theology from the Jesuits. After all, they did have a reputation as God's intellectual commando squad and I was ready for some serious deliberations about the "mysteries of the faith." This hankering after something more than the standard catechismal fare derived from my own aesthetic proclivities, but was also prompted by the climate of the times when old religious provincialisms and defensive authoritarian structures were collapsing in American life. These were, in fact, years when a spirit of rebellion was starting to transform the land in various ways. Alternative religious phenomena, and altered states of consciousness, were increasingly being discovered as interesting and vital issues. There had to be something more to all of it than hushed accounts of Padre Pio's stigmata, complicated neo-Thomist arguments for transubstantiation, hearty appeals to a "muscular Christianity," or loyal declarations that "we believe, goddamnit, precisely *because* it's so absurd."

The above is a prologue to a serendipitous turning point in my life (one that I was not able to act on till years later). It came about when, in my required sophomore honors class in theology, our young Jesuit instructor, in the spirit of the new Vatican Council sweeping through Catholic circles at that time, dramatically indicated that we were not going to use the regularly assigned textbook in dogmatic theology. Rather, he assigned us something from Gabriel Marcel's works on Christian existentialism and, more daringly, Mircea Eliade's *Sacred and Profane*. I had heard of Marcel before (a refreshing respite from catechismal apologetics, but still somehow too safe and precious), but Eliade was entirely foreign. I remember reading Eliade as a quasi-revelatory experience. Not only did Eliade cover a broad range of exotic topics, but also concluded with a discussion of the "science" or "history" of religions, a comparative discipline distinct from a theological or catechismal approach. Perhaps best of all, there was the delicious thrill of reading something that seemed both to explain and challenge everything I had learned about religion.

Although his background was Romanian Orthodox, it was no accident that I would discover Eliade at a Roman Catholic college in the 1960s. He had been embraced by liberal Catholic theologians (the Harper Torchbook edition of *Sacred and Profane* of 1961 includes a blurb by a Jesuit praising Eliade's emphasis on what was religiously "unique" in Christianity) and the English translation of his ground-breaking *Patterns of Comparative Religion* was published in 1958 by the well-known Catholic publishers, Sheed and Ward.[4] There is, in many ways, a very broad "Catholic" ("cosmic," "pagan," or "sacramental") sensibility in Eliade's work that allowed for his selective appropriation by theologians of a Christian existentialist bent. (This factor lends itself to the suspicions in the academy that Eliade was himself too much of a believer who disguised his global theologizing with the neutral rhetoric of the history of religions.) At the very least, he took religion and religions seriously—even "archaic," "primitive," "pagan," "superstitious," or "syncretistic" traditions (such as Catholicism itself, loosely speaking). Perhaps also because many different religions were treated with equal fascination and respect, it was possible to be less serious about those traditions making exaggerated claims of perfect seriousness.

It's hard to say now what exactly it was about Eliade that affected me. However, I am sure that it generally had something to do with his openness to bizarre new worlds of meaning, an embracing of forms of strangeness that even went beyond the strangeness of my own tradition. I was smitten by Eliade's raw curiosity, unfettered imagination, impressive erudition, fascination with the exotic, and his willingness to follow the historical and textual trail of an idea or movement without worrying about some preordained "Index" of allowable thought. Furthermore, Eliade's comparative approach actually interpreted the strange in accessible historical and cultural ways rather than relying on Scholastic sleight of hand, pious apologetic authority, or the "it's all an unfathomable mystery" ploy. Whatever it was, it was exhilarating for a wide-eyed and increasingly disloyal Catholic boy.

---

4. I believe I am correct in remembering that the jacket blurb to the Sheed and Ward edition of *Patterns* actually identified Eliade as a noted "Catholic theologian." Unfortunately I no longer have a jacketed copy of this book in my library. The original Sheed and Ward edition was published in 1958. [Prof. Girardot is correct. The cover of the third printing (October 1966) of the Meridian Books edition reads: "a study of the element of the sacred in the history of religious phenomena by a distinguished Catholic scholar."—Ed.]

Although I did not know it at the time, this textual encounter with the Eliadean counteruniverse would change my life. This definitive career change came about when, after years of studious self-effacement and a triumphant entrance into Dartmouth Medical School, I paused for the first time to consider my own deepest interests and motivations. The realization swept through me that I really wanted to pursue my long-simmering interest in religion. It was at this epiphanic moment of rare self-insight that I suddenly remembered reading Eliade three and a half years earlier. When catalogs from various programs arrived and I discovered that Eliade was not in France or Romania but at the University of Chicago, I knew immediately where I would go for graduate study. In January of 1966 therefore (a time when the concerted bombing of North Vietnam was just beginning), I left the wooded hills of Hanover, New Hampshire, to drive to the gray Midwestern city of Chicago where I would begin my exploration of the promise and possibility of strange religions first suggested by *The Sacred and the Profane*.

CHICAGO

No simple summation of my years in the history of religions program at the university of Chicago (from 1966 through the summer of 1970) is possible. Whatever I was undergoing in graduate studies was only a small part of a larger drama of political struggle and social-cultural change that was running through all aspects of American life. A new receptivity and experimentation regarding other forms of consciousness and spirit (encompassing politics and education, but also variously music, drugs, hair, clothing, and religion) were very much a part of these changes. What I had done in relation to leaving medical school and embarking upon a career devoted to the study of strange religions was already radical enough for a quasi-Catholic boy who had just left medical school and I spent the rest of the decade reclusively escaping into the obscure pleasures of Chinese alchemy, erotic Chinese pillow books, the "psychomental" aspects of Siberian shamanism, and Taoist chaos and gourd symbolism.

Amazing things were happening in American culture, but I will recount just a few stories relating to my graduate school years. These tales do not represent the most substantive events in my association with Eliade at Chicago—a relationship that was defined by my assistance with the new journal *History of Religions*, my role as his personal secretary (1967–1970), and his direction of my dissertation (along with Joseph Kitagawa and Anthony Yu). I have purposefully chosen memories that have a vague penumbra of meaning. To borrow an Eliadean principle of interpretation, "deep meanings" are often where we least expect them, especially since less serious experiences demand more imaginative forms of decipherment. However apparently frivolous, the episodes recounted here do suggest something of the "essential" Chicago Eliade of the 1960s and 1970s.

Eliade, fifty-nine years old in 1966, was on the threshold of his greatest success as a scholar and disciplinary pioneer in American higher education and had not yet suffered the ravages of arthritis or the structuralist and deconstructionist accusations of methodological sentimentality. Nor had his whimsical smile been darkened by whispers of moral and political duplicity. This was a cosmogonic and innocent time when Eliade was establishing himself, and his "creative hermeneutics," as the primary paradigm for an interdisciplinary academic approach to religion in tune with the radical openness and cultural breadth of the 1960s. More than anyone else at this time in the United States, it was Eliade who rescued the study of religion not only from a jealous Abrahamic God and a narrow provincial theology (in the mid-1960s Eliade was billed by *Time* magazine as the inspiration for the radical "Death of God" movement), but also from the reductive scientistic rationalizations of the secular academy. In this way, the newly vigorous academic study of religion (as an enthusiastically multicultural and interdisciplinary field) expansively transformed many existing theology departments in religiously affiliated schools and, even more notably, made inroads in numerous public institutions.

I will restrict myself to just two tales from this period. The first took place early in my career at Chicago when I was only a passive observer. I refer to an infamous "debate" between Eliade and Clifford Geertz, an anthropologist at Chicago who was just then attaining academic superstardom (soon after this, he would go on to the Center for Advanced Studies at Princeton). This event was staged at Jimmy's, a popular graduate student bar and hangout. I no longer remember the topic for this encounter (no doubt something to do with the perennial graduate student concern for "methodology") or very much of the actual event, aside from some dim memories that the articulate and combative Geertz clearly prevailed over an overly diplomatic and mumbling Eliade. All details of this artificial and awkward incident have passed away, but I still have a strong general impression that the real significance of this event was that it starkly dramatized the hierarchical vectors of political power in American graduate education at that time. As an exercise in the sociology of knowledge it was, therefore, revealing. Anthropology was an established discipline in the mainstream of university tradition and was one of the most elite of graduate programs at Chicago. The history of religions program, on the other hand, was suspiciously located in the Divinity School (suggesting a less than "objective" approach to the subject of religion) and certainly did not command the academic prestige of distinguished social science departments such as Anthropology.

It was this sense of the second-class and religiously tainted status of the history of religions students that was projected by the non-event in Jimmy's, a defensive judgment prompted by the argumentative facileness of Geertz and the presumptive arrogance of many the questions asked by anthropology students in attendance (often suggesting that historians of religions might actually be secret believers and, even worse, that they had not done any field work).[5] Eliade was always too "nice" to his antagonists and did not seem particularly bothered or disappointed by the event (he was mostly indifferent to whether the History of Religions Department was placed within the Divinity School or the university at large; although he was also a member of the university's distinguished Committee on Social Thought, he often suggested that, for all of its Christian and theological focus, the Divinity School was the better location for the comparative study of religion since, at Chicago, it upheld the methods of humanistic research while at the same time respecting the autonomy of religious phenomena).[6] Contrary to the assumptions of some anthropology students, he clearly honored the tense relationship between historical texts and existential contexts and regularly made use of anthropological research in his work, including Geertz's own work. Despite the debate, Geertz's interpretive method attended to the complex play of symbols in texts and contexts and was in many ways similar to Eliade's hermeneutics.

This experience also reinforced my growing awareness that an academic marginality had its advantages since, to take but one example, Eliade's work on shamanism from the outsider's standpoint of the comparative history of religions was at that time better than any anthropological work on the subject. His approach to a subject, especially those subjects ordinarily ignored as irrelevant or glossed over in silence, taught me the importance of exhaustive bibliographical research that disregarded any restrictive disciplinary boundaries or premature value judgments. Whereas many anthropological students seemed to read only other anthropologists, historians of religions at Chicago were imbued with an Eliadean methodological ethic that always took into account all available studies from every disciplinary perspective. This seems like an exceedingly simple matter, but within the academy it is a principle too often neglected by the more departmentally demarcated, politically connected, academically established, and intellectually self-sufficient disciplines.

My second story is a collage of my weekly meetings with Eliade in his office hidden away in the Meadville Theology School on Woodlawn and 57th streets. It was my habit to appear at the office late in the afternoon on a Thursday or Friday. This involved making my way up to the third floor and knocking on the oak door to the office. A slightly hunched and shuffling Eliade would hasten to open the door and then an unforgettable scene would present itself. The image was not of

---

5. Adding to the tension at the time was that Edmund Leach's acerbically negative article on Eliade from a quasistructuralist anthropological point of view had just appeared. "Sermons from a Man on a Ladder," *New York Review of Books* 7 (October 20, 1966): 400–414.

6. On Eliade's "niceness" see Martin Marty, "That Nice Man (Reminiscences of Mircea Eliade)," *Christian Century* 103 (1986): 503.

shelves or walls of books, but literally of an alternative world darkly illuminated by leaded windows at the rear of the room and totally overwhelmed by multiple hillocks of books. Amidst these rolling hills, there was a single narrow path that ran from the office door to an old wooden desk that was piled with scattered pipes, tobacco, random papers and correspondence, and more mounds of books. When brushed against, the mountainous piles could topple over, leading to a disastrous chain reaction among the many other mounds. Assuming a successful passage through these paper mountains, I would carefully place myself on the single chair by the desk and we would then proceed with the week's correspondence and with any other requests he might have for some library materials or for stylistically correcting the English of some of his recent writings.

What I particularly remember from these sessions is, first of all, the marvelous diversity of his correspondence and his emphasis on polite responses to even the most crackpot of queries (increasingly frequent toward the end of the 1960s) and that he steadfastly refused the vast majority of invitations for articles and speaking engagements. He was always generous and responsive to requests for bibliographical information, something that, as suggested above, was close to the very core of his being. I also remember being dumbfounded by Eliade's writing methods. Even when he was working on his most technical articles or books, he relied on his encyclopedic memory for assembling his notes and references (hence the importance of having his library envelop him in his office; amazingly he seemed to know exactly which pile contained a needed article or book). But most of all I recall his amiability in letting me babble on about many of my own eccentric questions and multifarious problems as a graduate student.

Especially impressive in all of these meetings was Eliade's readiness to help other scholars who wrote for various and sundry reasons (for instance, his fascination and delight with the correspondence and work of a brilliant young American Sanskritist, then known as Wendy Doniger O'Flaherty). Sometimes the results of these epistolary contacts had an impact that went well beyond the confines of his office. To take but one example of this, it is worth mentioning that, because of his groundbreaking work on alchemy and the fact that he could bring a comprehensive comparative perspective to the history of Chinese religions, he was invited by Joseph Needham to participate in the first international conference on Taoist studies held at Bellagio, Italy, in 1968. Because of Eliade's interest and conscientious patronage, these important papers were published in the *History of Religions* journal and were widely circulated in fields outside of Sinology. In many ways, Eliade's presence at this conference and the publication of the proceedings in a non-Sinological journal signalled not only the rise of serious Taoist scholarship, but also a revolutionary interdisciplinary appreciation of the overall significance of the history of religions for an understanding of Chinese civilization. This is a lasting contribution to world-wide Sinological scholarship (and the study of Chinese religious traditions has become one of the most vital areas in the contemporary study of China) that should not be overlooked in the current rush to denigrate the Eliadean legacy.[7]

The question may be asked whether he ever disclosed anything about his own religious beliefs concerning the ontological reality of God or the Sacred. There were some rumors that he periodically accompanied his wife to Romanian Orthodox services in Chicago and it is true that he was sometimes given to comments on the "Cosmic Christ" of Orthodox Christianity, but he scrupulously avoided talking about his personal religious convictions. It seems that he did not discuss such intimate religious matters with even his closer faculty colleagues at Chicago (at that time, Joseph Kitagawa, Charles Long, and Gerald Brauer). I had enough common sense to know that I should never ask him directly about such private matters, but when I started to read some of his literary works toward the end of the decade, it often seemed that his fantastic stories and novellas testified, albeit rather enigmatically, to his most closely held beliefs about the magical realism of human life. I did have occasion to obliquely discuss some of these matters in relation to his literary works, but was again greeted with a fleeting smile and with the frustration of his nodding agreement with almost anything I would say, no matter how contradictory. My own experience suggests that Bryan Rennie has mostly got it right.[8] That is, Eliade was certainly not a believer in God in any conventional theistic sense. Moreover, his references to a capitalized "Sacred" (and the "dialectic of the Sacred and the Profane") were primarily methodological statements about the creative human perception of religious meaning (which in its most basic sense has to do with our recognition of, and imaginative reaction to, the "strangeness" or "spookiness" of lived experience). But by interpreting Eliade's beliefs in this manner, I am most likely suggesting something about my own beliefs (as well as, no doubt, Bryan Rennie's) and therein lies the difficult hermeneutical rub.

I return to Eliade's enigmatic smile when some particularly arcane or paradoxical topic was raised in our conversations. Often these discussions had to do with

---

7. The Bellagio conference papers appeared in *History of Religions* 9 (1969–1970): 107–279. For a discussion of the interdisciplinary perspective of the comparative history of religions on the Sinological study of Chinese religions see my "Chinese Religion: History of the Study," in the *Encyclopedia of Religion* 3. New York: Macmillan, 1987, 312–323.

8. See Rennie, *Reconstructing Eliade*, 194, where he notes that "the young Eliade clearly stated that he 'didn't believe in God,' that he 'was a Christian though not a believer in God.'" Rennie is quoting Mac Ricketts's *Mircea Eliade: The Romanian Roots, 1907–1945*. Boulder: East European Monographs, 1988, 123. It should be said that Ricketts is referring to Eliade's autobiographical novel of his student years, *Gaudeamus*, which alludes to his relationship with his professor, Nae Ionescu. It is my guess that the later Eliade would not have added the qualification of being "a Christian."

methodological matters since it was typically his position to stress a historical and imaginative rather than a philosophical and analytical solution to a problem. Never did I witness any of the pomposity often associated with academic prima donnas or self-styled gurus (Bruno Bettleheim and Saul Bellow were particularly notorious at that time in Chicago). Nor did he consciously cultivate a circle of student disciples ("abject" or otherwise) since, aside from the inspiration of his historical curiosity and bibliographies, it was hard to know precisely what his method was. Certainly he did not demand or expect slavish adherence to any kind of party line concerning the interpretation of religious phenomena. Generally speaking, I was most deeply inspired by the magnanimity of his vision (what he would have called his "bird-view" of religious experience), his open-ended methodology, his respect for the contributions of other disciplines, his emphasis on the hard work of historical research (including adequate language skills) while also stressing the importance of a serious generalist approach to interpretation as opposed to the hyperspecialization of most disciplines, and his sense of irony about the strangeness of the total human enterprise. His mystocentric genius was to affirm the creative possibility of finding religious meaning in absolutely anything. These themes, I should say, are expressive of the culturally eclectic and transitional tenor of the late 1960s in the United States, an association that, perhaps like the associations of some intellectual movements in the late 1930s in Europe, alludes both to the artistic and cultural vitality and to the romantically self-deceptive and totalitarian danger of periods of rapid historical change.

Did I ever detect any intimations of darker secrets, something deeply and shamefully hidden from the naive American students so anxious to have exotic worlds of religious meaning opened to them? No, not really. Thinking retrospectively, however, I sometimes wonder whether there were not tiny clues of some embarrassing secret that escaped my interpretive radar. But such disgraceful associations from the distant past were mostly unknown at that time. It should also be obvious that an obsessive emphasis on detecting past secrets too easily lends itself to a creative hermeneutics of extreme exaggeration and mythic fabulation. I must admit, however, that it now strikes me as odd that amid the white heat of American political turmoil during the Vietnam period Eliade and I never, as I recall, discussed politics at all. I am as guilty as Eliade in this avoidance, but it is also true that Eliade affected the bumbling demeanor of the monkish and completely apolitical scholar who rarely read the newspaper or watched TV. By the late 1970s and early 1980s there were some indications from the strange lacunae and silences in his biographical writings (especially the first volume of his autobiography covering the years 1907–1938, which appeared in 1981) that his complete political disinterest was to some degree an artifact of his immigrant persona.

My awareness of the possibility of concealment was provoked sometime in 1967 or '68 when, as preparation for my German language comprehensive exam, I read the

German version of the story "The Secret of Dr. Honigberger," an effectively eerie and autobiographically suggestive tale about the investigation of the disappearance of a famous scholar who was learning how to practice secret yogic "powers" known as *sidhis* (one of which was the ability to become invisible).[9] At one of our weekly sessions I asked him whether or not the story had an esoteric level of meaning that suggested something about his own activities and experiences in India. Now, almost thirty years later, I can only disappointingly remember him smiling rather cryptically (or sadly), rapidly talking about the "historical Honigberger," and then quickly changing the subject.[10] I was left only with the dim impression that there were indeed some things in his early life that were best kept strictly private.[11]

NOTRE DAME AND BEYOND

As might be imagined at this point in my story, Eliade's Mona Lisa smile was, for me, gradually becoming too much of a Cheshire Cat grin. These feelings started to grow upon me as I was embarking—after marriage, a year and a half in Taiwan, and a child—upon my own academic career at Notre Dame University in Indiana in the 1970s. Some of my feelings at this time were the natural result of any young scholar's need to wean himself from the graduate school teat, a feeling that was heightened by my continuing indebtedness to Eliade and the strangeness of finding myself back within the Catholic fold. I had been hired sight unseen by Notre Dame with the special blessing of Eliade. Doubtlessly because of my Catholic pedigree, I was also perceived as a "safe" appointment for the first full-time position in comparative religions within the theology department. Unfortunately, however, I too cutely thought of myself at that time in Eliadean terms as some kind of "primordial Catholic," a foolishly self-styled (and redundant) identity that was not well received

---

9. I read the copy that was present in Eliade's own library (published under the title of *Nachte in Serampore* ["Nights in Serampore"], trans. by Günther Spaltman. Munich: Otto-Wilhelm-Barth Verlag, 1953). An English version (translated from the Romanian by William Coates) appeared in *Two Tales of the Occult.* New York: Herder and Herder, 1970.

10. It is worth mentioning that my other great disappointment concerning Eliade at about this time was his unwillingness to take a break from his work to go see Stanley Kubrick's religiously suggestive film, *2001, A Space Odyssey,* when it opened in 1967.

11. Even before the first accusations in the 1980s about his hidden antisemitism and involvement with the Romanian Iron Guard, my more general suspicions about a hidden life were confirmed by the appearance of Maitreyi Devi's haunting *roman à clef* about Eliade's disastrous Indian love affair in the 1930s and by Devi's surprise visitation of Eliade in Chicago some forty years later. See Maitreyi Devi, *It Does Not Die: A Romance.* Calcutta: Writers' Workshop Publications, 1976. There is a rich folkloric tradition about this incident among Chicago graduate students of the period.

by many in the department. I see now that the Eliadean interpretive trope of the "primordiality" or "archaicness" of just about anything was wearing thin for me as well as for some of my theological colleagues.

For much of the 1970s, as I started to publish and discover my own scholarly identity, I struggled to sort out my mixed feelings about Eliade. Eliade was even more famous and influential in the burgeoning professional world of the academic study of religion at this time than he was in the 1960s (though the Levi-Straussian structuralist and neo-post-structuralist criticism of Eliade's "phenomenological" and "essentialist" methodology was mounting; Jacques Derrida and full-blown postmodernist deconstructionism had not yet drastically altered the intellectual landscape). Despite my felt need to break from my intellectual father, I continued to be particularly enchanted by his literary works (I was, for example, the one who brought Eliade's novel, *The Forbidden Forest*, to the attention of Notre Dame University Press).

One response to these developments was my organization at Notre Dame in 1978 of a national conference devoted to the interrelationship of Eliade's scholarly and literary careers.[12] But the results of this generally successful conference only increased my simmering frustrations and uncertainties about the Eliade universe. Two memories regarding this period are particularly vivid. The first derives from Eliade's coming to Notre Dame on the last day of the conference to attend an unusual dramatic reading of his play, *The Endless Column*, about the famous Romanian modernist sculptor, Constantin Brancusi. He clearly enjoyed it and perhaps was even touched by its production at Notre Dame. Unfortunately, I was left with only a wry smile since he had to leave immediately after the production to return to Chicago.

A second related memory involves a hastily organized book dedication party at the University of Chicago in 1982 when *Imagination and Meaning* first appeared. By this time I had moved on to Lehigh University in Pennsylvania and in a giddy moment I planned to end the dedication ceremony in Chicago with a ritual presentation of a stuffed squirrel to Eliade. The reason for this weird gift was simply that I had used Eliade's fondness for American squirrels and cardinals to illustrate some key methodological points in the introduction to *Imagination and Meaning*.[13] In the spirit of these anecdotes, I decided that the usually solemn book dedication ceremony needed a lighter and more imaginative finale. With the special help of Chris Gamwell, then Dean of the Divinity School, I arranged therefore to have an actual stuffed squirrel presented to Eliade. I still think it was an appropriately funny

---

12. For a description of the conference, and some of the papers, see Norman J. Girardot and Mac Linscott Ricketts, eds., *Imagination and Meaning, the Scholarly and Literary Worlds of Mircea Eliade*. New York: Seabury, 1982.

13. "Imaging Eliade: A Fondness for Squirrels," *Imagination and Meaning*, 1–16.

and meaningful thing to do, but I also recall that Eliade himself seemed somewhat nonplussed when, in front of a bemused audience, I nervously presented him the rather mangy stuffed animal. In the end, he was able to wanly smile about the whole episode, but I had the distinct impression that he had other worries on his mind—as probably he did since he was by then suffering from a progressive arthritis that was making it painful for him to write.

This awkward event indirectly signalled my partial estrangement from the Eliadean world. No longer would I write or speak about Eliade, an informal vow that I have kept down to this very essay. I never made any dramatic "here I stand" declaration about these feelings, nor did I ever think that I had totally renounced my Eliadean heritage. It was really more of a matter of slowly finding, and steadily affirming, my own style as a writer, scholar, and teacher. Thus, the silly squirrel incident, I see now, really brought closure to feelings of alienation I had most powerfully experienced when, a year earlier, I was correcting the galley proofs of my book, *Myth and Meaning in Early Taoism*.[14] This work had been greatly expanded and revised since it was written as a dissertation under Eliade. What surprised and tempered me as a writer and scholar was that, after years of struggle to get the manuscript accepted and just when I thought there were no more corrections to make, I looked through the proofs and noticed what I had never clearly seen before—every other paragraph seemed to use the word "primordial" or some classic Eliadean variant. I went through the proofs in a frenzy to purge myself once and for all of the contamination of primordiality! This was an important moment for me since I finally felt some initiatory separation from Eliade, as well as experiencing that "powerful and obscure" emotion of discovering one's own authorial persona. It was not so much that I had rejected Eliade, but that I had now found my own voice and vocabulary (where a punned and alliterative cucurbitic chaos, strangeness, and spookiness have replaced the Eliadean primordial and his other Latinate expressions). *Myth and Meaning* is obviously inspired by an Eliadean perspective, yet in its published form it is very much my own interpretive and stylistic construct.[15]

---

14. *Myth and Meaning in Early Taoism, The Theme of Chaos (Huntun)*. Berkeley, Los Angeles, London: University of California Press, 1983. A corrected paperback edition appeared in 1988. In the preface to this book I wrote that (xv–xvi): "I learned from [Eliade] the humanistic significance, daemonic excitement, and scholarly toil of a history of religions that respects the strange contradictory meanings of religion in human life. Most of all I learned through him that religions often find their meaning in the interstices of the unexpected."

15. I should mention that two Eliadean interpretive devices—the "prestige of cosmogonic mythology" and the theme of "returning to the beginning"—were central to my argu-

I last saw Eliade in April 1985 in Washington, D.C., exactly one year before his death. The occasion was both the awarding of an honorary degree to him by George Washington University and a conference in his honor organized by Alf Hiltebeitel. This was a generally happy event—though with very few real smiles and distinctly punctuated by moments of profound melancholy. For myself it was not only a time to see Eliade and his wife, Christinel, after some three years, but also an opportunity to meet with old Chicago friends. I was struck by the degree to which disease and age had taken its toll. In particular, Eliade's hands were grotesquely twisted now with arthritically enlarged knuckles and his eyesight had grown worse. As he sadly confessed, it was becoming painfully difficult to write. To admit that writing, which had defined his whole life, was an almost impossible task was tantamount to saying that he was indeed on death's threshold. Most of all, amidst the forced happy-talk of the conference and reception, he seemed tired with a bone-deep physical, intellectual, and spiritual weariness. And even though I was not aware of it at the time, whispers about his Romanian past were starting to circulate.[16]

---

ment in *Myth and Meaning*. Again, it is worth noting how the perspectives of an outsider-comparativist (such as Eliade's views on mythology) have helped to reform an Orientalist discipline like Sinology that traditionally tended to emphasize the mythless nature of Chinese civilization. On the issue of Chinese mythology, see especially Anne M. Birrell, "Studies on Chinese Myth since 1970: An Appraisal," Parts I and II. *History of Religions* 33 (1994): 380–393; 34 (1995): 70–94.

16. For Eliade's description of this see *Journal IV*, 123–127. Constant themes throughout this phase of his journal are his physical ailments, his "worries" over getting his chaotic papers organized for posterity, and his general tiredness. In hindsight (and the fact that Adriana Berger, who would become one of Eliade's leading accusers, was working on his papers at this time), one can imagine that, in addition to all his other difficulties, the task of going through his papers was leading to certain anxieties about early "secrets." I also find it interesting that Eliade comments that at the conference I mentioned my fears "for the fate of the history of religions in the U.S. after [Eliade was] no longer alive" (127). Thinking about this now, I remember that the context for my concerns was the experience I had had with some Chicago graduate students during much of the 1980s. That is to say that, after Eliade's retirement at Chicago, there seemed to be a haughty rejection of anything having to do with Eliade or an "Eliadean" approach to the study of religion. History of religions students were now, interestingly enough, acting very much like the anthropology students in Jimmy's some fifteen years earlier. Much of this was natural enough in that this new, but still quite amorphous tradition, had now "made it" within the academy, yet the horrors of the job market created a climate of fear and extreme competition that made it mandatory to remain carefully *au courant* regarding the latest methodological trends. By the 1980s, it seems that Eliade was viewed as grievously dated and sentimentally old fashioned by many starting their careers at Chicago in the history of religions program.

Eliade died on April 22, 1986, just two months and two days before the summer solstice and St. John's Day.[17]

SMILES AT THE END OF MY STORY

The end of the millennium is upon us and the question remains as to why, after such a prolonged hiatus, I now find myself again writing about Eliade. With the steady drumbeat of damning accusations about his fascist sympathies (and the "rightist" affiliations of a whole generation of intellectual giants: Martin Heidegger, Carl Jung, Paul de Man, Joseph Campbell, and so on), there would seem to be every reason to be done once and for all with such "tainted greatness." I have no easy answer to this. Much like my creeping feelings of alienation during the '70s and '80s, the urge to reaffirm the best of the Eliadean legacy and spirit—while admitting the sins of his youth, his concealment of a shameful past, and his methodological shortcomings—has grown in me over the past few years. This occasion to break my silence results from the invitation to contribute to the present volume which, as a refreshing change of pace, seemed to take a carefully balanced approach to the whole murky issue of Eliade's past and his significance for the future of the study of religions. But how does one once again respond to the smile while hearing the whispers?

Even before this invitation, I was feeling the need to sort out my own confusions about the comparative method, the place of an interdisciplinary tradition of generalist scholarship in an age of politically correct specialization, and the surprising danger of teaching and studying seemingly ridiculous religious subjects such as the Elvis Presley phenomenon. All of these issues are epitomized by the Eliadean spirit and I simply felt it was time to return ritually to the mythic Creator. I am sure that my decision was also affected by my gut sense that, regardless of my awareness of the "secret" Eliade, the charges of incredible fascist depravity, intrinsic antisemitic evil, and lifelong duplicity now being heaped upon him do not fit with man I had known. Nor do I think that a compromised political past necessarily or completely invalidates all of one's life's work as a scholar. Somewhere in the course of these heated accusations, we need to remember the initiatory nature of a human life—that youthful transgressions can lead to atoning emotional and intellectual transformations in later life. In addition to this, the basic issues of fairness and proportional justice often seem to be blithely or polemically overlooked. Thus, in

---

17. For the significance of St. John's Day (and the evening before) for Eliade see Mac L. Ricketts (and Mary Park Stevenson), "Translators' Introduction," xi xv, in the English version of Eliade's *Forbidden Forest*. Notre Dame and London: University of Notre Dame Press, 1978.

all that has been written about Eliade's Romanian past, there has appeared to be little that was damning in the "smoking gun" way of de Man's wartime writings. Whatever the nature and extent of Eliade's involvement with ultranationalism in Romania in the 1930s, we should allow for the probability that his political and religious views evolved throughout his later life as a scholar in exile in Paris and Chicago.

Ambiguity concerning the degree of Eliade's culpability rules the record. And it is this root uncertainty that is probably the most accurate conclusion to draw from the evidence at hand (i.e., several writings nationalistically denouncing various minority groups, his association with, if not actual membership in, the fascist Legion of the Archangel Michael/Iron Guard, and his wartime actions as a "cultural attaché" in England and Portugal). Ambiguity can certainly be an invitation to the worst kind of delusive self-justification. But it can also function as the matrix for significant change and, in the best sense, a pretext for recognizing and renouncing an ignoble past. This kind of acknowledgment does not absolve Eliade's guilt, but it does, as an act of "creative hermeneutics," contextualize it and allow for some much needed interpretive discrimination. In the final analysis, there should be both a relentless rejection of all truly tarnished Eliadean artifacts and a sober recognition of what still has some real merit in the Eliadean approach to religious phenomena.[18]

The problem is that the ambiguity of the evidence too quickly lends itself to distorting extremes of muck-raking tabloidization or "see no evil" spin control. Once we are able to get beyond either a one-sided moral or methodological condemnation of Eliade, we may discover that he still has much to offer the study

---

18. The best discussion of these matters is found in Rennie, *Reconstructing Eliade*, 143–177. Rennie is too scrupulous in his analysis of Eliade's leading critics to be easily branded as a blatant Eliadean apologist, nor can he be accused of being biased because of former associations with Chicago. Based on my own experience with Eliade and his "secrets," I tend to agree with Rennie's sensible observation that (164) "if he [Eliade] did feel some general discomfort from his initial support of the Legion, but had no specific culpability to explain, would that not explain his reluctance to broach the subject in any way other than he did?" I also concur with Rennie's general conclusion that (165): "[t]he sum total of Eliade's involvement, while not entirely faultless, is mild, and can be seen as a moderating influence in the prevailing atmosphere [in Romania]. Eliade's case provides an example of how patriotism, manifested as ethnic nationalism combined with religious zeal, all too easily becomes violence, bigotry, xenophobia, and oppression. Eliade himself does not seem to have clearly analyzed the dynamics or implications of his own involvement. I would suggest that Eliade's brush with totalitarian ideologies in the '30s influenced his theoretical position as expressed in his later books as a reaction against such tendencies; that his perilous attraction to the extreme right in his younger years led to a far more mature position; that, in their own way, his later works were a repudiation of the exclusivism and ethnic superiority of the later Iron Guard."

of religion in a "post-Eliadean age." My renewed appreciation of Eliade does not imply that he is somehow immune from either scholarly or ethical criticism. Nor does it mean that his recommendations for the study of religion will not require careful revision, wary emendation, and deliberate alteration. Eliade never felt his own work was final or apodictic. But knowing how to go about this revisionary reclamation of Eliade is no straightforward task.

I have already suggested that legitimate moral issues concerning Eliade's past must be taken into account. Let me also indicate that, contrary to some popular conceptions, Eliade's methodology has much to recommend it for a postmodernist approach to the study of religious traditions. Indeed, the current rush to repudiate Eliade may be more symptomatic of problems related to the stunted professionalization and permanent "identity crisis" of the academic study of religion and its furtive struggle for institutional acceptance than with Eliade's supposed moral and intellectual unsuitability for the contemporary situation. It may be that our current inability to acknowledge the significance of Eliade's work is best understood in Eliadean terms of the increased opaqueness of the sacred (or of understanding itself) that comes through the fall into, and progressively profound capitulation to, the mundane demands of history—especially the retarded and defensive history of the academic study of religion. In an age of erasure, not only have the few past patriarchs in the history of the study of religion been wiped from the slate, but "religion" itself has evaporated for some as a meaningful category of analysis.[19] And all of this is transpiring while "religion departments" are institutionally trivialized and ignored.[20]

This kind of historical amnesia, philosophical fragmentation, methodological pluralism, political irrelevance, and *fin de siècle* fear is in keeping with these confusing postmodernist times, but these developments as related to Eliade sometimes seem to depend too much on the academic gamesmanship of those on the fast track of career advancement. Graduate students riding the crest of methodological fashion seem only to conclude that Eliade is morally reprehensible and methodologically outdated, and that the latter judgment depends almost entirely on the former.

---

19. See, for example, Russell T. McCutcheon's "The Category 'Religion' in Recent Publications: A Critical Survey," *Numen* 42 (1995): 284–309.

20. The meager history of the comparative history of religions in North America is largely defined by developments in higher education during the past thirty years. Despite the association of the comparative "science of religion" with the emergence of other humanistic sciences in the nineteenth century, we dare not forget just how recent it has been that the study of religion achieved departmental status in private and public universities in the United States. Even if we see Eliade's methods as hopelessly outdated and his personal character tragically besmirched, we nevertheless should acknowledge his far-reaching impact on the establishment of the nontheological study of religion today. In this sense, it is his editorship of the massive *Encyclopedia of Religion* (New York: Macmillan, 1987) that really sums up the accomplishments and failures of the academic study of religion at the end of the twentieth century.

In short, Eliade often appears to be dismissed because he is an unfashionable and politically incorrect dead white male with an unsavory past, not because of any careful assessment of his approach to the study of religion.[21] As Eliade himself might have bashfully put it, the learned public demands more than clever theories and a cynical hermeneutics of political suspicion in the study of religion. Instead of yesterday's "symbols" and "deep meanings," the graduate students of today are satisfied only with the collapse of religious meaning into the aporia of iconic surfaces, gendered tropes, power politics, performative flux, and pregnant silences. The irony is that Eliade, for all of his dated "essentialist" vocabulary and "phenomenological" concern with intentionality, would probably have agreed with much of this constructivist version of cultural and religious meaning.

Let me only suggest that, in keeping with my own experience, the ongoing significance of an Eliadean approach to the study of religion is its multidisciplinary nature, its unabashedly "comparative" sensibility, its concern for chaotic concreteness over abstract theory, its struggle to combine an outsider's and insider's understanding of religion, its romantic emphasis on the imagination and paradox, its interpretive usefulness (involving such organizing ideas and heuristic devices as "hierophany," "the prestige of creation mythology," "eternal return," "nostalgia for paradise," "the dialectic of sacred and profane," *coincidentia oppositorum,* and "returning to the beginning"), and its "unifying" principle of the "unrecognizability of the sacred."[22] Eliade is interestingly problematic not only because of his early political sympathies, but because he stands on the cusp between the modern (his concern for whispered "deep meanings") and the postmodern (his smiling acceptance of the role of aesthetic artifice and imaginative fabulation in all human meaning). It is not so much that Eliade actually believed in the gods or the sacred, but that he had faith in the human ability to perceive the meaningful strangeness communicated by the language of sounds, surfaces, and texts—that is, his affirmation that the human experience of reality is always clotted with a cosmology of signs and significations. Religion, like culture, has to do with the creative construction of meaning "even when it isn't there."[23] Eliade's approach was always perspectival,

---

21. For the academic politics behind much of the debate about Eliade (and the whole nature of the study of religion), see the journalistic article by Charlotte Allen, "Is Nothing Sacred? Casting Out the Gods from Religious Studies," *Lingua Franca* (November 1996): 30–40.

22. See Ricketts's discussion of the "unrecognizability of the sacred" as a "unifying theme" for Eliade in *Romanian Roots,* II, 1209–1211.

23. *No Souvenirs, Journal 1957–1969.* New York: Harper and Row, 1977, 34 (the entry for January 1, 1960). See also the discussion of this theme in Matei Calinescu, "Introduction, The Fantastic and Its Interpretation in Mircea Eliade's Later Novellas," xiii–xxxix in *Mircea Eliade, Youth Without Youth and Other Novellas.* Columbus: Ohio State University Press, 1988.

perceptional, and ambiguously (to employ an appropriately clumsy term) proto-postmodern. Eliade is not so much the end of the modern, but a partial anticipation of what we have come to call, rather apocalyptically now, postmodernism.[24] Let us therefore make rough and ready use of a rehabilitated and reconstituted Eliade while simultaneously remembering that we should not take such operations too seriously.

Despite all the understandable disappointment, embarrassment, and dismay regarding Eliade, we are incongruously left in a post-Eliadean age that calls for some semblance of an Eliadean approach to the study of religion. It is Eliade's value as a "sign" that continues to have meaning for the study of religions. The sad problem is that, for those who should know better, it is now forbidden that they should in any way invoke the tabooed name. In this sense, it is not so surprising to discover that, recently, only a few controversial and iconoclastic cultural warriors such as Camille Paglia have had the courage to speak appreciatively of Eliade and the importance of the history of religions for any humanistic course of studies.[25]

Let me end these reflections with one last small story. While in the midst of a great weeping and gnashing of teeth over my organization of a strange ritualistic baptism of a new art center at Lehigh University several years ago, I started to have strong misgivings about the whole affair. Perhaps it was best for me simply to stop any involvement in such silly activities that seemed to frighten so many in the university. While brooding about this one early spring morning outside my home along the banks of the Lehigh river, I found myself also trying to decide whether I should go ahead with a poster for the event advertising the appearance of the famous visionary outsider artist from Georgia, Howard Finster. The advertising copy used Finster's self-proclaimed identity as "God's Last Red Light" as a head caption and was printed on bright red stock. Glancing up as I was pondering the

---

24. See especially Rennie's intelligent discussion of Eliade's incipient "postmodernism" in *Reconstructing Eliade*, 213–259.

25. See, for example, Camille Paglia's comments on Eliade and the study of religion in *Vamps and Tramps*. New York: Vintage Books, 1994, 342 and xx–xxi. Besides Rennie's work already mentioned, it is worth citing Douglas Allen's "Recent Defenders of Eliade: A Critical Evaluation," *Religion* 24 (1994): 333–351; David Cave's *Mircea Eliade's Vision for a New Humanism*. New York: Oxford University Press, 1993; Norman Manea's "Happy Guilt: Mircea Elaide, Fascism, and the Unhappy Fate of Romania," *New Republic* (August 5, 1991): 27–36; Matei Calinescu's "Romania's 1930s Revisited," *Salmagundi* 97 (1993): 133–151; Ioan Culianu's "Mircea Eliade at the Crossroads of Anthropology," *Neue Zeitschrift für systematische Theologie und Religionsphilosophie* 27 (1985): 123–131; Carl Olson's *The Theology and Philosophy of Eliade*. New York: St. Martin's Press, 1992; and Daniel Pals's "Reductionism and Belief: An Appraisal of Recent Attacks on the Doctrine of Irreducible Religion," *Journal of Religion* 66 (1986): 18–36.

hue of these words, I suddenly saw a gaudy red cardinal flit in front of me and disappear into the trees toward the back of the house. I was immediately reminded of Eliade's smiling anecdote about cardinals and squirrels in Chicago, which I had written about almost twenty years previously. This ruddy epiphany seemed to me to validate both the advertising copy in my hands and my organization of the overall ritual event. And I suppose that I can say now that it also secretly forecast the writing of this essay. Such is my admittedly imaginative and nostalgic interpretation of this frivolous occurance in my backyard in Pennsylvania. But it is Eliade's inscrutable smile that reminds me that tiny "revelations" like this lie at the germinal core of religious meaning.

Chapter Eleven

METHODOLOGICAL, PEDAGOGICAL, AND PHILOSOPHICAL REFLECTIONS ON MIRCEA ELIADE AS HISTORIAN OF RELIGIONS

WENDELL CHARLES BEANE

ELIADE AND HISTORY-OF-RELIGIONS METHODOLOGY

It would not indeed be surprising if various scholars contemplating just what to do with Eliade were to discover that their task is not to write on behalf of "saving" or not "saving" Eliade, but rather to save themselves.[1] In terms of my own present disposition, it is, admittedly, reminiscent of the figurative remark of Shakespeare's Mark Anthony on the occasion of Caesar's death: that the former had come "to bury Caesar, not to praise him" (Act III, Scene ii). I submit, therefore, that, unlike Max Müller, whose thought some may be inclined to say has been irreverently put to rest, the method, thought, and insights of Mircea Eliade on the nature and study of religion are simply not going to be interred so easily.[2]

---

1. Should we imagine Eliade to be a venerable scholarly "palimpsest," assessing his work could (at the same time) be, as he suggested, like "poring over . . . your own genealogy and the past history of your own self. It is your history" (*Ordeal By Labyrinth: Conversations with Claude-Henri Rocquet*. Chicago: The University of Chicago Press, 1982, 121).

2. For a brief and informative summary of methodological remonstrances and trends illustrative of what I regard as "a premature dirge" for the Eliadean scholarly corpus, as well as other signs of the real precariousness of contemporary studies in religion, see Charlotte Allen, "Is Nothing Sacred?: Casting out the Gods from Religious Studies," *Lingua Franca. The Review of Academic Life* (November 1996): 30–40.

I must begin by insisting that there remains an inseparable relation between the romantic and the historical in the methodological study of the history of religions. The romantic element in the human being, as scholar or popular religionist, reflects the drive or thirst in us for being, meaning, and truth at the level of the universal. Unfortunately, a long-standing, conventional methodological misunderstanding of the term *romantic* is that it refers only to something without a basis in fact, that is, "fanciful," "fictitious," "visionary," or "quixotic." Have we forgotten the subtle historiographic implications of the very existence of the historical novel? "Historical," by contrast, refers to the occurrence of actual events, as opposed to the fictional, legendary, or poetic. While historiography aims to consider such events and their development, it also includes the task of grasping their significance within the larger framework of history as conceived by the historian. But as Eliade earlier noted, it is "the polyvalence of the term 'history' [that] has made it easy for scholars to misunderstand one another here."[3]

Just as Eliade in *Conversations with Claude-Henri Rocquet*, could say that "it is possible to recognize several great biblical myths in Marx and Marxism,"[4] (which has "romantic" overtones), we ought to consider that Eliade's so-called romanticism continues to haunt us because deep within ourselves we sense that his apprehensions and perceptions of what he called the sacred have something to do with unexplored dimensions in our inner being. For the notion of the sacred has not yet been completely shut out of consciousness; but, rather, it lingers due to the fact that it remains the driving force even behind the historicist, functionalist, even positivist critiques of religion. This means, therefore, that to the extent that any scholar or discipline endeavors to encompass the unlimited range of manifestations of religious phenomena in order to "tell the story" (Fr. *roman*) but, now, of what really happened, or what things really mean, through the use of philosophical propositions, historical criteria, or hermeneutical principles, such efforts will tend to reflect certain degrees of "romanticization."[5]

Thus all quests for "meaning, being, and truth" are, basically, "romantic" in orientation. Mircea Eliade's thought, then, reflects and takes account of the fact there is both an exhaustible (i.e., there are "limit-situations") and an inexhaustible (i.e., symbol-systems can "intercommunicate) dimension to the religious experi-

---

3. *Shamanism: Archaic Techniques of Ecstasy*. New York: Pantheon Books, Inc., 1964, xvi.
4. Rocquet, *Ordeal*, 155.
5. For an excellent and concise treatment of the distinction between the "classical" and the "romantic," which throws valuable light on this issue, see Nicolas Berdyaev, *The Beginning and the End*. New York: Harper Torchbooks, 1952, 188–194. He includes this remark: "In reality what really happens is that both ways are combined in human creative activity with some preponderance of one or the other" (193).

ences of human beings rooted in concrete historical reality.⁶ With regard to the tension between "historical consciousness" and "historical understanding," that concreteness has thus been characterized as a certain "historical situatedness."⁷

Eliade's methodology is not in fact anti-historiographic but his historiographic sense reflects a creative dialectic of the romantic and the historiographic, if by romantic one means the human desire—indeed, the human quest—to achieve an "ideal understanding" of religious phenomena;⁸ and thus we are being summoned by Eliade's thought to acknowledge that, to the extent that we are willing to confess that we are in search of such "ideal understanding,"⁹ we need not assume a vehemently antithetical posture before him, the man (though posthumously), and/or his oeuvres. The quest for the ideal understanding of anything or any number of

---

6. See my *Myth, Cult, and Symbols in Sakta Hinduism*. Leiden: E. J. Brill, 1977, 46.

7. Jacob Owensby, *Dilthey and the Narrative of History*. Ithaca and London: Cornell University Press, 1994, 137. On the basis of Peter Novick's remarkable work, *That Noble Dream: The "Objectivity Question" and the American Historical Profession*. Cambridge: Cambridge University Press, 1988, Owensby reminds us of "the declining fortunes of the notion of historical objectivity among professional historians" (137, n.1).

8. Wilhelm Dilthey, whose theory of understanding resembles Eliade's more than the latter seems to have realized says (in his essay, "The Understanding of Other Persons and their Life Expressions," in *Theories of History*, ed. Patrick Gardiner. New York: The Free Press, 1959, 213–225, esp. 219–220; cf. 221f), "[I]f it were possible, in the act of understanding, to set both principles, i.e., the outer principle of individuation, which is the alteration of mental life and its situation by the environment, and the inner principle of individuation, which is the peculiar emphasis of the various elements of the structure, in operation simultaneously, then the understanding of man, of his literary and poetic works, would become the pathway to the great secret of life. And this is in fact the case. In order to realize this, we must call attention to that element of the understanding which admits of no adequate description in logical formulae." Also see Owensby, *Dilthey and the Narrative of History*, 158f.

9. Just how this "ideal understanding" of life and things differs from Dilthey's system of historical understanding cannot be fully developed here. Nonetheless, Owensby's work (*Dilthey and the Narrative of History*) is an enlightening diachronic clarification, showing a potentially renewed relevance of the (recurrently controversial) Diltheyan system. But it is in Owensby's last chapter, "Historical Understanding and Historical Consciousness," where he undertakes a stimulating comparison between Dilthey and Nietzsche, that the apparent difference between Dilthey and Eliade might be discerned. In a word, the latter two, it seems, aver that "we construct the past as a framework for making action meaningful . . . the past is always constituted in its relation to the future, such that our actions are given a coherent context"(179). And they, of course, like Eliade, do not avow any such notion of "the Sacred as a metaphysical referent" (see Paden, in Rennie, *Reconstructing Eliade: Making Sense of Religion*. Albany: State University of New York Press, 1996, 24; cf. 21). Yet while Eliade can point to the venerated past as a coherent "orientation" in relation to which the present and the future can be creatively and meaningfully made "real" (sacred), unlike Nietzsche for whom a deconstructive-transvaluative rupture with the past means that the new breaks with

things, therefore, constitutes the prime archetypal motivation in all of us both as human beings and as scholars.

Thus, the history of religions field encompasses all the histories of the various religious traditions of humankind in their mythic, cultic, and symbolic manifestations, having as its aim the discovery of "universes-of-meaning." The use of the terms *sacred* and *profane*, contrary to what anti-Eliadeans may think, is not well understood should such terms be taken to refer to any rigid isolationist schematic that courts a kind of Cartesian methodological dualism. Hence, I have pointed out elsewhere that it is a matter of the sacred and the profane; and that, with Eliade, it is also not a matter of the past (the archaic) versus the present (the modern).[10] The "sacred" were better understood as phenomenologically descriptive of a qualitative dimension of human experience that Europeans have called "religious"; and the "profane" were better understood as phenomenologically descriptive of a quantitative dimension of human experience (life in the ordinary), which yet "conceals" (Eliade) the potentially "extraordinary."[11]

Eliade's thought thus summons us to a creative hermeneutical rediscovery of the respectability of the romantic dimension of the historical methodological task, not romanticism, as such! Consider the following insight from Fritz Medicus in his essay, "On the Objectivity of Historical Knowledge":

---

the old, Eliade would emphasize the process of "revalorization" (e.g., even the death of the gods does not mean the death of the sacred), whereby the sacred past is somehow newly "reactualized." Dilthey and Eliade, on the other hand, both share (1) an interiorist view of human identity that encompasses both a world-within and a world within-in-relation-to-a world-without (replete with concrete phenomena); and (2) an acceptance of the human capacity to master the art of "reproducing or reliving" the fragments (Dilthey, in Gardiner, 220) or the sacred power (Eliade) experienced by persons in the past through a process of ever-renewed, self-reflective imagination or creativity (Owensby, 153ff.: "*Nacherleben*"); and (3) a final recourse to "hermeneutics" (Owensby, 129ff., 180) as a fruitful enterprise but without the promise of absolute (historical) objectivity, yet a process which never ends. But, fundamentally, while Dilthey sees the presence of "an I-world relation prior to subjectivity" and correlative with a highly psycho-socio-historically conceived "lifenexus"(Owensby, esp. 40–45;72–78), Eliade sees the "sacred," as an original, [not derivative], "structural element of . . . [human] consciousness" (Rocquet, *Ordeal*, 153–154); but which has an ultimate capacity for transconscious ruptures that open the mind to the "Absolute." Importantly, for this term and "transconsciousness," see Guilford Dudley III, *Religion On Trial, Mircea Eliade and His Critics*. Philadelphia: Temple University Press, 1977, 63ff.

10. *Myths, Rites, Symbols: A Mircea Eliade Reader*, 2 Vols., ed. with W. G. Doty. New York: Harper Colophon Books, 1975, 24–25 (in both vols.).

11. On the "Romantic" origins of our modern understanding of "the concept of symbol," see Rennie, *Reconstructing Eliade*, 47f.

> Our statements about life are not "objectively" valid.... The certainty that life has of itself is immediate; and in so far as other certainties build on this one, they are the result of subjective reflection.... The mere getting of information about the external phenomena is not yet historical understanding.... Every present allows of a multitude of reconstructions of the past, each with a different perspective. Presentations of the same material can diverge without really contradicting one another; but they can even be mutually contradictory without one refuting the other.[12]

It is, after all, in this light that one should view the issue regarding Eliade's interpretation of the event of the Australian Achilpa's (Tjilpa's) understanding of the loss of their sacred pole.[13] Furthermore, if Medicus's statement be true, then Bryan Rennie's rebuttal to the claim of pansymbolism, that, then, "nothing can finally be described other than symbolically,"[14] implies its retroactive applicability to other fields of knowledge than religion itself. Not only is this so because, as Rennie says, " 'Reality' is itself an interpretative category," but because one needs finally to recognize the probability that "there is no absolute distinction between human and natural scientific facts. Inner states and physical processes alike may be facts for both types of science."[15]

The Marburg Statement and the Issue of Legitimation[16]

Novick reminds us that "a central problem for any new cognitive structure is to legitimize its epistemological foundation" (*That Noble Dream*, 3). What then was the Marburg Statement—a "Chalcedonian Creed" for the history of religions field?

---

12. In Raymond Klibansky and H. J. Paton, *Philosophy and History: The Ernst Cassirer Festschrift*. New York: Harper and Row, 1963, 138, 145, 147; on Medicus's last sentence, compare a remark by Carl R. Rogers ("Towards a Science of the Person," in T. W. Wann, *Behaviorism and Phenomenology: Contrasting Bases for Modern Psychology*. Chicago: University of Chicago Press, 1964, 129), that "Each Current in psychology has its own implicit philosophy of man.... It is not necessary to deny there is truth in each of these formulations in order to recognize that there is another perspective."

13. See David Cave, *Mircea Eliade's Vision for a New Humanism*, New York, Oxford University Press, 1993, 142–149. Eliade (in Rocquet, *Ordeal*, 143): "If I chanced on an interpretation different from my own, I was glad to find that it was possible to understand a given phenomenon from different viewpoints."

14. *Reconstructing Eliade*, 206. This groundbreaking revisitation of Eliade's methodology has both inspired and facilitated the range of my most recent personal thoughts as reflected in this chapter.

15. Owensby, *Dilthey and the Narrative of History*, 29.

16. See Zwi Werblowsky, "Marburg—and After?" *Numen* 7, 2 (1960): 2–3.

Or was it a methodological-programmatic myth? Was it, then (to paraphrase a memorable statement in Malinowski's definition of myth),[17] an intellectual charter of empiricist faith and methodological wisdom? Historically, we know that "creeds" and "charters," alike, have all been subjected, and oftentimes with good "Enlightenment-Reason," to blistering critiques due to the exigencies of historical change and human need. Can it be that the historians of religions gathered at the Tenth International Congress for the History of Religions[18] (or later echoed at Claremont) dared to imagine that their collectively declared fidelity to the use of scientific empirical methods of investigation of the phenomena of religion meant a commitment to a monolithic perspective of what constitutes "scientism" or "scientificism"; or that the association was to act as "monitor of the legitimacy of [methodological] truth-claims?"[19] I suspect that Eliade's signing of the Marburg statement should be considered in the light of three important considerations: (1) his awareness that "a rigorously scientific discipline" (Dudley) in the most general terms was at least something he could share with other attending scholars as an ideal platform from which to launch a concerted effort to bypass theological entrapment; (2) that in his mind it did not necessarily preclude the factor of "*methodological variability*";[20] and, I venture to say, (3) that an inevitable gerontological factor in the maturation of a historian of religion's thinking should not automatically disqualify that individual from pondering—and for that matter, publishing—what he or she apprehends it has all meant in terms of "being," "meaning," and "truth."[21] Let us also recall that

---

17. Cited in Eliade, *Myth and Reality*. New York: Harper and Row Publishers, 1963, 20.

18. Highlights of the platform's methodological issues are included in Dudley III, *Religion On Trial*, 20ff.

19. Novick (541, 540): recounting the views of "the most prominent antifoundationalist in recent years ... Richard Rorty." On Rorty (and others), William Dean, *History Making History; The New Historicism in American Religious Thought*. New York: State University of New York Press, 1988, 81–97, esp. 86; cf. 123ff. shows that historians themselves need to be concerned about "throwing out the baby with the bath water"; and it also invites a peculiar analogical interpretive interplay of the words *apostasy* and/or *heresy* regarding both the study of history and the study of the history of religions. The question of Eliade and methodological "heresy," as well as "the dogmatic position that the empirical method enjoys in the academy" are alluded to by Dudley III (*Religion on Trial*). "But then," he asks, "what is this heresy in the broader epistemological context of interpretation and understanding?" (118).

20. Beane, *Myth, Cult, and Symbols*, 17.

21. If, as it appears, Eliade used these terms after he signed the Marburg statement, it may reflect a (philosophical) shift in his field-understanding, but one that he did not thereafter develop systematically, even though they may be intentionally related to his use of language in "Methodological Remarks" and his "Observations on Religious Symbolism," i.e., "philosopher of religion"; "religious philosophy." Beane and Doty, eds., *Myths, Rites, Symbols*, II, 461.

within the phenomenological movement itself it has long been recognized that there continue to be variations in methodological orientation even with a larger concerted commitment to certain principles.[22] Spiegelberg himself notes that among at least seven of those principles three of them are implicitly generally accepted, but that the remaining ones are not accepted by all.[23] But this does not mean that no inroads into further understanding can be achieved by those exploring other methodological componential options.

All this is inseparably related to the issue of "legitimation," which refers to what is reasonable, logically correct, or justifiable in accordance with certain established rules, standards, or principles. However, the concept of legitimation is always subject to the same tension between synchronicity and diachronicity that the very Euro-American natural-scientific-historical tradition has predominantly espoused. Hence, as there are probably no political "Constitutions" that have not in the course of their historical development been subject to amendments, there are also probably no "Statements" of humanistic or religious purposes that have not felt the impact of what I prefer to call "historical change and human need." Marburg, therefore, represented a noble attempt on the part of virtual intellectual giants collectively to affirm, clarify, and safeguard certain principles and goals of research in the study of religious phenomena. This, of course, included (as aforementioned) the effort to bypass the temptation to "theologize" one's way through the superabundant maze of ideas, forms, and expressions and somehow to establish a unanimous commitment to a sound methodological-empirical enterprise. Yet, in the face of historical change and human need, can we honestly say that the scholars who decry Eliade the most have, on purely historicist, functionalist, even positivist grounds, given in any remarkable way a decisive thrust to the methodological progress already made in the discipline of the history of religions?[24]

---

22. S. H. Clark, *Paul Ricoeur*. New York: Routledge, Chapman, and Inc. 1990, 19, 24.

23. Herbert Spiegelberg, *The Phenomenological Movement: An Historical Introduction*, Vol. II. The Hague: Martinus Nijhoff, 1963, 653–701.

24. Hence Eliade's remark on "hermeneutical advance." *The Quest*, Chicago: University of Chicago Press, 1969, 36. Perhaps what might seem at first glance to be a potentially ground-breaking advance is explored by Hans H. Penner, "Holistic Analysis: Conjectures and Refutations," *Journal of the American Academy of Religion* 62, 4 (Winter 1994), 977–996. It appears that the "holistic implications," in principle, for the study of religion are generally helpful (pending the acceptance of the validity of a thesis of "the holistic, semantic, field of propositional attitudes" (990), his "principle of charity" being more acceptable (981ff.). However, with regard to this new "holism" as having anti-Eliadean implications (989), and esp. Penner's repetition of the typically erroneous (but probably widespread) negative dialectical understanding of sacred/profane (991), i.e., as if it were an "epistemic dualism," (978; cf. 987ff.), I have critical reservations: (1) it is not conclusive that Eliade's own idea of the

Should we not take all this seriously, then let us consider something more: that there may well be an analogical connection between a type of theological thinking and the type of historicist thinking that will prove rather ironic but certainly detrimental to the history of religions field. David Tracy, in his *The Analogical Imagination*, distinguishes three types of theological thinking: the foundational, the systematic, and the practical.[25] While all three of Tracy's "theologies" are related in some way to "a particular religious tradition," it is essentially the foundational type of theology that represents the tendency toward "the repetition of a *"traditionality of opinion"*[26] such as is held by normatively oriented religious institutions, in contrast to the "systematic" type that allows itself to "focus upon reinterpretation and new applications of tradition for the present."[27] Historians of religions should thus be wary of the possibility that in their well-nigh antiromantic approach to the study of religious phenomena, they do not lock themselves within a form of traditionality of methodological opinion to the extent that they are worthy of being designated as "methodological foundationalists" (but in the "fundamentalistic sense") when, in fact, what is needed is a creative hermeneutic much as Eliade espoused and embodied. For his methodological perspective was one wherein and whereby an acknowledged aspect of what it is to be human is linked to a positive apprehension of all other human and nonhuman phenomena (whether graphic, historiographic, or ideographic), to the extent that the Kitagawan "methodological schizophrenia" is assuaged.

---

sacred itself has no holistic implications if it is understood in Rennie's terms; see also *Reconstructing Eliade*, 27–42; note there: "heuristic device"; (2) the presence of "supernatural beings" as an entailed but exceptional, uniqueness-making component of "religious propositional attitudes" and as a feature for "our field of study . . . set[ting] it apart from other cognitive studies" (989) would seem noncontradistinctive since it is also integral to Eliade's "the sacred"; (3) the approach's one-dimensional, linguistic quality (993–995) is not even commensurate with symbolic-linguistic trends for understanding the nature of reality in modern physics; and (4) although it escapes radical positivism (narrowly), by insisting on an alternative yet irreducible datum: "natural, everyday truth-conditional semantics," it could paint itself into a corner; for instance, hypothetically, what would the implications be for a thesis of "the holistic, semantic, field of propositional attitudes" if in the near future an authenticated connection were established between the now phenomenologically understood experience of shamanic ecstasy and what is currently incubating in medical and psychological circles as the near-death and/or the out-of-the-body experience? That connection is dispassionately explored by Kenneth Ring, "Shamanic Initiation, Imaginal Worlds, and Light after Death," in *What Survives? Contemporary Explorations of Life after Death*, ed. Gary Doore, Los Angeles: Jeremy P. Tarcher, Inc., 1990, 204–215; 285.

25. New York: Crossroad (1981), Pt. I:2.
26. Beane, *Myth, Cult, and Symbols*, 71; italics added.
27. Tracy, *The Analogical Imagination*, 58.

It is indeed the sacred, in the sense in which Eliade uses the term, that opens to us the hermeneutic possibility of legitimately entertaining a theology of the history of religions, but not a history-of-religions-theology.[28] It is, of course, a history of religions theology of which Eliade has so often been accused; but it is actually a theology of the history of religions that the Eliadean perspective makes possible. In the more legitimate sense of the latter, there is implied that there is a necessary interdisciplinary foundation to any history of religions methodology. And I have lately been researching with increasing conviction the possibility that there may be some relevance of that interdisciplinary aspect to the current movement of "interreligious dialogue."

ELIADE AND HISTORY-OF-RELIGIONS PEDAGOGY

This is essentially a personal turn in this overall essay. As I contemplate the influence that Eliade has had on my teaching experience, two things come to mind. First, I wonder whether there are others, like myself, who may be undertaking such a testimony for the very first time in writing. Second, I have rediscovered what all serious teachers-and-scholars already know: that there tends to be a highly dynamic and creative tension between what one writes and what happens in the classroom, and vice versa.[29] In order to encapsulate, pedagogically, the sweep of Eliade's influence on me personally, I should say that it includes the following emphases: (1) the concept of the "sacred"; (2) the phenomenon of structures and changes in the history of religions; (3) the preeminence of the cosmogonic myth in the shaping of cultural worldviews; (4) the role of initiation in the transformation of human character; and (5) the element of creativity in the life of religious beings.

---

28. The statement that "there's the academic study of religion, and there's the religious study of religion—we believe in the academic study of religion (Donald Wiebe, in Allen, "Is Nothing Sacred" [supra, n.2], 32) is a blatant oversimplification of the issue, especially when one considers that the meanings of such terms are hardly static, that the term *academic* itself (Gr. *Akademia*) has a history, and that in the realm of contemporary pedagogy, it becomes an even more tenuous description of a "delicate balance" of influences. See Conrad Cherry, "Boundaries and Frontiers for the Study of Religion: The Heritage of the Age of the University," *Journal of the American Academy of Religion* LVII, 4 (Winter 1989), 823–824.

29. In commenting on "the didactic character of Eliade's work," at an earlier phase of his own studies, Lawrence Sullivan wrote that various general works, such as Eliade's *From Primitives to Zen*, "are service manuals which guide students through a labyrinth of materials and help younger scholars study religion as a whole"; in Lawrence Sullivan, "History of Religions: The Shape of An Art," in *What Is Religion: An Inquiry for Christian Theology*, ed. Mircea Eliade and David Tracy. New York: The Seabury Press, 1980, 82, 83, and n.20.

The Sacred

This category, which includes Eliade's concept of the "ambivalence of the sacred" and the nature of sacred symbols,[30] has been of invaluable help in introducing students to the larger world of humankind's religious experience; first, because it is a category that they have variously encountered in diverse contexts, sacred or (disguised as the) profane. Whether referring to something just "dear to the heart" or something outlandish to the mind, the notion of the sacred tends, consciously or unconsciously, to conjure up ideas of the qualitative value of a thing or a personal experience that stands apart from other "ordinary" experiences. Pedagogues who are wary of students being misled must consider that the idea of the sacred is itself a methodological metaphor. It is a metaphor for whatever Aboriginals, or any other religious beings, considered to be taboo on the one hand, and magnetic on the other. If the phenomenology of the sacred is as broad as Rennie says it is,[31] is also includes the Eliadean idea of the multivalence of sacred symbols ranging from personalistic conceptualizations (sky-gods/earth-mothers; "faineant" supreme beings/orishas), all the way to primal principles or, even, a pancosmic force (*Brahman*). But it matters not as long as the multiapplicability of the term *sacred* allows students both to associate that concept of the sacred with something in particular and/or with something that "is manifested"[32] through a form (hence: Eliade's "ambivalence of the sacred"); or something that can "affect my own individual life."[33] Yet a teacher must recognize that while it may be something that can be humanistically (intellectually) appreciated, it need not be something that can be personally (religiously) incorporated.

Structures and Changes in the History of Religions[34]

Eliade's essay strongly suggests "the ineradicable role which religion has played in the evolution of the human mind";[35] and it should, therefore, allow for the

---

30. *The Two and the One*. Chicago: University of Chicago Press, 1965, chap. V: esp., 201–208.

31. Hence, Rennie's response (*Reconstructing Eliade*, 98) to George Weckman, is that, for Eliade, " 'Sacred History' refers to that which is perceived as the real conditioning antecedent, thus myths about *illud tempus*, the Hebrew *Heilsgeschichte*, and finally the "plenary" history of the historicists, are all 'sacred history.' "

32. For the issue regarding the two usages, i.e., "is manifested"/"manifests itself," see Rennie, *Reconstructing Eliade*, 19.

33. Eliade, in Rocquet, *Ordeal*, 130.

34. in C. H. Kraeling and R. M. Adams, eds., *City Invincible*. Chicago: University of Chicago Press, 1960, 351–366.

35. Beane and Doty, eds., *Myths, Rites, Symbols*, Vol. II, 465.

making of tentative generalizations on vital historical-cultural-religious orientations.[36] Hence,

> [T]he truly amazing fact [is] that *an original dialectic of the sacred* occurred in the mind of humanity about their relation to the concrete landscape. This "landscape mysticism"... reveal[ed] itself... under the form of certain economico-religious orientations which may conveniently be delineated as (1) a mananimal solidarity... (2) a woman-plant mysticism... and (3) a man-woman, pastoral-agricultural complementarity.[37]

Eliade's view of these primary three "cultural moments" in human evolution (the Palaeolithic, Mesolithic, Neolithic, respectively) thus provides the teacher with a handy pedagogical paradigm[38] with which to affirm and describe to students the way in which humankind did in fact need religion as a sacred context in which to enshroud and enhance its unique survivability, adaptability, and creativity. Although we cannot really answer the question whether the emergence of *homo sapiens* and the religious consciousness was an absolutely synchronous event, we can at least say that, even if this is not the case, there was a time in history when "man-the-hunter became man-the-religious-hunter; woman-the-agriculturalist became woman-the-religious-agriculturalist."[39]

But more important is the way in which we can, anthropologically, still discern meaningful "survivals" of such primordial orientations. For when my students are asked to ponder the significance of the reference of John the Baptist to Jesus of Nazareth as "the *lamb* of God" (John 1:29; cf. Lev. 16)—even the symbolic nominals and mascots of our national athletic emblems—against the background of the archaic-totemic legacy of their forebears—the radiance of their countenances as they make the cultural-religious connection (or "revalorization" for Eliade) reminds one of nothing less than the amazement with which Helen Keller finally made the

---

36. Beane, in *Myths, Rites, Symbols*, xxvi.

37. See W. C. Beane, "Archaic Sacred Values and the Modern World," in *Communication* 4, 1 (1979) [49–72]: 59.

38. Eliade, *A History of Religious Ideas I*. Chicago: University of Chicago Press, 1978, 22–52. In *Myths, Dreams, and Mysteries*. New York: Harper Torchbooks, 1967, 178, he remarks, quite objectively, that "[w]e have no proof that religious structures are created by certain types of civilization or by certain historic moments. All one can say is that the predominance of this or that religious structure is occasioned or favored by a certain kind of civilization or by a certain historic moment."

39. Beane and Doty, eds., *Myths, Rites, Symbols*, Vol. II, 465. Theologians of orthodox persuasion, of course, will be inclined to maintain that humankindness and human religiosity were indeed absolutely synchronous phenomena as part of a unique act of creation within a monotheistic worldview.

association between her experience of sonic vibrations and the miraculous "feel" of water!

The fact that each of these otherwise "profane" cultural moments in world history underwent what I call "vital religious valorizations" means that it does not pay for the skeptic or the relativist merely to assert that humankind might well have done as well or better had the primeval, numinous landscape been experienced without any religious responses from prehistoric beings. The fact remains that humankind is what it is because it "refused to see nature as mere stones, bones and grass."[40]

THE PREEMINENCE OF THE COSMOGONIC MYTH

This element includes Eliade's insight into the ongoing validity of the "prestige of origins" and the existential validity concerning "the myth of the eternal return." The creation myths of civilization tend to lay out not only the foundations of the universe but also provide clues to the nature of human nature and the nature of human destiny.[41] But whether in religion (or developmental psychology for that matter) the return to "origins" constitutes a logotherapeutic review of one's history in order to reestablish one's being. This is certainly true among the three great "exclusive monotheisms" of Judaism, Christianity, and Islam. Of course, in the case of the Orient, we are presented with a medley of cosmogonic myths, alongside others that allow for no absolute beginnings, or, otherwise, entertain cyclical beginnings. In any case, however, the end of things (whether eschatologically or yugically conceived) tends to be explicitly or implicitly present in the beginning of things.[42] The Omega of history tends to be ensconced in the Alpha of history.

With regard to "the myth of the eternal return," there are those who have accused Eliade of having arbitrarily assigned what it essentially a progressive (noncyclical) Christian ritual to a foreign (archaic) world view. In fact, Eliade shows us how the Christian redemptive Eucharistic event (which, symbologically, includes the vital elements of creation, revelation, and redemption) both carries over and bypasses its archaic original heritage.[43] The Christian Eucharistic event, while theo-

---

40. Beane and Doty, eds., *Myths, Rites, Symbols*, Vol. II, 464.

41. Rocquet, *Ordeal*, 144; but then, Eliade notes that "the myth of the creation of the world does not always look like a cosmogonic myth, *stricto sensu* . . . ," *The Quest*, 75ff.; in this regard, see Dudley III, *Religion on Trial*, 73; and Beane, *Myth, Cult, and Symbols*, 175ff. for a Hindu exemplification.

42. "Even . . . the seeds of the destructiveness of the Kali Yuga are already sown in the Krita Yuga itself by virtue of the spiritual impoverishment implied in its potential for temporal diminution"; Beane, "The Nature and Meaning of Modern Religious Experience," *World Faiths Insight*, New Series 6 (January 1983): 24.

43. See Beane and Doty, eds., *Myths, Rites, Symbols*, I, 78ff.

logically understood to celebrate a unique—one time—occurrence of a redemptive theophany within a unilateral theory of historical time, nonetheless recurs within the calendrical cycle of "rehearsed" sacred events as a regenerative source of sacred power. It is, thus, phenomenologically a liturgical recurrence and not a historical recurrence, but this does not rule out the possibility that in the act of faith it can become a *reactualization* (Eliade) of sacred power. In this way the archaic and the postarchaic, the valorized and the revalorized, the linear and the cyclical aspects of supernatural *gesta* can be commonly yet variously understood and appreciated.

The Role of Initiation in the Transformation of Human Character

This aspect of Mircea Eliade's teaching has come home to a modern generation of adults many of whom can testify that, as young people, they did not really experience the typical processes of traditional initiations with the impact of living drama. And, in large measure, their children are growing in a world of technological wonders without experiencing the wonder of ontological transformation.[44] No doubt, in numerous cases, the recourse to the college or university fraternity/sorority, if not the "urban gang" is often all that many young people have left. With this last, oftentimes tragic, admixture of loyalty and violence such situations may seem to manifest not the mere "unrecognizability" but, indeed, the death of "miracle."[45] Having defined initiation as a religious phenomenon denoting "a body of rites and oral teachings whose purpose is to produce a decisive alteration in the religious and social status of the person to be initiated" ... [that individual] "has become *another*,"[46] Eliade later adds that

> initiation lies at the core of any genuine human life ... for two reasons. The first is that any genuine human life implies profound crises, ordeals, suffering, loss and reconquest of self, "death and resurrection." The second is that, whatever degree of fulfillment it may have brought him, at a certain moment every man sees his life as a failure.... The hope and dream of these moments of total crisis are to obtain a definitive and total *renovatio*, a renewal capable of transmuting life. Such a renewal is the result of every genuine religious conversion.[47]

---

44. See the subsection, "Initiation Into a Mode of Being," in Rennie's *Reconstructing Eliade*, 239–241.

45. Ierunca, "The Literary Work of Mircea Eliade," 347; see also Rennie, *Reconstructing Eliade*, 217f.: "The fact that the sacred fails to be manifested in certain experiences to certain people is ... characteristic of their religious culture ..."; Eliade, on loving (in Rocquet, *Ordeal*, 170), "the only form of behavior that really enables one to cope with evil ..."

46. *Rites and Symbols of Initiation*. New York: Harper Torchbooks, 1958, x.

47. *Rites and Symbols of Initiation*, 135.

To a large extent, though psychological studies (from the time of Freud)[48] reveal a certain acquaintance with lifecrises, even as they relate to religion, it may very well have been feminist theologians and writers who called our attention back to this largely "forgotten world" of initiations when they sought to revalorize the functions of "woman as religious symbol" in the history of religious thought and experience.[49] Be that as it may, informal censuses in my classes over the years have borne out the need for some kind of symbolic gestures that can at least approach the ontological significance that Eliade attributes to the role of the initiatic in human experience. For my students have almost unanimously favored some kind of special (ritual) valuation of life transitions for the young, even if among its dynamics, it should happen to fall short of, say, traumatic separation from the mother, a knocking out of a tooth, or the hearing of nightmarish sounds as among some tribal religions. To cite a single instance, in one class, entitled "Woman as Religious Symbol" (which I taught at Rutgers University), a student (on the occasion of her first experience of the menstrual cycle) told of having shared a festive meal with her family, received gifts, and an enlargement of social privileges by her parents. Of course, there are those who may say that this, minus what Eliade calls the ritual of an agony, a death, and a resurrection, was but a trivialization of a rite-of-passage tradition, and that it was certainly not tantamount to a remystification of a vital sacred function because it probably lacked the elements of traumatization and transformation associated with traditional *rites de passage*. But who is to say that what took place in what seems a largely interpersonal and communal context was not a creative and meaningful "survival" of what our ancestors intended.[50]

The Element of Creativity

This emphasis in Eliade's work can hardly be overestimated, for it means that, for him, the history of religious ideas includes an "occasionalistic" factor in that it involves an appreciation not only for what historical existence did to humankind but what humankind did for history:[51]

---

48. See "Traditional Techniques for 'Going Back,' " in Beane and Doty, eds., *Myths, Rites, Symbols*, 174ff.; on suffering, Vol.II, 430-431.

49. See, for instance, Penelope Washbourn's "Becoming Woman: Menstruation as Spiritual Experience," in Carol P. Christ, *Womanspirit Rising: A Feminist Reading in Religion*. New York: Harper and Row, 1979, 246–258.

50. See Eliade's (Rocquet, *Ordeal*, 158) comments on "dymystification" even within a rite of passage.

51. Beane, *Myth, Cult, and Symbols*, 11. Rennie, *Reconstructing Eliade*, 222, states the uncreative antithesis as "History is seen as making humanity rather than humanity as making history."

> [T]he revolutionary changes brought about in the economic realm and in social organization as a result of the development from the phase of food-gathering and hunting to that of proto-agriculture did condition the new religious valorizations of the world, but they did not "cause" them in the *deterministic* sense of the term. It is not the natural phenomenon of vegetation which is responsible for the appearance of mythico-religious systems of agrarian structure but rather the religious experience *occasioned* by the discovery of a mystical solidarity between [wo]man and plant life.[52]

The matter of archaic human creativity has, therefore, been restated this way:

> Traditionalist peoples' anticipations or apprehensions about that other dimension of Nature and of human nature (= the sacred) which occasions awe *and* devotion . . . were to them experiences which they allowed to influence, decisively, their conceptions of the world. It was not enough for them to *think*. To think at all was to think *creatively*, and it was at bottom the creative aspect of their approach to *the man-transcending-in-the-Given* that accounts for their display of a depth of mythical thought that surpasses some of our own.[53]

Pedagogically, all the previous emphases in Eliade's history of religions corpus no doubt confirm the manifest creativity with which he himself sought to approach the relations between history and religion, humankind and nature, and religion and culture. Such emphases, once again, establish the need to affirm the ineradicable role that religion has played in the evolution of the human mind. They also reconfirm in the light of our present time of technological revolution that modern humans are always in need of experiencing an *anamnesis* of the sacred.[54]

Like Freud, who became identified with the idea that humankind has suffered an "ontological shock" (ultimately symbolized by the reality of death), Eliade has seemingly caused various scholars, though impressed by his brilliance, to suffer a form of "methodological shock," insofar as they expected him to lead them further into the epistemological luxuries of the Enlightenment when it concerns making

---

52. *City Invincible*, 359. Italics added.

53. Beane, "Archaic Sacred Values," 52.

54. In an extremely penetrating essay, "Silence and Signification" (in Kitagawa and Long, *Myths and Symbols*, 146), which Charles H. Long subtitles "A Note on Religion and Modernity," he reflects on our present generation by noting that "it is not strange that in the nineteenth century, when the Western world admitted the death of its God, that at just this moment Western man sought him not in his own traditions and cultures but in the cultures of primitive and archaic peoples. It was from this silence that he tried to evoke once again *a sign of intimacy and relatedness to ontological meaning*." Italics added.

progress in understanding religious phenomena. Eliade, it turns out, seems to have "lived in another world."[55] Indeed, he tells us in his *No Souvenirs* that "my students seem to be saying: Give us a method and we will explain everything, we will understand everything."[56] In terms of the pedagogical impact he has made on the American scene, many students (which includes those taught directly or indirectly by him) continue to view him as having offered us a truly long-lasting methodological paradigm. Others, of course, have trepidatiously come to feel that they cannot methodologically go where he has gone without coming to grips with something in themselves that has decisive kinship with the so-called romantic; and others, still, have suffered a type of epistemological disillusionment[57] that has either led them into a form of quasitheological retreat (courting an "ecclesiastical" version of the Holy) or into another potential source of methodological danger—the temptation to capitulate without qualification to what is often called the "scientific" study of religion.

ELIADE AND THE HISTORIAN OF RELIGIONS AS PHILOSOPHER

> [T]he historian of religions also is led to systematize the results of his findings and to reflect on the structure of the religious phenomena. But then he completes his historical work as phenomenologist or philosopher of religion. In the broad sense of the term, the science of religions embraces the phenomenology as well as the philosophy of religion.[58]

> [R]eligion . . . does not necessarily imply belief in God, gods, or ghosts, but refers to the experience of the sacred, and, consequently, is related to the idea of *being*, *meaning*, and *truth*.[59]

Eliade opened the door to the prospect for the history of religions discipline to encounter philosophical questions when he said that "the historian of religions

---

55. See Novick, 526–537, esp. 531, on paradigm shifts. For his mention of Eliade, see ibid., 3.

56. *No Souvenirs, Journal, 1957–1969.* New York: Harper and Row, 1977, 2f.

57. Of course, there is always the recourse to what Nelson Goodman (Novick, 539) in another context calls, "a policy common in daily life and impressively endorsed by modern science: namely, judicious vacillation." This view, however, would need to be critically considered alongside Guilford Dudley III's in his *Religion on Trial*, 135ff.

58. Mircea Eliade and J. M. Kitagawa, eds., *The History of Religions: Essays in Methodology.* Chicago: University of Chicago Press, 1959, 88; in *The Two and the One*, the historian of religions "is completing his task as historian by a task of phenomenology or religious philosophy." It is hard not to infer that this requires a cumulative fund of reflective experience in the field.

59. Eliade, *The Quest* (Preface); *The History of Religious Ideas*, Vol. I (Preface).

completes his work as philosopher of religion." Here, however, we must note two very important things. One is that the use of "a task of phenomenology" requires that we remember that phenomenology itself is a *philosophical* methodology; but Eliade implies a decisive dimension of ultimacy by adding "or *religious* philosophy." Another is that it is not necessary in Eliade's case, as a historian of religions, to confine an assessment of his implicit understanding of the rubric "religious philosophy" solely to his phenomenological studies in their discernibly "descriptive" aspects. For it is highly probable that Eliade was speaking in a rather unselfconsciously "prophetic" way when he wrote those words.[60] He himself, then, had not undertaken to publish a philosophically focused self-assessment; and so during his "Conversations with Claude-Henri Rocquet," he was careful at one point in an extended answer to Rocquet's question, "But what is its [hermeneutics'] criterion of truth?" to say, "This is a purely a personal statement, mark you, and I am not presenting it as the *philosophical* consequence of my work as a historian of religions."[61] Nonetheless, the truly amazing thing is that it is in those "Conversations" that Eliade as philosophical historian of religions shines through so markedly. To those who might claim that looking for that aspect of Eliade should be confined to his scholarly works, let it be noted that, there, in those works, philosophical (not theological) intimations abound, though not, apparently, so profusely as in his novels. But the truth is that it is in the "Conversations" that Rocquet elicited from Eliade the very philosophical convictions or bases upon which he wrote about humankind's earliest historical-cultural-religious orientations.[62]

One of the best instances where Eliade exemplifies the historian of religions as philosopher outside the "Conversations" is a subsection of his *Myths, Dreams, and Mysteries*, entitled "Religious Symbolism and the Modern Man's Anxiety."[63] Calling our attention to a subtle analogy between Europe's folklorist *anamnesis* at the moment of death, Eliade likens Western civilization's obsession with historiography, "the historiographic consciousness of Europe," to an archaic human being's remembrance of everything just before foundering on the edge of death. Eliade is

---

60. Eliade to Rocquet (*Ordeal*, 187): "Your questions have sometimes forced me to rethink certain problems. In a way, you have forced me to recall large areas of my life. Too large, perhaps? That is the danger. . . . One cannot go deeply into everything one says." Did this include the "task of phenomenology" or/as "religious philosophy"?

61. Rocquet, *Ordeal*, 130, 131; italics added. He further says (132): "I made the decision long ago to maintain a kind of discreet silence as to what I personally believe or don't believe."

62. See Eliade, in Rocquet, *Ordeal*, 54–60: for "India's Three Lessons," esp., "the third discovery" (55f.).

63. *Myths, Dreams, and Mysteries*, 231–245.

careful, however, to specify that by "modern man" he means the man of unfaith, without "any living attachment to Judaeo-Christianity"; here: "the *Idolatry* of history."[64] Yet Eliade is not satisfied merely to label modern humankind's obsession in this manner without hope. *Angst* can be meaningfully overcome through its encounter with *anamnesis*. Modern humankind, too, is therefore capable of experiencing "a rebirth or resurrection," typically understood "as a rite of passage to another mode of being . . . [for even] Death [can be] the Great Initiation."[65]

This hope, then, that Eliade envisions is not one wherewith modern humankind should retreat into deeper anxiety and despair. Rather, it is a hope that would recapture "the attitude revealed by Krishna to Arjuna in the *Bhagavad-Gita*: namely, that of remaining in the world and participating in History, but taking good care not to attribute to History any absolute value."[66]

Although Eliade's writing here has a romantic-prophetic tone, it is really nondoctrinaire in its implicit philosophical force. Yet it may well also exemplify, again, his paradoxical nature as a scholar because of what seems its descriptive-normative tone.[67] And this particular tone I regard as pervasively epitomized in Eliade's use of the term: *the sacred*.[68] Now, this insistence on "the sacred" I regard as the minimally imperative intrusion of a proto-normative element in a field in which, eventually and inevitably, "the historian of religions recognizes a spiritual unity subjacent to the history of humanity" (*Quest*, 69). Here, I suspect that just as he alludes to the use of ancient Greek motifs (e.g., the Oedipus myth by Freud) to explicate modern humankind's psychological condition, perhaps Eliade was also thinking that the historian of religions' "task of phenomenology" is to present modern scholars of various disciplines still inquiring into the nature of human nature with a variety of optional models (Eurasian, African, Oceanian) for their reflection. But it certainly does not follow that the historian of religions must be committed to the monumentalization of philosophical neutrality, as if such a state of "disinterested scholarship"[69] were the pinnacle of academic achievement.

---

64. *Myths, Dreams, and Mysteries*, 242; see esp., his rendering of "two distinct ways" with reference to "modern man's passionate, almost abnormal interest in History," 233f.

65. *Myths, Dreams, and Mysteries*, 231, 234, 235, 242.

66. *Myths, Dreams, and Mysteries*, 242. The word "absolute" here is not, as some suppose, used in an antihistorical sense. For Eliade's essential objections to historicism, see Rennie, *Reconstructing Eliade*, 222.

67. Dudley III's brief discussion of this perspective (*Religion on Trial*, 135–138) is extremely crucial to my view of Eliade here.

68. See Rennie's incisive treatment of the controversy surrounding this term (*Reconstructing Eliade*, Pt. I: 1–3 et passim).

69. See "Consensus and Legitimation," in Novick, *That Noble Dream*, 61–85.

Toward what end, then, does the historian of religions study so many religious traditions? What does she do with the discovery that there are so many similar patterns and symbolic expressions of religious experience in the world? Does his historical-methodological commitment preclude the responsibility to ponder answers to a few of the very great questions of human existence, such as, What is the nature of reality?[70] What is the nature of human nature? What is the nature of human destiny? Reminiscent of Eliade and implying the "responsibility to ponder," Kurt Rudolf says that

> [a]lmost every term used in religio-historical work leads *out of the sphere* of the specialist's competence to *universal* questions which only the historian of religions can and should answer.... In the final analysis the object of study itself... calls for a science that encompasses and unites several methods of study. Such a study portends a needed and promising corrective to the increasing specialization of our age.[71]

To the question concerning the end toward which the study of so many religious traditions thrusts the historian of religions, I must first answer that it is to grasp and appreciate the structure and content of particular religious traditions; and, again, to compare and systematize those ideas and expressions in order to make such findings available to experts in other disciplines (i.e., theology, philosophy, science). Eliade's statements, therefore, support the position that the historian of religions has no irrefutable reason, permanently, to stay "out of the sphere" of normative philosophical contemplation. One might say that Eliade was the major scholarly force in laying the foundation for the integration of philosophy into the history of religions field. But I suspect, however, that Eliade was, consciously or unconsciously, aware that the cumulative effects of so much study naturally leads one into another dimension of scholarly experience: reflection. Moreover, if it be true that the more history-of-religions research one does, reflection becomes inevitable, then, perhaps, there is something inherent in the quest for such knowledge itself that motivates the transition from history-of-religions studies to "philosophical-religious" reflection.[72] And philosophical-religious reflection need not mean reflection within a field of dogmatic "preunderstanding," or "imposition," but, rather, a reflection that itself constitutes a creative exploratory process whose ultimate

---

70. In "Structures and Changes in the History of Religions" (Keeling, 366), Eliade used the terms *reality, truth, and meaning.*

71. *Historical Fundamentals and the Study of Religions.* New York: Macmillan Publishing Company, 1985, 58.

72. This obviously controversial remark would have radical implications for the tenor of any Marburg platform-revisited.

"end" remains unknown but perpetually open. Paul Tillich, in his essay, "The Significance of the History of Religions for the Systematic Theologian," remarks that "[t]he universality of a religious statement does not lie in an all-embracing abstraction which would destroy religions as such but in the depths of every concrete religion. Above all, it lies in the *openness* to spiritual freedom both *from* one's own foundation and *for* one's own foundation."[73]

Nonetheless, in conjunction with the question of the existence of so many resemblant patterns (or homologous structures) of religious experience and expression, it appears that such patterns are to be made known to theologians, especially, in order to allow them the opportunity to consider what their potentially ecumenical significance might be in the light of current interreligious dialogue.[74] But as to the question of whether the historian of religions has the responsibility to ponder answers to (any) of life's great questions, it appears that Eliade has to have understood "phenomenology" in a rather complex way to envision or to have used such phrases as "philosopher of religion," or "religious philosophy." In a word, it is a phenomenology that includes morphology, empiricism, epistemology, and hermeneutics.[75]

When Eliade, therefore, called for a "New Humanism," it would be "new" not only because it was not to be understood as a humanism in tension with "Religion" but rather a humanism that equates true humanity with true religion.[76] It would be new mainly because the searching scholar recognizes himself or herself in that very "historical situatedness" (Owensby) that so envelops us but which need not prevent us from developing a profounder understanding of humankind. Although in his most extensive excursus into the nature and ramifications of Eliade's theme of a New Humanism, David Cave concedes that the problem of nonfalsifiability remains, he insists that Eliade's larger purpose was to deal with a post-Enlightenment, twentieth-century "scientific technocracy" that engendered "a crisis of meaning and the absence of the transcendent. The root of this crisis was religious and its solution, Eliade believed, was also religious."[77] What is otherwise significant is that Eliade was not trying to interpolate the Christian "Incarnation" doctrine into his religious

---

73. Kitagawa, *The History of Religions: Essays*, 255; italics added (see Tillich's "fourth [systematic] presupposition," 242); "from one's own foundation" here could apply to any field, organization, or program that were conceived as capable of continuity-and-change.

74. See, for example, Gerald D. Gort et al., eds., *On Sharing Religious Experience: Possibilities of Interfaith Mutuality*. Grand Rapids, MI: Wm. B. Eerdmans Publishing Company, 1992); for Eliade's envisioning of the ecumenical possibility, see Rocquet, *Ordeal*, 107.

75. See Lawrence Sullivan, "History of Religions: The Shape of An Art," 83.

76. Note that Eliade can speak of "the true Asiatic, African or Oceanian . . ." in *Myths, Dreams, and Mysteries*, 244.

77. *Mircea Eliade's Vision for a New Humanism*, 93–94; and 25.

studies as some of his detractors have assumed merely on the basis of his Eastern Christian heritage. Yet what remains important for the history of religions discipline is the prospect that the *sophos* dimension of philosophy can be considered relevant to the discipline because, if with all our scholarly monographs we have not understood our species so much better, it may be due to the fact that we have shied away from where the cumulative evidence has been leading us. Not willing to consider the possibility (to use a favorite word of historian of religions, Charles H. Long) that the term *sacred* refers to an experienceable Unknown, as well as the "hierophanic" known, we have hesitated to make even tentative philosophical religious generalizations; not willing to consider that "*homo faber* was equally *homo ludens, sapiens*, and *religiosus*" (Eliade),[78] we have shied away from making tentative philosophical-anthropological valuations of the nature of human nature; not willing to consider that destiny does not always mean predestination, we have turned away from making tentative philosophicalethical revalorizations of archaic sacred values in relation to contemporary ideas of being, meaning, and truth.

In terms of the relation of the historian of religions to such philosophical concerns as "being," "meaning," and "truth," I propose the following philosophical-religious correlations, or vital links, between philosophy and the history of religions: being/consciousness, meaning/creativity, and truth/values. Since none of these elements is legitimately monopolized by either philosophy or religion, one must presuppose that here one is dealing with the prospect of a metanormative paradigm. The philosophical dimension of Eliade's thought is already manifested in the very way his assertions correlate with the three foregoing contiguous elements in human experience. He thus speaks to the question of the nature of being/consciousness when he says (reflecting both an archaic and a modern ontology) not only that

> the historian of religions is in a position to grasp the permanence of what has been called man's specific existential situation of "being in the world," for the experience of the sacred is its correlate. In fact, man's becoming aware of his own mode of being and assuming his *presence* in the world together constitutes a "religious" experience . . . (*Quest*, 9)

but that "the 'sacred' is an element in the structure of human consciousness, not a stage in the history of consciousness."[79]

He speaks to the question of meaning/creativity by calling our attention to humankind's essential nature as creative activity, that is, creativity: The great surprise is always the freedom of the human spirit, its creativity. "When you make

---

78. Cited in Beane, *Archaic Sacred Values*, 56.
79. *The Quest* (Preface); with slight variation in Rocquet, *Ordeal*, 153–154.

[a] . . . discovery, then, like Nietzsche discovering his Eternal Return, you may give a shout of joy! Because there again, what you have is an invitation to total freedom. You say to yourself: what extraordinary freedom one might gain, and what *creativity* as a result of such liberations!"[80]

Eliade speaks to the question of truth/values after looking back on examples of structures and changes in religious traditions, Occidental and Oriental, claiming that they

> illustrate the principle function of religion, that of maintaining an "opening" toward a world which is superhuman, the world of *axiomatic spiritual values*. These values are "transcendent" in the sense that they are considered revealed by divine beings or mythical ancestors. They therefore constitute absolute values, paradigms for all human activity. The function of religion is to awaken and sustain the consciousness of another world, of a "beyond" . . . [= "transconsciousness"]. It is thus through the experience of the sacred that the ideas of *reality*, *truth*, and *meaning* come to light . . .[81]

The utmost significance of these remarks by Eliade is that they have (to the surprise of some) a practical philosophical value. This intentionality beyond absolute detachment was intimated but not drawn out in another context when he said that "I do see our discipline as having a 'social function . . . '" (*Ordeal*, 107). For in terms of the truth/values correlation, we are desperately in need of becoming more aware that we must develop a sense of ecological-religious responsibility, as did our Stone Age ancestors, for our natural environment which is under the threat of continued pollution, deforestation, and species endangerment. This, Eliade would regard as a part of the creative process of the "*planétisation* of culture" (*Quest*, 69). Moreover, in terms of the meaning/creativity correlation we need to re-ask, if not to reconfirm, the answer to "the fundamental question" of "the meaning of existence" to which "religion is precisely a reply" (148, 149). But we must make the task of recovery an essentially creative process, in order to maintain a delicate balance between our technology and our spirituality. Finally, in terms of the being/consciousness correlation, the import here is to recognize that whatever "criterion of truth" (Rocquet) we adopt, if we are willing to concede that life also consists of affective truths, then it will not matter how much knowledge we have acquired but how that knowledge "may affect my own individual life"; not how that knowledge

---

80. Rocquet, *Ordeal*, 117,122; italics added. Some may consider the context of Eliade's latter statement simply astounding—yet it is (phenomenologically) true (154: "Quite right"; also see his comments on hermeneutics and creativity, 128f.).

81. "Structures and Changes in the History of Religion," 366; italics added.

casts "light on 'religious man' alone," but, more importantly, how it "enable[s] you, by a roundabout route, to find your way back to things nearer, more familiar to you . . ."[82]

The historian of religions as philosopher is thus a scholar who has rediscovered the ancient love of the *sophos* element of philosophy to the extent that he/she can overcome the hesitancy to generalize about the ciphers of sacred worlds. *Sophos*, here, of course, is conceived as a multivalent symbol of the convergence in the human mind of all the known ciphers of sacred human experience and the imaginative encirclement of them at their point of convergence, in order to draw out an essential meaning for the species as a whole. But that essential meaning requires, ultimately, that *sophos* be understood both as a rational and visionary truth-value for fully appreciating the sacred as a truly "Academic" enterprise.

Yet in the face of a largely "unfalsifiable" meaning extractable from humankind's long experience of the sacred, we are not obligated to be "right" or "correct" in every imaginative encirclement we have made.[83] But we are obligated to realize that even when we make it our aim to allow the ciphers to speak for themselves, we must accept the practical paradox of knowing that those ciphers are really speaking through us (= *re*-presentation); and this marks the inevitable but formidable presence of the task of a creative hermeneutics. Nonetheless, because of the superabundance of data and the maze of possible interpretations, we should expect there to be among various historians of religions (echoing Medicus, above, 169, n.12) "divergent" methodological perspectives in order to begin to comprehend so immense a horizon of possibilities.[84]

Should there develop an appreciative rediscovery of humankind's apprehension of the sacred, it would nonetheless remain incumbent upon us to accept that we cannot fathom the depth of the sacred because of its sheer inexhaustibility. Eliade's allusion to the sky as religious symbol is illustratively paramount in this regard: "[T]he sky . . . directly reveals a transcendence, a power and a holiness. . . . The

---

82. Rocquet, in Ordeal, 130; S9. Eliade (137): "This is why I am so very proud of being a human being, not because I am a descendant of that prodigious Mediterranean culture, but because I can recognize myself, as a human being, in the existence taken upon himself by an Australian Aborigine. And that is why his culture interests me, and his religion, his mythology"; originally cited in Rennie, Reconstructing Eliade, 127.

83. See the stirring remarks of Harvard's Nelson Goodman in Peter Novick's That Noble Dream, 538f.

84. See Dudley III, *Religion on Trial*, 141. Though his qualifying comments here are crucial, I am less concerned about potential "chaos" than the imperative initial general acceptance by historians of religions of the mutual respectability of "competing theories and paradigms." A newly advancing research program is inseparable from attitudes, which can indeed influence the prospects for developing "a common language" (loc.cit.).

symbolism of its transcendence derives from the simple realization of its infinite height. 'Most High' becomes quite naturally an attribute of... divinity."[85] Hence the sacred is both an ever-present and an ever-receding phenomenon; it, as the sky seen "above," is experientially near, yet it seems forever beyond our reach. Here one might be tempted to say that we are dealing with a "vague Somewhat" (van der Leeuw) or "Somebody" (E. B. Tylor). But just because humankind's experiences of the sacred manifest themselves in philosophical, mythological, sociological, and anthropological (or other) paradigms does not mean that such categories may not have a referent that continues to defy—to our wonderment or dismay—the comprehension of our intellectual-methodological traditions (e.g., the Euro-Americentric scientific tradition). The sacred, much like that highly elusive realm of modern science wherein lie subatomic realities that even now in the light of the Heisenberg "Principle of Uncertainty" appear to be characterized by a field in which it appears that we and they (subatomic realities) bear some highly elusive ontological relation, is, some might say, more like what Whitehead at one point described as the nature of religion: something that is "the greatest of present facts... and yet is beyond all reach."[86]

Let us contemplate what all this might mean for the future of the history of religions. In a scholarly sense, it means, to be sure, that it may remain our destiny to do our research in a (relatively healthy) state of methodological ambivalence, reminiscent of Eliade's reference to the ambivalence of the sacred itself. We must then deal with the concrete (e.g., documents, etc.) but, while remaining who and what we are, deal also with the discrete: the "hierophanic" encounter. In an existential sense, it could mean that, as we find ourselves to have been subtly affected, consciously or unconsciously, by the realization (as noted above) that there is something inherent in the quest for knowledge itself that motivates the transition from historical-religious studies to "philosophical-religious" reflection, we must also find the courage to make metanormative statements. It thus means that, as methodologists, we are destined to enjoy a certain amount of what I like to call "phenomenological freedom" (as opposed to what Eliade calls "philosophical timidity");[87] but we cannot claim to have methodologically penetrated and circumscribed with our mere intellects the entire field of the dimension of mystery that the sacred presents to us.

Thus, neither philosophy nor the history of religions can ever afford to ignore each other, nor either of them the concerns of theology (even though they also cannot afford to acknowledge its "dogmatic" proclamations), because all three of these fields have several very important things in common: (1) they all concern

---

85. Beane and Doty, eds., *Myths, Rites, Symbols*, Vol. II, 352–353.
86. *Science and the Modern World*. New York: Macmillan Publishing Company, 1931, 275.
87. Beane, *Myth, Cult, and Symbols*, 24; Eliade, *The Two and the One*, 195.

themselves with the same quest to know and understand the nature of being; (2) they all seek an answer to the question of the meaning of what it is to be a human being; (3) they all share an intellectual-apprehensive awareness that somehow there is a basic, fundamental, underlying truth that accounts for the apparent unity of all things; and (4) they all are becoming more drawn toward an interdisciplinary consciousness that is consistent with the foregoing "intellectual-apprehensive awareness." Too many modern scholars have forgotten why, in so many cases, Ph.D. graduates are called "doctors of *philosophy*," in so many disparate fields of expertise. In the ancient world, then philosophy, (*philein/sophos*) was never simply a matter of "*loving* wisdom" but, more so, of "loving *wisdom*." So it remains deeply regrettable today that numerous scholars have not contemplated the radical implications of the fact that so many of our graduates are not called, for example, doctors of science but doctors of philosophy. It is thus the *sophos* or *sophia* dimension of human intellectual exploration that did and still should imply that there is potentially an all-encompassing wisdom that comprehends the unity of all things. It matters not that Plato may have entertained more mystical notions of what the nature of ultimate reality might be; or that we may not in a given field of investigative endeavor be able to verify what we merely, now, apprehend. It does matter, however, whether modern so-called "Academicians" have lost that sense of intellectual exploration that remains ever open to new epistemological possibilities; or that the academician himself/herself must ever be an open-minded individual who dares to face without trepidation that dimension that historians of religions call the "sacred."

As for Eliade himself, he has been characterized as a scholar, poet, mystic, and even a shaman; and as a historian, phenomenologist, structuralist, and even a theologian. As in the case of all intellectual giants, the very range and profundity of this scholar's works will tend to make such viewpoints inevitable. And, like other renowned scholars in almost any field of endeavor, such personages will be challenged even more boldly after they have passed on. However, in Eliade's case (though he would draw back from the ensuing comparison—*Ordeal*, 187) during rather subjective moments when I am feeling patently disturbed about the recurrent clamor that will probably continue over his scholarly boldness, it occurs to me that the words of Nicolas Berdyaev may have some applicability:

> Of the greatest creative minds, for example, of Shakespeare and Goethe or of Dostoyevsky and Tolstoy, it is certainly impossible to inquire whether they were classical or romantic. Creative geniuses have always stood outside the quarrelling schools, and above them, although the disputing tendencies dragged them into their controversies.[88]

---

88. Berdyaev, *The Beginning and the End*, 188.

Chapter Twelve

Conversation with an Indian Nationalist and Intermezzo: Fragments from a Civil Revolt

Mircea Eliade

CONVERSATION WITH AN INDIAN NATIONALIST

On April 22, 1930, something happened to me which I relate here, not because it is a unique event or the worst thing that has taken place in the history of the Indian civil revolt, but purely and simply because it happened to me. From word-of-mouth, from newspapers, and from books, I know, and so do you, dozens of other episodes more cruel and more grave.

I was seated in a well-appointed Sanskrit bookstore in College Square, No. 4, close to the University, opposite a park with a lake and palm trees. There are at least two dozen such parks in Calcutta. I was happy because the fan was separating me from the torrid heat outside, because I was leafing through rare books, and because I was proud, like any white man who studies Indian philosophy in the hope that he will someday become a learned man.

From *India*. Bucureşti: Editura Cugetarea, 1934, 228–235. Translated by Mac Linscott Ricketts.

I had ignored the throng I met on the way there, massed in the park and on the streets. Another political rally. The same speeches will be delivered and new bands of students will set off to boycott English goods. We were in the midst of a civil disobedience movement; none of this was new to me.

I had seen a great many arrested, and, being white, I had time and again encountered hostile looks from Bengalis whom I should like to have had for friends. Very well, I said to myself, and hurried on toward the bookstore.

The twenty-second of April, please remember—a desolate month, sizzling and vacuous. A man cannot think on the street. He thinks only when isolated under the cool breeze of the electric fan. Outside there is an exasperating wilderness of noises and car horns, a desert in which you are aware of no one, although living beings assail you from all sides. Once you have put on your pith helmet and have descended the stairs, you know nothing except the number of the train you have to catch and the number of the station at which you want to get off. From Bhowanipore, where I am living, to College Square—a half-hour to an hour by train, with changes and waits. Vaguely I recall who I am, but my mind is incapable of a more strenuous effort than such a recollection. After a while, not even a memory, but only a half-conscious awareness of bodily fatigue and a longing for the delights of repose; the awareness of being a well-bred brute, with helmet and dark glasses, making his way forward through the heavy heat.

I prolonged my visit in the bookshop, more and more fascinated by my intelligence and learning. Suddenly, the noises from the park were throttled; then they became more ugly, unrestrained. The sound of marching feet reverberated from up the street; then shouts and howls from the crowd. Panic, with everyone in the park scattering in all directions. Then—a charge with *lathi* (those long, sinister riot sticks of the Indian police), more screams, more confusion. All this happened with the spontaneity of a nightmare. I barely had time to replace the books on the shelves and run to the door. From there I could see the police cavalry (the glorious Mounted Police) driving the student-citizen demonstration toward the broader streets. The chains of Bengalese students were being broken by the horses, sticks were striking right and left, at any one, any way. Cracked skulls and fractured limbs— these can be seen in any country. But there was something else, something one can see only in British India: children trampled underfoot by horses, children bleeding from hooves and police clubs.

The first of the wounded were brought into the very bookstore where I was standing. They were just children. Some were too shocked to be crying. They had come to the demonstration with little tricolor flags of rice paper, brought by the others just to shout "*Bande mataram!*" or to be used as shields by the demonstrators. The latter had calculated that the mounted police would not charge a crowd with children in it.

Several of them were unconscious. One had an eye gouged out, hanging from its socket like a bloody egg; around his neck, a collar of gore and dust. Another was screaming noiselessly, a scream which you could see in his mouth, which you expected to hear burst forth, and yet it did not—because it was turned into the rattle of a faint. Most of them had broken heads from the riot clubs and were weeping in the stifled way Oriental children have of crying when they don't know what hurts. Others...

The bookstore was filled with blood, groans, and water. A miniature hospital—as any Indian house ought to be, according to what a certain *Swarajist* said. I looked on, perhaps embarrassed by the color of my hands, furious and powerless, not knowing if I ought to leave, or try to help, or curse the English.

A young student wearing a *dhoti* of Khaddar approached me provocatively:

"Aren't you English?"

"No, thank God!"

"Does it amuse you?"

I was in no mood for a discussion. But the stranger continued, as though he felt an urgent need to insult the white race personified in the first white man to cross his path.

"And yet what they've done is futile. They can keep doing it. They can put us all in jail. But there are several hundred million of us. They don't have space for a thousandth part of us. The whole British administration would leap in the air if half a million volunteers were to be jailed... But what about our mothers, our women? Do you know what happened to them in Amritsar in 1919? They were assaulted with riot clubs! Yes, you can read that in the Congress Report. You can learn about it even without reading the report. Go to the villages and find out how the police operate. But what have they been able to do so far? Can they fight children? What they did is absurd, but panic got hold of them, that's what it was. They're acting with the fear of the man who knows he is playing his last card. Some Christians they are! And you're a Christian too, no doubt. How do you excuse these crimes?"

"I don't excuse anyone" I replied, when the young man repeated the question. "They are Sunday Christians, like all Europeans. They talk about Christianity, that's all. Please don't condemn a religion because of the actions of its so-called believers."

"But what you say is absurd, Sahib (this term, on the lips of a student, is mockery). Because, if your religion hasn't done more good than that in two thousand years, you should throw it out and find a better one! But you send missionaries here, to India. Why don't you start at home?"

"I don't understand why you keep mistaking me for an Englishman," I objected, embarrassed that a crowd of listeners was beginning to gather.

"But you're a European too. And if you aren't ashamed of what your brothers are doing in India, it means either that you aren't interested and therefore you're self-centered, or else that you're afraid, in which case you're a coward. Probably you're not concerned about anything except Europe. You Europeans are a glorious, civilized, infallible people! You are white. Pardon us, but we hate you to the point of contempt. *We* are the superior ones, no matter how much you praise yourselves for your books of philosophy which no one believes. We're superior because we know all about Europe, whereas you know nothing about India. Why did you come to India?"

"I, personally? To study Indian languages and philosophy."

"And will you not be ashamed of what you have seen a year from now?"

"I don't take sides with anyone," I replied, pressed against the door. "I'm apolitical. I intend to stay in India only a few years. I don't have time for anything else but study. What do you expect? You're a privileged person: you were born in India. You have time for politics as well as studies. I will return to my country."

"But politics in India is not *political*. Our struggle for independence, *swaraj*, is the necessary conclusion of our whole metaphysics. You know what the basic principle of Indian metaphysics and mysticism is: that no one can attain the path, the truth, freedom through another person. Our struggle is consistent with the fundamental premise of our philosophical consciousness: that just as the soul cannot achieve *mukta* except by its own effort, so India cannot become free except by its own effort. We do not accept help from outside. *Neither is it possible to give us help.* No one can intervene in the destiny of another. Not only does he not have the right, but it simply isn't possible. You know this from studying our philosophy. So then, how does England believe that she can interfere in the destiny of India, without producing and linking herself to fatal consequences?"

"Great Britain doesn't see the problem that way."

"So much the worse for her! She sees her domination as a divine act."

"But hasn't she given you, perhaps, a better administration?"

"Perhaps, Sahib, but this has nothing to do with the matter. We don't ask for an excellent administration. We ask for an administration *of our own*. I know it will not be as good, that it will be less decisive, full of deficiencies and abuses. But it will be *ours*. The British administration emasculates us, gives us the consciousness of slaves, makes us cowards. After a century of English domination, in spite of the trains, industries, and modern cities built by the English, the Indian people are on the verge of degeneration. The good life means nothing to an enslaved people. Those who think differently are already slaves."

"But India," I interrupted, "India has no national consciousness."

"In our case, the problem of nationalism does not arise, as it does for you in Europe. For Indians, India is not a country or a nation. There are too many races, religions, and castes. A European is lost in this 'chaos,' and he asks, what *is* India? Well, Sahib, India is for us Mother! Our national revolutionary slogan and the opening words of our national anthem are '*Bande Mataram!*' Bow to Mother. Ask any poor man, from any corner of India, what he calls India, and he will answer Mother. Our struggle is not an abstract one, for principles, nor one limited to specific demands. Our struggle is a crusade for the liberation of Mother from slavery. That's why it is not a political struggle, but a mystical one; we attain freedom, as the Mahatma says, through purification, through individual renunciation, through nonviolence, through agony. Our politics is an ascetic apprenticeship. Our politicians begin their career by a total renunciation of their work, wealth, and fame, and all earthly possessions. Our leaders are poorer than we. Political geniuses and political tactics are unnecessary for us. The Mahatma is not a genius, but a saint. He has no "tactical method," but he has sincerity. This even our most bitter enemies acknowledge. He is the only man who has succeeded in establishing sincerity in political conflict."

"But what if you don't succeed? Will you try other methods—European methods, for instance?"

"We, too, have our extreme left, our terrorist groups. We will resort to terrorism only when the Mahatma abdicates. But until then, we are bound by our promise to Gandhi: nonviolence."

"But terrorism is a method copied from Europe."

"Not at all. It is perfectly consistent with our philosophy and politics. You find it in the *Arthashastra*, a political treatise written three centuries before the Christian era. Nonviolence is on the *satvic* plane, terror is on the *rajasic*; the first uses contemplation, the other outbursts of energy. But both belong to the Indian consciousness."

"What if you attain nothing through terrorism?"

"Then *these* remain (he pointed to the wounded children) to try something else, or to try the nonviolent way again. You see, this is not a struggle of years, but of generations. India knows how to wait, because India does not forget. These little children will not forget the second campaign of civil disobedience. Even if we are stifled now, they will not be twenty years from now..."

An awkward silence. I took out my cigarettes and offered him one.

"No thanks, Sahib. My brother died in prison because he boycotted English cigarettes."

He smiled at me when I changed my mind and put the cigarettes away.

"If what I've told you has made you think, then try not to smoke any more English tobacco.... Good day, *Sahib*."

He saluted me and left, in the silence of the crowded bookstore. On that day of April 22, I wrote nothing in my notebook.

INTERMEZZO: FRAGMENTS FROM A CIVIL REVOLT

April–May, 1930

Gopal Chauddhuri, medical student, age twenty. He is tall, dark, handsome. His left hand is paralyzed, his left leg trembles. He was beaten from Monday night until the day before yesterday, Wednesday morning. He tells me:

"Write, man, write in French so the whole world will know. We threw ourselves down on the street. Not one of us raised a hand. Ghandiji knows that not one of us could raise a hand. They beat us first till we fell down, fainting, twelve or thirteen out of fifty of us. I came to in jail. When they began beating me, I fainted again. He was a Mohammedan policeman, and he beat us with a copper sword-sheath. After that, I don't remember anything. We all declared a hunger strike, without telling anyone. The last time I woke up, my body was covered with flies. Blood had been oozing all night . . .

Benoy Banerjee, high school pupil, son of a wealthy merchant of Dacca. He came secretly to Calcutta to tell in the main city about the Muslim horrors at Dacca. He was caught at a demonstration in the railway station, in the morning. The group he was with fled down a side street, when the cavalry charged. He doesn't know how it happened, but he was caught, alone, by a mob of Muslims. He was circumcised and his wound became infected immediately. Now he is delirious. The man next to him tells me: "At Dacca, Muslims began the uprising with the help of the police. They attacked houses, raped the women, and shot any who resisted. They burned whole neighborhoods, while the police looked on. The police intervene only when Hindus defend themselves with guns. Then they enter the houses and confiscate the weapons on the spot, arresting the men. The Mohammedans are armed; they are given free rein. All attempts of the Congress to make them stop fighting have failed."

"How did the fighting at Dacca begin?" I ask.

"It is not known. Probably, the way such fights usually begin. The police pay several loafers to throw a butchered pig into the courtyard of a mosque, at night. This is always enough to kindle a fire that no one can put out."

Shakuntala Das, student in physico-chemistry. She was in the boycott cordon at Bow-Bazar. Their orders were to hold hands tightly and not let anyone enter stores selling English goods. At eleven the cordons were charged by a squadron armed with *lathis*. She remembers very well that the hoofs struck her between the

---

From *Santier*. București: Editura Cugetarea, 1935, 155–174. Translated by Mac Linscott Ricketts.

breasts. Then she fainted. She is so terribly beaten that she can scarcely move. She doesn't know what happened to her. (The doctor tells me confidentially: raped repeatedly, contusions of the abdomen, genital organs beaten.)

Helen Majumdar, pharmacy student, second generation Christian, resident of Howrah. She took part in the boycott cordon on College Street. She cannot hear. Both her eardrums ruptured. Her upper lip split open, her mouth bloody. She holds a crucifix in her right hand.

Indira Chakravarti, philosophy student. Brother shot in 1928, father sentenced to ten years imprisonment in the same year. At the time of the morning charge, she was in the office of the University, under orders to gather up the wounded and get in touch with the Congress hospital. They were attacked inside the building. No one offered any resistance. The office was completely devastated, the girls arrested and beaten. She does not wish to say anything more.

I am an unwilling witness to the devastation of the Sikh quarter in Bhowanipore. The pretext was as follows: last evening an Anglo-Indian girl riding a motorcycle down Asutosh Mookerji Road, was accosted by several Sikhs. The same night the arrests and beatings began. At dawn I am awakened from sleep by a horrible uproar: horses, shouts, wailing. I went up onto the terrace to see better. The same well-known police technique: violent entrance into houses, blows struck to the right and left, provocation, destruction. Sikhs find it very hard to practice nonviolence. I am sure that not a few police were severely punished for this senseless devastation. Still I wonder, how can such strong and courageous men resist, how can they resist the temptation to cast aside Gandhi's orders and answer violence with violence?

How easily it would be for them to massacre the police squadrons. Reprisals, naturally, would follow. Machine guns would rattle, houses would burn. The masters of India are waiting for a true massacre which would justify a new Jallanwalla. How impatiently they wait to bring out the "white" regiments, to send tanks into the streets of Calcutta!

Discussion with D.* Revolted, clenching my fists, I tell him of the barbarities I have witnessed, powerless to do anything. I tell him how ashamed I am of my white skin, of my continent. D. is calm, disdainful, firm of speech.

"Don't get all worked up," he tells me. "Why did you watch the barbarities, if you knew you couldn't do anything, and if you knew you'd preserve them in your

---

*Almost certainly Surendranath Dasgupta, Eliade's philosophy tutor and host in India—Ed.

memory afterward? India will achieve its freedom some day, but not through nonviolence. This prolonged agony does no good."

Today's papers announce on the front page: 50,000 men in prison. Congress gives a larger number. In any event, the civil revolt is spreading like wildfire into all the states. Sen, whom I see before noon, is jubilant: "In a week there will I be 30,000–40,000 more sentenced to jail. If the revolution lasts a month, the government will have to give up holding people in custody; it will cost too much and there won't be room! Already primary schools and old army camps have begun to serve as prisons. Find a million volunteers in this land of over 350 million, and British domination will burst like a soap bubble!"

Sen takes me to Alipore, to attend the protest meeting of some four thousand women—the majority of them from among the "good people" of Calcutta. The women are marching en masse to the prison in Alipore, demanding to be locked up too alongside the nationalists. We meet them in large crowds, many led by students or volunteers who so far have escaped being arrested. They are stopped two kilometers from the prison. A regiment of Gurkhas and several English detachments from Fort William. As far as the eye can see—nothing but women. I don't know what is happening ahead of us. The women sit down. I hear that they are going to stay seated on the road and the field until the authorities agree to arrest them. The troops, so far as I can observe, are just maintaining their cordon; they are not attacking, not beating anyone. A delegation parlays with an English officer. Apparently the English have decided to practice nonviolence also! The Gurkha soldiers remain standing side by side, their rifles slung on their backs.

According to Sen, I must hide in order not to be observed. Already the people around us are looking at me suspiciously. Sen tells them that I am a French newspaper reporter sent to write about the civil revolt. He has to say this to every new group that surrounds us. From out of nowhere three student volunteers appear who offer to accompany me for the remainder of my visit. The visit, however, is of quite limited scope. I find it impossible to make my way through the throngs of women who remain seated or reclining on the ground, quiet or speaking in whispers, chewing pan or nursing babies. They have followed the classic procedure of such meetings: a great many women with suckling infants have come and have taken seats in the front rows in case of a charge by the mounted police. For some time now, however, this tactic has not worked. The police have received orders to attack, trampling over children and women alike. Today, however, the troops seem to be imitating the system of the revolutionists; they stand in front of them, nonviolent, only barring them with their bodies from going on toward the Alipore prison.

D. reproves me sharply on learning how I spent the day. In fact, he points out what a great responsibility he has: if the police arrest me, they will dismiss me from the university and his name will be besmirched, because he has sworn loyalty to His Majesty, Emperor of India, and he has no right to engage in politics. On the other hand, he knows what could happen to me in a group of Indians. I could be taken for an Englishman and be beaten to death. "You came here to study. You ought to have eyes and time for your books only. After you finish your studies, you can take up political news-writing, if you think you must learn this also from India. If you are concerned about the suffering of the world and of India in particular, I remind you that neither Sanskrit nor philosophy will alleviate it."

Several days ago, the mayor of Calcutta and the *Pandit* Jawarharlal Nehru, president of the Congress Party, were sentenced to six months in jail. The news precipitated a *hartal* (general strike) and meetings—brutally repressed. I am beginning to learn sensational details about the attack on the military depot at Chittagong. The attack took place on the night of April 18. The insurgents captured over five hundred rifles, a machine gun, and, it is said in whispers, a ton of munitions. There were several truck loads. The attackers were clever and careful; it is the only successful attack yet made on a British munitions depot. Dressed in officers' uniforms, the insurgents approached the sentinels, strangled them, and loaded their trucks till dawn. Only then was the alarm given. They were pursued and they exchanged rifle fire, but the pursuers lost their trail in the jungle. Six dead. In the Jungle of the Chittagong it will be very difficult to catch them, unless someone betrays them.

For the first time since the outbreak of the civil revolt, D. seems pleased. "From now on they'll have enough guns to terrorize the district administrators. The British power will weaken when it loses the confidence of the administrators."

On the street cars, Indian boys spit in the faces of Europeans. This is truly a revolutionary change. The prestige of the whites is crumbling. And it is by prestige that the British control India.

A few stupid, personal happenings. I walk through Bhowanipore alone, I am insulted by children. Once rocks were thrown at me. This evening, on a terrace next to the park, someone tossed a clay pot which landed two steps behind me. I laughed gaily as I told D. about it. I say, too, how lucky I am to be witnessing the rising of a new India. He is furious and forbids me to leave the house in the evening. Despite this, the attacks against me make me happy; they confirm the people's hatred of their oppressors. I understand what an invincible force this hatred is, this supreme collective effort against a foreign civilization, against a barbarian race and rule. Out of this effort will be born a new world. This incredible madness of India, to go forth unarmed against European tanks and machine guns! If they win—as I hope with all my soul they will—a new stage of history will begin. The spirit will prove itself once more invincible. Because the forces of Indian nationalism place their trust instinctively in spirit, in the magical power of suffering and nonviolence. How much this movement resembles Christianity of the first centuries, men very different from one another have observed. Probably this resemblance is not illusory.

This evening the city was aroused by the news that Mayor Sen and the nationalist leader Subhash Chandra Bose were beaten unconscious in the Alipore prison. The deed was committed this morning; the cause unknown. An enormous multitude in the streets; Alipore is under siege again. Gurkhas and English soldiers at all the street corners. In front of Fort William a row of tanks parades threateningly. I don't know what to do, where to go to see better and yet not endanger myself too much.

This evening, mass arrests. The meeting in College Square charged by mounted police. Almost all my fellow students, both male and female, are in jail. From Sen I have heard nothing, nor does D. know anything. The Congress Party Hospital has been evacuated. I hate quietly, with restraint—but atrociously.

From the French Consulate I request a pass to allow me to enter the prison. I obtain it with difficulty, but I discover I cannot very well make use of it. I can't get into Alipore because of the multitude outside. (I have forgotten to say that the nonviolence of the police, which had been viewed as such a joke at first, could not last twenty-four hours. At length they lost patience and charged the women with *lathis*, as usual.) Today, May 5, Gandhi was arrested. General consternation; *hartal*, meetings quickly dispersed. Repressions have reached a climax. All the Indian dailies are suspended; editors sentenced to six months in prison and fined a hundred thousand rupees. From *The Statesman* I cannot obtain any accurate information: it is an English imperialistic newspaper. People arrested in droves. The university is permanently closed. Horrible rumors are circulating which make me ill: guerrilla fighting in Chittagong (a hundred Indians, selected by lot, executed); military revolution at

Patna. Indeed, tickets for the train to Patna no longer are being sold. The reason: an epidemic of the plague. This is simple invention; every year there are plague epidemics in Patna and yet never until today have train tickets not been available. I don't know anything, and this uncertainty is getting me down. I've telephoned all my friends. Sen was arrested Saturday and given a six month's sentence. Sukumar is dead; when it happened is not known, but probably when he was taken to the police station the second time. Prescribed punishments have begun; in the villages women are violated with stakes, their genital organs ruptured. It seems to be a sure means of intimidation; it is a civilized way of impaling... as at Jallanwalla.

I cannot any longer obtain information from those who have been tortured. They are arrested immediately and sentenced automatically to six months' imprisonment. Some families have been allowed to retrieve their dead from the prison, to cremate them. It seems horrible to me that so many women are incarcerated. As many as fifty are put in a room together, with no water to drink or wash in, and they are not allowed to prepare food. The hunger strike is general throughout India. Gandhi has not been brought to trial. There is an article in the Indian Constitution giving the Viceroy permission to hold any person at his disposition, without charges. That is how Gandhi is being held now.

I can't find out anything now. However, I have succeeded in convincing D. to let me go to Benares. Sushil Kumar, who by some miracle has so far escaped arrest or injury, brings me the latest list of the dead. I cast horrified eyes over the names. Except for Sukumar, I have no friend among them. Kumar has. He points out the names and tells me how they died. One was killed on the street, trampled to death. I am no longer impressed. When so many women have died from being "raped" with stakes, what does a death on the streets mean, whether from hooves or *lathis*?

On the train I learned that fighting between communities has broken out; as usual, the Muslims have begun to butcher the Hindus, with police protection. My compartment companion, an Anglo-Indian, says to me, "Let them beat each other to death. They want independence, don't they?" I turn my head toward the window to keep from hitting him. Nevertheless, he continues.

"If things got worse, you'll see what good money you can make! They'll pay you a hundred rupees to escort a woman from one neighborhood to another, or from home to the railway station. Three years ago I was in Calcutta and a *marwari* gave me three hundred rupees to take his wife and daughter across the bridge at Howrah. If it had been night, maybe I could have come off with even more!"

———•·•———

Cawnpore. I'm writing in the station. It is a disaster greater than I had expected. From the train I saw flames above the whole Indian quarter. Before we came to a halt an English sergeant went through every compartment examining our identification papers. Luckily I have a French Consulate permit. We are waiting in the restaurant, to be told to what hotel we can go. We are permitted to go outside the station. A terrible crowd, bodies massed in front of the platform. Indians are not allowed to get off the train except by special permission. Volleys of rifle fire can be heard. I am told the police are not permitted to intervene. It is just a little fight between Hindus and Muslims. But last night houses burned the whole night through. Horrors are told me. Little children thrown alive into the flames, women split in half vertically, Turkish-style. I don't know what to believe. I meet two American reporters with photographic equipment. They come from Delhi. They tell me that there the civil revolt is going forward peacefully. Only the authorities beat and torture people. Inter-community fighting still has not erupted.

All the way to the hotel we are accompanied by a motorcycle escort. Streets empty, stores closed. Smell of smoke, dust throughout the city.

Europeans and Anglo-Indians have withdrawn into the neighborhood of the military camps. I encounter several Anglo-Indians displaying a severe, triumphant air. "At last, the true India shows itself!" There is no way to circulate on the side streets. Beyond the military cordons men venture at their own risk. If I only had an enterprising companion, only one...

Dr. Thomas Patel, Indian Christian, of the Indian Medical Service; he is past fifty, has married children; is not wealthy. He has been stationed in Cawnpore for several years. He tells me he has posted several telegrams to Delhi and Calcutta, begging the authorities to intervene. He posted one to the Viceroy also, but he believes that not one telegram was dispatched, because the police have no interest in intervening. On the contrary, these massacres in Cawnpore are a sure means of paralyzing the nationalistic campaigns. What he has seen: an armed band of Mohammedans, equipped with gasoline and benzene, attack houses, plunder them, and burn them. The men they shoot. Women they rape, then split them open vertically and throw them on the fire. They take children by the feet and toss them into the flames. This continued until the Hindus organized themselves into tight little groups, though they were inadequately armed. Then they attacked a Muslim quarter. They destroyed mosques, slit the women open, and threw the children into the fire. After that, fighting broke out across the whole city and spread into the villages. Men fight with what they can—some with fists and teeth. The doctor estimates the dead at some two thousand, the wounded at five or six thousand. As soon as the massacres began, the Anglo-Indian and European populace received orders to withdraw into the army camps. Troops have come out on the streets but only to keep the fighting from spreading into the Anglo-Indian quarter.

Night. From the terrace I see the sky bloodied in all directions. More of the same acrid stench of burnt thatch and putrefaction. Sounds of moaning, of alarm. Crackling of rifles. Now and then, a short, muffled crash. Houses collapsing, my neighbor informs me.

In front of the hotel, a patrol of English soldiers. The rare automobiles which pass have a soldier on the running board. A great many motorcycles go by. A young Anglo-Indian declares that if the "revolution" expands, all Anglo-Indians will be mobilized and armed. It was that way in 1925. He will receive, then, a carbine and a revolver, with enough ammunition to permit some innocent caprices.

"You walk down the street and if you see a light on a terrace, you take aim and shoot. One less black . . ."

What he saw at Cawnpore. "In front of the house, dear sir, lay a giant of an Indian with a knife in his back. Good shot! Right in front of our house. The whole street was full of blood, but there were few dead bodies. You could easily walk without tripping over them. The wounded had been taken away during the night."

I ask him why the fighting started, if the police, perhaps, had provoked it. He laughs.

"That's not true. They wanted to make a revolution with Gandhi. Then the Mohammedans said India was theirs. So to make everyone Muslims, they began catching Indians and circumcising them. If they'd had more time they'd have forced them to eat the flesh of the cow."

The fire spreads throughout India: Dacca, Patna, Cawnpore, Allahabad. Only in Gujerat is the civil revolution won peacefully. I learned that the Congress Party sent groups of volunteers, half Muslim and half Hindu, to pacify the centers of inter-community strife. The police did not want to let them in.

Here it has begun to smell of burnt flesh.

Part Five

APPLICATIONS

Chapter Thirteen

MIRCEA ELIADE'S VIEW OF THE STUDY OF RELIGION AS THE BASIS FOR CULTURAL AND SPIRITUAL RENEWAL

DOUGLAS ALLEN

Mircea Eliade was often described by scholars and in the popular press as the world's most influential historian of religion and the world's foremost interpreter of symbol and myth.[1] For example, an article in *Time* magazine identified Eliade as "probably the world's foremost living interpreter of spiritual myths and symbolism," and an article in *People Weekly* claimed that "Eliade is the world's foremost living historian of religions and myths."[2] Not unusual was the claim by Lawrence Sullivan that "Eliade has been the single most important individual in introducing the world to what religion means."[3]

---

1. The beginning of this chapter uses material from my preface to Douglas Allen, *Myth and Religion in Mircea Eliade*. New York: Garland, 1998. Most of this chapter uses material from chapter 11 of *Myth and Religion in Mircea Eliade*.

2. See "Scientist of Symbols," *Time* 87 (February 11, 1966): 68; and Giovanna Breu, "Teacher: Shamans? Hippies? They're All Creative to the World's Leading Historian of Religions," *People Weekly* 9 (March 27, 1978): 49.

3. Lawrence Sullivan is quoted by Delia O'Hara in the introduction to her interview with Mircea Eliade. See "Mircea Eliade" (interview of Eliade by Delia O'Hara), *Chicago* 35, 6 (1986): 147.

As influential as Eliade was as a scholar of religion, he has remained extremely controversial. Indeed, many scholars, especially those in the social sciences, have completely ignored or vigorously attacked Eliade's scholarship on religion as methodologically uncritical, subjective, and unscientific. Critics charge that Eliade is guilty of uncritical universal generalizations; reads all sorts of "profound" mythic and religious meaning into his data; ignores rigorous scholarly procedures of verification; and interjects unjustified, personal, metaphysical, and ontological assumptions and judgments into his scholarship.

Both Eliade's style and the contents of his scholarly studies add to the controversial nature of his scholarship. He never seems as bothered as critics think any serious scholar should be by his eclectic approach, by contradictions and inconsistencies in his writings, or by his mixing of particular scholarly studies with sweeping controversial personal assertions and highly normative judgments. Unlike the self-imposed limited approaches of specialists studying religion, he views his subject matter as the entire spiritual history of humankind. He often does many different things simultaneously, resists simple classification of his scholarship, and describes himself as "an author *without a model*."[4]

Adding to the controversial nature of his scholarship on religion is the fact that Eliade, while not hesitating to criticize the approaches of other scholars, never seems to feel the need to defend his work against the attacks of critics. In the Foreword to my *Structure and Creativity in Religion,* Eliade wrote the following: "For myself, I plan someday to dedicate an entire work to discussing the objections put forth by some of my critics, those who are responsible and acting in all good faith (for the others do not deserve the bother of a reply)."[5] But during the last year of his life, after noting that "methodological" criticisms brought against his conception of the history of religions had increased, Eliade wrote the following:

> The fault is, in part, mine; I've never replied to such criticisms, although I ought to have done so. I told myself that someday, "when I'm free from works in progress," I'll write a short theoretical monograph and explain the "confusions and errors" for which I am reproached. I'm afraid I'll never have time to write it. (*Journal IV*, 1979–1985, 143)

In my previous studies of Eliade—especially in *Structure and Creativity in Religion* and *Mircea Eliade et le phénomène religieux*[6]—perhaps my major original

---

4. See *Mircea Eliade, Journal IV*, 1979–1985, trans. Mac Linscott Ricketts. Chicago: University of Chicago Press, 1990, 41. For works by and about Eliade through 1978, see Douglas Allen and Dennis Doeing, *Mircea Eliade: An Annotated Bibliography*. New York: Garland, 1980.

5. Mircea Eliade, "Foreword" to my *Structure and Creativity in Religion: Hermeneutics in Mircea Eliade's Phenomenology and New Directions*. The Hague: Mouton Publishers, 1978, vii.

6. Douglas Allen, *Mircea Eliade et le phénomène religieux*. Paris: Payot, 1982.

contribution has been to submit that there is an impressive, underlying, implicit system at the foundation of Eliade's history and phenomenology of religion. Eliade is not simply a brilliant, unsystematic, intuitive genius, as extolled by some supporters, or a methodologically uncritical, unsystematic, hopelessly unscientific charlatan, as attacked by some critics. I formulated Eliade's foundational system primarily in terms of two key interacting concepts: the dialectic of the sacred and the profane, the universal structure in terms of which Eliade distinguishes religious phenomena; and religious symbolism, the coherent structural systems of religious symbols in terms of which Eliade interprets the meaning of religious phenomena. The essential universal systems of symbolic structures, when integrated with the essential universal structure of the dialectic of the sacred, constitute Eliade's hermeneutical framework and serve as the foundation for his phenomenological approach.

Eliade's systematic approach tends to be holistic, organic, and dialectical. The whole is more than the sum of its parts. No element can be understood in isolation but only in terms of its dynamic, mutually interacting relations with other key elements. New structures and meanings emerge through dynamic relations that cannot be found in any separate component part. The image of weaving, while limited, gets better at Eliade's approach than some analytic model of clear, linear progression.

My emphasis on the specific systematic nature of Eliade's theory should not convey the false impression that ambiguities, enigmas, and contradictions are for Eliade problems that need to be removed through rational systematic analysis. Just the opposite: Eliade often embraces and sustains ambiguities, enigmas, and contradictions as essential to mythic and spiritual life. When social scientists and other scholars look for clear definitions and linear progressive development in Eliade's writings, they are usually frustrated. Eliade often attacks other scholars who insist on clear definitions and linear development as employing rationalistic, scientific, positivistic, historicistic, naturalistic, or other reductionistic approaches that destroy the specific intentionality and nature of the religious world.

In this chapter, I focus on some of the boldest and most controversial claims in Eliade's theory of religion: his claims that the study of religion can serve—or even, must serve—as the basis for the cultural and spiritual renewal of modern human beings. I consider writings in which Eliade reflects on phenomena of the modern world in which the mythic and religious is often explicitly rejected.[7] I examine Eliade's proposals for overcoming modern anxiety, meaninglessness, and

---

7. In this regard, I shall not focus on Eliade's frequent claim that the sacred rather than being completely absent is frequently camouflaged, and hence unrecognizable, in the modern profane. By failing to recognize the concealed sacred, Eliade charges that modern human beings suffer from a self-defeating and dangerous Western provincialism. Eliade's extensive treatment of the camouflage of the sacred in the modern profane, including the modern unconscious, is presented as chapter 10 of my *Myth and Religion in Mircea Eliade*.

provincialism through a radical cultural and spiritual renewal. According to Eliade, such renewal can be achieved through a creative hermeneutics involving the rediscovering of our own symbolic and mythic structures and the authentic encounter with the mythic and religious world of "the other."

In these writings on the study of religion as a basis for cultural and spiritual renewal, Eliade is willing to take risks, to offer bold interpretations, and to make normative judgments about modern human beings, features of the contemporary world, and the nature of reality. Here we find levels of analysis, imaginative constructions, sweeping generalizations, and highly personal assertions that do not respect the defining features of specialized empirical and historical research. Eliade not only goes far beyond criteria of ethnologists and other social science specialists, but he also goes far beyond self-imposed disciplinary boundaries of almost all historians of religions and phenomenologists of religion.

There is a serious danger of misunderstanding my position arising from my focus in this chapter. I do not agree with Eliade's critics, who argue that his entire study of religion is based on his own religious orientation, on his normative assumptions and judgments, and on his assumed ontological and theological position. I also do not agree with several recent supporters, who argue that one cannot understand Eliade's study of religion without including his own personal, faith-oriented, humanistic, theological, or metaphysical commitments.[8] The vast majority of Eliade's scholarly writings on religion should be analyzed and assessed in terms of the history and the phenomenology of religion. In most of his studies, Eliade is attempting to interpret the religious meaning of phenomena for *homo religiosus*, not the religious meaning for Eliade.[9] However, in the following sections, Eliade often

---

8. See Douglas Allen, "Recent Defenders of Eliade: A Critical Evaluation," *Religion* 24 (1994): 333–351.

9. See the section entitled "Meaning for *homo religiosus* versus meaning for Eliade," in Allen, *Structure and Creativity in Religion*, 208–212. Eliade often asserts that he is interested in interpreting the believer as *homo religiosus*, but it is not clear what this term means. In *Myth and Religion in Mircea Eliade*, I attempt to clarify the meaning and significance of *homo religiosus* in Eliade's theory of religion. It would be false to identify *homo religiosus* with historically particular, flesh-and blood, individual, religious believers. *Homo religiosus* may be the subject of religious experiences of the sacred, but it is a type, a category, an essence, a view of human nature. As a generic, essentialized, universal category, *homo religiosus* is contrasted to *homo modernus*. In his formulations of *homo religiosus*, Eliade is involved in a complex process of imaginary idealization at a very high level of abstraction. He presents and argues for *homo religiosus* as this idealized, essentialized subject of religious experience. Critics charge that this idealized abstraction of essential sacred structures and meanings exists primarily in Eliade's head and is largely detached from the empirical, historical data of actual religious persons. My own view is that Eliade is primarily concerned with formulating a general theory of religion and not with presenting the meaning and significance of religion in the terms of the particular believer.

goes beyond the religious perspective of *homo religiosus*. He makes highly normative judgments in which he attacks the modern rejection of the sacred reality and the modern identifications with the temporal and the historical dimensions of reality. He makes ontological moves in which he affirms a religious orientation as more in touch with human nature and reality than modern, secular approaches. Since such analysis by Eliade often functions at the levels of metaphysics, ontology, and philosophical anthropology, there may be a danger in not realizing that Eliade's study of religion is usually formulated at the more descriptive and phenomenological levels of analysis.

THE RENEWAL OF MODERN HUMAN BEINGS

Not only does Eliade contend that modern, Western, historicistic, and other reductionistic approaches are inadequate for grasping the intentionality, deeper meaning, and ultimate significance of irreducibly religious data; he also contends that modern human beings and their Western cultures are in a condition of the most severe crisis. These two contentions are interrelated. As a reflection of the overall modern desacralized orientation, scholarly approaches that are inadequate for deciphering profound mythic, symbolic, religious structures and meanings exhibit the very same characteristics that define the ways moderns have repressed and denied much of their humanity and cannot solve their basic existential and historical crises. Both modern human beings, in general, and modern scholarly approaches, in particular, are in need of radical renewal.

Creative Hermeneutics

Eliade maintains that his scholarly discipline of the history of religions has a special role—even the most important role—to play in challenging Western provincialism and serving as an indispensable means for cultural renewal. The following passage is typical of Eliade's formulations.

> I see the history of religions as a total discipline. I understand now that the encounters, facilitated by depth psychology, with the stranger within, with that which is foreign, exotic, archaic in ourselves, on the one hand—and, on the other, the appearance of Asia and of exotic or "primitive" groups in history—are cultural moments which find their ultimate meaning only from the perspective of the history of religions. The hermeneutic necessary for the revelation of the meanings and the messages hidden in myths, rites, symbols, will also help us to understand both depth psychology and the historical age into which we are entering and in which we will be not only surrounded but also dominated by the "foreigners," the non-Occidentals. It will be possible to decipher the

"Unconscious," as well as the "Non-Western World," through the hermeneutic of the history of religions.[10]

Similarly, in the foreword to *Mephistopheles and the Androgyne,* Eliade submits:

> Hermeneutics—the science of interpretation—is the Western man's reply—the only intelligent reply—to the demands of contemporary history, to the fact that the West is committed (one might be tempted to say "condemned") to a confrontation with the cultural values of the "others." Now in this present situation, hermeneutics will find its most valuable ally in the history of religions.

When the history of religions assumes its proper hermeneutical role, it will allow us to recognize and interpret the deep structures and meanings of the "strange worlds" of two "others": the world of the unconscious—which is the plane of camouflaged mythic and sacred manifestation in modern consciousness—and the world of mythic, symbolic, sacred phenomena of archaic, Asian, and other non-Western cultures.[11] The true indispensable method of the history and phenomenology of religion is "creative hermeneutics." As seen in Eliade's frequent attacks on "reductionism" and in his distinguishing historical explanation from the interpretation of meaning, Eliade insists that the most important, antireductionistic, hermeneutical work must be done by the history of religion.[12] Historians of religion have been "timid" at the very moment when the history of religions should be exemplary

---

10. *No Souvenirs: Journal, 1957–1969,* trans. Fred H. Johnson Jr. New York: Harper and Row, 1977, 69–70. Also published as Eliade, *Journal II, 1957–1969.* Chicago: University of Chicago Press, 1989. See also Mircea Eliade, *Myths, Dreams, and Mysteries,* trans. Philip Mairet. New York: Harper and Row, Torchbooks, 1967, 7–12.

11. *Mephistopheles and the Androgyne: Studies in Religious Myth and Symbol,* trans. J. M. Cohen. New York: Sheed and Ward, 1965, 9-15. In *Journal III, 1970-1978,* trans. Teresa Lavender Fagan. Chicago: University of Chicago Press, 1989, Eliade states: "I am also convinced that under the pressure of history we will be forced to familiarize ourselves with the different expressions of extra-European creative genius, such as are found in Asia, Africa, and Oceania. As I've repeated over and over for thirty years, only the history of religions furnishes the discipline that can bring to light the meaning not only of traditional, but also of 'primitive' and Oriental civilizations. In a word, this is a discipline—such at least as I envision and practice it—that will contribute decisively to 'globalizing' culture" (226).

12. In chapter 1 of *Myth and Religion in Mircea Eliade,* I present Eliade's antireductionistic approach to the study of religion and his frequent attacks on different kinds of reductionism. In chapter 2, I formulate and assess the diverse claims of Eliade's reductionistic critics. In chapter 9, I examine the key distinction in the study of religion between interpreting religious meaning (Eliade's claim) versus providing historical and other explanations (reflecting the positions of most of Eliade's critics).

in the interpretation of the deep mythic symbolic meaning of "the other." Only the historian of religions can do this hermeneutical work "for only he is prepared to understand and appreciate the complexity of his documents." The road to creative synthesis leads through such hermeneutical work.[13] Eliade's primary justification for his claim that the history of religions is best equipped—or even only equipped—for this hermeneutical work is the following: the hidden, camouflaged, and "foreign" other is a mythic, symbolic, spiritual creation and can only be understood from an irreducibly religious perspective. In trying to understand the spiritualities of Asia and the archaic world, Westerners must engage in a genuine and fruitful dialogue that

> cannot be limited to empirical and utilitarian language. A true dialogue must deal with the central values in the cultures of the participants. Now, to understand these values rightly, it is necessary to know their religious sources. For, as we know, non-European cultures, both oriental and primitive, are still nourished by a rich religious soil. This is why we believe that the History of Religions is destined to play an important role in contemporary cultural life.

At this historical moment, how are we "to assimilate *culturally* the spiritual universes that Africa, Oceania, Southeast Asia open to us? All these spiritual universes have a religious origin and structure. If one does not approach them in the perspective of the History of Religions, they will disappear as spiritual universes." They "will not be grasped as spiritual creations; they will not enrich Western and world culture."[14] Eliade claims that "an encounter with the 'totally other,' whether conscious or unconscious, gives rise to an experience of a religious nature." It is "possible that the attraction of the unconscious and its activities, the interest in myths and symbols, the fascination of the exotic, the primitive, the archaic, and encounters with the 'others,' with all the ambivalent feelings they imply—that all this may one day appear as a new type of religious experience" (*Mephistopheles and the Androgyne*, 11–12).

This hermeneutical work is not some static, one-way interpretation of mythic symbolic structures and meanings of others. Modern human beings, their cultures, and the interpreters themselves will be profoundly changed by creative hermeneutics. A creative hermeneutics is "among the living sources of a culture. For, in short,

---

13. Mircea Eliade, "Crisis and Renewal in History of Religions," *History of Religions* 5 (1965): 5, 6, 9.

14. Mircea Eliade, "History of Religions and a New Humanism," *History of Religions* 1 (1961): 2; and Eliade, "Crisis and Renewal in the History of Religions," 16. These articles are reprinted as "A New Humanism" and as "Crisis and Renewal" in *The Quest: History and Meaning in Religion*. Chicago: University of Chicago Press, 1969.

every culture is constituted by a series of interpretations and revalorizations of its 'myths' or its specific ideologies. It is not only the creators *stricto sensu* who reassess the primordial visions and who reinterpret the fundamental ideas of a culture; it is also the 'hermeneuts.' " Hermeneutics leads to the creation of new cultural values. A "creative hermeneutics unveils significations that one did not grasp before, or puts them in relief with such vigor that after having assimilated this new interpretation the consciousness is no longer the same." "In the end, the creative hermeneutics *changes* man; it is more than instruction, it is also a spiritual technique susceptible of modifying the quality of existence itself. This is true above all for the historico-religious hermeneutics" ("Crisis and Renewal," 7–8). In this hermeneutical work of attempting to understand the existential situations expressed in the religious documents of the other, "the historian of religions will inevitably attain to a deeper knowledge of man. It is on the basis of such a knowledge that a new humanism, on a world-wide scale, could develop."[15]

This hermeneutical work of cultural renewal will be divided into two inter-related parts of the same overall creative hermeneutics. First, creative hermeneutics will allow modern human beings to uncover and understand mythic and symbolic structures that are already "buried" in their long "forgotten" spiritual history and in the unconscious of contemporary secular persons. Second, creative hermeneutics will allow moderns to engage in the confrontation, encounter, and dialogue with the mythic, religious, non-Western "other."

Rediscovering Symbolic and Mythic Structures

Eliade's studies of religion contain numerous attempts to identify, unconceal, and interpret the nature, meaning, and significance of religious phenomena. This section will only add some of his hermeneutical claims that modern, secular human beings have "forgotten" or are incapable of recognizing mythic symbolic structures that are already "there" in their spiritual histories and present unconscious. Moderns are a result of such past spiritual histories—a human cultural history of transhistorical essential mythic and symbolic structures for dealing with "boundary situations" and the deepest existential crises—and of the functioning of the mythic and symbolic structures of their unconscious. But imprisoned in the limited historical and temporal horizon of the modern mode of being, they are not aware of this. Through a creative hermeneutics, modern consciousness can be stimulated to overcome its "amnesia,"

---

15. "History of Religions and a New Humanism," 3. In *No Souvenirs*, Eliade maintains: "To the degree that you understand a religious fact (myth, ritual, symbol, divine figure, etc.), you change, you are modified—and this change is the equivalent of a step forward in the process of self liberation" (310). See also *No Souvenirs*, 233.

recognize what has been forgotten but remains at the foundation of constituted consciousness and being, and provide the means for cultural renewal and a deeper understanding of true human nature and the nature of reality.[16] Eliade maintains that "given the nature of the documents with which he works, the historian of religions is aware that his exegesis can eventually stimulate, through a curious process of anamnesis, the creative faculties of all those who passionately wish to know what the human spirit is capable of."[17] Matei Calinescu distinguishes the more skeptical and agnostic "unknowable" from Eliade's "unrecognizable" as a variant of the Platonic anamnesis, in which knowledge, in principle, is accessible to those who can recognize or "remember" it.[18] In his analysis of Eliade's "Nineteen Roses," Calinescu states that the central question of hermeneutics is linked with the broad question of memory as a way to mythical truth. After describing Eliade's literary techniques of anamnesis, such as attempts "to translate the dialectic of mythical unrecognizability into concrete, situational symmetries and oppositions," and the narrative unfolding of anamnesis in accord with the essential structures of initiation, Calinescu concludes that Eliade's fantastic of interpretation is a hermeneutic of trust and optimism.

> Eliade's fantastic of interpretation persuades the reader to look at images, symbols, metaphors, stories, or inventions as possible bearers of epiphanies or remembrances. By means of these devices the imagination breaks out of the amnesia in which modernity has trapped it to recall and revive lost worlds of meaning. The larger message of Eliade's fantastic prose is, in brief, that interpretation remains our best hope for an anamnesis of mythical truth.[19]

In his study of "Symbolism of the 'Centre,'" Eliade discusses how the history of religions could lead to a modern awakening, a renewal of consciousness, of archaic and other essential symbolic structures, whether still living or fossilized in religious traditions. What is needed is a more spiritual hermeneutical technique.

> One could equally call this a new *maieutics*. Just as Socrates, according to the *Theaetetus* (149 a, 161 e), acted on the mind obstetrically, bringing to birth thoughts it did not know it contained, so the history of

---

16. Since this topic of rediscovering and recognizing mythic and symbolic structures and meanings is so central to Eliade's studies of religion, I shall focus on only a few of Eliade's writings where he discusses this in terms of techniques and methods of anamnesis.

17. *Journal III*, 262. See also *Journal IV*, 54.

18. Matei Calinescu, "Imagination and Meaning: Aesthetic Attitudes and Ideas in Mircea Eliade's Thought," *Journal of Religion* 57 (1977): 4.

19. Matei Calinescu, "Introduction: The Fantastic and Its Interpretation in Mircea Eliade's Later Novellas," in *Youth Without Youth and Other Novellas*, ed. Matei Calinescu and trans. Mac Linscott Ricketts. Columbus: Ohio State University Press, 1988, xxx–xxxvii.

religions could bring forth a new man, more authentic and more complete: for, through the study of the religious traditions, modern man would not only rediscover a kind of archaic behaviour, he would also become conscious of the spiritual riches implied in such behaviour. (*Images and Symbols*, 35)

Eliade continues: "This maieutics effected with the aid of religious symbolism would also help to rescue modern man from his cultural provincialism and, above all, from his historical and existentialist relativism." Nonhistorical symbolic structures already exist in modern human beings;

> it is only necessary to reactivate them and bring them to the level of consciousness. By regaining awareness of his own anthropocosmic symbolism—which is only one variety of the archaic symbolism—modern man will obtain a new existential dimension, totally unknown to present-day existentialism and historicism: this is an authentic and major mode of being, which defends man from nihilism and historical relativism without thereby taking him out of history. For history itself will one day be able to find its true meaning: that of the epiphany of a glorious and absolute human condition. (35–36)[20]

In the controversial concluding section to his study of "mythologies of memory and forgetting," Eliade focuses on anamnesis and the modern passion for historiography. He uses his interpretation of traditional mythic treatments of memory and forgetting to disclose the deeper meaning and significance of this modern secular phenomenon. Eliade is concerned not with investigations into the meaning of history but rather with historiography itself: "the *endeavor to preserve the memory* of contemporary events and the desire to know the past of humanity as accurately as possible." From the nineteenth century on, historiography has played such a prominent role that it "seems as if Western culture were making a prodigious effort of historiographic *anamnesis*." With such a widening of the historical horizon, the modern "goal is no less than to revive the *entire past of humanity*."[21] Eliade finds

---

20. This quotation and many previous citations contain ontological moves and personal judgments, often on a highly normative philosophical level. Focusing on this quotation, much of contemporary philosophy, especially in its non-Eliadean antifoundationalism, would agree with Eliade about the problem of historical and existential relativism. But for those philosophers for whom such relativism is a serious problem, Eliade's claim that the reactivation and recollection of nonhistorical mythic and symbolic structures is the way to overcome relativism and nihilism will hardly seem like an adequate philosophical response.

21. *Myth and Reality*, trans. Willard R. Trask. New York: Harper and Row, 1963, 134–136. In *Myths, Dreams, and Mysteries* (233–235), Eliade interprets this "modern passion for historiography" as part of the modern awareness and anxiety in confronting history and one's historicity and as revealing, from a traditional religious perspective, an archaic symbolism of death.

much that is encouraging in this modern emphasis on historiography, not only in undermining Western cultural provincialism, but also "through this historiographic *anamnesis* man enters deep into himself. If we succeed in understanding a contemporary Australian, or his homologue, a paleolithic hunter, we have succeeded in 'awakening' in the depths of our being the existential situation and the resultant behavior of a prehistoric humanity." Such a historiographic anamnesis "finds expression in the discovery of our solidarity with these vanished or peripheral peoples" and in a genuine recovery of the past. This historiographic anamnesis, opening us to other perspectives, can be viewed as a way that moderns, unconsciously, defend themselves against the pressure of contemporary history, but "in the case of modern man there is something more. His historiographic horizon being as wide as it has become, he is able, through *anamnesis,* to discover cultures that, though they 'sabotaged History,' were prodigiously creative" (*Myth and Reality,* 136–137). This historiographical anamnesis of the modern Western world is only beginning. Though on a secular plane, without invoking religious myths or practices, this historiographic anamnesis continues a profound religious evaluation of memory and forgetting. There is this common element: "the importance of precise and total recollection of the past. In the traditional societies it is recollection of *mythical events;* in the modern West it is recollection of *all that took place in historical Time.* The difference is too obvious to require definition. But both types of *anamnesis* project man out of his 'historical moment.' And true historiographic *anamnesis* opens, too, on a primordial Time, the Time in which men established their cultural behavior patterns, even though believing that they were revealed to them by Supernatural Beings" (138). This interpretation of Eliade's creative hermeneutics, as consisting of such a rediscovery of mythic and symbolic sacred structures that then serve as the basis for cultural renewal, is both instructive but also potentially misleading. There is certainly the sense in Eliade's scholarly writings that the sacred is present, but buried and unrecognized, in our spiritual history and in our unconscious. Hermeneutics allows us to overcome our amnesia. The history of religions can stimulate our imagination, enlarge our consciousness, and allow us to recall and recognize the camouflaged sacred. The unconcealed sacred can then serve as the indispensable basis for modern Western and global renewal. In Eliade's theory of religion, in his hermeneutical framework for interpreting religious structures and meanings, and in his understanding of the specific orientation of *homo religiosus,* there is the sense that scholarly understanding, as well as spiritual growth, consists in remembering and recognizing what is already there, but has been forgotten. Trapped in the conditionings of the profane, human beings forget the mythic sacred essence that precedes their temporal historical existence. Modern persons have lost awareness of nontemporal, nonhistorical structures that are permanent essential structures of consciousness. Although the sacred and its universal mythic and symbolic structures constitute the human condition as such, modern Western cultures have forgotten this and seek, unsuccessfully, to resolve their deep existential and historical crises within the nonmythic, nonsacred horizon of historical temporality.

Such an interpretation can be misleading if it conveys a philosophically unacceptable sense of passivity on the part of constituting subjects. In his formulations of the dialectic of the sacred and in his theory of symbolism and myth, Eliade contributes to this unacceptable impression that sacred signs, images, symbols, and myths are just "there," waiting to be unconcealed, uncamouflaged, accurately remembered. As a nonhistorical atemporal "given," the sacred needs to be recognized, not created and constituted, by us. The sacred "shows itself." Modern human beings have forgotten this, and, misled by its camouflage in the profane, fail to recognize the sacred present in their unconscious and in contemporary phenomena.

Nevertheless, a more adequate interpretation of the rediscovery of mythic and symbolic structures, including an analysis of techniques and methods of anamnesis, emphasizes the sacred not as some passive given, but as a dynamic constituted given. There is also considerable evidence for this interpretation in Eliade's writings. For example, after stating that it is too soon to evaluate the contributions of structuralist approaches to the study of religion, especially to understanding the manifestation of religious creativity appearing in the flow of time and history, Eliade concludes *Australian Religions* with the following:

> And this is of a paramount importance; for the ultimate goal of the historian of religions is not to point out that there exist a certain number of types or patterns of religious behavior, with their specific symbologies and theologies, but rather to *understand their meanings*. And such meanings are not *given* once and for all, are not "petrified" in the irrespective religious patterns, but rather are "open," in the sense that they change, grow, and enrich themselves in a creative way in the process of history (even if "history" is not apprehended in the Judeo-Christian or modern Western sense). Ultimately, the historian of religions cannot renounce hermeneutics.[22]

Here we have the emphasis found throughout Eliade's writings on the imagination and creativity of human beings who dynamically unconceal hidden symbolic and mythic structures and constitute sacred meanings and significances. The sacred may "show itself," but *homo religiosus* is not some passive receptor. The dialectic of the sacred is a dynamic complex process of transfiguration and transformation. Mythic and symbolic structures are "given," but as unfinished and "open"; given to us in such ways that require our active participation as consti-

---

22. *Australian Religions: An Introduction.* Ithaca: Cornell University Press, 1973, 200.

tuting subjects. The given structures are creatively revalorized and reconstituted by concretely living human beings. What is remembered and recognized of the symbolic, mythic, sacred givenness is at least partially determined by specific historical and cultural conditions, and what is constituted as sacred meaning is at least partially determined by immediate, concrete, existential concerns. Therefore, in the general method for rediscovering mythic and symbolic structures, even in the specific emphasis on a sacred that has been forgotten and the indispensability of techniques of anamnesis, one need not endorse some passive remembrance of given, unchanging, sacred essences. Instead, anamnesis and recognition may be interpreted as part of a dynamic process of unconcealing and reconstituting sacred structures and meanings.

Of course, such an interpretation by itself does not clarify complex philosophical issues or justify bold epistemological and metaphysical claims. Philosophers, for example, continually reinterpret and debate what Plato may have intended by "anamnesis" and how this relates to his theory of reality. What precisely is meant by "recollection" of Forms or Ideas? What is the metaphysical status of the reality that is remembered? What is the relation between the forgotten ultimate reality and the world of appearances? By anamnesis, is Plato endorsing some bold metaphysical doctrine—perhaps even involving a belief in reincarnation—or is he making a more modest epistemological claim?

In short, in his assertions about hidden nontemporal, nonhistorical, mythic, and symbolic structures and the need for modern persons to remember the camouflaged forgotten sacred, Eliade often makes bold philosophical judgments and normative claims about reality. But he does not provide the clarification, analysis, and arguments to justify his philosophical position. One possible judgment is that such writings are hopelessly uncritical. The most generous judgment is that such writings, going beyond the disciplinary boundaries of the history of religions, the social sciences, and the phenomenology of religion, may serve as a catalyst for new, more comprehensive, more creative, philosophical reflection.

ENCOUNTER, CONFRONTATION, AND DIALOGUE

One of Eliade's most daring attempts at creative hermeneutics is his formulation of imagined encounters between modern Western and traditional non-Western cultures. Such encounters are indispensable for the creative renewal of modern culture. Eliade contends that "the prime phenomenon of the twentieth century" has been "the discovery of non-European man and his spiritual universe." Today "we are beginning to be aware of the nobility and spiritual autonomy of those civilizations. The dialogue with them seems to me more important for the future of European spirituality than is the spiritual revival which the radical emancipation of the proletariat could bring."²³ Eliade is not interested in establishing a dialogue with modern Western thinkers.

> Personally, I think that these [modern Western] cultural horizons are provincial. The crises and problematical issues of a Freud, Nietzsche, Marx, etc., have been left behind or resolved. As for me, I'm trying to *open* windows onto other worlds for Westerners—even if some of these worlds foundered tens of thousands of years ago. My dialogue has other interlocutors than those of Freud or James Joyce: I'm trying to understand a Paleolithic hunter, a yogi or a shaman, a peasant from Indonesia, an African, etc., and to communicate with each one. (*No Souvenirs*, 179)

The phenomenology and history of religions are essential for the imminent encounter and dialogue between the modern West and traditional non-Western cultures. In 1944 while still in Lisbon, Eliade observed that the whole world was being transformed, India would soon gain independence, and Asia was reentering history. But for him such events had much more than political significance.

> Soon there would become possible a new confrontation—on a footing of equality—between Oriental and Occidental spirituality. But the dialogue was possible only if the true Oriental spirituality—that is, its religious matrix—was correctly known and understood in the Occident. The phenomenology and history of religions, as I practiced it, seemed to me the most suitable preparation for this imminent dialogue. On the other hand, the archaic world—that of the "primitives" whom anthropologists had studied for a century—could not remain very long under its colonial guise. But for Occidentals, the understanding of archaic spirituality was even more difficult, because it presupposed a minimum comprehension of mythical thought.²⁴

Eliade's "encounters"—often described as "confrontations"—and "dialogues" between the modern West and the traditional Asian and archaic non-West are, for the most part, not genuine interactive encounters and dialogues. The modern West usually serves as little more than a foil for raising valuable non-Western critiques and alternatives. Occasionally Eliade indicates how the modern West might respond, but he usually has little time or patience formulating Western condemnations of premoderns as "primitive," backward, subjective, irrational, nonhistorical, and unprepared for the challenges of the contemporary world. He is not concerned with addressing contemporary crises in the non-Western world and the typical solutions the West proposes to resolve these crises. Instead he often formulates the

---

23. *Journal I, 1945–1955*, trans. Mac Linscott Ricketts. Chicago: University of Chicago Press, 1990, 163.

24. *Autobiography, Volume II: 1937–1960, Exile's Odyssey*, trans. Mac Linscott Ricketts. Chicago: University of Chicago Press, 1988, 107. See also *Journal IV*, 10–11.

encounter, confrontation, and dialogue around existential, historical, and cultural crises in the modern West. The encounter is intended primarily to give voice to archaic and non-Western perspectives, to critique and expose the limitations of modern perspectives, and to suggest possibilities for Western renewal if moderns listen and learn from the non-Western, mythic, religious "others." This hermeneutical encounter can be seen in two of Eliade's illustrations: modern anxiety and the modern response to "the terror of history."[25]

In his study of "Religious Symbolism and the Modern Man's Anxiety" under "The Encounter: A Test-Case," Eliade's interprets the nature, meaning, and significance of the extreme anxiety defining much of modern secular life as seen from "external," archaic and Indian, mythic and religious perspectives (*Myths, Dreams, and Mysteries*, 231–245). He explores how these non-Western cultures, with their basic religious structure, would understand and judge our modern Western crisis. In this encounter—which is almost entirely a one-way confrontation—the archaic and the Indian are not surprised by modern anxiety. They too analyze awareness of temporal and historical existence as generating anguish and anxiety as one confronts death and nothingness. What astonishes them is that modern persons affirm and remain at this experiential stage of temporality, historicity, and resultant anxiety rather than viewing it in relation to the symbolisms of initiation and as an indispensable rite of passage to another mode of being. In light of the mythic archaic perspective, this anxiety gains meaning and value not as an end but rather as a first transitional stage of initiation.[26] For both archaic and Indian, *"this anxiety is not a state in which one can remain; its indispensability is that of an initiatory experience, of a rite of passage."* Only in modern culture do we stop in the middle of the rite of passage without resolving the crisis generating our experience of anxiety (*Myths, Dreams and Mysteries*, 242–243).[27]

---

25. Because of limited space, I shall not present Eliade's detailed formulations and my analysis of these two illustrations. For my treatment of Eliade's illustration of the hermeneutical encounter arising from modern anxiety, see *Myth and Religion in Mircea Eliade*, 303–305. For my treatment of Eliade's illustration of the encounter arising from the modern response to the terror of history, see *Myth and Religion in Mircea Eliade*, 305–308.

26. See Eliade's interpretation of the initiatory significance of suffering, the symbolism of initiatory death, the other aspects of the myths, rituals, and symbolism of initiation in "Mysteries and Spiritual Regeneration," in *Myths, Dreams, and Mysteries*, 190–228, and the detailed treatments in *Rites and Symbols of Initiation: The Mysteries of Birth and Rebirth*, trans. Willard R. Trask. New York: Harper Torchbooks, 1965 and in *Shamanism: Archaic Techniques of Ecstasy*, trans. Willard R. Trask. New York: Pantheon Books, 1964.

27. Eliade states that by seeing ourselves from the archaic and Indian perspectives, we are able "to rediscover the initiatory meanings and the spiritual values of anxiety, meanings and values well known to certain European mystical and metaphysical traditions. But this is as much as to say that a dialogue with the true Asiatic, African or Oceanian world helps us to rediscover spiritual positions that one is justified in regarding as universally valid" (244).

Eliade's second illustration of "the terror of history" is a common theme in his scholarly works, journals, and literary creations.[28] He formulates an encounter and "conflict" between the archaic, antihistorical, mythic, religious conception and the modern post-Hegelian conception which seeks to be historical. More specifically, Eliade restricts this confrontation to one aspect of "the problem": "the solutions offered by the historicistic view to enable modern man to tolerate the increasingly powerful pressure of contemporary history." "How can the 'terror of history' be tolerated from the viewpoint of historicism?" (*The Myth of the Eternal Return*, 141–142, 147–150). After presenting some of the ways that traditional antihistorical religions have been able to endure and give value to the sufferings and tragedies of historical existence, Eliade reaches the following conclusion: "Whatever be the truth in respect to the freedom and the creative virtualities of historical man, it is certain that none of the historicistic philosophies is able to defend him from the terror of history." Human beings, who completely make themselves through history and who reject transhistorical, mythic, sacred models or who reject a freedom grounded in the Judaeo-Christian "category of faith," cannot defend themselves against the terror of history and cannot overcome their nihilism and despair (159–162).[29]

In terms of his traditional-modern "encounter," it is remarkable how quickly, and perhaps indistinguishably, Eliade often moves from presenting archaic, Indian, and other traditional views to endorsing them. And he sometimes endorses them not as specific traditional approaches to anxiety and meaninglessness or to the terror of history, but rather as revealing essential truths about the human condition, historical existence, and reality as such.

In formulating such creative hermeneutics through confrontation and dialogue, Eliade is not advocating that we simply return to some premodern conception. There is a sense of "return" as a rediscovery of hidden and forgotten mythic and symbolic structures and meanings. But for Eliade the renewal of modern human beings will involve unexpected "breakthroughs" and new spiritual creations. Through the creative hermeneutical encounter with the archaic and non-Western other, focusing on the terror of history and other existential concerns, modern

---

28. The most developed formulation is the chapter entitled "The Terror of History," in *The Myth of the Eternal Return*, trans. Willard R. Trask. New York: Pantheon Books, 1954, 139–162. In *Myth and Religion in Mircea Eliade*, I also examine Eliade's treatment of "the terror of history" in terms of his interpretation of "cosmic Christianity" (chapter 4), his personal and scholarly antihistorical attitudes (chapter 8), and his normative antihistorical judgments (chapter 9).

29. In *Structure and Creativity in Religion* and in *Myth and Religion in Mircea Eliade*, I emphasize that such normative antihistorical judgments about the terror of history involve an ontological stance and philosophical claims that go beyond perspectival boundaries of the history and phenomenology of religion.

culture will be renewed by rejecting major features of historical existence and by incorporating, in new creative ways, essential mythic and religious conceptions that disclose aspects of the universal human spirit.

THE RENEWAL OF PHILOSOPHY

Eliade contends that an understanding of myth and religion will not only allow us to understand traditional religious phenomena, the archaic, Asian, and other non-Western orientations. It will also allow us to understand better the unconscious, the imagination, dreams, fantasies, ideologies, aesthetic creativity, and other aspects of contemporary life. It will also allow us to establish a creative encounter and dialogue with the religious "other"; confront our own limited, self-deceptive, self-defeating, and dangerous cultural provincialism; and participate in a desperately needed Western and global cultural renewal.

When reviewing Eliade's generalizations and negative judgments about the modern mode of being in the world, it is tempting to classify him as antimodern premodernist. Most critics and some supporters have interpreted his scholarly approach as privileging an archaic ontology and endorsing a premodern, antihistorical, mythic, symbolic, cosmic, religious mode of being.

It is also possible to interpret Eliade's negative judgments about modernity as sharing characteristics with antimodern postmodernist approaches. "Postmodernism" is a very fashionable term among many contemporary philosophers, literary theorists, and other scholars, although the term tends to be very vague. It tends to resist any clear definition or coherent formulation because it often upholds the inviolability of differences and sees attempts at coherence as oppressive forms of intellectual and cultural hegemony. Nevertheless, the following assertions of much of postmodernism characterize Eliade's approach to religion. We must resist the tyranny and domination of the modernist idols of science, rationalism, and "objectivity." The Enlightenment gave us narrow, oppressive, hierarchical, reductionist projects of rationalistic and scientific hegemony. But rational scientific discourse is only one of the ways that human beings construct their "stories" about reality. The mythic religious narrative, as another autonomous way of constructing a story about truth, history, the human condition, and reality should not be reduced to scientific, rational, historical, and other nonmythic, nonreligious discourses. The mythic must be respected as one of many legitimate expressions of a multiplicity of irreducible, incommensurable stories about truth and reality. None of the particular stories mirrors or exhausts all of reality. Each of the stories has its own nature, structure, function, and significance; makes different claims about truth and reality; fulfills different emotional, imaginative, conceptual, and aesthetic needs for different people; and functions differently in different historical and cultural contexts.

Although Eliade sounds like this postmodernism when arguing against modern forms of reductionism, in many fundamental respects he clearly rejects such a postmodernist orientation. For example, Eliade insists on the need to respect "separate planes of reference," but he often violates this principle. He claims that we can only understand much of modern secular behavior in terms of a mythic religious plane of reference. In addition, Eliade, in his critique of modernity, is not simply insisting on a separate, mythic, sacred space so that he can tell an alternative story. He is not embracing some postmodernist relativism by endorsing the legitimacy of a plurality of irreducibly autonomous stories about reality. He makes universal absolute judgments about human nature, the human condition, and ultimate reality. Eliade may submit that "the scale creates the phenomenon,"[30] but he does not believe that all "scales" are equally legitimate. He judges the scales of modernity as inauthentic, provincial, incapable of solving their own existential and historical crises, and denying human and cosmic reality. He privileges a religious scale as providing access to the deepest structures and meanings of the human condition as such and reality as such. Therefore, from the above typical postmodernist perspective, Eliade would be criticized for formulating another universalizing, totalizing, essentializing, hegemonic project.

In this chapter and in previous works, I analyze Eliade's normative judgments that involve ontological and metaphysical claims functioning on a philosophical "plane of reference." I examine Eliade's philosophical assertions seen in normative judgments about *homo religiosus* as constitutive of essential human nature; about the meaninglessness and unreality of the modern mode of being; and about the sacred, transcendent, symbolic, and mythic structure of reality. On the basis of primordial, nonhistorical, mythic, and religious structures and meanings, Eliade makes bold philosophical claims about time and history, the true human mode of being, and ultimate reality. For example, the deep universal structure of the symbolic expressions of celestial flight and ascension, as found in experiences of ecstasy, is disclosed in shamanism and in numerous other mythic and religious phenomena, but also in dreams and fantasies of modern persons. This structure reveals an essential meaning of transcendence and freedom; an ontological abolition of the human condition. For Eliade this reveals a primordial, nonhistorical, universal dimension of the human condition that is coexistence with human nature.[31]

Eliade's makes the bold metaphysical claim that any human being "whatever else he may be free of, is forever the prisoner of his own archetypal intuitions,

---

30. See, for example, *Patterns in Comparative Religion*, trans. Rosemary Sheed. New York: World Publishing Co., Meridian Books, 1963, xiii.

31. See, for example, *Shamanism*, xiv; and *Myths, Dreams, and Mysteries*, 106.

formed at the moment when he first perceived his position in the cosmos." Eliade continues: the

> longing for Paradise can be traced even in the most banal actions of the modern man. Man's concept of the *absolute* can never be completely uprooted: it can only be debased. And primitive spirituality lives on in its own way not in action, not as a thing man can effectively accomplish, but as a *nostalgia* which creates things that become values in themselves: art, the sciences, social theory, and all the other things to which men will give the whole of themselves. (*Patterns in Comparative Religion*, 433–434)

Similarly, Eliade makes the philosophical claim that "certain primordial revelations can never disappear." Eliade continues that as long as we are part of the cosmic rhythm, "I don't think man can be changed." Eliade grants that we are conditioned by economic and social structures, and our specific religious expressions are conditioned. "But, nevertheless, we still assume that human condition here—here in this cosmos, whose rhythms and cycles are ineluctably given. So we assume our human condition on the basis of that fundamental experiential condition. And that 'basic' human being—it is permissible to call him 'religious,' whatever appearances may seem to say, because we are talking about the meaning of life."[32]

Scholars may question why a human being's becoming aware of her or his own mode of being in the world necessarily constitutes a religious experience; why a person who affirms a secular mode of being can never abolish his or her permanent religious nature; or why a concern "about the meaning of life" automatically makes a position "religious," even if the concern is expressed in nonreligious terms. As I have tried to show, Eliade can make such philosophical claims only because of his assumptions and normative judgments about the religious nature of the human condition, human nature, and ultimate reality.

In some of his writing, Eliade not only makes such philosophical assertions but he also submits that the history and phenomenology of religion themselves have great philosophical significance: They will provide the indispensable means for new, creative, philosophical reflection; as keys to the renewal of Western culture, they will provide the means for the renewal of Western philosophy; and they will contribute to the formulation of new philosophical anthropologies.

In 1976, Eliade observed that entries in his "secret journal" might reveal his own yearning for a philosophical work.

---

32. *Ordeal by Labyrinth: Conversations with Claude-Henri Rocquet*, trans. Derek Coltman. Chicago: University of Chicago Press, 1982, 116–117.

> The fervor with which I rework to better develop reflections inspired by the camouflaging of the sacred in the profane must have a deeper meaning, and I'm just beginning to have an inkling of it. This dialectic of camouflaging is infinitely more vast and goes much farther than all that I've been able to say about it up until now. The "mystery of the mask" is fundamental to an entire metaphysics, for it is the very mystery of the human condition. If it obsesses me so much, it is probably because I don't decide to go into it in more depth, to make a systematic presentation of it, to study it from its own unique perspective, that of philosophical meditation. (*Journal III*, 221)[33]

In *The Myth of the Eternal Return,* Eliade indicates that he will examine a certain archaic "metaphysical 'valorization' of human existence." He goes on to reaffirm his "old conviction that Western philosophy is dangerously close to 'provincializing' itself" by isolating itself from its own tradition, ignoring the problems and solutions of archaic and Oriental thought, and refusing to recognize any "situations" except those of modern historical human existence. "We hold that philosophical anthropology would have something to learn from the valorization that pre-Socratic man (in other words, traditional man) accorded to his situation in the universe. Better yet: that the cardinal problems of metaphysics could be renewed through a knowledge of archaic ontology." Such renewal can come from learning about "certain spiritual positions that, although they have been transcended in various regions of the globe, are instructive for our knowledge of man and for man's history itself" (*The Myth of the Eternal Return*, ix–xi). Once again, Eliade is not advocating that Western philosophy "return" to pre-Socratic archaic ontologies so that contemporary philosophers can reestablish premodern philosophies. Even if some of his imaginary "nostalgias" suggest that, Eliade rejects such an impossible task. Rather, he advocates that philosophers "return" to the archaic other—including the archaic as part of our spiritual history and the archaic within us—in order to revalorize and reconstitute transhistorical mythic and symbolic religious structures and archaic primordial metaphysical insights into the human condition as part of new philosophical reflections and creativity.

Eliade claims: "More than any other humanistic discipline (i.e., psychology, anthropology, sociology, etc.), history of religions can open the way to a philosophical anthropology." This is because "the sacred is a universal dimension" and the beginnings of culture are rooted in religion. In addition, even modern, radically secularized, cultural creations and values cannot be understood without knowing

---

33. Eliade concludes: "It is thus possible that these reflections, because of their intimate character, only amplify better, although indirectly, my remorse in betraying my vocation as a philosopher."

"their original religious matrix." "Thus, the historian of religions is in a position to grasp the permanence of what has been called man's specific existential situation of 'being in the world' for the experience of the sacred is its correlate. In fact, man's becoming aware of his own mode of being and assuming his *presence* in the world together constitute a 'religious' experience" (*The Quest*, 9).

According to Eliade, the history of religions must play a unique indispensable role in opening new perspectives for Western philosophy. The historian of religions

> will decipher and elucidate enigmatic behavior and situations, in brief, that he will advance the understanding of man by recovering, and reestablishing meanings that have been forgotten, discredited, or abolished. The originality and importance of such contributions reside precisely in the fact that they explore and illuminate spiritual universes that are submerged or that are accessible only with great difficulty. It would be not only illegitimate but ineffectual to disguise archaic and exotic symbols, myths, and ideas in a form already familiar to contemporary philosophers....
>
> [Such] a historico-religious creative hermeneutics would be able to stimulate, nourish, and renew philosophical thought. From a certain point of view, one could say that a new *Phenomenology of the Mind* awaits elaboration by taking account of all that the history of religions is capable of revealing to us. There would be important books to write on modes of existence in the world or on the problems of time, death, and dream, based on documents that the historian of religions has at his disposal. (63–64)

Eliade thus endorses a view of cultural and philosophical creativity and renewal in which our encounter with essential symbolic and mythic structures is a catalyst allowing us to burst open our self-imposed cultural boundaries and experience new ways of knowing, relating, and being.

On the level of greatest generality, Eliade's ontological moves and normative judgments—such as those about the human mode of being generally, the human condition as such, and reality as such—involve philosophical reflection on the level of analysis of metaphysics and philosophical anthropology.[34] They involve a normative philosophical "leap" beyond normal disciplinary boundaries of history of religions. Eliade's philosophical reflections and judgments are dependent on the special ontological status of essential, nonhistorical, universal symbolisms, as they are revalorized

---

34. In *Structure and Creativity in Religion*, esp. 223–246, I examine Eliade's philosophical assumptions, normative judgments, metaphysical claims, and directions for new philosophical anthropologies.

and reactualized through mythic narratives and other religious phenomena. These symbolisms and their mythic and other symbolic expressions disclose the deepest structures and meanings of our mode of being in the world. They serve as ciphers of reality, expressing the enigmas and ambiguities of being and the inexhaustible possibilities for philosophical reflection.

Eliade would maintain that his ontological moves, normative judgments, and philosophical claims are not subjective and arbitrary since they are informed by and consistent with the basic intentionality of the essential symbolic structures, as expressed in mythic and other phenomena of the sacred. Philosophical reflection must continually return to its ontological foundation. This is necessary not only to enrich and renew consciousness, but also to check that philosophical analysis, on levels of greatest generality, has not distorted the basic intentionality of the sacred that constitutes its philosophical foundation.

In suggesting how Eliade might verify such ontological moves and philosophical judgments, one may consider a notion of a "wager" from the philosophical hermeneutics of Paul Ricoeur.[35] On the level of philosophical analysis, Eliade is claiming the following. On the basis of the assumption of an irreducibly religious perspective, especially by reflecting on the fundamental symbolic and mythic structures of the sacred, I can frame general existential concepts. My belief is that these fundamental symbolic and mythic structures disclose the deepest structures of the human mode of being and fulfill their deepest function when they reveal essential structures of the sacred. The essential symbols and their mythic expressions, when understood as particular revalorizations of coherent, transhistorical, universal symbolisms, reveal the deepest structures of "the universal"; they "open out" to the most general structures of reality.

Now let us "wager" that such ontological concepts, formulated from the religious perspective, will reveal the nature of the human being and of reality better than the existential concepts framed in terms of some nonreligious perspective. We shall *verify* such a wager by showing that the primary symbolic structures of religious experience have the power to illuminate the fundamental structures of the human consciousness and mode of being *generally*, of the human condition *as such*. Indeed, such a level of ontological analysis will reveal that only by experiencing the symbolic structures of the sacred, only by renewing ourselves through new revalorizations of religious symbolisms, can modern Western human beings overcome their "terror of history" and their existential anxiety and live a truly meaningful existence (*Structure and Creativity*, 242–243).

---

35. See Paul Ricoeur, *The Symbolism of Evil*, trans. Emerson Buchanan. New York: Harper and Row, 1967, 355–357; Allen, *Structure and Creativity in Religion*, 236–243.

Eliade's philosophical reflections—grounded in his study of religion—involve normative judgments about the impoverishment and provincialism of our modern perspective and about the desperate need for creative "openings." These creative "breakthroughs" will allow us to "burst open" our limiting conditionings and open us to new universes of significant meaning. The modern "self" must establish a dynamic relation with the traditional, mythic, archaic, and non-Western, religious "other." It must also establish a dynamic relation with its own "other" through the rediscovery of the forgotten "other" in our own spiritual history and in our modern unconscious. Such self-other relations will enable us to burst open our limiting structures and conditionings, allowing us to recognize new creative possibilities and to construct new philosophical anthropologies.

A CRITICAL ASSESSMENT

In most of my previous writings on Eliade, I have taken a rather sympathetic approach to his study of religion. Taking a phenomenological approach, I have attempted to suspend my own value judgments, to empathize with Eliade's approach, and to reconstruct his methodology and the hermeneutic framework at the foundation of his study of religion. Sometimes my reconstruction has taken the form of modifying and revising Eliade's approach to deal with serious criticisms, and I have also offered many critical evaluations. In this concluding section, I shall express appreciation for Eliade's contribution in his bold formulation of the study of religion as a basis for cultural and spiritual renewal. But I shall devote more time to some of my criticisms of Eliade's controversial judgments and interpretations.

On the one hand, Eliade's interpretations and judgments about modernity, the contemporary world, and reality—based on, but going far beyond his theory of myth and religion as seen in his study of religious data—are often challenging, insightful, and serve as a catalyst for further reflection, creativity, and "bursting open" some of our self-imposed limitations and provincialism. On the other hand, the fact that Eliade is willing to take risks and has a remarkable imagination does not free his interpretations and claims from requirements of rigorous scholarly analysis. And to claim, as some supporters have done, that Eliade is a mystic or a shaman or a literary figure who is not bothered by inconsistencies in his writings or with other scholarly criteria does not mean that an assessment of Eliade the scholar, with his own claims to scholarly interpretations and judgments, is inappropriate.

It is important to reaffirm that formulations found in this chapter go beyond disciplinary boundaries of the history and phenomenology of religion. Therefore, these interpretations and judgments will be judged negatively by many historians and phenomenologists of religion if they restrict themselves to methods of verification and other scholarly criteria of their disciplines. Scholars endorsing social scientific and other highly specialized approaches to religion will be even more critical. The fact that Eliade's analysis often functions at the levels of metaphysics, ontology, and philosophical anthropology does not free his interpretations and judgments from scholarly criteria, including the scholarly requirements of those normative disciplines and approaches. Often Eliade's metaphysical and ontological judgments are startling, suggestive, and sources for further reflection. But even on this level of interpretation and judgment, he usually has not developed a rigorous and complete analysis. As he occasionally states, this may be a project for others to undertake.

In addition, in my view, Eliade's study of religion has led him to controversial interpretations and judgments about the contemporary world and the future of humanity that are sometimes reactionary. They may appeal to various traditional, hierarchical, scholarly orientations, but in terms of Eliade's own professed ideals and goals, they may fall far short. Eliade insists on the separation of planes of analysis and reality and the primacy of an irreducibly religious framework for his own study. But he does not hesitate to make personal and scholarly judgments about economic, political, social, and historical planes of reference. With his focus on religious cultures, on an irreducibly religious essence of reality, and on the truth of a largely nonhistorical and antihistorical mode of being in the world, Eliade ignores, deemphasizes, and even attacks legitimate economic, social, political, and historical values and struggles. Rather than leading to self-empowerment and liberation, many of his formulations—if left as stated—would reproduce hierarchical structures of domination and leave most human beings imprisoned in structures of powerlessness, poverty, class exploitation, and gender and racial oppression.

Eliade presents many valuable challenges, insights, interpretations, and judgments that critique real dangers of modernity: Western provincialism and its domination over and denial of the reality of "the other"; tyranny and hegemony of a narrow-focused scientism, technology, instrumental reason, and rationalism; domination and exploitation of nature; the fragmentation, alienation, and lack of meaningful relations; lack of awareness of profound symbolic and mythic structures for constituting a meaningful and significant mode of being in the world; repression and denial of the total human being and the diversity of reality; and overspecialization and lack of creative synthesis. But even these valuable contributions usually need to be reformulated and integrated and synthesized with non-Eliadean approaches to religion, the contemporary world, and reality.

I shall conclude by submitting that Eliade's philosophical reflections, ontological moves, and normative judgments, as bold as they are—with sweeping generalizations, essentializing claims, and universal philosophical judgments—are in certain basic respects too narrow and too limited! We have seen Eliade's claim that a creative hermeneutics of the history of religions can stimulate and renew philosophical thought leading to the creation of a new "Phenomenology of the Mind."

We may use Hegel's general structural analysis in *The Phenomenology of Mind* to illustrate why Eliade's philosophical formulations must be enlarged.

My relational view of self is not unrelated to Hegel's general structural analysis of the dialectical process of self-development and self-alienation.[36] To become a more sensitive, conscious, and ethical self, Hegel tells us that the self, while maintaining its autonomy as subject, must "objectify" and "externalize" itself in relating to that which is "other." Self-alienation may result either when the self defines itself internally and refuses to externalize itself and relate authentically to the external other; or when the self objectifies itself and then gives up its capacity as an autonomous subject, thus allowing itself to be defined as immanent, nontranscending other. Through this dynamic process of self-externalization, the relation to the other provides the necessary basis for the dialectical movement of self-transcendence; for the reconstitution of the new, more conscious, more fulfilled self.

Today "the other" must be broadened beyond any modern, Western self-claims to ahistoric, universal objectivity to include other concepts of self with their different worlds of meaning. Eliade is correct that empathizing with and relating to other concepts of self (other perspectives of human nature, etc.), created by other cultures and even in other historical periods, may serve as a catalyst to our own creative process of self-constitution and self-development. Such a creative, nonoppressive relation to the other is a necessary condition for our own dynamic process of self-constitution, freedom, and development. For those of us in the modern, technological, industrialized West, complex nonoppressive encounters with other concepts of self can reveal new worlds of meaning: different ways to free our imaginations and be more in touch with our emotions; to experience nature and the cosmos; to relate to death, time, and history; to understand myths and symbols often already influencing us; in short, different ways of understanding and creating and recreating our own selves and our relations to others. Eliade is correct that the modern West has suppressed, repressed, and silenced many voices of "the other" and that it is imperative that we establish a dialogue and learn from the "messages" of these others.

Nevertheless, Eliade's approach, involving some of the most controversial aspects of his study of religion, needs to be enlarged for at least three reasons: he dismisses or devalues achievements of modernity; he excludes the voices of many "others" suppressed by the modern West; and he does not address how "others" have been and still are suppressed in traditional religious cultures. For example, the class

---

36. This analysis is developed in Douglas Allen, "Social Constructions of Self: Some Asian, Marxist, and Feminist Critiques of Dominant Western Views of Self," in *Culture and Self: Philosophical and Religious Perspectives, East and West*, ed. Douglas Allen. Boulder: Westview Press, 1997, 3–26.

and gender voices of the majority have been suppressed in *both* traditional and modern cultures.

In his specific religious assumptions, ontological moves, and normative judgments and in his reaction against a secular mode of being, Eliade has devalued or dismissed too much that is valuable in the modern constructed "self" and in the diverse experiences of "the other." In his tendency to romanticize and idealize much of the premodern mythic—in contrast to sweeping condemnations and dismissals of the modern—Eliade focuses on what is negative while ignoring what is positive about modernity; and he focuses on what is positive while ignoring what is negative about premodern cultures. For example, as someone who is quite sympathetic to many of Eliade's condemnations of oppressive scientific reductionism and hegemony, I do not believe that science or rationality is inherently oppressive, exploitative, and dehumanizing. It is the social and historical forms that modern science and rationality have taken that allow us to understand their development as forces of domination; their definition and reformulation in terms of narrow models of instrumental reason; their institutionalization and commodification as instruments of dominant power relations. What is needed is not to devalue nonreligious science and rationality as illegitimate profane reductionism, but instead to demystify their ideological legitimations and to disclose and reconstitute their nonoppressive potential for self-realization, human development, and greater freedom and liberation.

Similarly, Eliade too easily dismisses modern secular democracy and minimizes the dangers of antidemocratic theocracies. I agree with many of his criticisms of self-alienation and meaninglessness under modern forms of democracy. But a more complex, dialectical analysis would reveal that modern forms of democracy not only display negative features but in other respects represent historical advances. I would suggest that the problem with modern forms of democracy, with their formal rights and freedoms, is that they aren't democratic enough! Because of economic, political, and historical reasons, they don't include, and intentionally exclude, substantive economic and political democracy. A self that has formal freedoms, but has little power and lives under conditions of extreme necessity, isn't very free. What is most defective in modern forms of democracy is not the superiority of premodern, hierarchical, antidemocratic, mythic and religious, economic, social, and political structures, but rather the fact that they don't address the real substantial issues of democratic empowerment.

To provide one other illustration, I agree with Eliade in his criticism of the impoverishment and dehumanization of the modern secular "individual." He is correct in demystifying modern secular ideologies about some exalted abstract individualism. But once again, Eliade, in his dismissal of the modern, too easily rejects what may reflect historical and social advances. Much of what is lacking in modern individualism is evident in the dichotomy of the individual versus society (versus other individuals, versus nature). What is needed is for new philosophical anthropologies to incorporate what is valuable in the modern conception of the autonomous individual self, while rejecting what is negative in modern relations that constitute the alienated individual self—alienated from nature, from any meaningful sense of community, and from much of one's own humanity. What is needed is not a simple rejection of the modern individual, but to reconstitute and enlarge our conception of what is authentically human in terms of the social individual: the individual who expresses the particular way one relates to the universal and who establishes harmonious organic relations with social reality, nature, and the cosmos.

Eliade is also too narrow in his formulation of "the other," even acknowledging that he has broadened "the other" to include the mythic, religious, archaic, and non-Western other and the mythic religious other in Western spiritual history and buried in the modern unconscious. But this process of self-constitution, dependent on providing culturally diverse contexts for creative encounters with worlds of meaning of the other, must be broadened. It must include others rarely addressed by Eliade in his study of religion, at least not in their defining economic, historical, and social forms: the disempowered and dispossessed, the oppressed and exploited, those on the "periphery," workers, women, gays and lesbians, peoples of color. And this applies not only to the West. The constructions of "archaic," Hindu, Buddhist, and other non-Western texts were not free from class, caste, gender, race, and other relations of power. This is why it is important that many contemporary scholars in India, for example, are focusing on culturally defined self-identities of "subalterns," women, peasants, tribals, and *dalits* ("the oppressed ones" or "downtrodden" Untouchables).

By establishing creative encounters with "the other," including cultural creations and concepts of self usually excluded or unrecognized by dominant modern and premodern traditions—Western, archaic, and Eastern—we create the possibility for increasing our sensitivity and awareness, overcoming some of our provincialism, "bursting open" our historically and culturally imposed limitations on what is valuable, significant, and even possible, and reconstituting new philosophical views of self and reality. In this regard, many of us have learned much from Mircea Eliade's writings on religion while we have also been highly selective, rejecting or reformulating some of his assumptions, methodological principles, interpretations, and judgments.

Chapter Fourteen

ELIADE'S INTERPRETATION OF SACRED SPACE AND ITS ROLE TOWARD THE CULTIVATION OF VIRTUE

DAVID CAVE

Eliade contributed to the study of religion by not attempting to define it. Instead he uncovered patterns of symbols through which humans perceived, interpreted, and experienced the sacred, that is, that which struck them as irreducibly real. These symbols include cosmic and natural symbols, such as the stars and planets, the sky, the moon, vegetation, and stones; symbols oriented in relation to the human body—up, down (vertical), front, back, left, right (horizontal), and the center; and temporal and spatial symbols (past, present, future; inner, outer, far, near, primordial, paradisiacal).

Of these symbols, those of symbolic space and time figure prominently in Eliade's studies, for he understood that one of humans' primary longings is to feel situated within the cosmos, to know and feel that they belong, that the world is a hospitable place. Humans seek a place upon which to stand and from which to create their world, individually and as groups. Those places and times that qualitatively affect meaning and the experience of the real, Eliade described as sacred places and times.[1]

---

1. It has been pointed out that Eliade's theoretical preoccupation with the anchoring of humans amidst the expanse and complexity of the world and within the merciless passage of time, was prompted in large part by his growing up during the social and political post–World War I upheavals in his native Romania. Philosophically as well, Eliade was responding to modernism's fascination with ceaseless change.

The study of sacred space and sacred time are popular subjects in academic and cultural discussions today, as is the study of virtue.[2] From these discussions, I am interested in how spatial patterns affect personal development. "What does sacred space actually do for me?" "Can it, and in what ways does it, shape my character?" And, "How does Eliade's understanding of sacred space shape virtue?" In answering these and the latter question in particular, I will evaluate the benefits and limitations of his interpretation of religion.

Eliade does not address virtue. Ethics and the moral life do not figure in his approach to the comparative study of religion and in the character of religion itself. Nor did discourses on ethics hold a strong place in his thinking overall. His lifelong Romanian friend, Emil Cioran, even wondered if Eliade had any sense of his own limits.[3] Eliade's colleague at the University of Chicago, Joseph Kitagawa, said Eliade underestimated the role of evil in human life.[4] To the puzzlement and amazement of both friends and critics, Eliade, mostly later in life, was quiet on some of the moral, ethical political issues of his day. His silence on the Holocaust is an example.[5]

However ethically mute, Eliade was, nevertheless, deeply concerned with making life meaningful and creatively productive. He had an unflagging confidence in human ability to persist and rise despite all odds. He believed all humans, not just the religious specialists and the charismatics, are fundamentally *homo religiosus*. Everyone has the potential to be religiously creative, and all people and cultures are equally valuable for the scholar of religion's careful study. Because Eliade believed in the potential of human character to develop, we can apply a study of virtue to Eliade's thought.

It is my thesis that Eliade's view of sacred space contributes to the cultivation of virtue in three ways: sacred places provide a forum for hearing or imagining narratives that articulate and define prescribed virtues; sacred places require virtuous actions to uphold the integrity of the places as sacred places; and, sacred places provide a means by which to experience the practice of a virtue.

Eliade's interpretation of sacred space for the cultivation of virtue is not complete, however. He does not account enough for, in his term, the "profane," those individual and societal factors at play that make and maintain a place as sacred and capable of forming the virtuous life. Because Eliade minimizes the significance of

---

2. Lee H. Yearley, "Recent Work on Virtue," *Religious Studies Review* 16, 1 (January 1990): 1.

3. See the chapter by Cioran in *Myths and Symbols: Studies in Honor of Mircea Eliade*, ed. Joseph M. Kitagawa and Charles H. Long. Chicago: University of Chicago Press, 1969.

4. Kitagawa mentioned this in a conversation with me in December 1987.

5. George Steiner, "Ecstasies, not arguments," *The Times Literary Supplement* 4, 565 (September 28–October 4, 1990): 1015–1016.

the profane, his interpretations inadequately develop the fact that sacred spaces can be profaned.

RELIGION AND SACRED SPACE

Eliade wrote on the symbolism of sacred space in defining the character of religion in *Patterns in Comparative Religion*, *The Sacred and the Profane*, and in a number of other monographs and books.[6]

According to Eliade, the religious mind creates a cosmos to give order to an otherwise chaotic world. Within the cosmos that a people create, there are places of meaning that command and are given inordinate attention. They command attention because they reveal themselves. Says Eliade, "[I]n actual fact, the place is never chosen by man; it is merely discovered by him; in other words, the sacred place in some way or another reveals itself to him" (*Patterns*, 369).

But sacred places are not just revealed. They are also enacted.[7] When a group repeats or reenacts through ritual their cosmogonic myth(s), the initial creative act of the gods or mythical heroes, they reenact creation itself, giving order to and empowering the place in which they live by setting it apart from other places not (yet) within the purview of their experience and understanding.[8] It is not difficult to imagine how initiating a project, coming into a new territory, or building a house, can be perceived as replicating the creation of the cosmos. A writer on architecture in America, Michael Pollan, in building "a place of his own," discovered how the act of building is like an initial creation. Choosing a site, drawing the blueprint, acquiring the materials, and starting the initial construction, is like creation itself. The first decision affects all resulting decisions, much in the same way as archetypes as primary plans do.[9]

---

6. See the section "Sites of the Sacred," in Mircea Eliade, *Symbolism, The Sacred, and The Arts*, ed. Diane Apostolos-Cappadona. New York: Crossroad, 1985 and my discussions of sacred space and of the symbol of the "center" in my book, *Mircea Eliade's Vision for a New Humanism*. New York: Oxford University Press, 1993, 140f.

7. Says Eliade, "We say a space can be consecrated by a hierophany, but man may also construct a sacred space by effecting certain rituals." Eliade, *Symbolism, The Sacred, and the Arts*, 109.

8. Some places are sacred precisely because they are beyond our experience and understanding. They are not ordinary, commonplace: Buddhist Pure Land, the heavens, a mysterious zone that is feared, are examples. Though these spaces are in ways unknown to us, they can nonetheless be sacred because they fit within a world outlook that gives them meaning.

9. *A Place of My Own: the Education of an Amateur Builder*. New York: Random House, 1997, 31. See also the philosopher of architecture, Karsten Harries, who refers to Eliade's position that to build any house is to create a cosmos in which one will act and carry out one's life. *The Ethical Function of Architecture*. Cambridge: MIT Press, 1996, 158.

If we suspend Eliade's sometimes overly abstract terms and mystical concepts (hierophanies, *illud tempus*, archetypes, experiencing the "really real"), he says simply that humans by nature desire to establish for themselves a meaningful place in which to dwell and live their lives. They want to feel part of a larger whole, rooted, centered, and, on occasion, freed from the confinements and mediocrity of the everyday and the commonplace. Religion is a matter of creatively placing oneself within the world. Eliade influenced the study of religion by encouraging students of religion to note those places and spatial concepts important to a people if the peoples' world and mindset were to be understood. Ed Linenthal, scholar of religion in America and of American sacred space, once told me it was through Eliade that he became a scholar of religion. The subject of religion did not have to be approached theologically, he found. One could study peoples' religious conception of the world as sacred contests over space.

In Eliade's conception, there are several components that make a place a "sacred" place: 1) the place has a quality or experience felt and interpreted to be distinctive and irreducible; 2) the experience is inherent to the place; 3) the experience, therefore, is not subject to human choice; 4) the place and what is done there (the rituals, for instance), are modeled on mythic patterns (on what the gods or culture heroes did in the beginning); and 5) the place is capable of transforming one: one comes into a different set of experiences from what one experiences generally.

To simplify these components into one sentence, sacred space is that space (or place) that commands excessive, discriminating attention and that orients and transforms a person or group such that their life, or a component of it, is perceived to be meaningful. The space "commands" attention because it discloses, "reveals," itself to humans; the attention is "excessive" because people engage in redundant and elaborate discourses (myths) and rituals in relation to it. The attention is "discriminating" because the space or place is concerned with boundaries (the sacred from the profane; the pure from the impure).[10]

Eliade has been justly criticized for making the meaning of symbols too transparent, as if the mysteries of the sun, moon, of the waters, of certain places, are discernible if one only has the eyes to see. I would agree with this criticism. Meaning is not so apparent as Eliade makes it out to be. When, however, Eliade refers to symbols as being experienced, as "striking" us, I feel he is on firmer ground. Even the Durkheimian approach to sacred space, which denies any inherent attributes to

---

10. Eliade, however, does not attend enough to boundaries. He is more interested in speaking of a place becoming sacred, and not on how it might be profaned. I will speak to this point later.

a place,[11] attributes a certain "feel" to a place that is regarded as sacred, though that feeling is itself a product of society.

Without getting into Eliade's understanding of the sacred per se,[12] for him the experience of the place precedes the societal categorization of the place. Regardless from where the experience of a sacred place arises (society or nature), once a place is collectively regarded as sacred it will have its distinctive feel.

VIRTUE AND SACRED SPACE

What is virtue? How is it defined? The two definitions of virtue I draw on are those of Alasdair MacIntyre, from his influential *After Virtue*,[13] and Lee Yearley, from his *Mencius and Aquinas: Theories of Virtue and Conceptions of Courage*.[14] MacIntyre defines virtue as human excellences informed by a tradition that are applied within "socially local and particular" contexts and are pursued for their own sake in fulfilling a "practice," a culturally recognized activity not unlike a professional vocation (*After Virtue*, 61, 126–127). He says, "[A] virtue is an acquired human quality the possession

---

11. On the difference between the Durkheimian and the Eliadean approach to sacred space, with corrective criticisms of the Eliadean, see David Chidester and Edward T. Linenthal, eds. *American Sacred Space*. Bloomington: Indiana University Press, 1995, 5–19. Here we read that those who approach sacred places primarily from the social, political perspective give less credence to a place as having its particular experiential quality. So speaking for the sociopolitical approach, David Chidester and Ed Linenthal qualify Eliade's "mystical" approach:

> Attention to the contested character of sacred space might provide a necessary corrective to . . . analytical naiveté, whether it takes the form of theological dogmatism or mystical intuitionism, that holds out for a view of sacred space as simply "given" or "revealed."
>
> [Our study] reopens the investigation of sacred space by creatively subverting Eliade's axioms. Sacred space may be set apart, but not in the absolute, heterogeneous sense that Eliade insisted upon. Against all the efforts of religious actors, sacred space is inevitably entangled with the entrepreneurial, the social, the political, and other "profane" forces.

12. See Bryan Rennie's discussion on Eliade's conception of the sacred, which Rennie defines as, "the intentional object of human experience which is apprehended as the real." Bryan S. Rennie, *Reconstructing Eliade: Making Sense of Religion*. Albany: State University of New York Press, 1996, 21 et passim.

13. Alasdair MacIntyre, *After Virtue*, 2ed. Notre Dame: University of Notre Dame Press, 1984.

14. Lee H. Yearley, *Mencius and Aquinas: Theories of Virtue and Conceptions of Courage*. Albany: State University of New York Press, 1990.

and exercise of which tends to enable us to achieve those goods which are internal to practices and the lack of which effectively prevents us from achieving such goods" (191). By "practice" he means

> any coherent and complex form of socially established cooperative human activity through which goods internal to that form of activity are realized in the course of trying to achieve those standards of excellence which are appropriate to, and partially definitive of, that form of activity, with the result that human powers to achieve excellence, and human conceptions of the ends and goods involved, are systematically extended. (187)

In practicing the virtues, one excels in and advances a "socially established" human activity. Virtues enrich individual life and social relationships. They help one do something better, more excellently.

MacIntyre stresses the importance that narrative gives to conceptions of virtue. The Heroic societies, for instance, passed on through narratives what it meant to be courageous. Narratives of virtue, says MacIntyre, point to a *telos*, to what constitutes the fulfillment of human life and of one's role and self-identity—in Homeric societies one's role and self-identity were synonymous (128–129). MacIntyre believes that modern society's rejection of tradition and of a *telos* to human nature, stressing instead the individual as distinct from and unbeholden to social institutions, has left society floundering in moral chaos. People have no parameters—intellectual, social, cultural—within which to evaluate competing ideas and ways to behave (21–35). Although MacIntyre recognizes it is impossible and unprofitable to recover the Heroic and Aristotelian worlds when people knew their place within society, knew what constituted their end, and had a general conception of virtue, he feels there are certain things that can be done to help us navigate through today's sea of moral disequilibrium: 1) recover the importance of instructional narratives; 2) provide social arenas for debating competing moral views; and 3) recognize that it is not impossible nor unenlightened to debate what are reasonable ends to human life.

MacIntyre shows that virtues are not abstractions divorced from our social and political life. One acts virtuously within a context and the context defines what the virtuous activity looks like. The violent heroism of Homer, for instance, is different from the nonviolent heroism of Martin Luther King's civil disobedience. MacIntyre, though, too closely embeds virtues within their social and political setting, thereby risking associating being virtuous with conforming to society's expectations.

Lee Yearley looks at virtue as a cultivated disposition defined in relation to a life plan. Virtue, he says, "is a disposition to act, desire, and feel that involves the exercise of judgement and leads to a recognizable human excellence or instance of human flourishing. Moreover, virtuous activity involves choosing virtue for itself and in light of some justifiable life plan" (*Mencius and Aquinas*, 13). Like MacIntyre, Yearley says virtues are practiced for their own sake and are informed by a narrative.

What I appreciate about Yearley's study, though, is that he defines virtues within world views and distinguishes virtue from conventional views of morality. Virtues occupy a middle ground between moral injunctions and world views, the former being the domain of philosophical or religious ethicists, and the latter of anthropologists and historians of religion. The study of virtue shares in the study of ethics and in the study of anthropology and the history of religions. Says Yearley, "Virtues connect with injunctions through their conceptual form and claims to universality and with ways of life through their embeddedness in particular cultural contexts" (11). Though virtues interrelate with both moral injunctions and ways of life, they are more shaped by a group's or culture's way of life than by any directive to follow a listing of moral rules. "Ways of life largely determine which virtues are expressed and how all virtues are ranked. Lists of virtues and their hierarchical order help distinguish ways of life," says Yearley (12). Anthropology and the history of religions, given to depicting ways of life, are able to contextualize the particular virtues important to a culture and describe what these virtues imply for those within that culture. Courage to Mencius differs from what courage means to Aquinas, but both agree that courage is a necessary virtue for the flourishing of individuals and of society.[15]

Virtues differ from conventional views of morality in that virtues are not tied to moral rules. Says Yearley,

> Conventional people believe that virtuous action rests on an allegiance to generally accepted rules and therefore provides predictable, reliable results. They fail to see that *real virtue rests on character, sensitivity to situations, and religious insight*. That difference can lead the conventional to declare unethical the activity of a truly virtuous person who attacks normal social or religious practice in the name of a higher vision. (20; emphasis added)

The practice and life of virtue does not conform to social or religious expectations. Virtue is the stage Confucius reached when he said, "at seventy I followed my

---

15. Yearley uses the typology of Jonathan Z. Smith of "locative" and "utopian" cosmologies to categorize the Mencian and Aquinian ways of life respectively. For Mencius, actions are undertaken within a closed system, and to uphold that system courage is needed to do what is necessary to sustain and further the social order of fifth century China B.C.E. And courage within the fourteenth-century medieval Christendom of Aquinas, meant the ability to do what God required to bring in the divine order that lay outside the boundaries of the present world. *Mencius and Aquinas*, 42.

heart's desire without overstepping the line" (*Analects*, II.4). Still living within society, Confucius focused not on social norms but sensed the way of Heaven.

Yearley adds that to lead the virtuous life one has a sense of what actions one is to follow to realize an overall vision. One is cognitively and experientially aware of a path to human flourishing. In following this path one does not suppress one's natural inclinations but through discipline, right thinking, and an initial adherence to certain moral standards, one molds one's natural inclinations into "dispositions" to virtue.[16] Informed by reason and emotional sensitivity, a disposition to virtue will act at the appropriate time, with the appropriate action, and with astute judgment.

To summarize by combining both MacIntyre and Yearley, virtue 1) builds upon and maximizes natural inclinations; 2) draws upon a narrative, a tradition; 3) acts within view of a life plan; 4) is rational and experiential (emotional); 5) is not tied to moral rules but exercises the latitude of judgement; 6) is practiced for its own sake, for its own internal rewards; and 7) leads to human flourishing, individually and collectively (or, referring to MacIntyre, to the flourishing of a "practice").

Let me now turn to a personal example to demonstrate how virtue ties to sacred space. I enjoy learning and would like to live within an overall vision to be a life-long student of the humanities and of religious studies in particular. I would like to learn, cultivate wisdom, and pursue the neo-Confucian heart-mind toward personal cultivation. And I want learning to be cultivated for its own sake, not for external rewards, such as being perceived as informed, competent, to get speaking engagements, be published, etc. In seeking this overall vision, my study, that is, the physical space of my office, where I think, read, and write, becomes a place for the cultivation of this vision and of the virtues necessary to pursue this vision. Discipline, for instance, would be a virtue that is required of me. I must discipline myself to come to my study and stay in the chair when I am tempted to escape the pains of study and go work in the yard, clean up the house, or go for a walk. I have the inclination to study, but I must make intelligent choices, exercise my will, and emotionally commit myself to the task of study if my inclination is to become an intelligent disposition to study. I must avoid the temptations to become complacent, haughty, and to seek the external rewards of personal recognition. In other words, I must avoid the vices. Instead, I must choose the internal rewards that come with refining my "practice." I must counter the above vices to pursue the internal rewards of learning.

---

16. Yearley defines dispositions as intelligent choices acting upon a real inclination. A disposition is different from a "propensity," which, similar to a habit, is likely to go with the grain. Having a propensity to smoke, I smoke, since it is easier than not smoking. A disposition, on the other hand, operates out of a complex set of choices and can go against the instinctual grain. *Mencius and Aquinas*, 106–107.

Whether I practice the virtues or settle into the vices, I can sense the difference between the two options. I know, I can feel, whether I am respecting the excessive and discriminating attention I am to give to my study and to the time I spend there, or whether I am escaping from the mental and physical discipline I need to keep. To others it may appear that I am pursuing a life of learning when, in fact, I may be idling my time away at my desk. But I can tell and sense if I am less than mentally and physically determined in pursuing the internal rewards consonant with the cultivation of wisdom. In other words, if I am indeed practicing the virtue of learning for acquiring wisdom, my rationale for following this virtue will be sound and my emotions will correspond appropriately. If my reasoning is unsound, I will sense the corresponding emotions that come with pursuing and settling for ill-conceived ends.

Eliade's approach to religion and to sacred space is relevant at this point to show the connection between sacred space and the cultivation of virtue.

ELIADE, SACRED SPACE, AND VIRTUE

As I said, in pursuing the virtues one not only exercises intelligent dispositions, one experiences the practice of these dispositions. If I practice the virtue of honesty, I will experience the internal rewards that come with being honest, regardless of how uncomfortable or painful the external responses to my honesty may be. Virtues are practiced for their own internal rewards. In doing so, one, in effect, creates one's own habitable cosmos. If I follow the virtue of honesty, I operate within a life plan that validates and gives purpose to my choices. These choices contribute to my flourishing as a human being and, by extension, to the flourishing of society. My rewards are not isolationist, but social and communal.

The experiential and holistic aspects of virtue—that is, that virtues are experienced and practiced within the framework of a life plan—apply to Eliade's approach to religion, vis-à-vis his view of sacred space. We see this in the following ways:

1. In the same way that virtues are practiced in light of a narrative, a *telos*, a life plan, so do sacred places share in a narrative. There is a story connected to a sacred place in which one or a group participates. If the place does not have a particular narrative associated with it, the place can be where one's dream life is cultivated or where a people's stories are told. In either case, it is at sacred places where other worlds are imagined and, through narrative and ritual, models of and for a way of life are articulated. One is provided with ideals inspiring exemplary behavior. Sacred places provide, therefore, forums for the verbal and symbolic articulation of ideal or paradigmatic behavior, interpreted and rationalized within an overall vision.

Granted, the mythical or historical narratives recounted and memorialized at a sacred place can inspire less than virtuous behavior. Visitors to the sacred ground of a memorialized battlefield can come away with nationalistic jingoism and aspirations for personal glory. One can argue, though, that these motivations inspire the desire for external rather than self- and other-promoting internal rewards.

2. Sacred space cultivates virtue in that to remain a sacred place the place requires ongoing excessive and discriminating attention, the kind of attention required, at least initially, of virtues. "If I am to uphold the integrity and sanctity of this place, my own behavior must be as scrupulous as the attention this place requires." "If my body is a sacred place and is not to be defiled, then I must abstain from defiling thoughts and actions."[17] Certain thoughts and behaviors (virtues) uphold the distinctiveness of a space as a sacred space, and by remaining and being upheld as sacred, this space upholds these thoughts and behaviors and the experience of them. One wants to make sure behaviors or thoughts are kept away that would conflict with the virtues (the vices) and thereby jeopardize the experience and interpretation of the place as a sacred place. The Christian home in Victorian America, as Colleen McDannell points out, was a place for the spiritual and moral instruction of children, separated from the perceived vices of a sinful society. The Christian house was its own world, combining aesthetics, virtue, and domesticity.[18]

3. Sacred space provides a context for the experiencing of virtues by putting those who enter a sacred space into a different experiential and temporal framework from ordinary experience and time. This framework is compatible to the experiential and temporal framework out of which a person practices the virtues. For virtuous activity arises not from prescriptive rules, but from a person's judgement and sense for what a situation requires. Says Yearley, virtuous actions rest on "character, sensitivity to situations, and religious insight" (*Mencius and Aquinas*, 20).

Let me explain with an example. The National Holocaust Museum in Washington, D.C., memorializes the tragedy of the genocide of the six million Jews under Nazism.[19] The museum's messages symbolize the inhumanity that was and can be waged between humans and by totalitarian ideologies even in our supposedly civilized and enlightened age. One of the virtues that is communicated through this

---

17. Becoming puritanical, prudishly moralistic would not be considered virtuous behavior. The discriminating attention I speak of here is the kind of attention that fits within the broader-than-moral-rules type of behavior that typifies the life of virtue.

18. Colleen McDannell, *The Christian Home in Victorian America, 1840–1900*. Bloomington: Indiana University Press, 1986, 32 et passim.

19. See Edward T. Linenthal's article "Locating Holocaust Memory, The United States Holocaust Memorial Museum," in Chidester and Linenthal, *American Sacred Space*.

memorial is the virtue of honesty. We (Americans, Westerners, non-Jews, Europeans, moderns, etc.) are confronted in this museum with stark reminders of what we have done and are capable of doing again. We have to be honest with our own evils and take responsibility for them. "[The museum]," says Ed Linenthal, "would remind Americans of the dangers of being bystanders, it would teach Americans where Christian anti-Semitism could lead, and it would impress upon Americans the fragile relationship between technology and humanistic values" (228). The architecture of and the textual and visual images within the museum all work together to have us perceive the need to be honest with ourselves and others. The Holocaust Memorial, separating us momentarily from the outside world, forces us to confront the stark judgment of the Holocaust. Says Linenthal,

> [James Ingo] Freed's building, from its outward appearance to its interior mood and insistence on certain ways visitors inhabit and move through space, is designed as a place of disorientation, a building that will force visitors to "leave" Washington, D.C. Ironically, then, while the location of the museum in the monumental core was deemed crucial for those who believed that Holocaust memory should be an integral part of the nation's memory, Freed's building has as its object the removal of visitors from Washington, so that they might be receptive to the story told in the permanent exhibition. The location of the museum asks visitors to "pay attention" to a crucial memory, and the attributes of the building inform you that you must, in order to pay attention, leave Washington. "I don't think you just ever walk into the door and there is just the Holocaust," Freed remarked. "You can't do it. You have to prepare yourself psychologically for it." Evocative architecture and the manipulation of interior space served as Freed's agent of spiritual preparation for the journey into the Holocaust. (241–242)

Sacred space can help shape our character for virtuous living by placing us in a setting that impresses upon us the message and experience of particular virtues.

To tie together the above three points, let me turn to an example from Mencius. In a meeting with King Hui of Liang, as Mencius and the king are standing on a patio overlooking a scenic pond, Mencius is asked if a good and wise man can enjoy the pond and the wild geese Mencius and the king see before them. Mencius responds, "only if a man is good and wise is he able to enjoy them. Otherwise he would not, even if he had them." Mencius goes on to quote from the *Book of Odes* about a king who built a terrace and a pond. Because the people were so delighted with it and with the king, they named the king's terrace the "Sacred Terrace" and his pond the "Sacred Pond." Not so for the tyrant Chieh, whom people called the Sun, since he said his rule would perish when the sun perished. If Chieh had built a terrace and a pond, the people would not care to enjoy the terrace and pond and the birds and beasts.[20] A virtuous ruler, according to Mencius, can enjoy, experience, and perceive, the distinctive character of the pond. A nonvirtuous ruler, such as the tyrant Chieh, could not; to him the pond would be an object, a means to show wealth, a place that cannot be attended to by a cold heart or a troubled conscience. In true Confucian fashion, virtue upheld for its own sake puts one in touch with Heaven and invites virtuous responses. The virtue of a wise king led the people to designate what he did as sacred. In Eliadean fashion, the king and the terrace and pond were hierophanic, connecting heaven to earth. So in Chinese cosmology, a virtuous ruler connects, through himself, heaven and earth.

SACRED SPACE AND VICE

In the same way as the profane is the flip side and counter to the sacred, so is vice the flip side and counter to virtue. As the sacred is defined in relation to the profane, so are virtues defined in relation to vices. "Virtues correct some difficulty thought to be natural to human beings, some temptation that needs to be resisted, or some motivation that needs to be made good," says Yearley. Virtues exist because there is some propensity or action that needs to be corrected (*Mencius and Aquinas*, 16). Instead of going with my drive to amass power and wealth for myself, I seek selflessness and generosity; instead of responding defensively or cowering to save myself from harm or embarrassment, I step forward courageously. Vices retard human flourishing by operating upon false premises and encouraging misguided emotions. Correct thinking and disciplined emotions are the way to virtuous living and to a more productive and deeply satisfying life.

So how do vices relate to sacred space and to Eliade's conception of sacred space in particular? Vices defile, or at least, retard human flourishing. They profane sacred space. To sacralize a space that has been profaned and to maintain the boundaries of sacrality, a person or group counters with corresponding virtues. In Eliade's estimation, the profane sphere is of chaos and meaninglessness, of spaces and action that have no perceived archetype after which they are patterned. They are spaces or actions that have yet to be consecrated, given meaning and order. In short, they have not been "corrected." Applying Eliade's view of the profanation and sacralization of space to human action, we can say that were a space not founded and made sacred, a person or group would wander aimlessly and react impetuously, having no mythic models to guide them and no spaces or places to ground and connect them symbolically to the surrounding cosmos. There would be no ethical order. In founding a sacred space, in contrast, humans move from being merely

---

20. *Mencius*, trans. D.C. Lau. New York: Penguin Books, 1970, I.A.2.

bestial to being of culture. Sacred space facilitates human flourishing. Conversely, a sacred space that is profaned through neglect, defilement, and ritual error, that is, through a violation of boundaries and procedure, hampers human flourishing; it perpetuates vice.

There are qualifications to Eliade's interpretation of sacred space and to how it cultivates, or fails to, the life of virtue. Eliade did not account enough for the role that everyday life plays in the creation of sacred space. Politics, economics, social practices are all present to some degree whenever a space is deemed to be and maintained as sacred. Moreover, in everyday life, people operate from mixed motives. They have moral failures and personal foibles. As William Paden says, "[W]hile Eliade showed how humans are compelled to organize worlds in the midst of chaos, his focus was more on the process of grounding those worlds in myth than on system or boundary maintenance and defense" in the "face of threatened or actual impurity, wrongness, or guilt."[21]

Just as there is no purely religious space, there is no purely virtuous action. So vices, in the end, are intertwined with virtues in establishing and preserving a space as sacred. And because vices are always present in some form within the sphere of virtuous action, the vices can be expressed to the point that they come to desacralize a place. While sacred spaces or places can contribute to virtuous behavior, they can also spawn corresponding vices. The battles over Palestine; the riots at Ayodhya, India, between Hindus and Muslims over a temple and a mosque; the evils depicted at the Holocaust Museum, are examples where the sacred and the profane conjoin, intermingle, clash. The Holocaust Museum is a sacred place today because there were profane evil actions under Nazism. Palestine is sacred precisely because it is a contested space; its very sacredness leads to contestation, as is the case for Ayodhya. The sacred and the profane work back and forth in creating, maintaining, and, at times, defiling a sacred space. They can both help cultivate virtue and perpetuate vice.

Eliade was not naïve about political oppression and individual failures of character, of social evils and individual vice. Eliade simply spent most of his theoretical and interpretive studies describing the nature and structure of the sacred and less on the nature of the profane. We may live out of unconscious mythic archetypes as Eliade suggests, but life takes place in the short term and through people of complex behaviors embedded in a historical setting. As a result, Eliade, though less so in his fictional writings, depicts a world difficult to relate to. Perhaps that

---

21. William E. Paden, "Sacrality as Integrity: 'Sacred Order' as a Model for Describing Religious Worlds," in *The Sacred and its Scholars*, eds. Thomas Idinopulos and Edward Yonan. Leiden: E. J. Brill, 1996, 9, 7.

is why when I taught a course on sacred space and students were presented with the neo-Durkheimian and the Eliadean approaches to sacred space, they sided with the Eliadean when it came to conceiving of sacred space as a space that commands some kind of power, but sided with the Durkheimian approach when it came to describing how sacred space works, is made, and is lived in.

CONCLUSION

Eliade gave us a language to understand our fundamental longing for a meaningful life. Sacred space is part of that language. His understanding of sacred space can help us advance human excellence. It can anchor narratives of meaning and cultural values. It is a physical or conceptual space that has or stimulates paradigmatic narratives and requires discriminating practices to provide a context for experiencing the internal rewards that come with following particular virtues.

Yet if such spaces or places are to be and remain sacred and help shape, thereby, the virtuous life despite opposing inclinations, we must know that such spaces or places do not come (solely) upon our unconscious archetypes, but are also the product of rational (i.e., political, economic, legal) choices, continuously evaluated, lest we too easily settle into a sacred rationalization of anachronistic beliefs and behaviors. The life of virtue is a deliberate one.

Chapter Fifteen

THE CONCEPT OF WORLD HABITATION

Eliadean Linkages with a New Comparativism

WILLIAM E. PADEN

Attackers and defenders have occupied a polarized center stage of the Eliade debate, giving the impression that the whole matter is an up-or-down, take-it-or-leave-it affair. But this disjuncture among historians of religion seriously risks stalemating the development of the very cause without which there cannot be any study of religion as such, namely comparative perspective. Fortunately there are other alternatives than defending an old comparativism and rejecting any comparativism.

Eliade's work is not something that stands or falls as a whole. It is well understood as a basic quarry of thematic studies, some of which may be pertinent, some not, some of which may be dated, some not—an eclectic resource from which one may legitimately make selections and choices for the continuous rebuilding of the analytical study of religion, and not something one has to justify or reject as a package. There are many Eliades and many contexts in which to give significance to facets of his work, and there remains the possibility of relating some of his categories to a broader, more contemporary model of comparative study.

Specifically, this chapter draws on a major theme in Eliade's work, which I consider particularly germane for the ongoing work of comparativism.¹ It is the concept of religious world habitation and the cross-culturally patterned ways such habitation takes place. This factor will become clearer if two discursive matrices are distinguished in Eliade's writings, both of them linked with the concept of the sacred. The first is the one most commonly associated with Eliade, where "the sacred" refers to hierophanies of the transcendent, manifest through some part of the ordinary or common (in Eliade's terms, "profane") world. It is the Eliade who sometimes speaks about "the fall and camouflage of the sacred" and who at places seems to associate his category of the sacred with the "Wholly Other" of Otto and other classical religious phenomenologies.² In this model, religion begins with the revelation of the sacred, with the "opening" of a human world to something supremely other, to the transpersonal cosmos, to the work of the gods.

But there is a second Eliade, a second voice, employing another model, and it this one I wish to focus on. Here are writings about the human capacity to constitute multiple worlds, where the concept "world" is clearly pluralistic and relativistic. Here is the language that every world is an "ontology," a "universe," a "cultural creation" analogous to the thousands of imaginal universes of art. Here Eliade is not theological at all, but postfoundationalist and to some extent postmodern.³ Here sacrality is a human value, not an epithet for divinity.

If the first matrix has been the one that has both attracted and repelled scholars of religion, I am not impressed that the second one has been as fully acknowledged as it should or that its relevance for the study of religion has been grasped. I agree with Bryan Rennie that the first matrix perhaps struck religion scholars as the most obvious because of their own cultural and theological associations with "the sacred."⁴ One can see how Eliade's writing would evoke the familiar overtones of the phenom-

---

1. A discussion of some prospects for such a model is found in my paper, "Elements of a New Comparativism," in *Method and Theory in the Study of Religion* 8, 1 (1996): 5–14. The response papers by panelists Marsha Hewitt, Donald Wiebe, and E. Thomas Lawson, and my reply to the panelists, are in the same issue.

2. Most overtly in his "Power and Holiness in the History of Religions," in *Myths, Dreams, and Mysteries: The Encounter Between Contemporary Faiths and Archaic Realities*, trans. Philip Mairet. New York: Harper and Row, 1967, 123–154. The essay was first given as a 1953 Eranos Conference lecture.

3. The postmodern aspect of Eliade has also been noticed by Bryan Rennie in his *Reconstructing Eliade: Making Sense of Religion*. Albany: SUNY Press, 1996, 232ff. [See also comments by Girardot (160ff.) and Allen (223) and the introductory essay to this volume—Ed.]

4. *Reconstructing Eliade*, 22. Rennie tries to counteract the theological image of Eliade and builds an impressive case for looking at Eliade's "the sacred" as a pattern of humanly perceived meaning rather than as a reified, independent reality.

enological theologies of Van der Leeuw and Otto. Readers scan texts in terms of the categories and horizons they already possess. The world-construction voice, though, has been less noticeable, if not obscured, because religionists on the whole have had little or no familiarity with the Durkheimian discourses about "the sacred" that influenced Eliade and that in fact have nothing to do with theological privileging.[5] Though this is not the place to argue it, I would maintain that Eliade's concept of sacrality ultimately owes more to the French School figures such as Georges Dumézil,[6] Marcel Mauss, and Roger Caillois, than it does to the Dutch, German, and Scandinavian phenomenologies and that it is a serious misunderstanding simply to lump Eliade and Otto in the same "theological" camp. Caillois's *L'Homme et le Sacré* (1939), in particular, gave Eliade a template for speaking of sacrality in a humanistic way quite at a remove from the trajectories of the Protestant phenomenologists.[7] The notion of the construction and maintenance of worlds by way of myth and ritual and the idea that religious worlds form around the irreducible category of the sacred, both resonate with the Durkheimian vocabulary.

---

5. For an analysis of Durkheim's use of "the sacred" see William E. Paden, "Before 'The Sacred' Became Theological: Durkheim and Reductionism," in Thomas A. Idinopulos and Edward A. Yonan, *Religion and Reductionism: Essays on Eliade, Segal, and the Challenge of the Social Sciences for the Study of Religion*, ed. Thomas A. Idinopulos and Edward A. Yonan, Studies in the History of Religions, Vol. LXII. Leiden: E.J. Brill, 1994, 198–210.

6. Dumézil, who had been a student of Mauss's, sponsored, edited and wrote a preface to Eliade's *Traité d'histoire des religions* (1949), even making the point there that the study of the sacred had already progressed from ideas about mana to the notion of religion as a system, an "explication du monde." "Preface de Georges Dumézil," in Mircea Eliade, *Traité d'histoire des religions*. Paris: Editions Payot, 1949, 5. Dumézil also had written about concepts of mythic time and space, "the Great Time," festivals as "openings" onto mythic time, and so forth. Cf. his "Temps et Mythes," in *Recherches Philosophiques*, vol. 5 (1935–1936), 235–251.

7. It will be evident to any reader of Caillois that Eliade's notion of the sacred has more affinity with his book than to Otto's Lutheran *Das Heilige*. At the beginning of *Man and the Sacred* there is even reference to Otto's book, mentioned appreciatively but said not to have gone far enough in delineating the morphology of the sacred. Eliade appears to repeat this reference at the beginning of *The Sacred and the Profane*, so that what innocent readers might conclude refers to a linkage between Eliade and Otto, is more an unabashed textual link with Caillois. In fact, Caillois's vocabulary generally reappears in Eliade: the distinction of "real-unreal" in the context of the sacred-profane; the idea of "religious man"; the profane world compared to the sacred "as nothingness is to being"; the sacred as "always more or less what one cannot approach without dying"; notions of primordial chaos, fluidity, and license prior to creation; periodic regeneration; statements such as "it is not merely the individual's mind that is fascinated by the sacred, but all of his being," and so forth. Otto is mentioned only twice in *Patterns in Comparative Religion*, neither time in reference to the concept of the holy. The second edition of Caillois's book (1949) was translated into English by Meyer Barash as *Man and the Sacred*. Glencoe, IL.: The Free Press, 1959.

I am not grounding this chapter on the analytic force of proving different historical or linguistic levels of Eliadean thought, and then maintaining that one of them is the "real" Eliade. Nor am I even certain that Eliade himself would have understood these distinctions. But I do find a constructivist, humanistic strain in his work that coexists with and often underlies his rhetoric about "the manifestations of the sacred," and I do think that the relevant Eliadean discourse for our present secular, comparativist generation is not Eliade-the-monist for whom a monolithic religious reality termed "the sacred" grounds all and manifests through all, but rather Eliade-the-pluralist interested in the myriad ways religious worlds are formed as cultural creations. With this distinction, and in this latter sense, I am unconvinced by the popular views that write off Eliade's work simply as ontological essentialism.

"WORLD" AS ELIADEAN CATEGORY

The first phases of religious phenomenology created inventories of the "forms" of its subject matter—expressions such as mana, taboo, gods, prayer, priesthood, sacrifice, and myth. This was a necessary part of the evolution of religious studies and its self-creation as a field of study, and much of Eliade's *Patterns in Comparative Religion*, with its encyclopedic, serialized organization of topics, illustrated this approach.

But something different developed in *The Sacred and the Profane*, whether Eliade was intending it or not. Here the act of worldmaking becomes the central theme. This is shown not by a listing of general religious *topoi* but by describing how a religious world per se is formed. For the constructivist Eliade, religious cultures create and inhabit their own "ontologies" through the media of space, time, nature, and human actions. This model does not presuppose a foundationalist reality that is then manifest in "the" world but rather describes multiple universes, or in Nelson Goodman's terms, world-versions.[8] It is the nature of a world to establish its own reality, its own mythic foundation, its own sacrality and archetypes. The history of religions shows an endless succession of such worlds, each grounded in its own categories of sacred time and space, each with its own calendars, its centering foci, and its pasts. Thus, when Eliade writes, "Every religion . . . is an ontology: it reveals the *being* of the sacred things and the divine Figures, it shows forth that which really is, and in doing so establishes a World which is no longer evanescent and incomprehensible,"[9] I would argue that these statements do not

---

8. *Ways of Worldmaking*. Indianapolis: Hackett Publishing Co., 1978.
9. *Myths, Dreams, and Mysteries*, 17–18.

represent any implicit ontology on the author's part and that they are primarily existential descriptions of how cultures construct their lenses.[10]

Eliade writes often of religious worlds as "creations" analogous to those of novelists and artists. As such, they are novel configurative expressions of the human spirit. This is a different point of emphasis than that of social scientists for whom a "constructivist" position means that the gods are "only" human inventions. Eliade wants historians of religion to understand these worlds in terms of their distinctive modes of behavior and world views—modes that are irreducible parts of religious world habitation.[11] The analogy would be the need to understand the artist's vision and not only his/her social circumstances.

For Eliade a world is not just a symbol system but a life space, built in the midst of chaos, a delineated region of habitation set apart from amorphous, uninhabited surroundings. The foundations of these spaces are ritually sacralized and given cosmic or supernatural significance and mooring. Humans create their worlds, inhabit them, and assume responsibility for them.

Sacrality is therefore not just something that manifests or shines through worlds or through the symbolic structures such as water, sky, earth, and trees, but also the factor that gives a world its standing against the forces of chaos. In this basic sense Eliade is linking religious worldmaking with the process of human worldmaking itself.

Several of Eliade's key comparative categories are integrally part of this fundamental human activity of building worlds. For example, humans construct sacred histories, create orientational centers, and renew the world through periodic rites.

---

10. From this angle I think there is more constructivism to Eliade's approach than the ahistorical, "morphological" position assigned him in the schema of different forms of comparison outlined in Jonathan Z. Smith's essay, "*Adde Parvum Parvo Magnus Acervus Erit.*" See *Map is Not Territory: Studies in the History of Religions.* Chicago: University of Chicago Press, 1978, 240–264.

11. This gives context to Eliade's controversial maxims about studying the phenomenon of religion/the sacred "in its own frame of reference." Understanding the role played by sacrality as a behavioral and signifying factor in the apparatus of someone's world view is a different idea than that of having to understand or accept a superhuman or "wholly other" dimension of reality in order to study religion viably. The first is a datum for analysis and comparative investigation; the second is a matter of religious intuition. I do not think there is much evidence that Eliade is asking religion scholars to have to "intuit" anything at all. Rather, his point is more that religious worlds have a sacred meaning to the insider and those meanings are categories that need to be understood as part of the structure of the very universes historians of religion describe. There is no privileged reality here, just the specific terms of the insider's system. I suspect that many of those who object to Eliade's idea of studying religion "at its own level" are doing so because of their mistaken assimilation of Eliade and Otto.

In this model, where what religion is "about" is worldmaking, the wide recurrence of these patterns is not due to their manifesting a transcending "other," but because they are the normal ways human organisms recall, focus, and renew their systems.

"WORLD" AS MATRIX FOR POST-ELIADEAN COMPARATIVISM

It will be useful here to give a more formal characterization of "world."[12] A world is the operating, lived environment of behavioral and linguistic options which persons presuppose, posit, and inhabit at any given point in time and from which they choose courses of action. World is here isomorphic with system, environment, cultural context, place, horizon, and to some extent, language and cognition. It does not necessarily imply systematization or sharp boundaries. It assumes that a world normally undergoes change, is syncretic, has moving and negotiable parts, and complex exchanges of power and gender relations. It is not a reification, but as an etic, comparative concept it directs attention to the discovery of the categories of the insider. It is metaphysically innocent.

The pluralistic concept of world not only marks a clear shift to a posttheological model of comparativism, but also provides a foundational term for addressing the main issue surrounding comparativism, namely, doing justice to difference as well as commonality. For the primary limitation of Eliade's comparative method was that while it identified common forms of world-building behaviors, it paid relatively little attention to what those behaviors showed about their specific worlds. He used data to exemplify the global ubiquity of the predefined patterns, rather than to direct attention to the way the examples illustrated differences in world composition among themselves. Thus, his cultural illustrations are mostly replicas of the pattern he wishes to illustrate—copies, as it were—of the same archetypes such as the Cosmic Tree, the Navel of the World, or the *axis mundi*. Even where he looks into subtypes of a theme—as in the case where ladders, towers, temples, ropes, and mountains are all shown to represent a central point of communication between earth and heaven—the method of comparison is the same.

It is this process of using historical examples only to illustrate or reproduce patterned archetypes and subtypes—as if the history of religion were like rolled dough

---

12. I am indebted to Goodman, op. cit., for the term *worldmaking*, though the genealogy of the concept of world here traces more to the philosophical phenomenologists Husserl and Heidegger. See also Michael Kearney, *World View*. Novato, CA: Chandler and Sharp Publishers, Inc., 1984. Kearney presents a crosscultural model of world views, differentiating universal forms—self versus other, classifications, causality, space and time, etc.—from the cultural contents of those forms. [Also worthy of mention in this context is Ninian Smart's idea of religious studies as "Worldview Analysis." See especially his *Worldviews*, 2nd ed. New Jersey: Prentice Hall, 1995,—Ed.]

to be submitted to cookie-cutter molds—that shows the limits of the old style comparativism. But as shown in the influential, wake-up-call works of Jonathan Z. Smith, comparison also should be a tool for yielding significant differences as well.[13]

The idea of worlds gives a frame for seeing both commonness and difference. On the one hand, religious worldmaking is a recurrent human endeavor with patterned resemblances discernible at a transcultural level. Regardless of particular differences of mythic content, religions build pasts, cultivate sacred histories in which exemplary figures set out prototypal behaviors or guidelines, engage spiritual beings, absolutize and cosmicize their own sacred objects and authorities, and renew their worlds through periodic rituals and festivals. Everywhere cultures conduct rites of passage, linking their members with the world order. Everywhere humans construct forms of sacred, moral order and set boundaries between what is right and wrong relative to the standards of their world order.

On the other hand, the notion of plural worlds can also underscore the difference between religious environments and make the plural nature of religious existence intelligible. It intrinsically locates religious activity in its own contexts, and it accommodates all the variables of sociocultural specificity that have been neglected by the old comparativisms. Every religious expression assumes a world, and it is the particularity of one's world-location that informs religious behaviors with meaning and gives special content, style, and nuance to any religious act.

Thus, in identifying both common forms of world-fashioning behaviors as well as their historically different sociocultural contents, this proposal would seem to parallel in some ways Jonathan Z. Smith's call for a comparativism based on "the integration of a complex notion of pattern and system with an equally complex notion of history."[14]

---

13. *Imagining Religion: From Babylon to Jonestown*. Chicago: University of Chicago Press, 1982, chs.1 and 2; *To Take Place: Toward Theory in Ritual*. Chicago: University of Chicago Press, 1987, 13ff.; *Drudgery Divine*. Chicago: University of Chicago Press, 1990, ch. 2.

14. Smith, *Imagining Religion*, 29. Although clearly there are differences, too. I am taking "world building" as a model for dealing with human universals, and saying that the content of "world" and the content of the patterns of world building get constituted by unique historical environments. Smith, by contrast, is more interested in the systematic grounding of comparison and patterns in forms of historical process that are culturally contiguous. He thus advocates "historicizing morphology" in an approach that compares three levels: 1) general, shared world view, holistic system of cultural, ideological, and mythic values and language; 2) individual national/religious systems or cultural complexes, which give their peculiar stamp to this world view; and 3) particular linguistic/textual manifestations of the interaction of the first two levels. Smith seeks a viable middle ground between the reduction of data to hierarchic, archetypal "essences" and comparing isolated motifs between religions. It seems to me that the notion of common, human behaviors of world building supplies that comparative matrix.

PATTERNS OF WORLD CONSTRUCTION

In the context just outlined—worldmaking both as common human activity and as specific cultural creation—consider now three elementary forms of world construction that are basic to Eliade's model but which need to be drawn out into broad daylight, as it were, and not hidden within his particularistic cosmological thematizations. I would argue that these categories are strategic to the analysis of any religious system.

Constructing and Performing Pasts. Historians of religion are finding a large body of sophisticated analysis in other fields that illumine or recontextualize the notion of "sacred histories."[15] That societies select and build pasts and form ways of conjuring these memories seems to me a universal case of human worldmaking behavior. I say "behavior" because myth making is not just a linguistic matter of texts and stories in semantic space, but an act of commemorating, enacting, and displaying. Every society makes genealogies and traditions and devises ritual and oral practices for recalling them. In this sense, the study of sacred histories could be informed by historical, sociological, and anthropological studies of past-building, orality, and techniques of communication such as mnemonics. Eliade's contribution, whatever his particular and controversial ideas about time, for example, archaic/cyclical myth versus historical time, is to have shown the mythic character of "histories" and the centrality of mythic pasts as a comparative concept.[16]

While making pasts is a common activity, every society makes a different one. In Eliade's writing the point of interest was the phenomenon *that* a certain culture ritually replicated its time of origins, *that* this group or that habitually stepped into the prestige of mythic time, or *that* a religion periodically recharged itself with the empowerment of its founding, divine words and acts. Yet again, the study of sacred pasts is not just a means to extrapolate universal themes, but also a key to revealing what makes a world its own and not another. Subgroups of Christians, Muslims,

---

15. Cf. Pascal Boyer, *Tradition as Truth and Communication: A Cognitive Description of Traditional Discourse*. Cambridge: Cambridge University Press, 1990. Boyer challenges the vague use of terms such as "tradition" and proposes a more empirical analysis of how actual cultures build worlds from actual practices and types of memory. On this see also Marcel Detienne's *The Creation of Mythology*, trans. Margaret Cook. Chicago: The University of Chicago Press, 1986; and Paul Connerton, *How Societies Remember*. Cambridge: Cambridge University Press, 1989. Patrick H. Hutton's *History as an Art of Memory*. Hanover, NH: University Press of New England, 1993 is a particularly fine overview of historical theories of the construction of the past.

16. Rennie, op. cit., does a fine job of sorting these factors out in chapters 7, 8, and 9, and his conclusions go in the direction of my own, namely that the construction of "historical" prototypes is a common human endeavor and not just an exotic belief of primitive societies.

or Buddhists divide amongst themselves according to different ways of reading their pasts: Pentecostalists and Catholics have diverse Christian genealogies; Shias stress what Sunnis ignore; Buddhist denominations each have their regularly rehearsed, unique sacred lineages. The study of mythic memory then becomes a gateway to investigating the socially specific nature and investment of the world-building process itself.[17]

Spatial Orientation. Just as religious cultures construct pasts, they make focalized, centripetal places in their environments. In correcting and going beyond Eliade's formulas, J. Z. Smith's *To Take Place* shows just how potent and differentiated the concept of space can be in the study of religion, and that, for example, the memorializing markings of the Tjilpa and the royal constructions of the Babylonians are not reducible to an identical Eliadean *axis mundi*.

Eliade gave examples of sacred space to show how it embodied cosmic archetypes. His Frazerian-style comparative method consisted of stating the theme, say, "Traditional kingdoms created worlds with a sacred Center and four directions extending from it," or, "The domestic house is homologous with an image of the universe," and then citing the incidence of this in different cultures. But little or nothing is revealed about the cultures or any other functions of space. The examples merely illustrate what we already know about the topic. Thus, in a New Guinea village the men's house, standing at the center, has a roof that represents "the celestial vault," and "the four walls correspond to the four directions of space," just as the interior of a Byzantine church symbolizes "the universe," and its altar symbolizes paradise, which lay in the East.[18]

But a comparative study of space reveals social structure and values too. It shows hierarchy, subordination, gender roles, egalitarianism. It shows local and national memory. The space of a medieval cathedral, a Quaker meetinghouse, and a contemporary Southern Californian megachurch reveal very different forms of world habitation and social dynamics. Where Eliade was interested in what space showed "upwardly" and cosmically, contemporary historians of religions are more apt to explore what space shows "downward" and laterally into the actual forms of social existence.

Periodic Renewal. A third pattern of world habitation emerging from Eliade's work is the periodicity of renewal rites. All cultures have periodic festivals or observances in which their central values are celebrated, made explicit, and given social catalyzation. These are times when the foundations of society, whether superhumanly

---

17. On the power of historical recollection to encode social values see the essays by Bruce Lincoln and Francisca Cho Bantly in Laurie L. Patton and Wendy Doniger, eds., *Myth and Method*. Charlottesville: University Press of Virginia, 1996.

18. *The Sacred and the Profane*, 46.

endowed or not, are renewed. Again, while Eliade's focus was *that* cultures returned to their cosmic foundations in regular festivals, this leaves the question of *what* it is each culture does and encodes that makes it different from other cultures. For the forms of world construction can be distinguished from their contents. Thus, it becomes of import not just to identify that cultures renew their worlds annually, though this does tell us something about the process of world habitation, but also that each system will have a different configuration of values that it is reaffirming. Thus, what is revealed "downward" is that the actual content or focus of the rites may variously have to do with the sacrality of hierarchic family relationships, or economic exchange alliances between villages, or the display of ideal military values, or meditative intensity, or the dependency of laity and monks on each other, or the prestige of the founder. And the fact that these traits are so highlighted in the renewal rites in turn shows us something about the group's central values. Far from the theme merely copying itself or obliterating historically contextual material, this approach to comparison delineates and underscores how worlds vary.

CONCLUSIONS

The concept of plural world habitation receives some direction and vision from Eliade but needs to be worked out on a broader canvas. It supplies a matrix for negotiating both common human realities and different culture-specific embodiments, thus helping to resolve the conceptual dilemma of how comparativism can deal with context. World, as a holistic concept that excludes nothing constitutive of the habitative situation of any human system, includes and integrates within its horizon the theoretical capital and complexity of metanotions such as "language," "history," "culture," "society," and "systems theory," and therefore connects what Eliade methodologically held apart.

Religion itself is shown to be a natural part of world experience. The comparative study of religious world habitation shows how natural it is that a religious world configures and experiences the universe through its own focal symbols and places, sees the whole of time in terms of its own history, finds the absolute in its own backyard shrines, and equates its particular moral order with the ultimate order of existence itself. Elsewhere I have argued that there is a sacrality attached to the maintenance of any world system, synecdochically coded in boundaries, territory, bonding, social roles, and authority, and this is itself a kind of universal connected to any culture's sense of the order of things.[19]

---

19. See W. Paden, "Sacrality as Integrity: 'Sacred Order' as a Model for Describing Religious Worlds," in Thomas A. Idinopulos and Edward A. Yonan, eds., *The Sacred and Its Scholars: Comparative Methodologies for the Study of Primary Religious Data*. Studies in the

Indeed, the time may be here for a reconsideration of the idea of universals—based now on the forms of human behaviors and world-building processes rather than on beliefs, meanings, or any referential content.[20] In the most primordial sense, humans all arrange and classify their world, create interdictions, and form connections with postulated, empowering objects. "Religion" as a concept has too often been interpreted apart from its function in this natural schema of behaviors, a recent exception being Walter Burkert's remarkable *Creation of the Sacred: Tracks of Biology in Early Religions*.[21]

In uncovering the coexistence of multiple worlds, the process by which ontologies are devised and applied, and all that can mean for our understanding of knowledge, we are afforded, I think, overdue lessons about the relativity of world to place, and the ability of world to recreate itself in unending, place-specific forms of memory, each with its own patterned observances, territories, and luminous objects.

History of Religions, Vol. LXXIII. Leiden: E.J. Brill, 1996, 318. In the same volume Veikko Anttonen's "Rethinking the Sacred: The Notions of 'Human Body' and 'Territory' in Conceptualizing Religion," 3664, examines sacrality from the point of view of cognitive boundarymarking. Hans Mol's *Identity and the Sacred: A Sketch for a New SocialScientific Theory of Religion*. Oxford: Basil Blackwell, 1976 remains a suggestive study of the connection of sacrality with identity formation. Roy A. Rappaport's magnum opus, *Ritual and Religion in the Making of Humanity*. Cambridge: Cambridge University Press, 1999, analyzes the function of ritual and mythic sacredness in the context of cultural evolution.

20. For one version of a reopening of the issue see Donald E. Brown, *Human Universals*. Philadelphia: Temple University Press, 1991, a compelling response to the era of anthropological focus on single cultures only, with a useful review of the history of the issue, of kinds of universals, and a fortyfour page annotated bibliography.

21. Cambridge: Harvard University Press, 1996.

Part Six

CONCLUSION

Chapter Sixteen

THE MEANING AND END OF MIRCEA ELIADE

BRYAN RENNIE

There is a great deal of research, serious thought, and conflicting recommendation in the preceding chapters. Many worlds are presented to us, and many different meanings offered. What will be the end of this? What meaning can be finally found for the texts of Mircea Eliade? How can we distinguish "truly tarnished Eliadean artifacts" from "what still has some real merit in the Eliadean approach to religious phenomena" (Girardot, above, 159).

In response to Roger Corless one can only accept that Eliade's thought did not produce any systematic schematic or arrangement of religions. However, the failure has been ours in that we failed to utilize the insights of the Eliadean position *or any other* to construct our own taxonomy. On the other hand the possibility remains that Corless has failed to register the full import of Eliade's thought and that there is something inherently religious about religions. What Corless calls "what-you-would-die-for-isms" (9) relate apprehensions of reality to the self.[1] To change one's religious views is to change one's view of the world so profoundly that one must change (one's view of) oneself. The self is constructed in parallel with the construction of the worldview in the familiar microcosm/macrocosm dynamic. To abandon one's religion one must indeed die in the sense that what survives is no longer "you"

---

1. On historical nature of the self, see Tim Murphy's "Eliade, Subjectivity, And Hermeneutics" in this volume, 35–47.

but some "other." It is the process of responding to and organizing elements of one's own life-experience as genuinely revelatory of the "really real" that Eliade seems to hold as the quintessentially religious act.

There is much of value to Russell McCutcheon's argument—I agree that insider judgments cannot simply be accepted at face value, I agree that religion cannot be "defined as an apolitical, autonomous, and irreducible intellectual and institutional pursuit" (22). However, McCutcheon seems to be so carried away by the momentum of his own insight that he is willing to advocate—or even insist upon—the rejection of all other insights. As he says, "all scholars of religion have a stake in the Eliade affair" and it is an affair in which there is much at stake since "Eliade has become a focal point for the on-going identity crisis in the field" (11 and 22, quoting Murphy). Why then is he so keen to "close the Eliadean era" (with dignity or otherwise)? To resolve the identity crisis in the study of religion perhaps, but certainly to gain greater advantage for his own analysis of religion as political—for a new subfield perhaps; the politics of religion. That is understandable and even admirable, but is it adequate justification of his rejection of Eliade, his terms, and his defenders? It is true that vaguely defined and imprecise terminology tends to obscurantism and as scholars we should analyze, rather than presume, conceptions of reality. Yet the understanding of electricity as a fluid was vague, imprecise, and eventually inadequate, but it was enough to give us the Leyden jar and to begin a process of effective analysis. Speculation is necessary to progress or at least to the development of more precise terms. In that process none of us can be as constantly critical as McCutcheon desires—not even McCutcheon himself. We cannot deal with every angle, every detail, and every possible fault in our own conceptions of reality, and because we fail to do so does not make our arguments wholly uncritical and unacceptable. One question must be borne before the critical mind: does anyone *not* believe that they know what is real and what is not to some degree? Does not any such claim presuppose a "privileged access to the nature of reality?" That does not necessarily preclude all reasoned argumentation, but it does introduce an uncritical element into any and every discourse. That is the point of an attempt to be critically appreciative as well as critically hostile. It is facile to accuse an author of being uncritical on the whole because he or she is uncritical in part. In order to explain further, let me borrow this rhetorical approach from McCutcheon (and so attempt to understand him in his own terms).

A major premise of McCutcheon's argument is that "the case of Eliade remains largely marginal" (12) and not discussed like the Heidegger and DeMan affairs and he concludes that it is because defenders of Eliade have dehistoricized the issue. However, an alternative explanation—that the case of Eliade's politics has remained marginal because no genuinely damning evidence has been forthcoming—is simply ignored. Perhaps if McCutcheon *did* have more interest in Eliade's culpability he would not be so willing to ignore such a possibility. To simply repeat that the distinctions and categories of Eliade and those who find some value in his work are "troublesome" while just as simply insisting that one's own are critical (or at least not uncritical), does not make it so. McCutcheon protests that David Cave tells us that Eliade's work can be understood on no level other than its own. Yet Cave does not actually claim that Eliade's work can be understood in no other way, but rather that he will analyze it in this way. One wonders how a "concern . . . to examine the visionary impulse behind the totality of Eliade's . . . work" (Cave, *Mircea Eliade's Vision for a New Humanism*, 3; quoted above, 14) implies that "Eliade's work is somehow *sui generis*, and can sufficiently be studied in its own terms" (McCutcheon, 14). To study Eliade in his own terms might be deemed valuable and illuminating without any insistence that this is the only way to study him, wholly adequate, or that he is thus somehow *sui generis*. Both Cave and McCutcheon, it seems, want to construct "the transcendental essence (i.e., the totality) to Eliade's so-called program of cultural and spiritual renewal" as McCutcheon says (15). Cave constructs it as a new humanism, McCutcheon as a crypto-political maneuver to secure Eliade's own advantage. The problem arises when one insists that one's own construction is exhaustive and any alternative is thus somehow misguided. Reconstructing Eliade or any other "in their own terms" simply allows a closer approach to the author's intentional world and reduces the intrusion of elements alien to that world. As explanation such a move encourages understanding.

Another area in which McCutcheon is less than critical and does less than justice to his sources is in accusing me of excluding myself from the class of secondary scholars and in implying that I claim some kind of privileged access to Eliade's "actual thoughts." I specifically raise the question of recreating anyone else's thought (*Reconstructing Eliade*, 1f., following references are to this work), and conclude that the analysis will never be anything other than my own interpretation. And by secondary scholars I intend only scholars who study other, particularly recent, scholars, rather than studying religious phenomena. As such I emphatically do include myself in the category of secondary scholars. It is odd, and rather uncritical, to assume that to talk of secondary scholars is somehow to be automatically excluded from amongst their number.

I agree with much of McCutcheon's reaction to attempts to depoliticize Eliade's nationalism, but since Eliade's political message was "Romania for the Romanians" (even though that is unjustifiable in the light of the impossibility of clearly delineating what it is to be Romanian without the oppression of minority groups) it is hard to see how that is relevant to Eliade's scholarship after he left that country. Since I specifically state that Eliade was "fiercely nationalist" (143), that such nationalism is "dangerous and disturbing" (151), and that it "easily becomes violence, bigotry, and oppression" (165), I do not understand how I can be held to "protect

Eliade of all accusations of fanaticism or nationalism" (above, 20). I do, however, argue that

> Eliade's case provides an example of how patriotism, manifested as ethnic nationalism combined with religious zeal, all too easily becomes violence, bigotry, xenophobia, and oppression. Eliade himself does not seem to have clearly analyzed the dynamics or implications of his own involvement. Our analysis is not complete, however, unless we take into account the irreducible pluralism of Eliade's later theories about religion in general and the sacred in particular. I would suggest that Eliade's brush with totalitarian ideologies in the 30s influenced his theoretical position as expressed in his later books as a reaction *against* such tendencies; that his perilous attraction to the extreme right in his younger years led to a far more mature position. (*Reconstructing Eliade*, 165)

I also agree that the assumption that religion is essentially personalistic and thus irreducible in unwarranted, misleading, and dangerous. But religion *is* personal in the sense that it is a characteristic of persons. My point here is that (my interpretation of) Eliade's analysis of hierophanies as a supposed revelation of the sacred, which is actually a manifestation of a structure of human consciousness, of a desire to remain in some kind of contact with what is perceived as the source of meaning and power is most assuredly not a privileging of the first person account (according to which it is an actual revelation of some transcendent Being).

I also agree that there has been a "general suspicion of theorizing, explanation, and analysis that abounds in the regnant discourse" (18). No doubt it was, at least in part, that fear that both provoked the prolonged hiatus in any serious attempt to evaluate Eliade and prompted Eliade himself to write in his tangled and ambiguous way. But if my analysis is accepted (not as Eliade's "actual thought," but as a good working understanding), then to theorize, explain, and analyze is precisely what Eliade does, although those elements are unsystematized in his work. Eliade himself can be seen as "primarily concerned with formulating a general theory of religion" (Douglas Allen, above, 210, n.9). It is deeply ironic that after such a vehement attack on Eliade McCutcheon makes a passionate call for theory (see especially his *Manufacturing Religion*, chapter 4). Perhaps it is the iconoclastic excesses of this "age of erasure" (Girardot, above, 160) rather than the privileging of insider reports by the "*sui generis* discourse" that has led to a paucity of theory.

I agree with McCutcheon that it would indeed be a feeble argument to defend Eliade against antisemitism by claiming that he only disliked "the Jews" as much as he disliked other nationalities such as the Hungarians and Bulgarians (above, 21). But it is a different matter to argue that Eliade was not antisemitic because the statements that have been given in support of accusations of antisemitism were themselves made out of context. The worst of his statements deploring the Jewish hegemony in Maramures and Bucovina are a rather stupid descent into nationalistic jingoism coupled with an equal abuse of Hungarians and Bulgarians. But they were not repeated and did not lead to any more culpable acts, so they are not a symptom of a "life-long antisemitic ideology." The distinction between blind and fanatical nationalism and the nonvirulent (but still misguided, in my opinion) variety is not baseless: one leads to violence, the other to reconsideration. The former attempts to justify the unjustifiable, the latter does not. My point is to explain Eliade's position by historicizing and contextualizing it and to point out that he was not historically involved in this violence.

It is certainly true that there are "weak arguments, unfounded assertions" (22) to be found in the works of Eliade's defenders including myself (though I don't accept that term without qualification). I have read very little that didn't have some weak arguments and unfounded assertions. But throughout McCutcheon's chapter, his understanding of explanation shifts in a way that puts me in mind of Bertrand Russell's "conjugations of irregular verbs": I am firm, you are stubborn, he is pig-headed; I reassess, you change your mind, he vacillates. In this case McCutcheon explains, Cave and Olson defend, Rennie excuses. Since explanation is, in McCutcheon's words, to contextualize and historicize, then from my point of view I explain Eliade's behavior in connection with the Romanian right wing of the late thirties. I do not seek to excuse it, save to say that he was not as deeply embroiled as many of his compatriots, that he has not been found in possession of any smoking guns, and save to say that this is not adequate grounds to neglect the theorizing of this scholar.

We *should* be concerned with religious legitimations of power and authority, but not exclusively. We need to ask also why these particular strategies of legitimation are found to be compelling by this particular individual. How does McCutcheon legitimate his own authority to recommend the end of the Eliadean era? He does so by presenting himself as critical and others as uncritical and their classifications, distinctions, and categories as "troublesome." Am I right in assuming that this implies by contrast that his categories are trouble-free? As we have seen, they are not.

There is nothing wrong with the politics of religion as an academic discipline, but once again, it is a part and not the whole. Any attempt to divorce the whole field of the study of religion from political implications is willful ignorance, but any attempt to subsume the study of the religion under the study of politics is misclassification, akin to studying Indo-European languages as a form of Greek. It is in forcing this inappropriate classification, subsuming religion under the political, that McCutcheon is led to uncritical analysis of the writings of those he perceives as defenders of Eliade. Were he to recognize that their desire to address Eliade as an object of the study of religion is not only as legitimate as his own desire to address the political, but in fact structurally very similar, he might be able to read and understand them more accurately.

Robert Segal's chapter is a rather precise example of the contrary of the method I have recommended. Rather than inquiring as to how Eliade understood his own claims on myth and the universality of religion, Segal sets out to undermine that understanding. No doubt this is in support of an understanding that Segal himself promotes. Whatever the motive, it is the *mis*understanding of Eliade's statements that leads irresistibly to Segal's conclusion. An inspection of the argument will, I think, substantiate my assertion.

First, Eliade does not claim that myths "explain" the origin of present-day phenomena in the way that Segal uses the term—allowing him to conclude that "Eliade takes myth to be foremost an explanation of the physical world, in which case it clashes with natural science, which Eliade . . . equates with modernity" (32). As Segal actually quotes him, Eliade takes myth to "narrate," "relate," or "tell" an event *in illo tempore* that relates how and why a present reality came to be (26). Myth does not "explain" in the manner of the natural sciences (itself a very difficult thing to adequately describe), but gives a narrative that connects the present reality to characters, events, places, and things in the familiar mythic world that are held in high esteem.[2] For myths "[t]o tell how things came into existence is to explain them and at the same time indirectly to answer another question: *Why* did they come into existence?" (*Sacred and Profane*, 97). It is not an explanation of the natural world but an explanation of how, for example, we can take certain things to be "natural" while others are not, that is the very ground and basis of mythico-religious phenomena.

In this light those narratives identified by Eliade as modern myths do "explain" present phenomena. Both Marxist ideology and psychoanalysis narrate contemporary situations and locate them within the extended matrix of their own theoretical worlds. It is somewhat more difficult to describe literature, drama, and popular fiction as similarly "explaining" the present by referring it to a mythical "past" (i.e., non-present—I will discuss Eliade's conception of *illud tempus* further). However, anyone who has ever sought to make sense out of a contemporary situ-

---

2. In order to be truly mythic a narrative has to be familiar, hence my earlier conclusion regarding the longstanding tendency to study as myths exactly those narratives that are held by other peoples to be revelatory of the real, but are not so held by ourselves. The concept of "myth" was thus formed as "other peoples' myths" rather than as "myths" *tout court*, (see Wendy Doniger's *Other Peoples' Myths*) and it is in correcting this misapprehension that Eliade's consideration of myths has diverged from the conventional understanding of the word (*Reconstructing Eliade*, 76).

ation by relating it, say, to an episode of *Star Trek* is—thus understood—indulging in mythic functions.

Second, while it is unquestionably true that the provision of exemplary models is central to Eliade's understanding of myth, Segal's argument that these modern myths do not provide such models is forced. Obviously Marxism (it is a significant flaw in Segal's paper that he does not directly rebut the mythical status of Marxism) does provide models for behavior as does psychoanalysis, and in stating that "[b]y no coincidence it is nowadays a commonplace to ask whether children who harm, even kill, others have taken their cues from movies" (31), Segal himself affirms the exemplary status of popular culture. Of course, it is not only in such extreme and undesirable instances that films, for example, so function. Whenever one behaves in any way influenced by an admired fictional character one succumbs to mythic influences as Eliade conceives it. If I try to be as logical and to reason as carefully as Sherlock Holmes, for example, I appeal to myth.

In his treatment of the putative mythic status of psychoanalysis Segal again misunderstands Eliade's position. While it is true that Eliade does take "dreams, reveries, fantasies, and so forth" as "private myths" and while psychoanalysis "employs [such] myth as a vehicle for returning to the past" (28), this is not the extent of Eliade's claim that psychoanalysis bears the stamp of myth. It is not these private myths encountered in psychoanalysis that make it mythic, rather it is the very structure of (1) constructing a narrative in which a present reality is located in and explained by a theoretical world, (2) providing a model for behavior that includes a "return" to that theoretical world for the cure (renewal, restoration) of the subject, and (3) the actual "return" in memory to that supposed event, which is seen as more significant, more "real" than the present world of experience, especially given our inability to otherwise account for whatever behavior has prompted the analysis.

Nor is the fact that "while private myths may well carry one back to the character-forming, precedent-setting time of childhood, no gods are to be found in this private primordial time" damaging to Eliade's position, as Segal insists (29). Since Eliade has stated that a relation to the sacred does not "necessarily imply belief in God or gods or spirits . . . it is the experience of a reality and the source of an awareness of existing in the world" (*Ordeal by Labyrinth*, 154), the absence of gods is inconclusive. It is the encounter *in illo tempore* with something more "real," more significant, more powerful that makes the experience mythic and religious. In psychoanalysis the infantile neurosis is the "center" of the adult affliction. The characters and events encountered in a return via memory to that "time" are the center of the psychoanalytic reconstruction of the patient's very self. It is, to be sure, an example of the "fall" of mythological structures into historical time, but it is nonetheless mythic as so conceived.

Segal asks whether "the stories in modern drama, film, and literature . . . trace the establishment long ago of a natural or social phenomenon of any kind that continues to exist today?" (30). He points out that "any precedent that present-day stars set would not hark back to primordial time. . . . Consequently, getting close to the stars does not require going back in time" (32), revealing another constitutive misreading of Eliade's texts. Sacred time "is a *mythical time*, that is a primordial time, *not to be found in the historical past*" (*Sacred and the Profane*, 72; emphasis added). Obviously this "primordial time" is not located in any long-gone historical era of our known world, but is notional, conceptual or imaginary. Eliade's use of the word *time* in this context is not historical but metaphorical. *In illo tempore* might be as well replaced with *in illo loco*, or, as William Paden is keen to tell us, in another world.

By thus misunderstanding Eliade's ideas, it is possible for Segal to conclude that Eliade fails to show that modern myths exist. In fact it is correct that they do not, as Segal defines myth. However, as Eliade defines myth its presence in the modern world is hard to deny. The advantage of the interpretation that I propose is that it seeks for coherence in the thought of another and thus presents some hope of understanding that other, rather than seeking for incoherence in the hope of propagating the interpreter's own understanding. It seeks to undermine the specious binary religious/nonreligious, which unavoidably invites the "centering" and privileging of one member over the other. This meaning can serve the end of understanding the other and avoiding self-centering.

I sincerely look forward to seeing further elaborations of Tim Murphy's ideas. His comments on Eliade's ethnocentrism are important and his spirited attack on ethnocentrism is admirable. That "a number of examples of this ethnocentricity could be marshalled" indicates that Eliade did fall prey to ethnocentrism. Studies that apply the thought of Edward Said and Michel Foucault are increasingly bringing to light the pernicious influence of latent ethnocentrism, often concealed beneath a motivation to understand the other ("they are just like us") that is finally imperialist. Given Murphy's analysis, I am skeptical of the possibility of avoiding all ethnocentrism. He admits that even the "genealogical difference" that he commends as a replacement to universal subjectivity "does not eliminate ethnocentrism, but it reduces its power over us" (47). If we cannot eliminate ethnocentrism then it must remain a matter of degree and disposition. Becoming aware of its hidden workings especially in our favored texts—perennial support to our self-centering— is thus a matter of great importance.

Murphy goes on to point out that "[b]y arguing that the sacred is a category of consciousness, then, Eliade is not only evoking this historical concept [consciousness] within *Religionswissenschaft*, but he is claiming that the sacred (and therefore religion) is part of the very structure of human being" (38). This cannot be denied. However, it is "part of the very structure of human being" to ascribe reality to certain elements of our experience and to construct our worldviews around this "center."³ In so doing we ascribe less reality (truth, meaning, power) to other elements of our experience. These are the claims that make a claim to be universal human truths revealed by the data of religious phenomena. It is thus not the case that "all historical manifestations [are] manifestations of the sacred," nor that "the universality of religion . . . allows one to see all historical manifestations as manifestations of the sacred" (38). Rather, while they are all potentially manifestations of the sacred, all historical manifestations are necessarily party to the dialectic of the sacred and the profane, some are seen as hierophanies, some are seen as manifestations of the profane, which are simultaneously and unavoidably concealments of the sacred. For Murphy, this universalization of the sacred and of religion leads to a neglect of actual distinctions. "In short, Eliade's move to inclusiveness is bought by the elision of the difference in the other" (44). This is a criticism levelled also (but on different grounds) by J. Z. Smith in *Map Is Not Territory*. Murphy's point is that, given the historical nature of the self, humanity *is* its interpretations, its various self-articulations, thus we cannot appeal to unity, but must rather appeal to difference as the basic trope of our discourse on historical identity. Yet Murphy seems to make a strong disjunction between unity and difference—to consider them mutually exclusive. The historical nature of the Western concept of subject is not an adequate warrant for such a conclusion. Eliade's "philosophical foundation for the *simile in multis*" (39) need not rely on some essentialized concept of the human spirit but can be grounded on a similarity of behavior and of environment (not to mention biology). Thus restored, the concept of unity in difference can even allow us to use the very fact that "humanity *is* its interpretations" to stand as an example of that unity—we are *all* our interpretations.

As I have said, I think it valid to relate Derrida's "longing for the uninterrupted fullness of presence" with Eliade's "longing to live as close as possible to the Sacred" as Murphy does. But that this "forces phenomenological hermeneutics into its narcissistic, ethnocentric quest to find sameness in all forms of otherness" (45) is only true when it is untempered by any awareness of the relationality of the Sacred. That is, when *my* Sacred is taken to be the only possible presence—which is precisely what Eliade's work warns us that we cannot assume.

Murphy certainly demonstrates the importance of philosophy, and the dangers of neglecting it. In order to understand the development of the study of religion

---

3. It may well be the genealogy of these centers, or, rather, of the family-trees of knowledge descended from, or dependent upon, them, which Murphy would have us trace. And "the appearance of the subject [that] in Western history represents a dramatic 'paradigm shift' in human self-understanding" (72) could be seen as an interiorization of the *axis mundi*, the sacred center.

we need to understand the philosophy of the era. In order to advance our own understanding of religion we need to be philosophically astute.

Carl Olson's contribution is to make a useful and suggestive reference to the philosophy of Gilles Deleuze, who "attempts to develop a philosophy of difference" (73). From the Deleuzean perspective, the ultimate unity *is* difference, this supports the claim that the disjunction between unity and difference is not strong and that they are not mutually exclusive. Of course we need to recognize both to make any accurate analysis of the complexities of human religious behavior, and any tendency to emphasize one will doubtless provoke criticisms of our neglect of the other. Yet any analysis that does neglect one at the expense of the other is not thereby rendered nugatory—unless, that is, one subscribes to a belief that there *is* an actual, real, singular, and exhaustively correct analysis that is thereby lost. It may be the case in certain scientific analyses of macro-level physical phenomena that there is such an analysis, but I can only concur with Olson's quotation of Eliade to the effect that "[n]either the history of religions nor any other humanist discipline ought to conform—as they have already done too long—to models borrowed from the natural sciences, still more as these models are out of date (especially those borrowed from physics)."[4] In the case of the study of religion, to emphasize difference at the expense of similarity puts us in a position from which the worlds of the other become inaccessible to us. To apply a model from the natural sciences of a singular and absolutely correct analysis of the real (or sacred) risks making religious worlds as mutually incommensurable as differing scientific paradigms in Thomas Kuhn's *Structure of Scientific Revolutions*.

However, I cannot agree with the comment made by Olson (73 n. 33) to the effect that Eliade "shares with the neo-Kantian and Enlightenment philosophical tradition a number of convictions such as the following: the universe is intelligible; truths are fixed, uniform, permanent, absolute, and universal; religion is a *sui generis* reality that is unique and irreducible." Given the reading of Eliade that I have made, although the mass of religious humanity might insist on constructing the cosmos in this way, Eliade insists that "absolute reality" involves the *coincidentia oppositorum*—the transcendence of all oppositions. The conviction Olson attributes to Eliade involves inherent dualities—intelligible/unintelligible; fixed/floating; uniform/heterogeneous; etc.—that deny the basic intuition of the *coincidentia oppositiorum*. As I have just argued, the "reality" that makes religion *sui generis* is the human relation to our environment, not any independent thing in that environment.[5]

---

4. *The Quest*, 60f., above, 70.

5. The interested reader should consult Olson's "Mircea Eliade, Postmodernism, and the Problem of Representational Thinking." *Method and Theory in the Study of Religion*, 11:4 (1999): 357–385, and my response, 12:3.

Norman Girardot takes a renewed look at the style of study represented by Eliade, seeing much of value in it yet acknowledging the need for a contemporary revaluation. Among his accolades are that Eliade "took religion and religions seriously—even 'archaic,' 'primitive,' 'pagan,' 'superstitious,' or 'syncretistic' traditions.... Perhaps also because many different religions were treated with equal fascination and respect, it was possible to be less serious about those traditions making exaggerated claims of perfect seriousness." Further, "Eliade's raw curiosity, unfettered imagination, impressive erudition, fascination with the exotic, and his willingness to follow the historical and textual trail of an idea or movement without worrying about some preordained 'Index' of allowable thought" (147) constituted a needed liberation of an otherwise hidebound discipline. It "rescued the study of religion not only from a jealous Abrahamic God and a narrow provincial theology... but also from the reductive scientific rationalizations of the secular academy" (149), and it is still required today to make sense of the otherwise incomprehensible data of religious phenomena. It is to the credit of Eliade's approach that he "always took into account all available studies from every disciplinary perspective. This seems like an exceedingly simple matter, but within the academy it is a principle too often neglected by the more departmentally demarcated, politically connected, academically established, and intellectually self-sufficient disciplines" (150).

Despite the advice of Corless and McCutcheon in this volume and Ninian Smart elsewhere that we are at the end of the Eliadean era and should be prepared to go beyond it, Girardot is more inclined to state that

> Eliade's approach was... ambiguously (to employ an appropriately clumsy term) proto-postmodern. Eliade is not so much the end of the modern, but a partial anticipation of what we have come to call, rather apocalyptically now, postmodernism. Let us therefore make rough and ready use of a rehabilitated and reconstituted Eliade while simultaneously remembering that we should not take such operations too seriously. (161f.)

Wendell Beane's personal observations, drawn from years in the classroom, are similarly valuable. One of our most important tasks is not just to generate theory but to generate theory that is translatable into classroom practice. I will not here go into the ends and structures of a pedagogy informed by a possible "Eliadean paradigm." Suffice it to say that Beane has given us some valuable clues.

His discussion of the Marburg platform raises important issues, not only concerning the integrity of Eliade's position but also concerning the possibility of a Marburg platform revisited. It is, perhaps, unfortunate that Beane does not go into the details, but space was limited. What form might a revisited platform take today? What content would it have and who would sign it?

Beane issues a resounding call for the return of an avowedly philosophical element in the history of religions; not the philosophy of religions as it is often constituted today, but a philosophical anthropology, a religious philosophy focused on being, meaning, and truth as revealed in the data of the history of religions. I can only agree. Our discipline is a historical study, but so informed by the fluid construction of self-consistent world/systems that it must also be a philosophical study. Just as various departments of the history of science or the philosophy of science have realized that you cannot have one without the other,[6] so our discipline needs to recognize more openly that what we do is the history *and philosophy* of religion.

Douglas Allen is certainly one who explicitly combines philosophy with his history of religion. Although I am largely in agreement with his interpretations of Eliade, I wonder whether Eliade's analysis of archaic views are, like all analyses, inescapably like "interpretations of the Gita"[7] that always tell us at least as much about the interpreter as about the Gita. Allen perceives contradictions in that

> Eliade insists on the need to respect "separate planes of reference," but he often violates this principle. Especially in his ontological moves and normative judgments, he reduces modern secular phenomena to religious interpretations and explanations. He claims that we can only understand much of modern secular behavior in terms of a mythic religious plane of reference. (224)

These contradictions could, perhaps, be resolved if Eliade's claims are seen as religious rather than normative.[8] That is to suggest that they are Eliade's personal responses to the hierophanic elements of his life-experience and as such, for him, irresistible, but not required of his readers. The question, then, is whether the term *normative* is at all helpful. Is the implied distinction between, for example, the religious believer who claims that there is no god but Allah (normative), and the academic who proposes as a supportable theory that all expressions of a divine being are reducible to the human experience of society (non-normative) really warranted?

---

6. I am particularly thinking of the Department of the History and Philosophy of Science at the University of Pittsburgh, one of the most influential in the field, but I am sure that there are others.

7. "Interpretation is frequently more revealing of the interpreter than of the Gita itself." Aurobindo Ghose, in Ralph McDermott, *The Essential Aurobindo*. New York: Schocken Books, 1973, 109.

8. *Norma* is Latin for a carpenter's or mason's square, hence "establishing or setting up a norm or standard." *Oxford English Dictionary*. For further discussion of this issue see my review of Allen's *Myth and Religion in Mircea Eliade* in *Religion* 30:1 (2000).

The distinction that the former is thought to be true in all possible circumstances and is thus a rule for all people, while the latter is not, does not hold. Both could be made as absolute truths. It might be objected that the conditions of defeasibility are radically different in each case: faithful Muslims would die before rejecting their declaration of faith, whereas the academic need only read a powerfully written refutation. Is that what makes one "normative" while the other is not? But this, on closer consideration, seems to be a circular and unfalsifiable objection bent on supporting an a priori affirmation; the Muslim is religious, the academic is not. We might want a real difference between the two types of claim, but we thus ourselves constitute that difference in our own world of meaning. I suspect that we all know people who have been devout religionists at one time but who have changed their faith. Likewise, we all know academics who have insisted upon a cherished theory despite all rational disproof, and who would, we suspect, go to their graves before they would recant. The "normativity" of the assertion depends upon our personal response to it, and historically, religious "rules" have not been "normative" in the sense of applicable to all and sundry.

I suggest that it is Allen's reticence to grapple with the equation of the sacred and the real that draws him into a cul-de-sac concerning normative judgments. Given this equation I am loath to accept that Eliade ever does, in fact, talk about "reality as such" (222, 224, 227) but always reality as expressed by... or as perceived by... Quite possibly reality as seen by himself—but his philosophy apparently makes him aware that this is a necessarily subjective claim. This permits Allen to talk of "an irreducibly religious essence of reality" (230) as a ("normative") ontological claim, where for me it remains a matter of definition. "Reality" is a matter of ascription, not of privileged access to the genuine ontology.

Allen concedes that "Eliade would maintain that his ontological moves, normative judgments, and philosophical claims are not subjective and arbitrary since they are informed by and consistent with the basic intentionality of the essential symbolic structures, as expressed in mythic and other phenomena of the sacred" (228). Yet even this concession, with its apparent equation of subjective and arbitrary, misses the mark of the system that he and I agree is implicit in Eliade's thought. All judgments are subjective since they are made from within the lifeworld of the incarnate subjectivity. Yet they are not arbitrary as they are informed by the experience of that lifeworld.

Thus Eliade's assumptions—though assumptions they are—are not "unjustified," etc. (208), but explicitly corroborated by his study and interpretation of the history of religion. Allen passes too lightly over his own phrase "Eliade's philosophical reflections—*grounded in his study of religion*—" (229; emphasis added). Without historical support for philosophical speculation anyone can be accused of making unjustified assumptions. We need both the historical and the philosophical, both the actual and the ideal, both the romantic and the scientific, and Allen's chapter is a useful return to a philosophical approach where it has been lacking.

In his consideration of "sacred space and its influence on the formation of virtue," David Cave makes it readily apparent that there are certain categories of human nature that are simply not directly amenable to naturalistic treatment: virtue, conscience, etc. These can be explained in naturalistic terms but only at the expense of their operation as categories of thought, especially in narrative. If one explains conscience in behavioristic terms of stimulus-response conditioning, one no longer responds to the category of conscience per se but to these categories; one translates the meaning into different terms. Perhaps one might be right that the new terms are better, but they are not terms that one's subject, or popular thought, employs. How, then, does the employment of the new term improve one's understanding of one's subject or of popular thought? When our questions are; why does the subject believe in the operation of a "conscience"? What difference does this belief make? How does the world appear to someone who does employ this category?—then it is fruitless to explain the term as the product of stimulus-response conditioning. This might accomplish two things: (1) it might explain our own beliefs concerning "conscience," and (2) it might explain (what we take to be) the origins of conscience. But if our purpose is to answer the above questions, we will have accomplished nothing. Further, the "religious" nature of the prestige of origins was one of Eliade's most significant insights. No doubt the employment of terms in the same manner as a religious subject can lead to accusations of "religious" rather than "objective" behavior or thought. This has never been denied. To deny this is to fall foul of the fallacy of complex question—"Don't you see that you are thinking religiously now?"

The point is that all thought that recognizes values, all hierarchical organization of relationality, and especially all thought that communicates values and relations by means of narrative structures is "religious" according to the understanding encountered in Eliade's writings. The divide between "religious" and "secular" is socially constructed. It operated effectively in societies that sought to break the power of the institutional Church over political government, or vice versa, but it is not itself a "natural kind." To see humanity as *homo religiosus* never implied that institutional religion should govern our political and social institutions.

William Paden shares an estimation of Eliade's usefulness and applicability with Cave, and although we agree on that, he and I differ in certain significant details in our analysis. Paden takes very seriously my claims that "Eliade is not a theologian but a humanist for whom religious activity is a form of world-interpreting imagination."[9] Thus, that "the transcultural similarities in religion are not such by

---

9. Review of *Reconstructing Eliade, Method and Theory in the Study of Religion* 9:3 (1997): 314.

virtue of any theological-essentialist referent... but because they reflect common and sometimes universal human situations and activities" (315). So "Eliade's work provides a critique of any single model of the world." Clearly, "[t]here is no single world or 'history' to be taken for granted, but rather inexhaustible version of world and history" (314f.). However, Eliade's

> use of the terminology of the sacred is more eclectic and less systematic than Rennie takes it to be.... One does not have to force Eliade into *either* a theological mould *or* a non-theological one, as he participated in and blended several kinds of discourses... the idea that religiousness is "the expression of the fact of our embodied existence in the world..." makes the category too wide and vacuous. (316)

No doubt it is true that I have focused exclusively on one voice from a complex and polysemic text and I have insisted on the ubiquity of the structures that Eliade defines as religious. I have indeed attempted to defend Eliade—especially against appropriation by the extreme right. However this may be, I do share Paden's belief that conceiving of religions as different worlds is a move of considerable importance and utility. The most important effect of the analysis of Eliade that I have attempted to lay out in my work is that it allows, or, rather, positively encourages, movement among these worlds. It has long been an element of Romantic thought that we have access to alternative worlds. This was indicated, for example, by Samuel R. Levin in his *Metaphoric Worlds*.[10] Levin argued that it is a more coherent interpretation of the Romantic use of metaphor that, rather than inviting an accommodation of the metaphorical expressions to a fixed world, it invites an accommodation of the world to the expression. That is to say, we can change worlds.

One of several implications of what Rachela Permenter has identified as Romantic Postmodernism is that, in the simplest possible terms, it avows a both/and rather than an either/or mentality; conjunction rather than disjunction. On the other hand J. Z. Smith insists that in the symbol of the *omphalos*, the navel of the world, "it is the disjunctive rather than the conjunctive which is to the fore."[11] My point is that is a matter of interpretation. The modernist interpretation will tend to the disjunctive, the postmodern to the conjunctive. Of course, this position, to be consistent, must apply to itself. It is not one or the other, but both conjunction and disjunction. The old world is never completely ended by the new but is surpassed and re-created within it. Thus, the Romantic Postmodern attitude does not

---

10. Samuel R. Levin, *Metaphoric Worlds: Conceptions of a Romantic Nature*. New Haven: Yale University Press, 1988. See my review, *Style*, 24:4 (Winter 1990): 638–642.

11. *Map is not Territory*, 98; *To Take Place*, 122 n. 2.

attempt to replace, but to embrace, modernity. It is not a case of either modernism or postmodernism, either romanticism or scientism, but both one and the other. The modern world does not stand completely apart from the archaic or postmodern. The secular modern mind is not fundamentally different from the religious. These oppositions are constructs, temporarily necessary for classification and ordering, but finally ephemeral. If we take these distinctions too seriously, alternative worlds become inaccessible to us.

As I mentioned in the introduction (xxiv), my title for this section, and the subtitle for the anthology as a whole, has been taken from Wilfred Cantwell Smith's classic, *The Meaning and End of Religion*. Here Smith has argued that the word *religion* is finally so misleading and confusing that it should be dropped entirely in favor of some other term or terms (Smith suggested "faith" and "tradition"). It certainly seemed inconsistent that Smith himself did not follow what seemed to be a serious suggestion. He proceeded to use "religion" in his own later book titles. But simply to malign Smith for inconsistency and incoherence would be to fail in the object of creative hermeneutics as I have conceived it. The word *religion*, for all its faults is so firmly entrenched, so commonplace, so familiar, and so enmeshed in the English language, that Smith would have been a fool indeed to imagine that a single book, no matter how well researched and well argued, could succeed in exorcising it. It would be more respectful of Smith's intelligence to assume that he did not really hope for the rejection and abandonment of the word, but, in stating his point as he did, for a deeper understanding of it. Eliade is structurally comparable to "religion" in Smith's text in the sense that there religion was the object of interpretation. Here it is Eliade. There it was "religion" that was confusing and potentially misleading. Here it is Eliade. There it was "religion" whose end was recommended even as it was articulated. Here it is Eliade. Like "religion," Eliade—or rather the texts he left behind—may be misleading and confusing. But like "religion" he cannot be exorcised from our world. The texts are there, the terms are in circulation, scholars use his categories, the past is enfolded in the present. Like religion, Eliade will not go away. In calling for the end of the Eliadean era writers such as McCutcheon and Corless articulate their own positions well but finally their appeal is hopeless and Eliade must be put to another end. All such calling for an end should come under the scrutiny applied by Jacques Derrida in his paper "Of an Apocalyptic Tone Newly Adopted in Philosophy."[12] Here he questions "the fact of

---

12. "Of an Apocalyptic Tone Newly Adopted in Philosophy," in *Derrida and Negative Theology*, ed Harold Coward and Toby Foshay. Albany: State University of New York Press, 1992, 25–71.

telling, foretelling, or preaching the end, the extreme limit, the imminence of the last" (47). He goes on, "[E]ach time we ask ourselves where they want to come to, and to what ends, those who declare the end of this or that, of man or the subject, of consciousness, of history, of the West or of literature" (51, and in this case of "the Eliadean era"). Of course, "every apocalyptic eschatology is promised in the name of light" (50). "Whoever takes on the apocalyptic tone comes to signify, if not tell, you something. What? The truth of course" (53).

To understand this self-aggrandizement, this self-centering in others we need to see it in our selves. Kant does it with his elevation of the mystery of pure practical reason ("the mystery at once domestic, intimate, and transcendent, the *Geheimnis* of practical reason, the sublimity of moral law," 38). Empiricists and historicists do it with the presumed access to the authorities of nature and history. We make our sacred real by making sense of it. We construct a coherent world and bring into the realm of empirical experience what properly does not belong there. Kant warns us of the "presentiment of the sun," the "glimpse behind the veil of Isis," the "rustling of the garments of the goddess Wisdom" (41), whose voice calls to us in the marketplace. But there is also the perspective on nature, the view of history—now, perhaps, more convincing than the vision of God, but still the unveiling, revealing, apocalyptic hierophany. It is the centering of the peripheral and it is the centering of the self. Kant considers this an abuse of metaphor but, following the Romantic metaphoric of Levin (above, 277) and, I suggest, Eliade, it may in fact be the use of metaphor—the construction of worlds. Schlosser, attacked by Kant, takes the Romantic side. He talks of "this prosaic age in which the highest wisdom is to see nothing but what lies at our feet and to assume nothing but what we can grasp with our hands" (44). The rational Kant would have us claim an empirical accessibility only to what is empirically accessible. But history (and, arguably, nature) is not. Neither of them "lie at our feet" any more than the constructed worlds of the other. In treating Eliade as I do I hope to further the ends of an increased understanding between people of differing cultural worlds by destabilizing the binary oppositions of religious/secular, them/us and thus making these other worlds more accessible.

Apparently, those who "believe in" Eliade's thought, who make positive valorizations of it, either along the lines I have suggested or in some other way, are those who can use it. Douglas Allen for personal renewal, David Cave for the cultivation of virtue, and William Paden for the comparison of religious world habitation. Those who don't believe in it, can't use it. To them it remains meaningless and pointless. This itself is an example of the coherence I perceive in Eliadean thought: the hierophanic revelation of meaning and significance in something—in this case in the writings of Mircea Eliade—is dependent upon the preparation of the subject to recognize that hierophany. Once recognized, subjective though this recognition may be, the hierophany empowers the creative application of the now "sacred" (i.e., meaningful, significant, real, true, powerful) item. Failure to recognize the significance corresponds to the inability to accord a positive valorization to the phenomenon in question and leads to the dismissal of that phenomenon as insignificant, meaningless, powerless—even possibly malign—in short, profane.

CRISIS? WHAT CRISIS?

One thing that becomes strikingly obvious in this debate over Eliade is the consistency and coherence of the various scholars involved. Although there is much talk of crisis in the field today it would appear that this could be largely attributed to external circumstances. As Norman Girardot has pointed out, the whole academic enterprise is challenged (144). This challenge has been brought about externally by new developments in culture, politics, technology, and in the administration of the academy. But, internally, there seems to be a desire to be in crisis—perhaps because it indicates a time of "revolutionary science" in which paradigms are changing, much is at stake, fortunes are to be made, and excitement is high. In fact, it appears to me that there is a paradigmatic understanding of our field, possibly not well articulated, but quite well established, and, if my analysis is at all correct, strongly influenced by the works of Mircea Eliade. All sides of the debate that has focused on Eliade seem to agree on an important range of issues, which would indicate that the field is, in fact, surprisingly healthy and coherent. Both pro and con desire the advent of a position in which the dominant culture of the Western world is refused any claim to "natural" superiority. All sides regard ethnocentrism as an ill if it implies the provincial privileging of "us" over "them." Although there is disagreement over Eliade's role in right-wing oppression of minorities, all are agreed that such oppression is culpable. All seem to desire a fair and evenhanded appreciation of both sameness and difference in the treatment of other cultures, including the awareness and diminution of the ethnocentrism that is regarded as an inescapable historical fact. One manifestation of this is the recommendation given by both Roger Corless and Norman Girardot that systems should not be taken too seriously (42, 317).

There seems also to be a high degree of consensus on the return to philosophy in the study of religion. Our discipline is properly constituted as the history *and philosophy* of religion in which the data can only be properly processed in the self-conscious awareness of our own historical and philosophical situatedness. We need both the historical approach to uncovering reliable data and the philosophical approach to a sensitive analysis of that data in the full awareness that our worldviews often play a very active role in constituting what is taken to be data.

There is, perhaps, some disagreement over whether we should understand religion or resist it. Conceived of in the way I have suggested, it is not religion that should be resisted—that would be tantamount to resisting our own innate nature, to denying the presence of the past in the present—rather it is the *abuse* of religion. This is an abuse to which all human systems are prey. It is the tendency to dogmatism and provincialism, to the oppression of the other, which is validated by a worldview that, finally inconsistently, draws a hard line between them and us. In the previously mentioned article, Derrida is, as usual, not merely critical, not only negative. "Each of us is the mystagogue *and* the *Aufklärer* of an other," he points out ("Apocalyptic Tone," 45). Thus, the proposal is not somehow to step off this merry-go-round ("shall we thus continue in the best apocalyptic tradition to denounce false apocalypses?" 59), to refuse the play of actual and ideal that constitutes the truth, but to recognize it for what it is—the human constitution.

Bibliography

MAJOR WORKS BY MIRCEA ELIADE
(for a more complete and detailed bibliography see Bryan Rennie,
Reconstructing Eliade, State University of New York Press, 1996)

Metallurgy, Magic, and Alchemy. Paris: Guenther, 1936.

Cosmos and History: The Myth of the Eternal Return. Princeton: Princeton University Press, 1954.

Patterns in Comparative Religion. London: Sheed and Ward, 1958.

Rites and Symbols of Initiation. London: Harvill Press, 1958.

Yoga, Immortality, and Freedom. London: Routledge and Kegan Paul, 1958.

The Sacred and the Profane: The Nature of Religion. London: Harcourt Brace Jovanovich, 1959.

Myths, Dreams, and Mysteries: The Encounter between Contemporary Faiths and Archaic Realities. London: Harvill Press, 1960.

Images and Symbols: Studies in Religious Symbolism. London: Harvill Press, 1961.

The Forge and the Crucible. London: Rider and Co., 1962.

Myth and Reality. New York: Harper and Row, 1963.

Shamanism: Archaic Techniques of Ecstasy. London: Routledge and Kegan Paul, 1964.

The Two and the One. Chicago: University of Chicago Press, 1965.

From Primitives to Zen: A Sourcebook in Comparative Religion. New York: Harper and Row, 1967.

Patañjali and Yoga. Trans. Charles Lam Markmann. New York: Funk and Wagnalls, 1969.

The Quest: History and Meaning in Religion. Chicago: University of Chicago Press, 1969.

Zalmoxis, the Vanishing God. Chicago: University of Chicago Press, 1972.

Australian Religion. London: Cornell University Press, 1973.

Myths, Rites, and Symbols: A Mircea Eliade Reader, ed. Beane, W. C., and W. G. Doty. New York: Harper and Row, 1975.

Occultism, Witchcraft, and Cultural Fashions. Chicago: University of Chicago Press, 1976.

A History of Religious Ideas, vol. I, *From the Stone Age to the Eleusinian Mysteries.* Chicago: University of Chicago Press, 1978.

What Is Religion? (ed. with David Tracy). Edinburgh: T. and T. Clarke, 1980.

A History of Religious Ideas, vol. II, *From Gautama Buddha to the Triumph of Christianity.* Chicago: University of Chicago Press, 1982.

Ordeal by Labyrinth: Conversations with Claude-Henri Rocquet. Chicago: University of Chicago, 1982. Trans. Derek Coltman.

The History of Religious Ideas, vol. III, *From Muhammad to the Age of the Reforms.* Chicago: University of Chicago Press, 1985.

Symbolism, the Sacred, and the Arts, ed. Diane Apostolos-Cappadona. New York: Crossroad, 1986. Trans. from French by Diane Apostolos-Cappadona and Frederica Adel, Derek Coltman, and from Romanian by Mac Linscott Ricketts.

Encyclopedia of Religion (Editor in Chief). New York: Macmillan, 1987.

Dictionaire des Religions (with Ioan Culianu). Paris: Plon, 1990.

OTHER WORKS CITED

Abrams, M. H. *The Mirror and the Lamp: Romantic Theory and the Critical Tradition.* New York: Oxford, 1953.

Allen, Douglas. *Myth and Religion in Mircea Eliade.* New York and London: Garland Publishing Inc., 1998.

Anderson, Walter Truett. *Reality Isn't What It Used to Be: Theatrical Politics, Ready-To-Wear Religion, Global Myths, Primitive Chic, and Other Wonders of the Postmodern World.* Harper San Francisco, 1992.

———. *The Truth about the Truth: De-Confusing and Re-Constructing the Postmodern World.* J P Tarcher, 1995.

Anttonen, Veikko. "Rethinking the Sacred: The Notions of 'Human Body' and 'Territory' in Conceptualizing Religion." In Thomas A. Idinopulos and Edward A. Yonan, eds., *The Sacred and its Scholars: Comparative Methodologies for the Study of Primary Religious Data.* Studies in the History of Religions, Vol. LXXIII. Leiden: E. J. Brill, 1996, 36–64.

Barfield, Owen. *Romanticism Comes of Age.* Middletown, CT: Wesleyan University Press, 1967.

Beane, Wendell. *Myth, Cult, and Symbols in Sakta Hinduism.* Leiden: E. J. Brill, 1977.

Bercovitch, Sacvan, and Myra Jehlen, eds. *Ideology and Classic American Literature.* New York: Cambridge University Press, 1986.

Bloom, Harold. *The Breaking of Vessels.* Chicago: University of Chicago Press, 1982.

———. *The Ringers in the Tower.* Chicago: University of Chicago Press, 1971. Brighton: Harvester, 1980: 245–264.

———, and Mireille Cale-Gruber. *Hélène Cixous Root-prints: Memory and Life Writing.* Trans. Eric Prenowitz. Paris: Editions des femmes, 1994. New York: Routledge, 1997.

Boyer, Pascal. *Tradition as Truth and Communication: A Cognitive Description of Traditional Discourse.* Cambridge: Cambridge University Press, 1990.

Brown, Donald E. *Human Universals.* Philadelphia: Temple University Press, 1991.

Burgin, Victor. "The End of Art Theory." In *The End of Art Theory: Criticism and Postmodernity.* Atlantic Highlands: Humanities Press International, 1986.

Capps, Walter H. *Religious Studies: The Making of a Discipline.* Minneapolis: Fortress Press, 1995.

Caputo, John D., ed. *Deconstruction in a Nutshell: A Conversation with Jacques Derrida.* New York: Fordham University Press, 1997.

Chai, Leon. *The Romantic Foundations of the American Rennaissance.* Ithaca: Cornell University Press, 1987.

Chidester, David. "Anchoring Religion in the World: A Southern African History of Comparative Religion." *Religion* 26 (1996): 141–160.

———. " 'Classify and Conquer': Friedrich Max Muller, Indigenous Religious Traditions, and Imperial Comparative Religion." Unpublished paper, 1996.

Cixous, Hélène. *Illa.* Paris: Editions des femmes, 1980.

———. "The Laugh of the Medusa." Trans. Keith Cohen and Paula Cohen. *Signs* 1 (1976): 875–899. Rpt. Eds. Elaine Marks and Isabelle de Courtivron. *New French Feminisms.*

Clifford, James. "Histories of the Tribal and the Modern." In *The Predicament of Culture: Twentieth-Century Ethnography, Literature and Art.* Cambridge: Harvard University Press, 1988.

Connerton, Paul. *How Societies Remember.* Cambridge: Cambridge University Press, 1989.

Couliano, Ioan P. *The Tree of Gnosis: Gnostic Mythology from Early Christianity to Modern Nihilism.* Trans. H. S. Wiesner and the author. San Francisco: HarperSanFrancisco, 1992.

Cromphout, Gustaaf van. *Emerson's Modernity and the Example of Goethe.* Columbia: University of Missouri Press, 1990.

Deleuze, Gilles. *Difference and Repetition.* Trans. Paul Patton. New York: Columbia University Press, 1994.

———, and Felix Guattari, *A Thousand Plateaus: Capitalism and Schizophrenia.* Trans. Brian Massumi. Minneapolis: University of Minnesota Press, 1988.

Derrida, Jacques. "Structure, Sign, and Play in the Discourse of the Human Sciences." In *Writing and Difference.* Chicago: University of Chicago Press, 1978.

———. "The Ends of Man." In *Margins of Philosophy.* Chicago: University of Chicago Press, 1982.

———. "Form and Meaning: A Note on the Phenomenology of Language." In *Margins of Philosophy.*

———. "Différance." In *Margins of Philosophy.*

———. *Of Grammatology.* Trans. Gayatri Spivak. Baltimore: Johns Hopkins University Press, 1976.

———. "Like the Sound of the Sea Deep within a Shell: Paul de Man's War." *Critical Inquiry* 14 (1988): 590–652.

———. "Biodegradables: Seven Diary Fragments." *Critical Inquiry* 15 (1989): 812–873.

———. "Of an Apocalyptic Tone Newly Adopted in Philosophy." In Harold Coward and Toby Foshay, eds., *Derrida and Negative Theology.* Albany: State University of New York Press, 1992.

Detienne, Marcel. *The Creation of Mythology.* Trans. Margaret Cook. Chicago: The University of Chicago Press, 1986.

Dillard, Annie. *Teaching a Stone to Talk: Expeditions and Encounters.* New York: Harper and Row, 1982.

Dilthey, Wilhelm. *Pattern and Meaning in History.* New York: Harper and Row, 1961.

Durkheim, Emile. *The Rules of Sociological Method.* Trans. Sarah A. Solovay and John H. Mueller. 8th ed. Chicago: University of Chicago Press, 1938.

———. *The Elementary Forms of the Religious Life.* Trans. Joseph Ward Swain. London: George Allen and Unwin, 1954.

———, and Marcel Mauss, *Primitive Classification.* Trans. Rodney Needham. Chicago: University of Chicago Press, 1963.

Eagleton, Terry. "Capitalism, Modernism, and Postmodernism." *New Left Review* 152 (1985): 60–73.

Eichner, Hans. "The Rise of Modern Science and the Genesis of Romanticism." *PMLA* 97 (1982): 8–30.

Evans-Pritchard, E. E. *Theories of Primitive Religion.* Oxford: Clarendon Press, 1965.

Falck, Colin. *Myth, Truth, and Literature: Towards a True Postmodernism.* Cambridge: Cambridge University Press, 1989.

Foucault, Michel. "Nietzsche, Genealogy, History." In *The Foucault Reader.* Ed. Paul Rabinow. New York: Pantheon Books, 1984.

Frazer, James George. *The Golden Bough: A Study in Magic and Religion*, 3 Vols. 3rd ed. London: Macmillan, 1951.

Freud, Sigmund. *Moses and Monotheism.* New York: Vintage Books, 1939.

Fuller, Margaret. *Woman in the Nineteenth Century.* Boston: John P. Jewett, 1855. New York: W. W. Norton, 1971.

Gadamer, Hans Georg. *Truth and Method.* New York: Crossroad Publishing Co., 1989.

Geertz, Armin W., and Jeppe Sinding Jensen. "Tradition and Renewal in the Histories of Religions: Some Observations and Reflections." In Armin W. Geertz and Jeppe Sinding Jensen, eds. *Religion, Tradition, and Renewal.* Aarhus, Denmark: Aarhus University Press, 1991.

Girardot, Norman J., and Mac Linscott Ricketts. *Imagination and Meaning: The Scholarly and Literary Worlds of Mircea Eliade.* New York: The Seabury Press, 1982.

Godlove, Terry. "Religious Discourse and First Person Authority." *Method and Theory in the Study of Religion* 6 (1994): 147-161.

Goethe, Johann Wolfgang von. *From My Life: Poetry and Truth (Parts One to Three).* Ed. and trans. Douglas Miller. The Collected Works, Vol. 4. Princeton: Princeton University Press, 1995.

———. *Scientific Studies.* Ed. and trans. Douglas Miller. The Collected Works, Vol. 12. Princeton: Princeton University Press, 1995.

Goodman, Nelson. *Ways of Worldmaking.* Indianapolis: Hackett Publishing Co., 1978.

Gray, Ronald D. *Goethe the Alchemist: A Study of Alchemical Symbolism in Goethe's Literary and Scientific Works.* Cambridge: Cambridge University Press, 1952.

Hamacher, Werner, Neil Hertz, and Thomas Keenan, eds. *Wartime Journalism, 1939–1943.* Lincoln: University of Nebraska Press, 1988.

———. *Responses: On Paul de Man's Wartime Journalism.* Lincoln: University of Nebraska Press, 1989.

Harris, Marvin. *The Rise of Anthropological Theory: A History of Theories of Culture.* New York: Columbia University Press, 1969.

Hassan, Ihab. *The Dismemberment of Orpheus: Toward a Postmodern Literature*. New York: Oxford, 1971.

Hayles, N. Katherine. *Chaos Bound*. Ithaca: Cornell University Press, 1990.

Hegel, G. W. F. *The Phenomenology of Spirit*. New York: Oxford University Press, 1977.

Heidegger, Martin. *Being and Time*. New York: Harper and Row, 1962.

———. *Basic Writings*. New York: Harper and Row, 1977.

———. "The Age of the World Picture" and "The Word of Nietzsche: 'God is Dead.' " In *The Question Concerning Technology and Other Essays*. New York: Harper Torchbooks, 1977.

Hoy, David. "A History of Consciousness: from Kant and Hegel to Derrida and Foucault." *History of the Human Sciences* 4:2 (1991).

Husserl, Edmund. *Ideas: General Introduction to Pure Phenomenology*. Trans. W. R. Boyce Gibson. New York: Collier Books, 1931.

Hutton, Patrick H. *History as an Art of Memory*. Hanover, NH: University Press of New England, 1993.

Idinopulos, Thomas, and Edward Yonan, eds. *The Sacred and its Scholars: Comparative Methodologies for the Study of Primary Religious Data*. Leiden: E. J. Brill, 1996.

Irigaray, Luce. "When Our Lips Speak Together." Trans. Carolyn Burke. *Signs* 6 (1980): 69–79.

Jardine, Alice A. *Gynesis: Configurations of Woman and Modernity*. Ithaca: Cornell University Press, 1985.

Johnson, Kent, and Craig Paulenich, eds. *Beneath a Single Moon: Buddhism in Contemporary American Poetry*. Introduction by Gary Snyder. Boston: Shambhala, 1991.

Jonas, Hans. *The Gnostic Religion: The Message of the Alien God and the Beginnings of Christianity*. 2d. ed., rev. Boston: Beacon Press, 1963.

Kant, Immanuel. *The Critique of Pure Reason*. Trans. Friedrich Max Müller, London: Macmillan, 1900.

King, Ursula. "Historical Phenomenological Approaches to the Study of Religion." In Frank Whaling, ed. *Theory and Method in Religious Studies: Contemporary Approaches to the Study of Religion*. New York: Mouton de Gruyter, 1995.

Kitagawa, Joseph M. *The History of Religions: Understanding Human Experience*, AAR Studies in Religion 47. Atlanta: Scholars Press, 1987.

———, and Charles H. Long, eds. *Myths and Symbols: Studies in Honor of Mircea Eliade*. Chicago: University of Chicago Press, 1969.

Kuhn, Thomas. *The Structure of Scientific Revolutions*. Chicago: University of Chicago Press, 1962.

Lang, Andrew. *The Making of Religion*. London: Longmans, Green, 1898.

Lawrence, D. H. *Phoenix II: Uncollected, Unpublished, and Other Prose Works*. Ed. Warren Roberts and Harry T. Moore. 1959. New York: Viking, 1968.

van der Leeuw, Gerardus. *Religion in Essence and Manifestation*. Princeton: Princeton University Press, 1964.

Lévy-Bruhl, Lucien. *Primitive Mentality*. Trans. Lilian A. Clare. London: George Allen and Unwin, 1923.

Lincoln, Bruce. *Authority: Construction and Corrosion.* Chicago: University of Chicago Press, 1994.

———. "Theses on Method." *Method and Theory in the Study of Religion* 8 (1996): 225–227.

Long, Charles H. *Significations: Signs, Symbols, and Images in the Interpretation of Religion.* Philadelphia: Fortress Press, 1986.

Lyotard, Jean-Francois. *The Postmodern Condition: A Report on Knowledge.* Trans. Geoff Bennington and Brian Massumi. Minneapolis: University of Minnesota Press, 1984.

Mack, Burton. "Caretakers and Critics: On the Social Role of Scholars Who Study Religion." Unpublished paper presented to the Seminar on Religion in Society, Wesleyan University, September 14, 1989.

Manea, Norman. *On Clowns: The Dictator and the Artist.* New York: Grove Weidenfeld, 1992.

Marty, Martin. "That Nice Man (Reminiscences of Mircea Eliade)." *Christian Century* 103 (1086): 503.

McCutcheon, Russell. "The Category 'Religion' in Recent Publications: A Critical Survey." *Numen* 42/3 (1995): 284-309.

———. "A Default of Critical Intelligence? The Scholar of Religion as Public Intellectual." *Journal of the American Academy of Religion* (1997).

———. *Manufacturing Religion: The Discourse on* Sui Generis *Religion and the Politics of Nostalgia.* New York: Oxford University Press. 1997.

———. Review of Bryan Rennie, *Reconstructing Eliade. Religion* 28:1 (1998): 92–97.

———. *Critics not Caretakers: Redescribing the Study of Religion,* Albany: State University of New York Press, 2000.

Mellor, Anne K. "Blake's Portrayal of Women." *Blake: An Illustrated Quarterly* (1982–83): 148–155.

Merleau-Ponty, Maurice. *Phenomenology of Perception.* New York: Humanities Press, 1962.

Mitchell, W. J. T. "Visible Language: Blake's Wond'rous Art of Writing." In *Romanticism and Contemporary Criticism.* Ithaca: Cornell University Press, 1986, 46–95.

Mol, Hans. *Identity and the Sacred: A Sketch for a New Social-Scientific Theory of Religion.* Oxford: Basil Blackwell, 1976.

Morris, Brian. *Anthropological Studies of Religion: An Introductory Text.* Cambridge: Cambridge University Press, 1987.

Müller, Max. *Chips from a German Workshop.* Vol. I. *Essays on the Science of Religion.* New York: Charles Scribner, 1869; reprint Chico, CA: Scholars Press, 1985.

———. *Introduction to the Science of Religion.* London: Longmans, Green, 1873.

———. *Natural Religion.* London: Longmans, Green, 1890.

Murphy, Tim. "*Wesen und Erscheinung* in the History of the Study of Religion: A Poststructuralist Perspective." *Method and Theory in the Study of Religion* 6:2 (1994): 119–146.

———. Review of Carl Olson, *The Theology and Philosophy of Eliade*: *Method and Theory in the Study of Religion* 6, 4 (1994): 382–389.

Nietzsche, Friedrich. *On the Genealogy of Morals: A Polemic.* New York: Vintage Books, 1967.

Norris, Christopher. *Derrida.* Cambridge: Harvard University Press, 1987.

———. *Paul De Man: Deconstruction and the Critique of Aesthetic Ideology*. London: Routledge, 1988.

———. *What's Wrong with Postmodernism: Critical Theory and the Ends of Philosophy*. Baltimore: Johns Hopkins University Press, 1990.

Olson, Carl. *The Theology and Philosophy of Eliade*. New York: St. Martin's Press, 1992.

———. "Mircea Eliade, Postmodernism, and the Problematic Nature of Representational Thinking," *Method and Theory in the Study of Religion* 11:4 (1999): 357–385.

Otto, Rudolf. *The Idea of the Holy*. New York: Oxford University Press, 1958.

Paden, William. "Sacrality as Integrity: 'Sacred Order' as a Model for Describing Religious Worlds." In Thomas A. Idinopulos and Edward A. Yonan, eds., *The Sacred and Its Scholars: Comparative Methodologies for the Study of Primary Religious Data*. Studies in the History of Religions, Vol. LXXIII. Leiden: E. J. Brill, 1996.

———. *Religious Worlds: The Comparative Study of Religion*. Boston: Beacon Press, 1994.

Palmer, Richard. *Hermeneneutics: Interpretation Theory in Schleiermacher, Dilthey, Heidegger, and Gadamer*. Evanston: Northwestern University Press, 1969.

Patton, Laurie L., and Wendy Doniger, eds. *Myth and Method*. Charlottesville: University Press of Virginia, 1996.

Person, Leyland. *Aesthetic Headaches: Women and a Masculine Poetics in Poe, Melville, and Hawthorne*. Athens: University of Georgia Press, 1988.

Preus, J. Samuel. *Explaining Religion: Criticism and Theory from Bodin to Freud*. New Haven: Yale University Press, 1987.

Rajan, Tilottama. *Dark Interpreter: The Discourse of Romanticism*. Ithaca: Cornell University Press, 1980.

———. *The Supplement of Reading: Figures of Understanding in Romantic Theory and Practice*. Ithaca: Cornell University Press, 1990.

Rennie, Bryan. "The Diplomatic Career of Mircea Eliade: A Response to Adriana Berger." *Religion* 22:4 (1992): 375–392. Trans. Lidia Rosu as: "Cariera diplomatica a lui M. Eliade—un raspuns Adrianei Berger," *Jurnalul Literar* (Bucharest) 5–8 (feb–mar 1993): 1, 4–5.

———. "The Religious Creativity of Modern Humanity: Some Observations on Eliade's Unfinished Thought." *Religious Studies* 31:2 (1995): 221–235. Trans. Raluca Podocea as: "Creativitatea religioas a umanitii moderne," *Jurnalul Literar* nr. 9–12 (aprilie 1994): 4–5.

———. *Reconstructing Eliade: Making Sense of Religion*. Albany: State University of New York Press, 1996. Translated into Romanian by Mirella Balta, Gabriel Stanescu, and Stefan Stoenescu as *Reconsiderându-l Pe Mircea Eliade: O nouă viziume asupra religiei*, Criterion Publishing, 1999.

———. "Manufacturing McCutcheon: The Failure of Understanding in the Academic Study of Religion." *Culture and Religion* 1:1 (2000).

———. "Mircea Eliade: A Secular Mystic in the History of Religions." In *The Unknown Remembered Gate*, Eliot Wolfson and Jeffrey Kripal, eds. New York: Seven Bridges Press, 2000.

Rescher, Nicholas, and Robert Brandon. *The Logic of Inconsistency: A Study in Non-Standard Possible World Semantics and Ontology*. Oxford: Blackwell, 1980.

Ricoeur, Paul. *The Symbolism of Evil.* New York: Harper and Row, 1967.

de la Saussaye, D. Chantepie. *Manual of the Science of Religion.* Trans. Beatrice S. Colyer-Fergusson. London: Longmans, Green, 1891.

de Saussure, Ferdinand. *Course in General Linguistics.* Trans. Wade Baskin. New York: McGraw-Hill, 1966.

Schneidau, Herbert N. *Sacred Discontent: The Bible and Western Tradition.* Berkeley: University of California Press, 1977.

Shapiro, Gary. *Nietzschean Narratives.* Bloomington and Indianapolis: Indiana University Press, 1989

Sharpe, Eric J. *Comparative Religion: A History,* 2nd ed. La Salle, IL: Open Court, 1986.

Sheehan, Thomas. "Heidegger: The Normal Nazi." *New York Review of Books.* (January 1993): 30–35.

Shepard, Paul. "A Post-Historic Primitivism." In *The Wilderness Condition: Essays on Environment and Civilization.* Max Oelschlaeger ed. San Francisco: Island Press, 1992.

Silverman, Hugh. *Derrida and Desconstruction.* New York: Routledge, 1989.

Smith, Jonathan Z. *Map Is Not Territory: Studies in the History of Religions.* Leiden: E. J. Brill, 1978.

———. *Imagining Religion from Babylon to Jonestown.* Chicago and London: University of Chicago Press, 1982.

———. *To Take Place: Toward Theory in Ritual.* Chicago: University of Chicago Press, 1992.

Solomon, Robert. *Continental Philosophy Since 1750: The Rise and Fall of the Self.* New York: Oxford University Press, 1988.

Sontag, Susan. "Against Interpretation." *A Susan Sontag Reader.* New York: Farrar, Straus, and Giroux, 1980.

Spencer, Herbert. *The Principles of Sociology,* 3 Vols. New York: D. Appleton and Company, 1898.

Strauss, Erwin. "Born to See, Bound to Behold . . ." In *The Philosophy of the Body: Rejections of Cartesian Dualism,* ed. Stuart Spicker. Chicago: Quadrangle Books, 1970.

Strenski, Ivan. *Religion in Relation: Method, Application, and Moral Location.* Columbia: University of South Carolina Press, 1993.

Taylor, Charles. *Philosophical Arguments.* Cambridge: Harvard University Press, 1995.

Tiele, Cornelis P. *Elements of the Science of Religion,* 2 Vols. New York: Charles Scribner's Sons, 1897.

Tilly, Charles. *Big Structures, Large Processes, Huge Comparisons.* New York: Russell Sage Foundation, 1984.

Tracy, David. *The Analogical Imagination: Christian Theology and the Culture of Pluralism.* New York: Crossroads, 1981.

Tylor, Edward B. *Primitive Culture: Researches into the Development of Mythology, Philosophy, Religion, Language, Art, and Customs.* 2 Vols. 3rd ed. New York: Holt, 1883.

Waardenburg, Jacques. *Reflections on the Study of Religion.* The Hague: Mouton Publishers, 1978.

———. "Religion between Reality and Idea." *Numen,* Vol. XIX, Fasc. 2–3 (1972).

Wach, Joachim. *Sociology of Religion.* Chicago and London: University of Chicago Press, 1971.

———. *Types of Religious Experience, Christian and Non-Christian.* Chicago: University of Chicago Press, 1970.

———. *The Comparative Study of Religions.* Ed. Joseph M. Kitagawa. New York and London: Columbia University Press, 1969.

Weber, Max. *The Theory of Social and Economic Organization.* Trans. A. M. Henderson and T. Parsons. New York: Free Press, 1947.

———. *The Sociology of Religion.* Trans. Ephraim Fischoff. Boston: Beacon Press, 1964.

Werblowsky, R. J. Zwi. "The Comparative Study of Religions—A Review Essay," *Judaism* Vol. 8 (1959).

Whitford, Margaret. "Luce Irigaray's Critique of Rationality." In Morwenna Griffiths and Margaret Whitford, eds., *Feminist Perspectives in Philosophy*, Bloomington: Indiana University Press, 1988, 109–30.

Wolin, Richard. *The Heidegger Controversy: A Critical Reader.* Cambridge: MIT Press, 1993.

Contributors

DOUGLAS ALLEN is associate professor of philosophy at the University of Maine at Orono. He gained his Ph.D. from Vanderbilt University and has studied at Yale and Benares Hindu University. He has published *Structure and Creativity in Religion: Hermeneutics in Mircea Eliade's Phenomenology and New Directions* (The Hague, Mouton, 1978); "Eliade and History," in the *Journal of Religion* 68 (1988): 545–565; *Mircea Eliade et le phénomène religieux* (Paris: Payot, 1982); and, with Denis Doeing, *Mircea Eliade: An Annotated Bibliography* (New York and London: Garland, 1980). Professor Allen's recent book, *Mircea Eliade on Myth and Religion* was published by Garland Press in 1998.

WENDELL CHARLES BEANE is professor of history of religions at the University of Wisconsin Oshkosh and does comparative research in his approach to the study of the major world religious traditions. He studied history, French, and pastoral theology at Howard University. He has been an elder in the United Methodist Church since 1961. A student of Mircea Eliade and a graduate of the University of Chicago (Ph.D.), he has been a fellow of the American Institute of Indian Studies and, at present, teaches world religions, Hinduism, issues in contemporary world religions, perennial myths, and modern mysteries; a seminar on comparative-religious views of suffering; religion, faith, and healing; and comparative mysticism. He was awarded the Distinguished Teaching Award in 1990, and the University of Wisconsin Board of Regents Award for Teaching Excellence in 1992. He has written scholarly articles for international journals, such as *History of Religions* (Chicago), *Religious Studies* (Cambridge), and *World Faiths Insight* (London). He is the author of *Myth, Cult, and Symbols in Shakta Hinduism* (E. J. Brill), and editor (with W. G. Doty) of *Myths, Rites, Symbols: A Mircea Eliade Reader*, 2 Vols. (Harper and Row). He has delivered papers before the American Academy of Religion, the Society for the Scientific Study of Religion, the University of Wisconsin Madison Annual Conference on South Asia, and the National Medical Association. He has traveled widely and has spoken on various subjects ranging from Biblical mysteries and spirituality to meditation and mysticism. He is a former chair of the Department of Religious Studies and Anthropology at the University of Wisconsin Oshkosh and was a visiting scholar at Andover Newton Theological Seminary for the year 1992–1993. He is currently writing a book, entitled *Interreligious Dialogue from a Christian Perspective: Problems and Prospects*.

DAVID CAVE grew up in Argentina, the son of missionary parents. He has a Ph.D. from Lutheran Theological Southern Seminary in South Carolina with a dissertation on Eliade involving research at the University of Chicago and Indiana University. This dissertation was revised and published as *Mircea Eliade's Vision for a New Humanism* (New York: Oxford University Press, 1992). He has also written "The Domicile in the Study and Teaching of the Sacred, Using the Methodological Assumptions of Jonathan Z. Smith and Mircea Eliade" in *The Sacred and its Scholars: Comparative Methodologies for the Study of Primary Religious Data*. Eds. Thomas Idinopulos and Edward Yonan (Leiden: E. J. Brill, 1996). He is currently teaching at Chatfield College, St. Martin, Ohio.

ROGER CORLESS is professor of religion at Duke University. He has a B.D. from King's College, University of London, and a Ph.D. in Buddhist studies from the University of Wisconsin-Madison, with a specialty in the Pure Land tradition. He has published four books and more than fifty articles on Buddhism, Christian spirituality, and Buddhist-Christian dialogue. He is a co-founder of the Society for Buddhist-Christian Studies.

MIRCEA ELIADE, the focus of this volume, was born in Bucharest, Romania, in 1917. He read extensively in Romanian, French, and German, and learned Italian and English to read Raffaele Pettazzoni and James George Frazer. He studied philosophy at the University of Bucharest from 1925–1928 and produced a master's thesis on Italian Renaissance philosophers from Ficino to Bruno. In 1928 he sailed to India in order to "universalize" the "provincial" philosophy he had inherited from his European education. He studied Sanskrit and philosophy under Surendranath Dasgupta, author of the five-volume *History of Indian Philosophy* (Motilal Banarsidass 1922–55). He returned to Bucharest in 1932 and successfully submitted his analysis of yoga as his doctoral thesis.

Invited to give the 1956 Haskell Lectures on "Patterns of Initiation" at the University of Chicago, he later assumed the chair of the History of Religions Department there and stayed until his death in 1986. Eliade was undeniably influential in the academic study of religion, author of more than twenty major books and hundreds of articles, founder of the Chicago journals *History of Religion* and *The Journal of Religion*, editor-in-chief of the ubiquitous *Macmillan Encyclopedia of Religion*, and instrumental in the development of the history of religions at the University of Chicago. Eliade is also the object of serious criticism. (For a concise background study, see Bryan Rennie, "Eliade, Mircea" in the *Macmillan Encyclopedia of Philosophy*, 1997.)

NORMAN GIRARDOT has been full professor in the Religious Studies Department of Lehigh University in Pennsylvania since 1989. He received his M.A. and Ph.D.

degrees from the University of Chicago, of which he is a fellow, in 1968 and 1974 when Eliade taught there. He was Eliade's secretary for several years.

Professor Girardot is a specialist in Chinese religions and he authored *Myth and Meaning in Early Taoism* (University of California Press, 1983). He was the special editor for China for *The HarperCollins Dictionary of Religions*, edited by Jonathan Z. Smith and William Scott Green (San Francisco: Harper, 1995), to which Professor Girardot contributed 34 entries on China. He also contributed five entries to *The Macmillan Encyclopedia of Religion* (New York: Macmillan, 1987), of which Eliade was the editor-in-chief, including entries on "Chaos," and "Marcel Granet" as well as three entries on Chinese religion.

Professor Girardot's work on Eliade includes the organization of a national conference at the University of Notre Dame in 1978 on "Coincidentia-Oppositorum: the Scholarly and Literary Worlds of Mircea Eliade." This resulted in the publication of *Imagination and Meaning: The Scholarly and Literary Worlds of Mircea Eliade* (New York: the Seabury Press, 1982), edited by Girardot and Mac Linscott Ricketts, to which Professor Girardot contributed the preface and "Imagining Eliade: A fondness for Squirrels," pages 1–16.

Professor Girardot also claims responsibility for a series of eight "Prankish and Quasi-Shamanic Productions of Public Ritual Events," including most recently the Lehigh University First Presleyterian Church of Elvis the Divine Revival in April 1996 which was featured in an article in the *Religious Studies News,* volume 11, number 4, November 1996.

ALLAN W. LARSEN has a Ph.D. in philosophy from Duquesne University in Pittsburgh and has done post-doctoral research in Heidelberg, Germany. He has a special interest in philosophical phenomenology and religious studies and has served as the president of the Philosophy and Religious Studies Association of the Pennsylvania State System of Higher Education. He has published papers on Martin Heidegger and Nicolai Hartmann and has reviewed *Reconstructing Eliade: Making Sense of Religion* for the journal *European Legacy*. His analysis of Eliade's phenomenology was presented to the Annual Conference of the International Society for the Study of European Ideas in Haifa, Israel, in the summer of 1999.

RUSSELL MCCUTCHEON is from Port Colborne in southern Ontario, Canada (on the north shore of Lake Erie, close to Niagara Falls). He did his undergraduate work in life sciences at Queen's University but switched areas after that and finished his Ph.D. at the Centre for the Study of Religion, University of Toronto, in January of 1995.

McCutcheon's particular area of interest is in the history of the study of religion itself, that is, in the methods and theories that scholars use to define, describe, compare, and explain religion. His work involves the study of religious scholars and their research. He employs tools derived from the fields of literary criticism, postmodernism, and the study of politics, and he has been greatly influenced by the work of such critics as Michel Foucault, Edward Said, Fredric Jameson, Noam Chomsky, and Terry Eagleton. His first book came out in the spring of 1997: *Manufacturing Religion: The Discourse on Sui Generis Religion and the Politics of Nostalgia* (Oxford University Press). It is a materialist or political critique of the manner in which scholars have generally defined, or constructed, religion as an item of discourse and knowledge and includes an extensive critique of Eliade. Since 1990, McCutcheon been a co-editor of *Method and Theory in the Study of Religion* and is co-editor of Mouton de Gruyter's *Dictionary of Religion, Society, and Culture*.

TIM MURPHY is a graduate of the History of Consciousness Program at the University of California, Santa Cruz. He has published a number of articles and reviews in the areas of theory and method and is currently Mellon Postdoctoral Fellow in the Department of Religion at Case Western Reserve University in Cleveland, Ohio. With Russell McCutcheon, he is co–editor of the *Council of Societies for the Study of Religion's Bulletin*. Among his publications are: "Wesen und Erscheinung in the History of the Study of Religion: A Poststructuralist Perspective," in *Method and Theory in the Study of Religion*, 6/2: 119–146, 1994; "Is a Psychology of Religion Possible? A Critique of the Taxonomy of Religion in William James' *The Varieties of Religious Experience*," in *Paradigms*, 7/2:1–10, Spring 1992; "The Concept of Entwicklung in German Religionswissenschaft Before and After Darwin," in *Method and Theory in the Study of Religion*, 1998; and many reviews, particularly in *Method and Theory*.

CARL OLSON is full professor and former chair of the Department of Religious Studies at Allegheny College, Meadville, Pennsylvania. He is the author of *The Book of the Goddess Past and Present: An Introduction to Her Religion* (New York: Crossroads Publishing Company, 1983); *The Mysterious Play of Kali: An Interpretive Study of Ramakrishna* (Atlanta: Scholars Press, 1990); *The Theology and Philosophy of Eliade: A Search for the Centre* (London: Macmillan Publishing Company, 1992); and *The Indian Renouncer and Postmodern Poison: A Cross-Cultural Encounter* (New York: Peter Lang Publishing, 1997).

Professor Olson's articles on Eliade are: "The Fore-Structure of Eliade's Hermeneutics," (*Philosophy Today* (Spring 1988): 43–53; "The Concept of Power in the Works of Eliade and van der Leeuw," (*Studia Theologica*, Vol. 42 (1988): 39–53; and "Theology of Nostalgia: Reflections on the Theological Aspects of Eliade's Work," (*Numen*, Vol. XXXVI, Fasc. (1989): 98–112). He has also published over 100 journal articles, essays in anthologies, and book reviews, and has been the holder of the National Endowment for the Humanities chair at Allegheny College (1991–1994).

WILLIAM E. PADEN has his Ph.D. in the history of religions from Claremont Graduate School (1967), he is professor and chair of the religion department at the University of Vermont. He is the author of *Religious Worlds: The Comparative Study of Religions* (Boston: Beacon Press, 1988; 2nd ed. 1994), which has been translated into Japanese and German, and *Interpreting the Sacred: Ways of Seeing Religion* (Boston: Beacon Press, 1992). Of his many articles, of particular relevance is "Before the Sacred became Theological: Rereading the Durkheimian Legacy" in *Religion and Reductionism: Essays on Eliade, Segal, and the Challenge of the Social Sciences for the Study of Religion*, edited by Thomas A. Idinopulos and Edward Yonan (Leiden: Brill, 1994).

RACHELA PERMENTER is Associate Professor of English, Slippery Rock University of Pennsylvania. With a dissertation on Herman Melville, D. H. Lawrence, and postmodernism, her work has been focused on romanticism and nonduality, including its relationship to Native American literature and feminism. Her publications include "The Blakean Dialectics of *Blade Runner*," "The *Piano* on (Dis)location," and "Pythagoras and Nonduality: Melville among the Pre-Socratics." She is currently completing a book-length study to be entitled *Traditions of Nonduality: The Romantic Thread in Postmodernism*.

BRYAN RENNIE was born in Ayr, Scotland, in 1954 of Scottish and English parents. He developed an interest in world religions during his final years at grammar (high) school and went to the University of Edinburgh to pursue that interest in 1973. He holds B.A., M.A. and Ph.D. degrees from the University of Edinburgh in religious studies. A revised version of his doctoral dissertation on Eliade was published as *Reconstructing Eliade: Making Sense of Religion* in 1996. He has also published articles on Eliade in *Religion* and *Religious Studies* and contributed to *Method and Theory in the Study of Religion* and to *Zygon*. He organized a session on Eliade for the national conference of the American Academy of Religion in 1996. He is the editor of this volume.

MAC LINSCOTT RICKETTS is now retired. He was full professor and chair of the Department of Philosophy and Religion at Louisburg College in North Carolina. He studied the history of religions under Eliade at Chicago, where he received the M.A. and Ph.D. degrees with a dissertation on the Native American trickster figure. He also taught at Duke University.

He is the author of "Eliade and Altizer: Very Different Outlooks" (*Christian Advocate* [Oct. 1967]: 11–12); "Fate in the Forbidden Forest" (*Dialogue* 8 [1982]:

101–119); "In Defense of Eliade: Bridging the Gap between Anthropology and the History of Religions" (*Religion* 1 no. 3 (1973):13–34); "Mircea Eliade and the Death of God" (*Religion in Life* 36 no. 1 [Spring 1967], 40–52); "The Nature and Extent of Eliade's 'Jungianism' " (*Union Seminary Quarterly Review* 25 no. 2 [1970]: 211–234); "On Reading Eliade's Stories as Myths for Moderns," an unpublished paper read at the Midwestern Modern Language Association, Cincinnati, Ohio, 1982; and the two-volume *Mircea Eliade: The Romanian Roots 1907–1945* (New York: Columbia University Press, 1988).

Ricketts has translated Eliade's major novel, *The Forbidden Forest* from Romanian into English (University of Notre Dame Press, 1978) as well as Eliade's journals (volumes I and IV) and his *Autobiography* (volumes I and II). He has also translated much of Eliade's Romanian scholarship and most of his fictional work, although these translations are as yet unpublished. He is currently translating the remainder of Eliade's journals and writing an account of Eliade's life from 1945 on.

ROBERT SEGAL is reader in religious studies at the University of Lancaster, England. He is one of the foremost scholars of mythology in the world and the author of *The Poimandres as Myth*, *Joseph Cambell: An Introduction*, and *Explaining and Interpreting Religion*. He has also edited a six-volume compilation of *Theories of Myth*.

Subject Index

Alipore, 200
American Academy of Religion, x, 11 n, 79 n
Amritsar, 192
Anamnesis, 215–19
Anthropology, 40, 44–45, 62, 69, 149
Archaic culture, humanity, society, 25
  hunter/gatherers, 53
  See also "Primitive"
Archetypes, 69, 238, 254
Aristotelianism, 50
Arthashastra, 195
Axis mundi, 113, 254

"*Bande mataram*," 192, 195
Bhagavad-Gita, 182
Bhowanipore, 192, 197
Buddhism, 5

Calcutta, 191, 196, 198–99, 201–02
Catechism classes, 146
Catholic upbringing, 145
China
  the "three religions" of, 5–6
  Chinese Buddhism, 6
Christianity, 6
  Christian anti-semitism, 245
Cinema Paradiso (film), 31
Civil disobedience, 191, 240
  second campaign of (India, 1930), 195
Coincidentia Oppositorum, xii, xiv, 12, 107, 161
Comparison
  the comparative method, xix, xxi
  the new comparativism, xxiii
  an Eliadean approach to the comparative study of religion, 145, 147
Consciousness, 37, 45–46

Constructivism
  in Eliade, 253 n.10
  of meaning, 161
  social construction of reality, xiii
  world/cosmos construction, xxiii, 237
Creativity as the essential nature of humanity, 185–86

Dacca, 196–97
Death of God theology, 149
Deconstruction, 108, 155
Democracy, 232
Diaspora studies, 96

Ethnocentrism, xviii, xix, 40, 47, 75, 270
Ethnography, 64
Eucharist, the, 145, 176
Evolution, 69–70

Fascism (and Nazism), 12, 16, 19, 144
Feminist theology, 178

Genealogy
  Nietzschean/Foucaultian, xviii
Grail, Holy, 28

Hermeneutics, 13, 38, 212–13, 215, 217–18
  creative, xvi, 15, 68, 149, 159, 168, 172, 187, 211, 213–14, 219, 222, 227, 230, 278
  Eliade's, 37, 43–44
  principles, 166
  "total hermeneutics," 43, 68
Hierophany, hierophanies, xii, 12, 67, 69, 102, 108, 161, 238
Higher education, 144

Historicism, historicist, 56, 171–72, 222
Historiography, 181, 216–17
History
    complex nature of, xiii, 255
    the fall into, 100, 110, 112
    sacred histories, 256–57
History of Religions, 7, 168–69
History of Religions (Journal), 148, 151, 152 n. 7, 157 n.15
Holocaust, the
    Eliade's silence on, 236
    National Holocaust Museum, 244–45
Homo Religiosus, xiii, 12, 210–11, 217–18, 224, 236
    as *homo faber, ludens,* and *sapiens*, 185
Humanism
    the new humanism, 15, 40, 184, 214

Illud Tempus (*in illo tempore*), xii, xv, 26, 53, 238, 268–69
Initiation, 177–78
Iron Guard, the, 16, 19, 97, 144, 154, 159
Islam, 6

Jainism, 5
Jallanwalla, 197, 201
Judaism, 6

Legion of the Archangel Michael, the, 97, 159
Lisbon, 220

Magic, 62, 69
Magic realism, 96
"Man," 40, 44–45
Manichæanism, 8
Marburg Statement, the, 169–71, 273
Marx, Karl, 7
    Marxism, 27, 71
Meaning, 39, 161
    for *homo religiosus,* the insider, 210, 253 n.11
    religious, 163

Memory. *See* Myth, of memory; Jung, "collective memory"
Methodology, 15, 18, 38, 40, 59–60, 67, 153, 155, 160, 170
    Eliade's, xi, 152, 165–69
    not anti-historiographic, 167
Modernity, 32, 35, 215–16, 223
    modernism, 278
    modern West, 25, 61, 211, 218, 220–21
    modern world, 209
    modern humanity, 25 n.1, 30, 182, 210 n.9, 211, 213–16
    modern literature, 27
Morphology, 60, 184
    morphological classification, 72
Mysticism, 38
Myth, xii, 98
    camouflaged or concealed, 28, 29–32
    cosmogonic, 176
    eschatological, 27, 71
    of memory, 216–17, 257
    as model for behavior, 26, 269
    modern myths, xviii
    as true, 50

Nationalism, 191–95
Nazism. *See* Fascism
Nobel Prize for Literature
    Eliade considered for, 92
Nonduality, 103, 107, 113, 115

Orthodox theologians, 175 n.39
Other, the, 40–44, 75, 177, 223, 231–33

Phenomenology, xviii, 13, 36, 44, 66, 171, 180–81, 184
    descriptive, 168
    Eliade's phenomenology, 40–58
    epoché, 20
    hermeneutics, 45–46
    method, 49–50
    reenactment, 56
    structures, 40
    of religion, xviii, 209

Subject Index

Philosophers' stone, the, 109–110
Philosophy, 189, 271–72
    the distinction between philosophy, literature, and religion, xix–xx
    and the history of religions, 181, 274–75, 280
    philosophical anthropology, 38, 40, 44–45, 211, 226–29, 233, 274
    of religion, 180
Postmodernism, 97 n. 6, 107, 277–78
    and Eliade, xiii–xiv, xiv–xv, xiv n.11, 160–162, 223–24, 250, 258, 272 n.5, 273
    and Romanticism, xx, ch. 8, 277
    approach to the study of religion, 160
Poststructuralism, 97 n.6, 115
"Primitive"
    culture, 25
    See also Archaic culture, humanity, society
Provincialism, 211
Psychoanalysis, 28
    See also Jung, Jungian psychology

Reductionism, 212 n.12, 223
Religion
    academic study of, 144
    African, 6
    as creative location in the world, 238
    Greek, 6
    Hindu, 6
    nonbelievers, 25, 182
    as natural part of world experience, 258
    opposition between religion and non religion, xiv
    "primitive," 72
    South American, 6
    as *sui generis*, understood "in its own terms," "at its own level," "in its own frame of reference," 13–14, 253 n.11, 264–65
    as worldmaking, 254
Romanticism, 36, 100, 166, 168, 180, 277–79

Eliade's romantic forebears, xiv
Eliade's romanticism, 166, 182
"primary faith," 105
and postmodernism, xx
Romania, 19, 55

Sacred, the, 12, 98, 113, 152, 166, 168, 173–174, 218, 235
    camouflaged or concealed, 71, 81, 168, 218–19, 250
    dialectic of the sacred (and the profane), 69, 152
    identity of the sacred and the real, xi, xii
    Otto's and Eliade's, 250
    and the secular, 20
Science
    natural, 70, 75
    of religion, 7
    scientism, 278
Science fiction, 30
Shinto, 6
Simile in multis (the one in the many), 39
Sikhism, 6
Social construction of reality. *See* constructivism
Subject, the, 35, 52, 231
Surrealism, 28
Symbolism, 235
    religious, 209
    water, 109

Taoism, 6
    Taoist studies, 151
Teaching (pedagogy), 173–75
"Terror of history, the," 221–22, 228
Theravada Buddhism, 6
Tibetan Buddhism, 6
T'ien-t'ai Buddhism, 6 n.4
Transubstantiation, 146
Truman Show, The (film), 107, 115

Unrecognizability (of miracle), 215
Universals, 259, 271

University of Chicago, 147
  Committee on Social Thought, 150
  Divinity School, the, 149–50

Vajrayāna, 103
Verstehen, 39, 65–66
Virtue, 236
  defined, 239–40
  and discipline, 242
  and narrative, 240, 243–44
  and sacred space, 239
  and vices, 246

World
  as creations, 253
  creative placement in, 238
  other world(s), 98–99, 116
  worlds, ix
  worldmaking as universal, 257–59
  worldviews, xv

Zen Buddhism, 106

Name Index

Allen, Douglas, xxii, 13, 162 n.25, 274–76, 293
   Structure and creativity in Religion, 208
Arjuna, 182
Augustine, Saint, 7

Baird, Robert D., 67 n.24
Beane, Wendell Charles, xxi, 273–74, 293
Berger, Adriana, 13, 20
Blake, William, 97, 114
Bloom, Harold, 100, 104
Bose, Subhash Chandra, 200
Boyer, Pascal, 256 n.15
Burkert, Walter, 259

Calinescu, M., xix, 87, 98, 110, 112 n.40, 162 n.25, 215
Callois, Roger, 28, 251
Campbell, Joseph, 32, 158
Cave, David, xxii, 13–21, 162 n.25, 184, 276, 294
Chai, Leon, 100
Chidester, David, 22 n.8
Cixous, Hélène, 103, 109, 115
Coleridge, Samuel, 98
Comte, Auguste, 65, 70
Confucius, Confucianism, 5, 241–42, 246
Corless, Roger, xvi, 21, 263, 278, 294
Culianu (Culiano), Ioan Petru, 3–4, 7–8, 67 n.24, 162 n.25
   The Tree of Gnosis, 6

Dasgupta, Surendranath, 197 n, 199–201
Deleuze, Gilles, 73–74, 272
Derrida, Jacques, xiv, 12 n.1, 44–45, 107–108, 115, 155, 271, 278, 281

Descartes, René, 50, 53
Devi, Maitreyi
   It Does Not Die, 87, 154 n.11
Dilthey, Wilhem, 37–39, 46, 167 nn.7–9
Doniger (O'Flaherty), Wendy, 151, 268 n.2
Dudley, Guilford III, 67 n.24, 168 n.9, 170, 180 n.57, 187
Durkheim, Emile, 64–65, 69, 72, 238, 248, 251
Dumézil, Georges, 251

Eliade, Christinel, 157
Eliade, Mircea, 294
   allegations of antisemitism, 21, 154 n.11, 266
   antihistorical judgments, 222 nn.28-29
   literary work, xix–xx, ch. 7, Part III, 215
   mistaken as Catholic theologian, 147 n.4
   nationalism, 17, 19, 265–67
   normative judgments by, 208, 224, 275
   personal religious convictions, 152
   as philosopher, 57
   pluralism, 266
   politically incorrect, 161
   politics, 13, 16
   politics of nostalgia, 13
   sentimentally old fashioned, 157
   system in his thought, 209
   works:
      "Adio!" (Goodbye), 85, 110, 143
      Australian Religions, 37 n.4, 43, 218
      Autobiography, 16–17, 87, 220 n.24
      Bengal Nights, 88–89
      "Cosmical Homology and Yoga," *xi*
      Cosmos and History (The Myth of the Eternal Return), 27 n.5, 113, 222, 226

Eliade, Mircea, works: *(continued)*
  Eliade Guide to World Religions, The,
    3–9
  Encyclopedia of Religion, 3, 160 n.20
  Endless Column, The, 80, 155
  Essential Sacred Writings from around the
    World, 3–9
  Forbidden Forest, The, 79, 82–84, 155,
    158 n.17
  Gaudeamus, 152 n.8
  History of Religious Ideas, 7–8
  Images and Symbols, 27 n.5, 102, 215–
    16
  Journal I, 220 n.23
  Journal II, 67 n.21, 69
  Journal III, 226
  Maitreyi, 88–92, 95
  Man Who Could Read Stones, The, 109,
    113–114
  Men and Stones, xx, 99, 104, 109–114
  "Methodological Remarks on the Study
    of Religious Symbolism," 68 n.26
  Miss Christina, xx, 104
  Myth and Reality, 26 n.3, 27 n.5, 52,
    216 n.21, 217
  Myths, Dreams, and Mysteries, 25 n.2,
    26–27, 27 n.5, 28, 40 n.11, 181
    n.63, 216 n.21, 221
  "Nineteen Roses," 215
  No Souvenirs, 80, 161 n.23, 180, 212
    n.10, 214 n.15, 220
  Nuntă în cer (Marriage in Heaven), 90,
    95
  Occultism, Witchcraft, and Cultural
    Fashions, 27 n.5
  Old Man and the Bureaucrats, The, xx,
    84, 89, 104, 108–109
  Ordeal by Labyrinth, xi, 67 n.22, 165
    n.1, 166 n.4, 169 n.13, 181 nn.60–
    62, 186, 225 n.32, 269
  Patterns in Comparative Religions, xii, 7,
    27 n.5, 37 n.5, 67 n.20, 72, 147,
    224, n.30, 225, 252
  Quest, The, xx, 27 n.5, 37 n.6, 39, 43,
    171 n.24, 180 n.59, 182, 186, 213
    n.14, 227
  Rites and Symbols of Initiation (*Birth and*
    Rebirth), 27 n.5
  Sacred and the Profane, The, 26 n.4, 27
    n.5, 28, 30, 52, 98, 146, 148, 251
    n.7, 252, 257 n.18, 270
  Șarpele (The Serpent), 99
  Secret of Dr. Honigberger, 154
  Shamanism: Archaic Techniques of Ecstasy,
    67 n.23, 69, 166 n.3, 221 n.26, 224,
    n.31
  "Structure and Changes in the History
    of Religion," xi
  Tales of the Sacred and the Supernatural,
    85, 96 n.5
  Two and the One, The (*Mephistopheles*
    and the Androgyne), 25 n.1, 105 n.25,
    180 n.58, 212–13
  Two Tales of the Occult, 80, 82, 154 n.9
  Youth without Youth, 87, 89, 99, 161
    n.23, 215 n.19
Emerson, Ralph Waldo, 98, 111

Frazer, James George, 32, 61, 69–70
Freud, Sigmund, 7, 28, 41–42

Gadamer, Hans Georg, 46, 51
Gandhi, (Mahatma), 195–96, 200–01, 203
Geertz, Armin, 13
Geertz, Clifford, 149
Ginsberg, Allan, 95, 106, 115
Girardot, Norman, xxi, 110, 263, 273,
    294–95
  Myth and Meaning in Early Taoism, 156
Goethe, Johann Wolfgang von, 63, 96,
    102, 113, 115–116
Goodman, Nelson, 252, 254 n.12

Hegel, Georg Wilhelm Friedrich, 36, 40
Heidegger, Martin, 12, 21, 36, 50, 54,
    158, 264

Husserl, Edmund, 44, 50–54, 57

Irigaray, Luce, 103

Jensen, Jeppe Sinding, 13
Jonas, Hans
  The Gnostic Religion, 6
Jung, Carl Gustav, 29, 32, 99 n.11, 158
  Jungian psychology, 29
  "collective memory," 99

Kant, Immanuel, xi–xii, 279
  neo-Kantian philosophy, 73
Kerouac, Jack, 105 n.26, 115
Krishna, 182
Kierkegaard, Søren, 52
Kristensen, Brede, 35
Kuhn, Thomas, x, 272

Larsen, Allen, xviii, 295
Lawrence, David Herbert, 97, 105
van der Leeuw, 37–38, 188, 251
Lévy-Bruhl, Lucien, 61, 69–70
Lewis, C. S., 85
Lincoln, Bruce, 18, 21
Lyotard, Jean-François, 107

de Man, Paul, 11, 158–59, 264
Mauss, Marcel, 65, 251
McCutcheon, Russell, x, xvi–xvii n.17, 264–67, 278, 295–96
  Manufacturing Religion, 11 n, 14
  Critics not Caretakers, 23 n.10
Mack, Burton, 18
Manea, Norman, 20, 162 n.25
Melville, Herman, 97, 113, 115
  Moby Dick, 109
Mencius, 241, 245
Merleau-Ponty, Maurice, 36, 49, 57
Muhammad, 4
Müller, Friedrich Max, 62
Murphy, Tim, xviii, 11, 13, 22–23, 263 n.1, 270–71, 296

Nāgārjuna, 103
Nagel, Thomas, 35
Nehru, Jawarharlal, 199
Norris, Christopher, 21–22
Nuesner, Jacob, 8

Olson, Carl, xv n.16, xix, 16–21, 272, 296
  Theology and Philosophy of Mircea Eliade, The, 16, 162 n.25
Otto, Rudolf, 37, 250–51
  Idea of the Holy, The, 37 n.7

Paden, William, xxii, 167 n.9, 247, 276–77, 297
Padre Pio, 146
Pals, Daniel, 162 n.25
Penner Hans, 50
Permenter, Rachela, xx, 277, 297
Plato, 6
Proudfoot, Wayne, 18
Popper, Sir Karl, 35

Rajan, Tilottama, 95, 101
Rennie, Bryan, 15–21, 152, 174, 250, 256 n.16, 277, 297
  Reconstructing Eliade, x, xii, xv, 19–20, 97 n.7, 105 n.25, 152 n.8, 159 n.18, 162 n.24, 167 n.9, 169 n.14, 171–72 n.24, 174 nn.31–32, 177 nn.44–45, 178 n.51, 182 nn.66, 68, 239 n.12, 265
Ricketts, Mac Linscott, xix–xx, 16 n.5, 20–21, 95 n.1, 98 n.8, 297–98
  Romanian Roots, 161 n.23
Ricoeur, Paul, 56, 228
Rudolf, Kurt, 183
Ryba, Thomas, x, n.5

Said, Edward, 42, 270
de la Saussaye, Pierre de Chantepie, 64, 72
de Saussure, 107
Segal, Robert, xvii, 18, 268–70, 298

Schleiermacher, 37, 46
Sharpe, Eric J., 63
Shelley, Percy Bysshe, 98, 111, 115
Smart, Ninian, 3, 9, 67 n.24
Smith, Jonathan Z., xix, 59, 73, 241 n.15, 253 n.10, 255, 257, 271, 277
Smith, Wilfred Cantwell, xxiv, 8, 278
Strenski, Ivan, x, n.5, 13, 20, 67 n.24
Sullivan, Lawrence, 173 n.29, 184 n.75, 207 n.3

Tiele, Cornelius P., 63
Tillich, Paul, 184
Tracy, David, 172
Tylor, Edward, 32, 61, 69–70, 188

Wach, Joachim, 35, 37, 66
Weber, Max, 65–66
Wordsworth, William, 103, 115

Yeats, William Butler, 97, 105